BEGINNING TO READ
AND THE SPIN DOCTORS OF SCIENCE

BEGINNING TO READ AND THE SPIN DOCTORS OF SCIENCE

The Political Campaign to Change America's Mind about How Children Learn to Read

■ ■ ■

DENNY TAYLOR

National Council of Teachers of English
1111 W. Kenyon Road, Urbana, Illinois 61801-1096

Staff Editors: *Michael Greer and Kurt Austin*

Interior and Cover Design: *Jenny Jensen Greenleaf*

Cover Art: *Keith Haring*, "Labyrinth, 1989" © The Estate of Keith Haring

NCTE Stock Number: 02751-3050

It is the policy of NCTE in its journals and other publications to provide a forum for the open discussion of ideas concerning the content and the teaching of English and the language arts. Publicity accorded to any particular point of view does not imply endorsement by the Executive Committee, the Board of Directors, or the membership at large, except in announcements of policy, where such endorsement is clearly specified.

Library of Congress Cataloging-in-Publication Data

Taylor, Denny, 1947–
   Beginning to read and the spin doctors of science/Denny Taylor.
      p.   cm.
   Includes bibliographical references (p.   ) and index.
   ISBN 0-8141-0275-1 (pbk.)
   1. Reading—Research—United States. 2. Literacy—Political aspects—United States. 3. Reading—Law and legislation—United States.
   I. Title.
LB1050.6.T38 1998
428.4'07'2073—dc21   98-9526
                                                                                      CIP

DEDICATION

This book is dedicated to the memory of Lilian Janye Hawkins, known to her family as Ginny, who was born in 1889 at Penylan Fields on the Varteg, a coal mining village in South Wales.

Ginny received her education in the Wesleyan Schoolroom and became a pupil teacher at the Varteg School. She was concerned about the poverty that surrounded her and, even though she was not allowed to vote, she stood on a soapbox to denounce the conditions in which the miners and their families were forced to live.

On August 30, 1926, Ginny was a member of the mass picket to protest against those who crossed the line and worked in the mines during the General Strike. She was extremely lucky not to be convicted and imprisoned for illicit assembly along with two of her school friends who also participated in the picket.

Ginny, who was my great aunt, died when she was quite young, but she did live to see women over 30 get the vote in 1918 and women over 21 in 1928.

In each generation there are teachers who struggle for emancipation and for an emancipatory pedagogy. Perhaps the most we can expect of these courageous teachers is that they will teach the next generation how to participate in the struggle in whatever form it takes. In this task I know that teachers are succeeding, for in writing this book I have talked with many teachers whose courage and determination easily equals Ginny's. With this in mind I also dedicate this book to them.

To the teachers who struggle for emancipation today, and for all the teachers who, being mindful of the courage of their predecessors, will continue the struggle for the emancipation of future generations, please accept this book in recognition of your important work.

CONTENTS

ACKNOWLEDGMENTS

Writing is a social process, but it is also a selfish act. I began writing *Spin Doctors* after I visited the exhibit hall at the 1997 IRA Convention. I wanted to write a short paper on phonemic awareness research, and I talked with Sharon Murphy about the possibility of publishing it in *Language Arts*. "Keep it short," she said, "twenty pages, double spaced." I called Sharon several times at the beginning of June 1997 to discuss my progress on the piece. "It's a bit long," I told her, "but I should be finished by next week." But by then I was getting up at 5 a.m., working until 11 or 12 p.m., and grabbing for a notebook at 2 a.m. When I reached sixty pages, I called Sharon. "It's a book," I said. Sharon laughed as if she knew already, and she offered encouragement and even commiserated with me.

It was my fiftieth birthday in May, and I was taking the summer off. David and I were going to the UK to spend six weeks with my mother. "I promise I won't bring any work," I said to Lizzy on the telephone. She said she couldn't imagine me coming home without some work to do, so she wasn't surprised when four file boxes of papers arrived at her house the day we flew in, and she didn't seem to mind when I set up shop in her living room and got up early to work. A week after we arrived at my mother's house, we packed up and took ourselves off for a month in a stone cottage on Exmoor in Devon. There was one big room downstairs, and we set up a writing area near a window. As it rained almost continuously the first week we were there, I spent each day writing. David had brought a second laptop computer, and Lizzy had lots of books to read as well as the manuscript of a book that our son Benjamin had sent her. Lizzy read her grandson's book, and she didn't seem to mind that I was spending so much time writing, and I love her for that. She has always supported me selflessly, even when I behave selfishly.

David supports me in the same way. I know there were many times during the early stages of this book when he spoke to me and I didn't hear what he was saying. Other times he worked with me through the evenings, reconstructing the statistical analyses used in the various studies that I was focusing upon. David and I have done this kind of work together since I was a graduate student at Teachers College in the late 1970s. The work reminds me of an archeological dig, except that it takes place at the kitchen table where papers can be spread out and we can "dig" into the numbers in the statistical analyses that we are trying to reconstruct. David and I share an immense interest in this kind of analytical work. But while I enjoy figuring out the conceptual frames which undergird the statistical analyses that are used in research studies such as those presented in this book, David becomes immersed in the mathematical applications. Someone recently called him "a numbers man." If we go to the symphony, he knows how many violinists are in the orchestra, and if a member of the chorus does not return after the intermission, David will whisper to me that one of the chorus is missing. When we work together, I am fascinated by the way in which he reads mathematical formulae; his appreciation of numbers rivals my appreciation of text. But what I like most about this work that we sometimes do together is the camaraderie. Above all David and I are good friends, and I think that is the way it is supposed to be. When I am tired and writing has become tedious, we have a cup of coffee. When the documentation that I am reading is disturbing, we go for a walk and David listens to me. He reads what I write, fixes the computer when it freezes up, and helps me beat deadlines which occur all too frequently.

Picture this scene and then add to it the endless telephone calls, the e-mail messages and faxes, and the express packages that seem to arrive continuously. Much of the documentation I have used in *Spin Doctors* has been sent to me. Many of those who have supported me are not mentioned by name in the book, but they have both my appreciation and my admiration. Others have more visibility. Ken and Yetta Goodman, who are tireless in their support of teachers, children, as well as public education, encouraged me, even though *Spin Doctors* has taken me away from writing their biography. As with so many educators, my work is on hold so I can respond to the political events that are taking place which critically affect the ways in which young children are taught to read.

Karen Smith at NCTE also helped me enormously. We talked often about the Reading Excellence Act, shared information, and discussed ways in which we could respond. When H.R. 2614 was going through the House of Representatives, Karen offered me encouragement as I prepared packages of the documentation that I had gathered while I was writing *Spin Doctors* to send to every member of the House Committee on Education and the Workforce. Later, CELT reimbursed me for the $600 in postage that was needed to send the documentation to the Committee. I am grateful for this financial support but even more for the message that CELT is deeply committed to issues of social justice and equity when it comes to teaching young children to read.

While I am writing and the telephone rings and faxes arrive, Karen Onofrey and Michele Ebersole are at the library finding documents for me. I have bits of citations, last names, an endless stream of requests. Karen and Michele look for the information and, however obscure or difficult the reference, they manage to find what I need. They also organize all my documentation, filing it logically, and finding it when logic escapes me and I panic at the loss of a particularly important document. Karen and Michele also check the direct quotations against the original documents, and Karen, going above and beyond what any research assistant should be expected to do, checks the quotes from the eight hours of videotape recordings of the May 8, 1996, meeting of the Education Committee of the California Assembly. We laugh about that now, but it truly was an awful job.

When Benjamin comes to stay, he brings with him his friend Brandon Ward, and they also pitch in. Ben and Brandon are both writers, and they sit at the kitchen table, one with the transcript of the pre-summit meeting of the Texas Business Council and the other with the *Spin Doctors* chapter on Texas, and they read back and forth, checking quotes one against the other. In the breaks we sit and talk about their writing. Ben talks of his poetry as personal narrative and he says, "I don't try to be offensive, but sometimes the things that happen are offensive so why not write them down?" I think about *Spin Doctors* and of statements that researchers and politicians have made that are offensive about children or their teachers, and I have cold feet about writing them down. But I get back to work, and when Benjamin and Brandon leave we carry on the conversation on the telephone, and Brandon sends me notes on hip-hop and rap that I use to respond to one of the most offensive quotes that I have included in the book.

I send a rough draft of the manuscript to Michael Greer at NCTE, and he writes to tell me that he thinks NCTE would be interested in publishing. This is the beginnings of a friendship that will last long after the publication of the book. He makes ten copies of the manuscript and sends them to five members of the editorial board and to five independent reviewers. I continue writing and I talk with Michael often on the telephone. There comes a time in writing when everyday conversations no longer make sense, and as few people know what I am writing it becomes difficult to talk with anyone about anything that is not connected to the book. So Michael, who is also a writer, talks with me about the chapter that I am writing, he introduces me to John Barth's *Lost in the Funhouse*, and we play with the idea of the funhouse as a labyrinth and we connect it up with Umberto Eco's library, and it makes us both laugh. Then I go back to my computer ready to write. More than anything I am grateful to Michael for the many hours that he has spent on the telephone talking about the book, for making me laugh, and for entering the labyrinth with me.

I did not know most of the reviewers, but I thank them for their generosity in responding in such detail to the manuscript. Even the critical comments were helpful, and I tried to respond to each point that was made. I did recognize the extremely helpful review by Dick Allington, and you will find in the endnotes that with his permission I have included some of the comments that he made. Michael O'Loughlin also read the manuscript and wrote a review which raised several issues that I attempted to address. I am especially grateful for the encouragement that Michael continues to give me, and for the ways in which his writing has informed my understandings of the struggle that we share to create opportunities for both teachers and children to work together in ways that are truly emancipatory.

My final thanks go to Michele Ebersole, Andrea Garcia, and Alan Flurkey, who are reading the page proofs as I write. I am inspired by their generosity, vitality, and enthusiasm. They are the next generation of teachers in schools and universities, and it is also for them that I write. If there have been times when I have lost my purpose, it is young scholars like them that encourage me. But in the end I alone take responsibility for what I write.

AUTHOR'S NOTE

"In this Orwellian hall of mirrors," Donald Lazere writes, "can anyone judge who is telling the truth and who is lying? Individual readers can only check the source texts on both sides and judge for themselves, daunting as this effort has been made by increasingly sophisticated techniques of obscuring such judgements" (p. 681).

By sticking as closely as I can to what is written and what is said, I have tried to put before the reader as much original documentation as the pages of a book will allow me to do. It is important to note that some of the direct quotations that I have used in *Spin Doctors* are too long to be included in their entirety. Thus, there are occasions when I have used the interjection of "the speaker/author states" to mark a break in the text. On several occasions I have advised the reader to refer to an original source. Most of the documents are available within the public domain.

Unfortunately, as the book is typeset I still have not been able to obtain the primary data from the Houston reading studies. Although the research was funded by the federal government and therefore should be in the public domain, all requests to obtain this documentation have been rejected.

However, as the page proofs arrive I have received two more documents which are of critical importance to the reconstruction of the NICHD Houston reading studies on which political decisions have been based. The first is the Annual Performance Report of the elementary campuses of the school district in which the NICHD reading studies were conducted, and the second is the long-awaited *Journal of Educational Psychology* article which focuses on this NICHD research. Both original documents, which are discussed in Appendix 2, add further evidence of the inherent bias of the studies in favor of Open Court and what counts as "scientific evidence" and "reliable, replicable research."

In which it is explained that the end of the book can only be found at the beginning

■ ■ ■

"Please do not tell anyone what happens today," Umberto Eco says, "we are irresponsibly playing, like atomic scientists trying dangerous scenarios and unmentionable war games."[1]

The game we are playing is not ours, and it is risky for us to participate. Some of us have been silenced, while others have been ridiculed. What we are going to do is enter a labyrinth and go on a journey through documents filled with land mines that are quite likely to explode.[2] In the country in which this war game takes place, there are also reports in newspapers and magazines and on radio and television about a small group of government scientists who have discovered that a terrible illness is afflicting millions of the nation's children, and that only "reliable, replicable research" will provide a cure.[3]

Politicians who believe this little group of otherwise quite insignificant researchers are publicly outraged when they are told that the sickness has been allowed to infect so many children throughout the land. So the politicians make speeches, and pontificate on the importance of reliable, replicable research. They hold hearings and pass laws which they secretly hope will increase their chances of re-election, especially if they can persuade voters that they have found a cure and got rid of the infection that is debilitating the nation's children.[4]

Large corporations, focused solely on their revenues and profits, recognize the financial possibilities of a country at war *and* plagued by disease, and tempt the little group of scientists with lucrative deals to produce "scientific treatments" which they can sell at enormous profit. Meanwhile, behind the scenes, powerful political lobbyists in conservative think tanks and right-wing foundations pull everyone's strings.

"National Institutes of Health researchers now consider reading problems a major public health threat," Marego Athans writes in an article in the *Houston Chronicle* entitled "Schools fail to teach kids how to read," which includes quotes from right-wing conservatives and references to the Bible and the religious right.[5]

Marilyn Jager Adams, who is described as a Harvard scholar, is quoted by Athans as saying, "This is totally fixable. The data indicate that the ability to learn to read is remarkably independent of ethnicity and parental education, and children's IQ."

Adams is then quoted as stating that "[e]verything we can measure says it depends on what they learn, which depends on what we teach them. And consistent with that, we have all these programs demonstrating that classroom instruction can make all the difference."

"But reading instruction in this country has been buffeted for decades by a vitriolic war," Athans declares, "a war in which firm evidence is often ignored in favor of fads and shifts in political winds."

G. Reid Lyon is also quoted. He is described by Athans as a leading authority on reading and chief of the child development and behavior branch of NIH's National Institute of Child Health and Human Development in Bethesda, Maryland. "It's horrible," Lyon says, "so counterproductive. It takes away from the professional dialogue, from children, in terms of getting the best practices to them."

But many educators, including myself, do not agree with the researchers from NICHD that reading problems are a major public health threat, and we resist Lyon's search for pathology. In "The Reading Wars," which was published in the *Atlantic Monthly*, Nicholas Lemann writes that many educators consider Lyon "a nightmarish figure." Lemann is correct in his assessment, but he doesn't seem to understand what it is about Lyon that disturbs so many educators.[6]

One example of what many of us regard as "horrible" is Lyon's view of the language abilities of inner-city children. "The language interactions that they've had at home are nil," Lyon says. "They've never even heard these sound systems. Are they lousy readers? A lot of them are. Are they genetically predisposed? Some of them are, making that combination a tough one to treat."[7] Many of us find it impossible to discuss "best practices" with Lyon because he holds such a deficit view, or perhaps more accurately a racist view, of inner-city children.

In another article on reading in the *Houston Chronicle*, entitled "Battling Illiteracy," Melanie Markley writes of the research of Barbara Foorman that was conducted in Houston, and which has been used as the "scientific" basis of state laws and national legislation that mandate phonemic awareness training and the teaching of systematic explicit phonics in public schools across the United States.

Markley notes that Foorman is now the head of the new Center for Academic and Reading Skills (CARS) which was dedicated by Governor Bush, and that Foorman has been joined at the center by her co-researcher in the Houston reading studies, Jack Fletcher. "The facility's opening in the Texas Medical Center underscored the governor's thrust to recognize reading as a public health issue," Markley writes. "Calling illiteracy 'one of the most tragic childhood diseases,' he said it poses a long-term health risk that requires serious scientific scrutiny."

"Many in the education field, however, find it inappropriate to shift reading into the domain of scientific research," Markley then states, adding, "[c]hildren, they say, are not lab specimens." Markley follows this statement with a quote from Foorman.

"The belief systems are so strong that even though those same people would go to their doctor and expect their drugs to go through clinical trials before they popped them into their mouth, they don't expect their reading methods to have gone through those kinds of trials," Foorman is quoted as saying. "They have their beliefs about what is best for children, and they suspend science. It just doesn't seem to enter that realm of their decision making."

The ultimate irony, of course, is that it is precisely because we are *not* willing to reject what science has taught us about how young children learn to read and write that we cannot accept Foorman's scientifically indefensible NICHD reading studies. The difficulty that we face is that while the media has been fed sound bites on the importance of the research, educators have been systematically denied access to the data.[8] My own requests for information were dismissed by Fletcher as not serious, and he told me that I should ask myself "the purpose of the questions."

My answer is quite straightforward. While members of the research community have been repeatedly denied access to the primary data, and while both Lyon and the principal investigators have declined to answer critical questions, state laws have been passed based upon the research, and the United States House of Representatives has used Foorman's research as a basis for the Reading Excellence Act, which awaits a hearing in the Senate as this book goes to press.

Thus, there are serious ethical issues regarding the presentation of this research to policymakers at the state and national level, and these issues should be addressed before any further legislative action is undertaken which relies even in part on the NICHD Houston Reading Studies conducted by Foorman, Fletcher, and Francis, and which have been actively promoted by Lyon.

In *Beginning to Read and the Spin Doctors of Science*, I have analyzed all the information I have been able to obtain on the Foorman studies, but even as I write the prologue more documentation has come to light, and we are in a race to make public the information that politicians need to evaluate their false definitions of "reading" and "reliable, replicable research."

What is not commonly known is that the key results of the Foorman studies, which have been widely disseminated by the media, combine the scores of first- and second-grade children with widely different test scores into one common "average" straight-line result. Nor is it widely known that it is the meaningless comparison of these "averaged" straight lines for the four "treatment" groups that is used by Foorman and her colleagues to support the finding that Open Court and direct instruction in systematic explicit phonics is a superior method of instruction.

Examining the data for first- and second-grade children separately allows us to compare the test performance of first-grade children exposed to a year of Foorman treatments with the test performance of first-grade children, now in second grade, who had no such exposure. Examination of the data in this way provides some important results which refute the major reported findings of the study.[9]

First, the data for the direct instruction group show there is no significant difference between (1) the scores on Foorman's word reading test achieved by the first-grade children after one full year of the Open Court basal reading program, and (2) those children beginning second grade who had not had Open Court during their first-grade year and who had only the school district's preexisting reading curriculum.[10] *This is a flat contradiction of Foorman's claim that the children in the Open Court/Direct Instruction group outperformed the school district's existing reading curriculum.*

A second important finding for the Open Court/Direct Instruction group is that there is no significant difference between (1) the scores on Foorman's phonological processing tests achieved by the first-grade children after one full year of the Open Court basal reading program, and (2) those children beginning second grade who had not had Open Court and who had only the school district's pre-existing whole language program.[11] *The bottom line is that the school district's preexisting reading curriculum, before Foorman, before phonemic awareness training, and before systematic, explicit phonics, was just as effective as the Open Court/ Direct Instruction reading program.*

A third important finding is that in the other three groups, the beginning second graders, who had not received any instruction in Foorman's study, scored significantly better on her word reading test than the first-grade children who had been subjected to a full year of her reading "treatments."[12]

"A child who comes into the direct instruction group has the opportunity to grow," Foorman tells the Education Committee of the California Assembly, "that's not the case in these other groups, to the same extent. That's an alarming picture. You'd expect to see improvement and when you don't see improvement you've got to ask yourself is this a curriculum disability that we are creating?"

Unfortunately, it is clear from the data that it was Foorman's quasi-experimental treatment which had a negative impact on the word reading scores of the first graders, and we have to ask if it is not Foorman's study which created the "curriculum disability" to which she refers.

Just as there is no comparison of the first- and second-grade data, there is also no consideration given to the effects of the sample bias in Foorman's study in favor of Open Court/Direct Instruction. Based on the table that presents the May achievement test results for the four treatment groups, for the Open Court/Direct Instruction group there were approximately 55 percent of children in the tutorial group and 45 percent in the nontutorial group. Keep in mind that Foorman describes the tutorial group as being in "the bottom 20 percent," and the nontutorial group as "between 20 and 30 percent" on the district's emergent literacy survey. In sharp contrast, for each of the three other treatment groups, more than 80 percent of the children were in the tutorial group and less than 20 percent were in the nontutorial group.[13]

Did this sample bias toward the inclusion of more lower-achieving children in these other groups affect the scores on Foorman's word reading test at the beginning of her study? Apparently it did. Both the first- and second-grade children in the Open Court/Direct Instruction group scored higher on the word reading test than the children in the other three treatment groups at the beginning of the year, and for the second-grade children, in particular, the differences in the test scores are highly significant.[14] Did this sample bias affect the scores on Foorman's word reading test at the end of her study? Yes it did, and Foorman herself provides the evidence.

In the draft of the paper for the *Journal of Educational Psychology*, Foorman and her colleagues state, "In the case of tutorial, children who received tutoring read fewer words correctly in April than those who did not receive tutoring." Foorman explains, "This seemingly paradoxical finding is most likely due to the fact that tutoring was provided first to children who had the lowest scores on the district's emergent literacy survey."

Compounding this sample bias, the second graders in the Open Court/Direct Instruction treatment group were also given a double dose of Open Court, thus ensuring that this particular group of children, who started the year with a clear advantage over the children in the other treatment groups in terms of their scores on Foorman's word reading test, ended the year with even higher scores than they would have obtained without this extra instruction.

The presence of such a clear sample bias in favor of the Open Court/ Direct Instruction treatment group, whether intended or unintended, is critical evidence which confounds the entire study, and which renders its key reported finding, the "superiority" of the Open Court/Direct Instruction treatment, totally meaningless.

In a letter to the editor of *Education Week* defending the research of NICHD and the research of Foorman and her colleagues, Lyon writes of the "scientific standards" to which the studies of NICHD must adhere. "The study," Lyon states, "and those conducted to replicate the findings, must attempt to falsify the hypotheses and refute the theories that guide the investigation."

But Foorman and her colleagues made no attempt to falsify their hypothesis or refute their theory that training in phonological awareness and direct instruction in systematic explicit phonics is effective in improving beginning reading instruction. They failed to examine the effects of a clear sample bias on the word reading scores, the phonological processing scores, and the end-of-year achievement scores. They ignored the fact that there was no significant difference in test scores between children at the end of the first-grade Open Court/Direct Instruction treatment and the beginning of second grade who had only experienced the district's existing reading curriculum. And they disregarded the negative effect their study apparently had on the test performance of the children in the three other groups.

The effects of these findings have implications not only for national and state legislatures but also for the work of (1) the National Academy of Science Committee, of which Foorman is a committee member, and that is soon to publish a report on preventing reading difficulties in young children; (2) the National Reading Panel that is being established by NICHD, which sponsored Foorman's research; and (3) the Learning First Alliance, which is developing a position statement on early reading, the executive summary of which is being used in states such as Washington and Michigan to influence the legislature.

But the full impact of the research cannot be fully understood until consideration is given to the influence of the Foorman studies at the local level. School districts are changing the way in which young children are taught to read based upon the findings of Foorman's research. The school district in which Foorman conducted her research has *not* adopted Open Court. The basal reading program is used in a few classrooms and in others as a resource with a variety of other materials. "Open Court gets too hard too quickly," a teacher in the district explains. Nonetheless, many school districts across the country have jumped on the bandwagon and have adopted Open Court.

"There is full adoption of Open Court in K–2," Ann Lippincott writes in an e-mail message about what's happening in Santa Barbara, "despite the teachers' protest, strong protest, against it. There is a memo that actually tells teachers that they must teach Open Court for 2.5 hours a day. Kindergarten gets some slack because with 2.5 hours of Open Court and 1 hour of math, there is no time to eat a snack, have a recess, or even hear a story or sing a song." Lippincott continues, "All children get English Open Court. And the memo goes on to say that the teachers don't need to worry about teaching science or social studies because Open Court has that built in. You can imagine how upset the science and social studies educators are in our community. To assume that Open Court can do all this is very dangerous."[15]

In Sacramento, Open Court has similarly been adopted throughout the school system. Deborah Anderluh, a staff writer at the *Sacramento Bee*, states that "[t]he program lasts two to three hours a day, with half that time spent in whole group instruction."[16] Anderluh then adds, "The detailed scripting, combined with the oversight of roving coaches, means that from school to school, teachers are presenting basically the same lesson at a given grade level in a given week."

"Part of the reason for choosing Open Court is that studies have found it to be successful with poor, urban student populations," Anderluh reports that the head of the district's new Learning and Literacy Department, Kathy Cooper, told her. "A year-long study in Houston schools, involving 374 first and second graders, pitted Open Court students against two other programs," Anderluh continues. You know the rest.

In a country in which school children are pitted against school children, a small group of government scientists, hiding in their fortress of impenetrable numbers, claim they have discovered that a terrible illness is afflicting millions of the nation's children, and that only "reliable, replicable research" will provide a cure. Politicians make speeches and pontificate on the importance of such research, and the media makes their findings front-page news. Large corporations market "scientific treatments" and make immense profits, while behind the scenes powerful political lobbyists smile cynically at one another as they congratulate themselves on the success they have had at pulling everyone's strings.

Beginning to Read and the Spin Doctors of Science is about the political campaign that is taking place to change the minds of Americans about how young children learn to read. The book begins with a close look at the empirical research on phonemic awareness training and the teaching of systematic, explicit phonics which is being used to support a cultural shift in our national psyche about language, about literacy, and about learning. After that the book focuses on the ways in which research studies on early reading instruction are being used by the federal government, as well as state governments, to support this new mythology which has turned early reading instruction into a massive business of unprecedented commercial worth.

My purpose in writing *Spin Doctors* is to reconstruct the underlying assumptions of the political arguments that trouble and divide us, and to discover how the arguments are conceived and how they are shaped. I want to provide those who read this book with opportunities to raise fundamental questions about the character and purpose of "the reading wars." I want to break down the barriers that are being erected between our epistemological understandings of how children learn to read and the pedagogical practices that arise from current political pressures and commercial interests.

I will argue that the contention that phonemic awareness must be taught directly and that children need explicit systematic instruction in phonics is less of a scientific "fact" than an exercise in political persuasion. Politically, what we value is a product of the choices that we make, but choosing becomes very difficult when the arguments are so skewed. Within this context I will argue that the media coverage of "the reading wars" is biased, and that the press has misled the public by selectively providing information that is inaccurate, false, fallacious, and, at best, is nothing more than spin doctoring.

Before you turn the page, let me take a few more moments and share with you the way in which I have written *Spin Doctors*. Most of us would agree that "the battle" taking place over how young children should be taught to read is being fought in the public arena and the rhetoric that is being used is not that of the academy. For this reason, I have resisted writing in an academic discourse style which would smother what reporters have written and politicians have said with layers and layers of dry, overanalyzed, albeit scholarly, interpretation.[17]

Instead, what I have tried to do is to stay grounded in the immediacy of the situation, to *re*-present not represent, to *re*-collect not recollect events which critically affect our understandings of how young children learn to read. I have tried to focus on the conversations and arguments that are taking place, and in *re*-presenting them I have attempted to *re*-create the dialetics and dialogics in a multivoiced, multileveled, polyphonic (excuse the pun) narrative, that is often colloquial and which, unfortunately, might at times be considered too argumentative.

My own interpretation of the text is that it is edgy and often polemic, in ways that reflect that I am both personally and politically immersed in the events that are taking place. For this reason I would urge you to view this work not as a historical account but as a book which, of necessity, is unfinished and incomplete because it tries to capture the immediacy of the situation.[18]

In October 1997, while the House of Representatives discussed the Reading Excellence Act which defines research on reading in such a way that it excludes the research of some of this century's most renowned scholars in the field of education, a commemoration was held to remember filmmakers, actors, and writers who were blacklisted during the McCarthy era by the House Un-American Activities Committee. One of those who spoke in memory of his blacklisted father was the writer and producer Tony Khan, who calls himself "a child of the blacklist."

"I saw it kill him," Khan says, "and I saw the silence kill him." Khan talks of the lessons of that period. "Better do what you can to head the fear off at the pass before it gets to town," he says, "because once it gets to town it's almost too late. You don't know what you are going to do until the time comes, whether you are going to have the guts or not, and don't think you do know before you're tested because there are a lot of surprises and most surprises are unpleasant." He pauses and then continues, "When it comes to the blacklist the other thing we learned is that it can happen in the world's greatest democracy. You don't have to have a policeman pointing a gun at your head to make you do something that takes you very close to a police state."

This is the immediacy of the situation of which I write. Teachers have been silenced and speak of intimidation, educational researchers have had their work blacklisted, and some have been personally vilified.

"It's 1984 only it's 1997," says Lee Grant, who was blacklisted during the McCarthy era, only now it's 1998.[19] To capture the immediacy of the situation you might want to begin by reading the chapters on Texas or California, or go straight to the chapter on Washington, D.C. Then you might want to go back to the beginning of the book and consider the research that is behind the events that are taking place. Wherever you begin, keep in mind Keith Haring's labyrinth on the cover of *Spin Doctors*. I spent a lot of time looking at it as I wrote the book.

1

In which we are told training in phonemic awareness is the key to reading success

■ ■ ■

In Atlanta, Georgia, at the International Reading Association's 1997 Annual Convention, the exhibit hall is full of teachers. There is music, laughter, neon light, and vivid color, from purple, scarlet, and cadmium yellow to ultramarine, pamphlets to collect, games to play, and prizes to be given away. Smartly dressed sales associates beckon to teachers and invite them to take a look at the new reading programs they are selling. In years past, the publishers of children's literature drew teachers in with posters of illustrations from the latest story books in artists' subtle shades. But this year things have changed. Now teachers are given samples of phonemic awareness products and letter-cluster charts to post on their classroom walls.

"When you get home," the salesperson says as she gives a teacher a chart, "you need to take a razor and cut out the first two consonant digraphs." The salesperson laughs. "We made a mistake. We're reprinting, but you can use this chart if you cut out the cheese." She points to the wedge of yellow cheese with *ch* beside it.

"Is that a treble clef or a chord?" the teacher asks, pointing to the picture of a musical notation with a *ch* beside it—the other consonant digraph she is supposed to cut out.

"Good question," the salesperson says, laughing. "I don't know. I'd just cut it out."

The McGraw-Hill exhibit for Open Court includes a big beautiful box in bright primary colors. It's the Phonemic Awareness and Phonics Kit, complete with teacher's guide, phonemic awareness cards, phonics cards, sound spelling cards, learning framework cards, activity sheets, individual sound/spelling cards, letter cards, alphabet flash cards, outlaw word flash cards, phonemic awareness and phonics audiocassettes, and take-home phonics minibooks. It is a bonanza for teachers who have been told that they must shift away from holistic and process-oriented instruction to systematic, intensive, explicit, direct instruction in phonemic awareness and other scientifically based methods of teaching young children to read.

"The program is based on the latest scientific research," the salesperson says, as she introduces the teacher to the sales executive who works in her region. The sales executive gives the teacher his card.

At Scholastic the exhibit is as enticing as Hansel and Gretel's gingerbread house in reds, yellows, and blues, and smiling sales representatives greet teachers as they step inside. An entire section is devoted to the phonics and phonemic awareness exhibit, and there are lots of advertisements, pamphlets, and samples for teachers to take.

"Research shows that 11 to 15 hours of training in phonemic awareness is the key to reading success," the phonics pamphlet states authoritatively.

"Is there a difference between phonics and phonemic awareness?" a teacher asks. It's noisy and the salesperson appears not to hear her question, so she doesn't get an answer; instead, the still-smiling salesperson stretches out her arm with more pamphlets for the teacher to take.

"At Literacy Place young readers get skills instruction that is explicit and systematic, with an emphasis on phonics, phonemic awareness and other cueing systems," one of the publicity pamphlets gushes.

Another brochure touts Scholastic Spelling as "the only program based on powerful new research on how children learn to spell." Tucked into this pamphlet are pictures of the authors. There's a picture of researcher Barbara Foorman smiling, and a short blurb that tells teachers that she has been awarded four National Institute of Child Health and Human Development grants to study dyslexia and other reading problems.

We plan to direct public and private funds to programs that introduce teachers to the work of these outstanding scientists

In Texas, Barbara Foorman and her colleagues demonstrated that an explicit focus on teaching phonemic awareness skills increases the test scores of the children participating in their research studies. "What we're doing here," Foorman says, talking about her research, "is getting these economically disadvantaged low achievers almost up to the national average with just good classroom instruction."[1]

In California, Bill Honig, the former State Superintendent of Schools, states that Foorman's research frames the debate. "It's like in science when you get a theory," he explains, "and you have evidence to back it up and the results are what you predicted, you know you have something."[2]

Like Honig, the California State Board of Education is impressed with the kind of research that Foorman is doing, and a Reading Program Advisory is created to help develop a balanced approach to teaching reading for children in pre-kindergarten classrooms through third grade.[3]

"Research has shown repeatedly," the Reading Program Advisory states, "that phonemic awareness is a powerful predictor of success in learning to read." Quoting Keith Stanovich in one of his definitive studies, "Matthew Effects in Reading," the California Board asserts that "phonemic awareness is more highly related to learning to read than are tests of general intelligence, reading readiness, and listening comprehension."

Then, with reference to Marilyn Jager Adams—who is the author of the government-sponsored report, *Beginning to Read,* as well as an author of *Open Court*—the Board expands upon this indisputable finding of empirical science: "The lack of phonemic awareness is the most powerful determinant of the likelihood of failure to learn to read because of its importance in learning the English alphabetic system or learning how print represents spoken words."

The Advisory Board continues with a reference to Adams by stating categorically, "If children cannot hear and manipulate the sounds in spoken words, they have an extremely difficult time learning how to map those sounds to letters and letter patterns—the essence of decoding."[4]

Back in Texas at the Houston Reading Conference, Darvin Winick, a member of Governor Bush's Business Council and a senior business executive who voluntarily works on public policy, states his case: "The rules of engagement are stated and clear," he tells the teachers who have gathered there.[5] "Full public disclosure of the scientific bases for program development and well-defined experimental procedures are expected. We will measure and report the results." The teachers in the audience are silent. "Last year we spent considerable time and energy reviewing the scientific literature on reading. We searched the country for good researchers. Fortunately, we had resources available to do this, and we are very comfortable in our ability to discriminate."

A few teachers smile; others nod their heads.

Winick continues, "Our search identified a group of highly competent researchers and teachers, including those associated with the National Institute of Child Health and Human Development." It's Winick's turn to smile as he tells the audience that Governor Bush's Business Council is especially proud that fellow Houstonians Barbara Foorman and her colleagues are a part of NICHD. "We plan to direct public and private funds to programs that introduce teachers to the work of these outstanding scientists."

Winick looks serious. "In reading—and this is stern, and I know that, and I mean to be, and I understand this is not the most popular kind of talk—but in reading, too many people seem to ignore what works and to stress dogma rather than data.

"Frankly, and honestly, we find the ongoing debate over reading ideologies unproductive. We are much less interested in the dogma. We do intend to follow empirical data on what is effective.

"You shake your head no, but that's the policy in Texas."

It is imperative that this information be made available to every superintendent and charter school leader

In Massachusetts, John Silber, Chairman of the Massachusetts Board of Education, sends a copy of the report that contains the scientific base to which Darvin Winick refers to every school superintendent in the state. The report, *30 Years of NICHD Research: What We Know about How Children Learn to Read*, was prepared by Bonnie Grossen, who is associated with DISTAR and direct instruction. The report focused upon the research of the National Institute of Child Health and Human Development (NICHD)—the group that funded Foorman's research that Winick mentioned.[6]

"As you know," Silber writes in his letter to Massachusetts school superintendents, "many claims have been made in recent years supporting a variety of new methods and techniques for teaching children to read. All too often, however, the evidence has shown that these methods, when used to the exclusion of all others, have failed."

After comments about California's "dramatic about-face," Silber writes, "The enclosed report documents the findings of a long-term, scientific study commissioned by the National Institute of Child Health and Human Development. Commissioner Robert Antonucci and I have discussed this report, and we both feel it is imperative that the information it contains be made available to every superintendent and charter school leader. I urge you to circulate this to your principals, teachers, and all others in your schools who are involved in teaching children to read."[7]

In the report, Grossen states categorically that 40 percent of people in the United States have "reading problems severe enough to hinder their enjoyment of reading" (p. 5). She goes on to state that "treatment research has shown that appropriate early direct instruction seems to be the best medicine for reading problems" (p. 6). And she states unequivocally that classroom teachers should take the following steps to prevent reading problems:

1. Begin teaching phonemic awareness directly at an early age (kindergarten);
2. Teach each sound-spelling correspondence explicitly;
3. Teach frequent, highly regular sound-spelling relationships systematically;
4. Show children exactly how to sound out words;
5. Use connected, decodable text for children to practice the sound-spelling relationships they learn;
6. Use interesting stories to develop language comprehension (these are teacher-read stories to build children's oral language comprehension).

"To appreciate fully the significance of the NICHD findings," Grossen writes, "it helps to understand the level of scientific rigor used to guide the formation of conclusions from the research." Grossen states that "each research study within the NICHD network must follow the most rigorous scientific procedures." She emphasizes that researchers for NICHD use the "true scientific model," and she criticizes other studies for their lack of scientific rigor. Grossen argues that it is the "usual nature of research in education" to present "untested hypotheses" as "proven theories" but that "in a true scientific paradigm, theories are tested by doing everything to try to prove the theory incorrect" (p. 2). Grossen goes on to explain that "researcher bias is reduced by the sheer number of people involved in the NICHD program."

This proposition reminds me of Winick's concern about data and not dogma. The more empirical the research studies, the lower the chance for error. As one study confirms the findings of another, the database grows and the conclusions become irrefutable. Publishers of basal readers and phonemic awareness programs are counting on it. States are investing all their money in these published programs. New laws are being written based upon this empirical evidence. In California, for example, the "ABC Bills" mandate the teaching of phonics and spelling, and the California Task Force of the State Board of Education has insti-

tutionalized the systematic and synthetic teaching of phonemic awareness based upon the scientific proof provided by the research.

The remedy for the problem must
be more of a "surgical strike"

But what if these eminent researchers got it wrong? What if there were
fundamental problems inherent in the design of the studies that they
conducted? If that were the case, the sheer number of researchers or
studies wouldn't help them. While it is true that many researchers have
conducted phonemic awareness studies, most of these studies are inter-
connected and interrelated and one study invariably builds on another.
A cites B in support of her rigorous scientific procedures; B cites C; C
cites A, B, and D; D cites B; and B then cites them all, including himself, in support of his arguments. Thus if the research studies of A and B
are fundamentally flawed, so must be the research of C and D. Neither
Winick's well-defined experimental procedures nor NICHD's replication of studies to test their theories will overcome this difficulty.

One statement in Grossen's report with which I agree is that "in a
true scientific paradigm, theories are tested by doing everything to try to
prove the theory incorrect." At a time when publishing companies are
making statements about scientific evidence for their phonemic awareness programs and when states such as California, Texas, Massachusetts,
North Carolina, and Virginia are using the findings of these research
studies to change the ways in which young children are to taught to read
and write in schools, it is imperative that we examine the evidence and
test the theories in which Bill Honig and Darvin Winick have put their
faith.

Whether in schools or in universities, we must accept the responsibility to respond to the research—not with ideological arguments, but
with a thorough analysis of the data and the documentation on which
decisions are being based. This is the task we must set for ourselves,
whether we agree or disagree, whatever our philosophy. We must examine the facts and ask: Is the research responsive to the social, cultural,
and intellectual lives of children? How was the research conducted?
What are the ethical issues? Were the scientific procedures rigorous?
Were the tests and measurements relevant to the stated objectives of the
studies? Were the hypotheses properly tested? Were the theories proven?
What does the research really indicate? Correlation or causation? Are
there alternative explanations for the results? What is the impact of the
research on the lives of children and their families?

And if, when this is done, we find that the theories we have tested are scientifically defective, filled with unsubstantiated assumptions and insupportable "evidence," and are essentially just "spin," then we must ask ourselves, what are the consequences for children of the widespread use of these studies in determining how they should be taught to read? In *Beginning to Read and the Spin Doctors of Science*, I will explore some of the possibilities.

Let's return now to my proposition that if A cites B; B cites C; C cites A, B, and D; D cites B; and B then cites them all, including himself, in support of his arguments, and B's (or A, C, or D's) research rationale and statistical procedures are fundamentally flawed, then this finding places in jeopardy the research findings of A, C, and D.

In my search for phonemic awareness studies on which to base my analysis, it has become clear that while there are many researchers who have contributed to the research base on the importance of phonemic awareness in learning to read, there are only a small number of researchers whose studies are central to the idea that we should *specifically* teach phonemic awareness skills to young children.

One of these researchers is Barbara Foorman, who consistently references Marilyn Jager Adams and Keith Stanovich, both of whom also agree that phonemic awareness should be specifically taught. In *Beginning to Read*, Adams relies heavily on the research studies conducted by Stanovich. She discusses no fewer than eight of his articles in her report, and in her bibliography she makes twenty-six references to his work, including "Matthew Effects in Reading: Some Consequences of Individual Differences in the Acquisition of Literacy," which received the Albert J. Harris Award from the International Reading Association, is also referred to by Foorman, and is one of the most-cited research articles in support of the proposition that variation in phonological awareness is causally related to the early development of reading.

"The remedy for the problem must be more of a 'surgical strike,' to use a military analogy," Stanovich writes in "Matthew Effects in Reading," adding, a few sentences later, "identify early, remedy early, and focus on phonological awareness" (pp. 393, 394).

The research of Foorman and Stanovich is also discussed in Grossen's report on the research of NICHD—which is hardly surprising, since both receive research funding from that institute. Adams's government report is also mentioned. Because the research of Foorman and Stanovich and the report written by Adams are also frequently referred to and relied upon by governmental agencies at the national, state, and local levels, I have begun my evaluation of the research on phonemic awareness with an analysis of some of their work. The Foorman studies that are a part my analysis are those referred to by Honig and Winick, which are also relied upon by the states of California, Texas, and North Carolina.[8] They are also the studies referred to by Grossen in the NICHD research circulated by John Silber to every superintendent in the state of Massachusetts.

In my analysis of Stanovich's research, I have begun with "Matthew Effects in Reading," and I have also read the reports of a number of the studies to which he refers in that article.[9] "Even more popular has been my work on Matthew Effects in the reading development," Stanovich writes in his "Distinguished Educator" article in *Reading Teacher.* "The term Matthew Effects derives from the Gospel according to Matthew: 'For unto everyone that hath shall be given, and he shall have abundance; but from him that hath not shall be taken away even that which he hath' (XXV: 29). It is used to describe rich-get-richer and poor-get-poorer effects that are embedded in the educational process" (p. 281).

In addition, I have also read many of the studies which now refer to "Matthew Effects" as if Stanovich's arguments and conclusions are indisputable. Thus the corpus of data for this analysis goes well beyond what I consider to be just the primary studies in phonemic awareness.

Since I am trained in both anthropology and psychology, I will present a synthesis of my analysis from two very different perspectives. I begin with an exploration of empirical research in which reading is regarded as a psychological process and the emphasis is on reading words.[10] This is an "in-the-head" viewpoint on young children learning to read, which, as Adams states, "depends as much on [children] detecting invariants as on attending to distinctive or differentiating features" (p. 203). Learning to read is "the creation or strengthening of associations"—visual, auditory, motor, or conceptual—"to interlink the printed appearance of words with one's knowledge of their sounds, contexts, functions, and meanings" (p. 206).

Then I will explore the research on phonemic awareness from the sociocultural perspectives of practical intelligence and everyday cognition. Such a viewpoint takes the research out of the child's head, considers learning to read (and write) from the perspective of literacy as social and cultural practice, and draws upon research in literacy but also on the work of many other scholars whose work is relevant to our understandings of the reading process and how young children learn to read.

"Speech," Oliver Sacks explains in an essay, "natural speech, does *not* consist of words alone, nor of 'propositions' alone. It consists of *utterance*—an uttering-forth of one's whole meaning with one's whole being—the understanding of which involves infinitely more than mere word-recognition" ("The President's Speech," p. 81). Similarly, reading is more than decoding the sounds that letters and groups of letters represent, or even of reading words. I can decode and "read" entire paragraphs in Spanish — but that doesn't mean that I understand what the text *means*.

"Reading, then," Alberto Manguel writes, "is not an automatic process of capturing text in the way photosensitive paper captures light, but a bewildering, labyrinthine,[11] common and yet personal process of reconstruction. Whether reading is independent from, for instance, listening," Manguel continues, "whether it is a single distinctive set of psychological processes or consists of a great variety of such processes, researchers don't yet know, but many believe that its complexity may be as great as that of thinking itself" (p. 39).

You might think that much of this sounds like a dry intellectual treatise, a silly argument between academics and nothing more, but as I found out as I was writing *Beginning to Read and the Spin Doctors of Science*, politics doesn't stop at the schoolhouse door.

In which phonemic awareness research is analyzed from an experimental psychological perspective

■ ■ ■

My analysis of the documentation begins with an examination of the research on phonemic awareness from an experimental psychological perspective.[1] I focus primarily on the foundational work of Keith Stanovich and his co-researchers Anne Cunningham, Barbara Cramer, and Dorothy Feeman, who participated with him in different phonemic awareness studies. What I have found, you will see, is that in these phonemic awareness research reports and articles, other studies are selectively and misleadingly cited out of context to support the argument that explicit training in phonemic awareness is the key to reading success.

I have also reviewed the published accounts of many of the experimental studies that Stanovich and Foorman reference to support their proposition that explicit phonemic awareness training is the key to reading success.[2] To some degree, all of these experimental studies: (1) were based on the assumption of cultural uniformity; (2) focused on aggregates of children; (3) separated children's everyday lives from their performance on isolated cognitive tasks; (4) artificially disconnected the forms of written language from the functional meanings of print; (5) assumed that children's early cognitive functions work from abstract exercises to reading as meaningful activity; (6) depended on cognitive tests that have no value outside the testing situation; (7) assumed the transfer of learning; and (8) totally disregarded the critical relationships that exist between teachers and children. Further, a critical review of a number of key studies that are frequently cited reveals that some of the research used to support the direct training argument does not support this proposition. Some studies actually provide contradictory evidence.

To support the statement that studies are selectively and misleadingly cited out of context, I will focus on one of the landmark articles in phonemic awareness research — "Matthew Effects in Reading" by Keith Stanovich. In this paper Stanovich discusses the literature on individual differences in the cognitive skills related to reading, and he uses his critique of the literature to support the hypothesis that slow development in phonemic awareness "delays early code-breaking progress and initiates the cascade of interacting achievement failures and motivational problems" (p. 393).

"The cycle of escalating achievement deficits must be broken," Stanovich asserts, "in a more specific way to short-circuit the cascade of negative spinoffs" (p. 393).

To bolster his argument for phonemic awareness training, Stanovich writes, "a growing body of data does exist indicating that variation in phonological awareness is causally related to the early development of reading skill." In this context he states, "most convincing, are the results of several studies where phonological awareness skills were manipulated via training, and the manipulation resulted in significant experimental group advantages in reading, word recognition, and spelling" (p. 363).

One of the studies that Stanovich cites in support of this statement is by Swedish researchers Åke Olofsson and Ingvar Lundberg, a study in which the "long-term effects" of phonemic awareness training in kindergarten are evaluated. "Great variances, ceiling effects, and group heterogeneity created many difficulties in evaluating the training effects," Olofsson and Lundberg write in the abstract of their paper. They state in their discussion of methodological problems that "the increase in precision gained from an elaborated statistical analysis may be rather small compared to the uncertainty introduced by the post-test treatment delay and the lack of randomization often occurring in practical settings. However, this is no excuse for not trying to make the best of the situation."

In discussing their testing protocols, these researchers caution that "[I]n addition, we must consider the effects of violating the assumptions about normally distributed scores and homogenous error variances. Distributional violations have generally small effects but unequal variances in combination with unequal group sizes may seriously affect the statistical significance tests."

In an examination of their "preschool test protocols," Olofsson and Lundberg observe, "the children with negative development almost without exception passed the tests very fast rendering test-administer's remarks like 'fast' and 'very fast.'" They go on to state, "On some test protocols the assistant had made notes like 'ants in the pants.'" The researchers then talk about letter-name bias and comment that "some children completely refused to utter phonemes or certain phonemes but could silently make the correct synthesis."

Olofsson and Lundberg observe that a great number of children had already reached a high level of phonemic awareness before starting school and before participating in their phonemic awareness training program. Interestingly, they also found some nonreaders who had "complete ability" with their phonemic awareness test. How could this be explained? Olofsson and Lundberg do not answer this question.

Olofsson and Lundberg conclude, "The ability to predict the effect of, for example, a four-month or a two-semester training program is limited. However, the results found here suggest that a longer training program in combination with an examination of the children's total alphabetical environment could yield important information about the parameters in the development of phonemic awareness."

By juxtaposing statements made by Stanovich with those of Olofsson and Lundberg, it is possible to gain some appreciation of the ways in which studies are selectively and misleadingly cited out of context. Clearly, there is much to be learned from the research of Olofsson and Lundberg, but their research does not provide strong support for Stanovich's argument. Contrary to the claim by Stanovich that this study provides "most convincing" evidence that training in phonemic awareness is "causally related to the early development of reading skill," the most that Olofsson and Lundberg say is that "the children who participated in the phonemic training program seemed to have benefited from it to some extent. At least they improved their scores on phonemic synthesis tests in school."

The misleading use of citations might seem like a small problem— but consider the larger context. "Matthew Effects in Reading" is relied upon by both Adams and Foorman, and it is also relied upon by the state of California to justify the "ABC Bills" and to mandate that children receive phonemic awareness training. NICHD has used "Matthew Effects in Reading" in the report that Silber sent to every school superintendent in the state of Massachusetts. But when the references are checked, they are often problematic. Much of what is stated by Stanovich is little more than "spin doctoring" to support an argument with which many researchers and teachers who have spent their lives observing children's early literacy development would strongly disagree.

Let me provide another example. Once again I will stick closely to the text to avoid overinterpretation. In "Matthew Effects in Reading," having "established" causation between phonemic awareness and early reading development—at least to his own satisfaction—Stanovich goes on to discuss the concept of "reciprocal causation." He cites the work of Linea Ehri, which suggests that reading acquisition itself facilitates phonological awareness. He adds references to Charles Perfetti, and to Richard Wagner and Joseph Torgesen, and then states that "the situation appears to be one of reciprocal causation." But none of the references Stanovich provides supports this proposition.

"Such situations of reciprocal causation can have important 'bootstrapping effects'" Stanovich states, without any evidence to back him up. Then comes the spin. "However, the question . . . is not which direction of causality is dominant. The essential properties of the model being outlined here are dependent only on the fact that a causal link running from phonological awareness to reading acquisition has been established, independent of the status of the opposite causal link" (p. 363).

Unfortunately for this argument, the articles that are cited do not establish conditions of reciprocal causality; in fact they do not even establish causality. At best, and even then subject to the many limitations and problems inherent in the various studies, all that they establish is a possible correlation, and correlation is *not* causation—in either direction. But let's suspend judgement for a moment and say, "Okay, we accept that there is an apparent correlation between phonemic awareness and reading acquisition, and that this may imply a causal link one way or the other." By what leap of faith can we then discard one of these two possibilities and accept only the other, as Stanovich does when he states that "the causal link running from phonological awareness to reading acquisition has been established independent of the status of the opposite causal link?"

More importantly, how do we end up with the definitive conclusion that the direction of this phenomenon of reciprocal causation is unimportant? Clearly it is of national importance. School districts across the country are being told by state governments to shift direction in reading instruction, so how can it not be important? Where's the data to support Stanovich's "one way" causal link conclusion that explicit teaching of phonemic awareness will lead to reading acquisition? Certainly not in "Matthew Effects in Reading," nor in any of the other papers that I have read on phonemic awareness.

However, if we continue to suspend judgement and put aside the severe limitations of experimental research studies, we could still find empirical evidence that contradicts the position that Stanovich has taken. In a paper published one year after "Matthew Effects in Reading," Perfetti, Beck, Bell, and Hughes write, "What is clear is that learning to read can begin in a variety of ways, most of which may require only minimal explicit knowledge of speech segments. Thus, the rudimentary ability to manipulate isolated segments may be necessary for significant progress in reading. However, *it is reading itself*, we suggest, that enables the child to be able to analyze words and to manipulate their speech segments. It is not that the reader performs such manipulations on the orthography. Rather, learning some orthographic principles *through reading* enables the discovery of parallel phonemic principles" (p. 317, emphasis added).

A final example of selective and misleading referencing that will provide a context for a critical analysis of the Barbara Foorman studies that have received national attention is Stanovich's contention that "Although general indicators of cognitive functioning such as nonverbal intelligence, vocabulary, and listening comprehension make significant independent contributions to predicting the ease of initial reading acquisition, phonological awareness stands out as the most potent predictor" (p. 363). To support this statement Stanovich quotes a research study that he conducted with Anne Cunningham and Dorothy Feeman.[3]

In this study these researchers administered a series of tests to first-, third-, and fifth-grade children who attended a "predominantly middle-class" elementary school. The children were given tests of general intelligence—the Picture Peabody Vocabulary Test (all groups); the Raven's Colored Progressive Matrices (1st and 3rd grades); and the Raven's Standard Progressive Matrices (5th grade). Then there were timed decoding tests with words and pseudowords—*lat, wuck, mip, mish*—and vocal reaction times were assessed. Then the children were tested for reading comprehension with the "stimuli" for each group consisting of three paragraphs taken from the 1972 Revised Edition of the Diagnostic Reading Scale. Then there were two phonological awareness tasks for the first graders—"the strip initial consonant task" and the "phonological oddity task." In addition, the authors state that "All of the children had completed other cognitive tasks that were part of another investigation." Notably, there is no discussion of the effects of all this testing on the children.

In analyzing the tasks that were given to the children in this testing situation, we might begin by asking a critical question raised by Sylvia Scribner.[4] "To what extent does the (experimental) task selected for study share at least some characteristics with other tasks?," Scribner asks, with regard to the phenomena being studied. In other words, are these laboratory tasks representative of the ways in which young children encounter print in their everyday lives? *Is this reading? Lat. Wuck. Mip. Mish.* I would think not. If the pseudowords were timed, would that reflect everyday uses of print? Definitely not. Knowing how contrived the paragraphs are on the Diagnostic Reading Scale, is this task representative of authentic reading tasks? Almost certainly not. Given these difficulties, can we generalize from the completion of these tasks? I suggest not. The researchers do not establish cross-task commonality on these arbitrarily selected laboratory tasks. Given that the tasks have no generalizability, Scribner encourages us to focus on the children and ask ourselves whether the researchers can make generalized statements based on the performance of such a small number of individual children. Intuitively, we might answer, we don't think so.

The importance of statistics should not be overestimated

But we don't have to answer intuitively; we can answer analytically. If we examine the statistical procedures we can question whether the research supports the proposition that phonological awareness stands out as the most potent predictor of the ease of initial reading acquisition. Before we examine the statistics, however, let me say that I am convinced that one of the reasons the phonemic awareness research has gone unchallenged is that most of us are not comfortable in critiquing statistical studies. For my own part, I am fascinated by mathematical representations and by the problem solving involved in statistical analysis, and fortunately, over the years I've had considerable support in my analysis of reading studies which rely heavily on the use of parametric statistics. I've consulted with a statistician who has a Ph.D. in statistics, is a fellow of the American Statistical Association, was awarded a senior research fellowship in statistics at the National Institute of Standards and Technology, and has received many awards for his work in statistics. I've also worked closely with a scientist with considerable expertise in engineering statistics who has spent the last fifteen years critically analyzing the uses and misuses of statistical procedures in commercial settings. Experimental psychologists use the same basic parametric statistical procedures to study the cognitive functioning of children as engineers use to assess the failure rates of mechanical components in nuclear power plants and commercial aircraft.

 The study Stanovich cites to support the proposition that "phonological awareness stands out as the most potent predictor" of "ease of initial reading acquisition" violates three fundamental properties of parametric statistics. The first property is that the sample on which measurements are being made is a *random* sample from both the specific population being studied and the population to which the results are being generalized. The "sample" in Stanovich, Cunningham, and Feeman's study is in fact highly subjective and selective with 56 first-grade children, 18 third-grade children, and 20 fifth-grade children drawn from a middle-class elementary school.

In the published article, Stanovich, Cunningham, and Feeman recognize that this situation is problematic: "The sizes of the third- and fifth-grade samples were small, rendering tentative any conclusions from the results of these groups" (p. 298). Unfortunately, this caveat does not appear when the study is cited in "Matthew Effects in Reading," nor in Adams's *Beginning to Read*.

The second fundamental property of parametric statistics on which the experimenters based their analysis is that both the population and the sample are normally distributed with respect to the attribute being studied. The experimenters do not present their raw data nor do they show how the various test results are distributed. But with such small numbers of children, it is highly unlikely that the scores were normally distributed. The lack of a normal distribution is problematic.

"Low power and non-normal distributions of test scores lie behind the limited application of statistical tests," Olofsson and Lundberg write in the article cited earlier. Then they add that "the importance of statistics should not be overestimated." Non-normal distributions raise all kinds of questions about the data, but even if the sample distributions were normal, the experimenters' statistical inferences and conclusions would still *only* apply to their limited and subjective sample and *not* to any broader population—which is the answer to Scribner's question.

The third fundamental property of parametric statistical analysis involves the use of an interval scale. Using a strategy that is typical of most of the experimental research on phonemic awareness, Stanovich, Cunningham, and Feeman use variables and test measurements which are both qualitative and subjective, that are at best ordinal, and convert them into number-assigned, interval scales in order to use parametric statistical procedures.

In further support of these arguments, I refer you to Sidney Siegel's *Nonparametric Statistics for the Behavioral Sciences*. The third chapter focuses on parametric statistics—the kind of statistics used in phonemic awareness studies. Siegel presents a clear discussion of the assumptions, problems, and dangers inherent in the use of parametric statistical tests in the behavioral sciences. Siegel's discussion supports the criticisms stated above that, in general, the manner in which the sample is drawn, the nature of the population from which the sample is drawn, and the kind of measurement or scaling which is employed to define the variables involved, *all preclude the use of parametric statistical methods*.

Siegel also lists the conditions which must be satisfied before *any* confidence can be placed in *any* probability statement obtained by the use of parametric tests (p. 19) and notes that "these conditions are ordinarily not tested in the course of the performance of a statistical analysis. Rather, they are presumptions which are accepted, and their truth or falsity determines the meaningfulness of the probability statement arrived at by the parametric test." He further notes that the "scales used by behavioral scientists typically are at best no stronger than ordinal" (p. 26), and that the inappropriate use of "interval" scales results from the "untested assumptions" made by investigators, including the assumption that the underlying distribution is "normal" (p. 27).[5]

Siegel concludes his discussion by noting that "the assumptions which must be made to justify the use of parametric tests usually rest on conjecture and hope, for knowledge about the population parameters is almost invariably lacking" (p. 32). This certainly applies to the study of Stanovich, Cunningham, and Feeman.

But other assumptions are also made that are particularly problematic. In this study the researchers quite literally discarded data. For example, in their test of "decoding speed"—the naming of 20 real words and 15 pseudowords—they simply discarded all incorrect responses and all responses where the "subjects" took longer than 3 seconds to name a word. How many of the 35 individual words did each "subject" get right in less than 3 seconds, and how many responses from the "subjects" were discarded? Did they discard just a few answers from a few children, many answers from a few children, or many answers from many children? We don't know, because the experimenters don't say, but in another of their speed tests, they admit to discarding 20 percent of the children's answers as "inappropriate" before analyzing the remaining data.

In the "decoding speed" test, Stanovich, Cunningham, and Feeman also proceed to analyze the remaining data, with the result that the "subjects'" response times on this decoding test were highly correlated with their reading comprehension as measured by the Metropolitan Achievement Test. The magnitude of the effect that inclusion of the discarded data would have had on this correlation is unknown, but the correlation would obviously be reduced, perhaps even to insignificance. The researchers further claim that this "decoding speed" test had a high "split-half reliability" (Spearman Brown Corrected), when in fact George Ferguson, in *Statistical Analysis in Psychology and Education*, states categorically that this reliability measure should not be used with speed tests (p. 367).[6]

Given the statistically inappropriate procedures which Stanovich, Cunningham, and Feeman use throughout this study, and their "selective" use of some of the data, the reliance on this study in "Matthew Effects" to support the proposition that phonological awareness stands out as the most potent predictor of the ease of initial reading acquisition seems highly questionable.[7] But the problems with this research go even deeper.

Mechanical models break down hopelessly before the sheer creativity of the brain

"One of the reasons I'm against mechanical models," Oliver Sacks tells interviewer Wim Kayzer, "is that they are too physicalistic and too reductive and too impoverished and too boring, and I think they break down hopelessly finally before the sheer creativity of the brain."[8]

Kayzer asks several questions, and Sacks continues talking about the brain. "It's not a library. It's not a granary. It's not a computer." Then, speaking of memory, Sacks asserts, "memories are constructions and not xeroxes, not facsimiles, not reproductions." A few minutes later he says, "There is no snapshot of how things are. Whatever comes into the mind always comes in a new context and in some sense is colored by the present. This doesn't mean that it is distorted, but it is against any mechanical reproduction."

The research studies on phonemic awareness that I have reviewed are too physicalistic, too reductionist, and too impoverished. The theories on which these studies are founded do break down whenever I have observed or worked with a young child who is learning to read. The brain is not a library; it's not a granary; it's not a computer. And children do not produce mechanical reproductions when they are learning to read.

In which phonemic awareness research is analyzed from a sociocultural perspective

■ ■ ■

I am now going to shift my focus to explore the central characteristics of phonemic awareness research from the perspective of research on practical intelligence and everyday cognition. This analysis builds on the work of Michael Cole, Anne Haas Dyson, Emilia Ferreiro and Ana Teberosky, Jean Lave, Barbara Rogoff, Sylvia Scribner, Lev Vygotsky, and James Wertsch, all well-known scholars who are highly regarded for their scientific research.

From the perspective of research on practical intelligence and everyday cognition, the major criticisms of phonemic awareness research are as follows:

1. Experimentation rests on the assumption of cultural and social uniformity.

Jean Lave argues that the concept of cultural uniformity "has served as a mandate to treat culture in cognitive studies as if it were a constant, as if nothing essential about thinking would be disturbed if its effects were controlled experimentally."[1] The assumption of cultural uniformity is a fundamental theoretical weakness in phonemic awareness research. Ignoring the social, cultural, and intellectual lives of children invalidates the measures.

Inspired by the ideas of Vygotsky, Luis Moll explores the concept of the cultural mediation of thinking in his research which focuses on Spanish-speaking children in school and at home with their families.[2] "This social thing called literacy has come to possess you," Moll says, "you find it unthinkable to live without it, and for most of you, reading has become a substitute for life." To explain the concept of cultural mediation, Moll quotes Scribner, who was his colleague and friend, as if in conversation with her.

"Vygotsky's special genius," Scribner writes, "was in grasping the significance of the social in things as well as people. The world in which we live is humanized, full of material and symbolic objects." She gives as examples signs and knowledge systems, for example, "that are culturally constructed, historical in origin and social in content." She continues, "Since all human actions, including acts of thought, involve the mediation of such objects," which she describes as tools and signs, "they are, on this score alone, social in essence. This is the case, whether acts are initiated by single agents or a collective and whether they are performed individually or with others."[3]

"To put it succinctly," Moll writes in his to-and-fro with Scribner, "people interact with their worlds, which are 'humanized, full of material and symbolic objects,' through these mediational means, and their mediation of actions through cultural artifacts, *especially language in both its oral and written forms* plays a crucial role in the formation and development of human intellectual capacities. Notice that the central point is not simply about the importance of tool and symbol use by human beings, it is a stronger claim than that, it refers to the essential role of cultural mediation in the constitution of human psychology."[4]

In phonemic awareness studies, children do not interact with their world. Their lives are dehumanized, and researchers ignore or remain unaware of the role of cultural mediation in the early reading development of young children. In positivistic research there is a total lack of recognition that literacy—I prefer to talk about both reading and writing—is embedded in everyday activities, or that the use of complex symbolic systems is an everyday phenomenon constitutive of and grounded in the everyday lives of young children and their families.[5]

2. There are no children in the phonemic awareness studies, only labels, aggregates, and measures.

In these studies children are referred to as "normals," "good readers," "poor readers," "disabled readers," "passive organisms," and "subjects," subscript i in a mathematical formula, and "cohorts." Nameless, faceless, they are phenotypes, data points on a scatter plot, "phonologically disabled," "phonologically deficient," and "limited English proficient." In one study children are identified as 70 percent African American, 16 percent Hispanic, 5 percent Asian, 9 percent White, and 15 percent ESL, but that is all. They are anonymous, their lives unknown. They are identified only by their participation in federal lunch programs, segregated by their socioeconomic status, ethnicity, and race or by their scores on some artificial test. Irrespective of what is happening to them, they all receive the same "treatment," and there is a total disregard of the social, political, and economic circumstances in which young children live their everyday lives.

To meet Erik and Alejandra and Marisela in studies of early literacy development, we must turn to the research of Emilia Ferreiro and Ana Teberosky.[6] To learn more about the literacy development of Jameel and Ayesha and William, we must read Anne Haas Dyson.[7] In fact, there are numerous longitudinal studies of children's early literacy development that are disciplined and systematic in their data collection procedures and rigorous in their scientific analysis, and these provide counterevidence to the reductionist empirical studies of phonemic awareness and early reading development.[8]

3. In phonemic awareness research, there is a complete separation of children's everyday worlds from their performance on certain isolated cognitive tasks.

Such an approach to the study of language and literacy is problematic, and the difficulties are underscored by James Wertsch, who writes, "Like Vygotsky and Bakhtin, I believe that it is often difficult if not meaningless to isolate various aspects of mental processes for separate analysis" (p. 14). The phonemic awareness research ignores the social and cultural embeddedness of human learning.[9] The research disregards the considerable body of work which explores the social and cultural literacy practices of very young children. For example, in her discussion of the social consequences of written formulas, Anne Dyson provides a powerful example of the ways young children search for meaning in isolated cognitive tasks.[10]

"This is a story about AbcdefGhiJklMnoPQRstuvwXYz," a first grader writes, "One day there was a A. And One DaY There was a B. And One Day there was a c. I like aBcdefGhiJKlmnoPQrstuvwxY and Z The End"

Even so, as Dyson states, "A quick story about ABC would not be likely to engender an intense response from one's peers." The social fabric of learning breaks down. Mapping the smallest units of sound onto the smallest units of print is an irrelevant activity. It's hard to read a story about a digraph or a schwa.

4. In phonemic awareness research, the form of written language is separated from the meaningful interpretation of the text.

There is no text. The practice of investigating the mapping of isolated sounds onto decontextualized units of print has no purpose for the reader. It is a meaningless exercise. You cannot have an opinion about a digraph, you cannot express how you feel about a diphthong, and you cannot deepen your knowledge of your everyday world with an "øū" or an "ēÿ." Children cannot discuss the phonemic awareness exercises that are prescribed to them within the sociocultural contexts of their everyday lives. Vowel digraphs have no meaning in time and space. No transactions can take place.

"Recall," Louise Rosenblatt tells us, "that the text is more than mere paper and ink." Then, referring to the reader, she states, "The physical signs of the text enable him to reach through himself and the verbal symbols to something sensed as outside and beyond his own personal world."[11]

In *Family Literacy*, the first of my own longitudinal studies of young children learning to read and write, I stated, "The children's increasing fascination with both writing and reading was well evidenced in the present research, and their fascination with print seems to occur when they become highly sophisticated in their functional utility of print." And then, as if I was preparing to write *Spin Doctors* almost twenty years later, I wrote, "Developing metalinguistic awareness of written language forms was added to the literacy agenda of the children. But still, the activities were meaningful in their everyday lives" (p. 77).

In *Growing Up Literate* the same applies. Except of course in school, where the African American children who participated in the longitudinal study sat in highly controlled situations—"(I) don't *want to see anybody with a blank scrap paper.*" "*Don't let me see you rushing through this.*" "*Get busy young lady. Now!*"—doing meaningless phonemic awareness exercises, even though they were reading and writing in out-of-school contexts and even though written language was functional in their everyday lives (p. 105).

We cannot reduce children's lives to a meaningless exercise. As Ferreiro states, "the process by which a child arrives at an understanding of a particular type of representation of spoken language, e.g., alphabetic writing, cannot be reduced to the establishment of a series of habits and skills."[12]

5. Phonemic awareness research is based on the false assumption that children's early cognitive functions work from abstract exercises to meaningful activity.

To the contrary, as Vygotsky states, "We have found that sign operations appear as a result of a complex and prolonged process subject to all the basic laws of psychological evolution. *This means that sign-using activity in children is neither simply invented nor passed down by adults:* rather it arises from something that is originally not a sign operation and becomes one only after a series of qualitative transformations" (emphasis in the original).[13]

An example of these Vygotskian evolutionary processes and qualitative transformations in a child's early reading and writing is provided by the story of Nicola, whose teacher participated in the Biographic Literacy Profiles Project (BLiPP), a longitudinal study of early literacy development which lasted from 1986 to 1994.[14] Nicola was sexually and physically abused by her father for the first three years of her life. In kindergarten Nicola was supported both socially and academically by Sharron, her teacher, who did not force her to practice phonemic awareness drills, or make her participate in other rehearsal-for-reading exercises. There were no "surgical strikes," to quote Stanovich, and there was no "quick remedy."

Nicola used writing as one of the ways in which she coped with the difficult circumstances of her everyday life. She wrote letters to her teacher and took telephone messages even though she did not know the letters of the alphabet and was unable to transform the sounds of language into their written form. But then, over the period of a year her scribble-like writing began to include letter-like forms. She began to connect letters with sounds. She used a pointer to point to the words in the big book stories that she "read" to the other children in the class and eventually she began reading some of the words in her own interpretation of the story.

But Nicola's ability to communicate through print had far deeper significance in her everyday life than just learning to read. When she was angry or afraid she expressed how she felt in print. On one occasion when her teacher was away and she was taught by a man, she wrote all over her face, her arms, and her legs. Through print, she expressed her anger and her grief, and eventually the ways in which she had learned to use print helped her to improve her sense of well-being.

I think of Nicola when I read the phonemic awareness research. If this approach to reading is going to be successful, it has to work for even the most fragile of our children. That it does not work for them is emphasized by what happened to Patrick, who received systematic, intensive instruction in phonics when he was in first grade.[15]

"Identify early, remedy early, and focus on phonological awareness," Stanovich states, and Patrick's school did exactly that. Patrick was identified and separated from the other children in his class as he received one-on-one instruction in DISTAR. Reading became a series of alphabetic drills and phonics skills. During vacations Patrick would come to my house and we would read books together. But during the school year there were often times when he quite literally just stopped reading.[16]

"Everything that was wonderful was constantly overshadowed by the difficulties that Patrick experienced in school," his mother says. Then she laughs. "I cried a lot. I got frustrated, and the frustration came out in tears a couple of times because I just felt like Patrick was never going to be allowed to grow up."

6. In phonemic awareness research, the tests given to children provide measures which are of no value outside of the testing situation.

In their discussion of social constraints in laboratory and classroom tasks, Denis Newman, Peg Griffin, and Michael Cole state, "The key to making claims in the laboratory is the psychologist's control over the task and the conditions under which the subjects undertake the task."[17] These researchers go on to state, "Whether laboratory settings are used for testing cognitive theories or for administering psychological tests, the cognitive processes modeled in them and the cognitive accomplishments tested are thought of as representing more than esoteric games. . . . But the constraints on activity used to create model systems render them systematically dissimilar to the systems of activity created in the society for other purposes"[18] (pp. 172–73).

Wertsch expands upon this argument. Citing studies by Donaldson, Rogoff, Cole and Scribner, Lave, and Rogoff and Lave, he states, "In general, these studies have shown that children and adults who were not thought to have a particular ability on the basis of an assessment in one context did in fact demonstrate that ability in other contexts" (p. 94). This has consistently been my experience as an ethnographer working with children and their families or with children and their teachers in school. In the Biographic Literacy Profiles Project, which lasted for more than eight years, I was continually working with teachers whose observations of children reading and writing in classroom settings did not support the findings of the tests that were administered to them.

Ironically, the test with which we had the most difficulty was the Woodcock-Johnson Revised—the same test that is used in many of the phonemic awareness studies I have included in my analysis, and the same test that was used by Foorman and her colleagues in the NICHD reading studies which are being used across the country to rationalize the new emphasis on teaching decontextual skills. During the course of the eight-year project, we were continually responding to children's deficits and "deficiencies" that were identified by the Woodcock-Johnson, but which were not evident in the disciplined and systematic documentation of children's reading and writing in classroom settings.

"That was the problem," one of the teachers with whom I worked for many years commented in a recent conversation. "We were always trying to counter the ways in which children's reading abilities were being tested in isolated situations. On tests like the Woodcock-Johnson, kids scored really low, but, for example in their everyday reading and writing, they did have the ability to encode and decode."

One of the children with whom we worked who was evaluated using the Woodcock-Johnson was an eleven-year-old boy called Bobby who had been to many schools. "Eight," he says, "That ain't helpful at all. That's dreadful because I didn't learn much."

"We're talking about a child who is working in the superior range and the retarded range," the psychologist tells us after he has tested Bobby. "I wouldn't be surprised if there were some perceptual-motor difficulties."

Bobby experienced difficulties on the Woodcock-Johnson with the subtest on blends. So when the psychologist labeled him learning disabled, one of the areas on which he was supposed to work was "blends." But when his teacher and his student support team examined his work, they found evidence of his use of blends in his writing in the initial, medial, and final positions. They documented the different kinds of blends that he was using and presented them to the child study team. Everybody agreed that the low score on the Woodcock-Johnson was an aberration of the test, and did not reflect Bobby's ability to use blends in his writing or to "decode" them in his reading.

As Barbara Rogoff states, "Skills that children seem not to possess in laboratory tasks thus appear well developed when these same children meet similar problems in familiar contexts" (p. 2).[19]

7. *In phonemic awareness research, there is an underlying assumption that there will be a transfer of learning from isolated phonemic awareness exercises to reading texts.*

This assumption is reminiscent of the late sixties and the alphabetic paradox which Phil Gough referred to as an "infamous fact."[20] In "The Cooperative Research Program in First Grade Reading Instruction," Guy Bond and Robert Dykstra reported that knowledge of the alphabet is the single best predictor of reading achievement.[21] But as Jay Samuels pointed out, there were no studies, and no evidence to support the proposition that specifically teaching the alphabet facilitated learning to read.[22] The question that was raised was whether the children who knew the alphabet were ever specifically taught the alphabet, and if they weren't, then why should we presume that other children will profit from such instruction?[23]

At about the same time in the sixties, there was a "phoneme-grapheme-correspondences-as-cue-to-spelling-improvement" movement; and a major study was undertaken at Stanford University which produced over 10,000 pages lists, analyses, and statistics regarding the subtle grapheme-phoneme correspondences in the American-English language. The purpose of this study was to reform language arts programs in schools across America—sound familiar?—and to help improve school spelling programs. Paul Hanna and his many colleagues who participated in the study produced a tome of 1,716 pages. Figure 3.1 has been adapted from their 22-vowel classification of graphemic options representing phonemes. Figure 3.2 is from the 30-consonant classification.

Just as specifically teaching the alphabet did not work, neither did the attempts that were made to improve spelling through specifically teaching the phoneme-grapheme relationships identified by the Stanford researchers. It didn't work for the reasons discussed earlier. There was a complete separation of children's everyday worlds from their performance on these isolated cognitive tasks. The form of written language was separated from the meaningful interpretation of the text. And the approach was based on the false assumption that the child's early cognitive functions progressed from abstract exercises to meaningful activity.

Unfortunately, it is the children that we have made most vulnerable, and it is children like Nicola and Patrick who are the victims of this form of instruction. Many children entering school have already developed a sensitivity to the ways in which the sounds of language are mapped on to units of print, but for a variety of reasons some children have not had the opportunity to develop this sensitivity. So too with the alphabetic principle. Instead of providing these children with the opportunity to sing songs, learn rhymes, listen to stories, and write their own texts in the ways that their friends have begun to learn to read, we do something quite different. Based upon experimental research and reductionist analysis we break language down into some of its smallest component parts and teach these parts artificially, nonsensically, but with great specific-

Frequency and Percentage Tabulations of Phoneme-Grapheme
Correspondence in American English: 22-Vowel Classification

PHONEME	GRAPHEME	FREQUENCY	PERCENT
/E/		2,538	
	E	1,765	69.54
	EE	249	9.81
	EA	245	9.65
	E-E	62	2.44
	I-E	44	1.73
	I	38	1.49
	IE	33	1.30
	EA-E	30	1.18
	IE-E	23	0.90
	EI	16	0.63
	EE-E	9	0.35
	EI-E	6	0.23
	EY	6	0.23
	AE	5	0.19
	OE	5	0.19
	EO	2	0.07
/E2/		198	
	E	64	32.32
	EA	49	24.74
	EE	36	18.18
	E-E	27	13.63
	IE	14	7.07
	I	3	1.51
	IE-E	3	1.51
	EI	2	1.01
/E3/		3,646	
	E	3,316	90.94
	EA	139	3.81
	A	94	2.57
	E-E	79	2.16
	AI	4	0.10
	IE	4	0.10
	EO	3	0.08
	U	2	0.05
	A-E	1	0.02
	A-E	1	0.02
	AY	1	0.02
	EA-E	1	0.02
	EI	1	0.02
/E5/		2,170	
	E	1,666	76.77
	O	268	12.35
	A	168	7.74
	U	31	1.42
	U-E	23	1.05
	I	8	0.36
	Y	4	0.18
	E-E	1	0.04
	OU	1	0.04

Figure 3.1

Frequency and Percentage Tabulations of Phoneme-Grapheme Correspondence in American English: 30-Consonant Classification

PHONEME	GRAPHEME	FREQUENCY	PERCENT
/CH/		564	
	CH	313	55.49
	T	175	31.03
	TCH	61	10.81
	TI	13	2.33
	C	2	0.35
/F/		2,019	
	F	1,580	78.25
	PH	242	12.02
	FF	177	8.76
	LF	9	0.44
	GH	8	0.39
	FT	3	0.14
/G/		1,338	
	G	1,178	88.04
	GG	67	5.00
	X	42	3.17
	GUE	21	1.56
	GU	19	1.42
	GH	10	0.74
	TG	1	0.07
/J/		982	
	G	647	65.88
	J	218	22.24
	DG	51	5.19
	D	32	3.25
	DJ	16	1.62
	GI	14	1.42
	GG	2	0.20
	DI	2	0.20
/K/		4,712	
	C	3,452	73.25
	K	601	12.75
	CK	290	6.15
	CH	142	3.01
	X	80	1.75
	CC	76	1.61
	QU	27	0.57
	Q	20	0.42
	LK	14	0.29
	CQ	3	0.06
	KH	3	0.06
	SC	3	0.06
	CCH	1	0.02
/SH/		1,537	
	TI	820	53.35
	SH	398	25.89
	CI	81	5.27
	SSI	51	3.31
	SI	38	2.47
	C	38	2.47
	CH	34	2.21
	T	30	1.95
	S	20	1.30
	SS	9	0.58
	SC	6	0.39
	SCI	5	0.32
	X	3	0.23
	CE	2	0.13
	SCH	2	0.13

Figure 3.2

ity. This is not the same activity. The smaller the subparts the greater the difficulty.

8. *The direct application of experimental research on phonemic awareness to classroom situations changes the relationships that exist between teachers and children.*

Developing phonemic awareness in reading and writing classrooms in which teachers and children form literate communities has different social, cultural, and intellectual significance than developing phonemic awareness in classrooms in which instruction takes the form of predetermined lesson plans that are given to children and used to control their learning. The difference is easily made apparent by contrasting the work of children in these two types of classrooms. The following examples of children's work from reading and writing classrooms are taken from data I collected in the 1980s when I was participating in the Biographic Literacy Profiles Project. The children whose work is represented here live in low-income neighborhoods and attend two different "financially challenged" schools. In the first example, Leigh, who teaches kindergarten, is writing about Trevor's literacy development for the months of November and December.[24]

"Trevor continues to experiment with different topics in his drawings with houses and family appearing frequently," Leigh writes. "One time, he called upon a familiar nursery rhyme—the Old Woman Who Lived in a Shoe—for inspiration (November 21)."

For a while Leigh focuses on Trevor's art and his oral description of his pictures before she talks about his writing. "Trevor continues to label with beginning sounds—'K' for 'Christmas' (December 6), 'S' for 'sun' (December 13)." Then she writes, "He is often able to determine words that begin like the one he is attempting to write, saying, for example, 'House. It starts like horse and hot-dog' (November 7). Or, 'Bubble starts with 'B', but I don't know how to make it' (November 14)."

Leigh adds, "He has begun collaborating with friends on letter formation. One day, he first assisted George in writing 'T'—easy for a boy named Trevor! Then, he asked George how to write a 'p'. Copying the example George made for him onto his own paper (November 17)."

In the project, teachers observed children's early literacy development on a daily basis, and they used these observations as a basis for instruction. They wrote notes about a few children each day, and notes about every child at least once a week. The second example which follows is taken from the quick notes that Martha, a kindergarten teacher from a different school, wrote as she observed Michael on October 11.

Michael, who had been in kindergarten for approximately six weeks, was talking about what he wanted to be for Halloween.

"I want to be Superman," Michael says, "but I don't know how to write it down."

"Well, what do you hear when you say Superman?" Martha asks him.

"S!" Michael says, and writes it in his journal.

"What else?"

"E." Michael writes *E* and then he writes a *P*.

"What else?"

"P and I already wrote that."

"What else?"

"M." Writes *M*. "I'm all done!" Michael pauses, then adds, "I think."

Every so often, Martha gathers up her notes and synthesizes the literacy development of the children in her classroom. In March she documented the transformations that had taken place in Melanie's reading and writing.

"Melanie is starting to make sense of the sounds of letters and connect them to her writing," Martha notes. "She is changing from random strings of letters to strings of letters with more and more accurate sounds represented. On February 2, she wrote I S P C R S Y Q Y—'I was playing on the swing set with Jakey.' On February 15, she wrote, I (write backward Z) S K E—'I was skating.' Suddenly she got it!" Martha writes, her excitement clearly visible in her notes. "Since then beginning, middle and ending sounds are all represented, as well as vowels. They seem to be coming all at once. On March 14, she wrote I W S T K A W—'I was taking a walk.' On March 17, I W S G

W E N

M A G P H—'I was going to my club house.'"

Martha ends by stating that Melanie's pictures "continue to be colorful and closely illustrate the sentences that she writes."

Now contrast the Vygotskian evolutionary processes and qualitative transformations in the reading and writing histories of these kindergarten children with the intellectually poverty-stricken activities that were given to Patrick when he was in first grade.

On one workbook page that he was given sometime in October or November, there is a picture of a boy eating a hamburger. Underneath is a sentence (I presume it is a sentence even though it doesn't start with a capital letter): "s me at." Underneath, this "sentence" is written twice in broken lines, and Patrick has traced them. Twice. He then traced the letters *t*, *r*, and *d* in lines across the bottom of the page. It is unclear to me why these letters appear with "s me at," and I wonder if Patrick had any idea why they appeared that way.

"Cc" is printed at the top of another workbook page—now sometimes called "activity sheets." On this torn-out page, Patrick has written a "c" beside a picture of a camel, a cowboy, and a candle. Underneath there are more pictures, and he has written a "c" to go with "age" to make cage, and a "c" with "up" to make "cup." But then beneath these pictures there are other pictures. One is of a mask, and Patrick has written an "m" to go with "ask," and another is a picture of some jacks and he has written a "j" to go with "acks." I still don't know why these pictures of a mask and some jacks are on the page which is supposed to be about the initial consonant "Cc." But it must have been okay because on the "Nn" page there is another mask, and after Patrick has written "n" to go with "ail" and "n" to go with "et," he has written "m" to go with "ask." He must have been correct because when his "m" didn't sit on the line, his teacher wrote over it with a bright red marker. I guess that makes what he wrote correct and incorrect at the same time, and once again I have no idea what he made of that.

Sometimes Patrick didn't have to write. The instructions on one page state, "Say the short sound of e. Name the pictures. Color the ones with the ˇ sound of e." I wonder what coloring has to do with reading and why, if Patrick was having so much difficulty, he was being taught phonetic notations that he would never need if he was given the opportunity to read. Even so, on this page Patrick had colored a bell, an elephant, and a pen, and other pictures of "short e sounds" as well.

I have several entire file drawers filled with similar workbook pages which Patrick dutifully completed. Then there are other workbook pages on which he had to draw lines to match letters, and others on which he drew lines to match pictures and some to match words. On some workbook pages he had to fill in boxes with single letters to match the letters in the boxes on the left hand side of page. Patrick also had to copy from the board. On one piece of lined paper he wrote, "can, can, mat, mat, pan, pan, pan, pan, pan, rat, rat, rat, rat, mat, mat mat mat." On another page "Al ran to Dot. Dot ran and ran." On . . . and on . . . and so on . . . ad infinitum and ad nauseam.

I am unable to take notes when I observe children in classrooms that rely on commercial skills programs, even if the materials are not as impoverished as those that were given to Patrick. In such classrooms children are not active learners. It's impossible to document the evolutionary processes and qualitative transformations that take place as children learn to read and write if all they have to do is follow directions. Their literacy histories are interrupted and written language is fractured when it is handed down to them piecemeal by adults.

In such situations children are, as Paulo Freire states, "anaesthe-tized" and left "a-critical and naïve in the face of the world" (p. 152). In such situations teachers lose their status and become technical aids with predetermined lesson plans that they must use to "teach" children. This is what happened to the African American children who participated in the research project that was published in *Growing Up Literate*. What is so sad about this situation is that children who often had many impor-tant responsibilites in their families were forced to sit and copy from the board, fill in dittos, and practice for tests. In their classrooms they did not have the opportunity to create their own literate environments. They were denied ownership of their own literate lives, their personal and shared histories, and they did not have the opportunity to learn to use print in ways that would eventually give them access to the literacies of the world outside of their own community.

In which we find Foorman's research does not support the NICHD proposition that "phonological processing is the primary area where children with reading difficulties differ from other children"

■ ■ ■

As NICHD relies heavily on the research of Barbara Foorman and her co-researchers David Francis and Jack Fletcher to support the proposition that "phonological processing is the primary area where children with reading difficulties differ from other children," I will focus my response on their research studies, and I will use the criteria for "scientific rigor" presented in Grossen's report on NICHD research. First, I will examine the studies themselves and ask the questions introduced in Chapter One. I invite you to join me in considering these questions. Is the research responsive to the social, cultural, and intellectual lives of children? How was the research conducted? Were the scientific procedures rigorous? Were the hypotheses properly tested? Were the tests and measurements relevant to the stated objectives of the studies? Were the theories proven? What does the research really indicate? Correlation or causation? What are the ethical issues? Are there alternative explanations for the results? What is the impact of the research on the lives of children and their families?

I will then review some of the essential elements of "the true scientific model" that Grossen presents in her report on NICHD research that are seen as essential before any findings are "finally considered incontrovertible." Then, as suggested by Grossen, I will contrast the findings of the Foorman studies and her interpretation of those studies with other scientific evidence on human learning and how young children learn to read and write.

The stated purpose of the study was to determine to what degree early intervention "can reduce the morbidity of social and cognitive risk factors"

Foorman and her colleagues received a series of grants from NICHD. The most recent series of five studies (HD28172), which focus on early intervention for children with reading disabilities, began in 1993 and is funded through 1998. This is the series of studies which supposedly show that training in phonemic awareness is the key to reading success and the research that has been presented at both the state and national level as well as widely disseminated by the media.

Before presenting my analysis, it important for you know that in fairness to Foorman and her colleagues I sent them a request for further information which focused on the design of the Houston studies, data collection procedures, and analysis and interpretation of the data. I received a response which stated that the "material" that I was using represented "preliminary analyses" and that I should consult the article which is to appear at some undisclosed date in the *Journal of Educational Psychology*. My request was forwarded to Reid Lyon, the director of NICHD, who also responded by referring me to the journal article which at that time had yet to be published. Lyon writes of "ongoing intervention studies" which are being conducted "to supplement existing protocols so that reliable intermediate results inform possible changes in direction or that questions that arise from the initial phases of the studies can be addressed and answered in the context of the ongoing study."[1]

The response from Foorman, Fletcher, and Francis and the response from Lyon are highly problematic. State laws have been passed based upon the research of Foorman and her colleagues and, as I write, the U.S. House of Representatives Education and Workforce Committee is considering similar legislation at the national level. Given that Foorman and her colleagues and Lyon now refer to the findings of the Houston studies as "preliminary" and "the initial phase" of ongoing studies, there are serious ethical questions that the academic community needs to address about the way in which the data has been presented both at the state and national level and the way it has been used to pass laws on how children can and cannot be taught to read and, by default, to write.

Whatever documentation is presented in the *Journal of Educational Psychology*, it will be too late for academic debate. Under the circumstances it seems entirely appropriate and necessary for me to focus on the "preliminary" documentation, because it is these "initial" findings that are being used to change the teaching of beginning reading throughout the United States. Let me now present my analysis of the studies to support my argument that the research is nothing more than spin doctoring, and that the findings of the studies are, in fact, totally misleading to all of those who are concerned about supporting children's early literacy development.

Foorman and her colleagues experimented with five "treatment" studies.[2] The first study focused on kindergarten children who were "at risk for reading problems because of social, cultural, and other factors related to literacy." The stated purpose of the study was to determine to what degree early intervention "can reduce the morbidity of social and cognitive risk factors."

The second study "provided early interventions for children with identified reading disabilities." The children in this group were entering second and third grade, and they received instruction either in synthetic phonics, a combination of synthetic and analytic phonics, or whole words.

The third study focused on "children enrolled in Chapter 1 programs in grades 1 and 2 who are underachieving in reading." These children received "one of two types of interventions representing a reading recovery program and a curriculum-driven, practice orientation."

The fourth study reversed the order of the curriculums "to determine the efficacy of curriculums based on synthetic phonics, analytic phonics, or whole language if preceded or succeeded by another curriculum."

The fifth study was designed to cross the interventions developed in studies one and two "to determine if interventions are equally effective across children with identified learning disabilities and children who are low achieving and also at cultural risk."[3]

Culture is flat, a constant variable.
Everybody has it, nobody is different.

Let's focus on our first question: Is the research responsive to the social, cultural, and intellectual lives of children? In most of the studies on phonemic awareness that I have read, there is a major problem with cultural uniformity. Culture is flat, a constant variable. Everybody has it, nobody is different. In the Foorman studies there is also an assumption of cultural uniformity. No attention is paid to the possibility that the treatments might have different significance for children whose cultures are European, African, Hispanic, or Asian American, or that the tests may not be applicable or appropriate for these children.[4]

For example, in the first study the kindergarten children were taught the Lundberg, Frost, and Peterson phonological awareness curriculum that was "translated" by Adams. Lundberg and his colleagues developed the training program in Denmark and tested it on Danish children who were a part of "a homogeneous school system" living on the island of Bornholm, which they describe as "a fairly isolated island in the most eastern part of Denmark."[5]

In this program the children listened to nursery rhymes and then took part in phonemic awareness exercises. For the "substitute sounds activities" the children listened to the nursery rhyme "Little Miss Muffet," and then they were asked to listen for the beginning sound /m/ in Miss Muffet. For the "segmentation activities" the children listened to "Polly Put the Kettle On" and the children were asked to join in. The children were then asked to identify the two names in the nursery rhyme. Then the children joined in, repeating the beginning sound, "P-P-P- Polly put the kettle on . . . S-S-S-Sukey take it off again." So what's the problem?

The problem is that the children in Foorman's study do not live on a remote Danish island. The program assumes cultural uniformity among the children attending Houston's elementary schools. It is colonialism of the very worst kind.[6] There is never an excuse, whatever the purpose, for taking the traditions of one culture and imposing them on another. Where's Langston Hughes? "Sure, I'm Happy! Take it away! Hey, pop! Re-bop! Mop! Y-e-a-h!"[7] Or Nikki Giovanni's rap poem, "when I take my rainbow ride, you'll be right there at my side, hey bop hey bop hey re re bop"?[8] Or the "Sawdust Song" from Puerto Rico, or "Gee Lee, Gu Lu" from China, or the American jump-rope song, "Red, White, and Blue"?[9] Children from every culture have a rich heritage of songs, rhymes, and games, and they enjoy them just for the pure pleasure of saying the poem or singing the song. Fortunately, sharing these rhymes helps them develop phonemic awareness without artificially pulling the rhymes apart.

"It appears that different social groups draw their children's attentions to the sounds in words through nursery rhymes in much the same way," Morag Maclean, Peter Bryant, and Lynette Bradley write. "The lack of any social effect on knowledge of nursery rhymes, the variable which interested us the most, was surprising. It suggests that this knowledge which, as we have seen, is widespread among 3-year-olds, is common to all types of families."[10]

As language and culture are inseparable, if there is cultural uniformity in the phonemic awareness research it follows that there is language uniformity. In research which focuses on mapping the smallest units of sounds onto the smallest units of print, I have found no research which focuses on the differences in the ways children speak. In recent years the use of the word "dialect" has been increasingly criticized, for as Edward Kamau Braithwaite puts it, "the word 'dialect' has been bandied about for a long time, and it carries very pejorative overtones."[11] However, the research on children's first language or home language which took place in the 1960s and 1970s was sensitive to the pejorative connotations, and tried to shift the thinking of educators.

Writing in 1976, Frank Riessman states, "Many of the compensatory programs of the sixties were based on the presumption of verbal and cognitive deficits." He states that there was no basis for this "linguistic-cognitive impoverishment." Riessman refers to two points made by Ralph Ellison in 1964. The first is that "human beings cling to the language that makes it possible for them to control chaos and to survive in the situations in which they find themselves." The second is that "the way to teach new forms or varieties or patterns of language is not to attempt to eliminate the old forms but to build upon them while at the same time valuing them in a way that is consonant with the desire for dignity that lies in each of us." Riessman concludes, "Thus, if we deny or take away the student's language, we deny and diminish a crucial aspect of the student who uses it."[12] Both Riessman and Ellison could be writing today in response to the phonemic awareness research.

"What complicates dealing with and accepting phonological difference is that there is an artificial phonology, sometimes based on spelling," Ken Goodman argues in a paper he wrote at the end of the 1960s, "that confuses many teachers on what is acceptable dialect"(pp. 63–64). He adds, "Ethnocentrism permeates attitudes toward language. We think of our own speech as natural and that of others as funny-sounding. This gets entangled with feelings of superiority towards those in lesser social and economic hierarchies" (p. 66).

"What do we do if the child pronounces the sound differently?" a teacher asks, at a meeting on phonemic awareness.

"You get him to repeat it," the teacher is told, "until he gets it right."

"[T]he conception of reading as deciphering not only inhibits reading but creates other problems as well," Ferreiro and Teberosky argue, as if attending this meeting. "Attempts at establishing phoneme-grapheme correspondences lead to 'proper' (or 'correct') pronunciation, the pronunciation form of the dominant social classes within the society and the only one supposed to permit access to written language" (p. 282).

This is certainly the case in the Foorman phonemic awareness research studies. Dialect is simply ignored; it doesn't exist. I have found only one reference to dialect, and that is in a synthesis paper for all the studies, in which Foorman and her colleagues note that in the studies on children with reading disabilities, "[a]ny instructional attempt to circumvent phonological processes lacks a firm theoretical basis." Later, they write in the synthesis paper, "The onset-rime unit facilitates reasoning by analogy . . . and might reduce dialect interference because the medial vowel is anchored to the remaining consonants in the rime" (p. 8).

In addition to dialect differences, Foorman and her colleagues pay very little attention to the difficulties their experimental tasks might present for children for whom American English is a second language. They state in the proposal that children who were expected to "exit the Limited-English-Proficiency designation within the course of the study in which they are participating" were included in their sample. However, we know nothing of how these children coped with the batteries of tests, and there are very few references to them.

"Whites had higher scores on orthographic processing than Hispanics, meaning that whites were better at recognizing and producing less predictable spellings than Hispanics," the experimenters state, and then they comment that, "[t]his result is not surprising, given the more direct correspondence between sound and symbol in Spanish compared to English, and, therefore the greater likelihood that Hispanic children would produce more phonetic errors" (p.10).[13]

Children's first languages in a nutshell. Foorman and her colleagues did not take into consideration or study the ways in which children speak in their experiments. They ignored the phonemes of every test-taking child. They did not consider the varying degrees of complexity of tasks for children whose first language or language form was not "standard" American English. In such situations, where children speak another form of the language or another language, think what they are expected to accomplish in speed tests to reproduce the sounds of the pseudowords as the experimenters have predetermined they should—even when the experimenters don't have to work out the pronunciation of the pseudowords because they have real words to guide them. Think of the transpositions, the transmutations. Eliza Doolittle would have a fit![14]

To ignore the first languages of children, which Labov might refer to as sharply differentiated linguistic subsystems,[15] means ignoring what he calls "the original dictionary entries that determine the categories of the phonological system [which are] acquired in their most consistent form from the original care-givers when language is first learned" (p. 136).[16] This is quite an indictment of Foorman and her colleagues, who were supposed to be focusing on the phonological awareness of young children.[17]

In addition to the assumption of linguistic and cultural uniformity in these studies, there is another view of culture that is even more problematic. "Culture" is also regarded as a "risk factor." In the proposal for these studies Foorman and her colleagues write of children with identified learning disabilities "who are low achieving and also at cultural risk" (p. 2). They also talk of interventions to "reduce the morbidity of social and cognitive risks factors" (p. 2). Morbidity is a word I associate with the medical profession, with doctors and disease, and as I wasn't sure what the researchers meant by the word, I looked it up in a dictionary. "Morbidity" means the state of being unhealthy, unsound, contaminated, pathological, or degenerative.

These references to culture bring into sharp focus the differences between (1) social theorists whose research on young children learning to read and write is framed by social and cultural perspectives of practical intelligence and everyday cognition, and (2) experimental psychologists who believe, as Adams does, that learning to read is "the creation or strengthening of associations" — visual, auditory, motor, or conceptual — "to interlink the printed appearance of words with one's knowledge of their sounds, contexts, functions, and meanings" (p. 206). These two views of scientific discovery are diametrically opposed and critically affect every aspect of the research endeavor.

"[T]he social system in which the child is embedded . . . channels cognitive development," Rogoff writes. "The culture and the influence of socialization agents are not overlays on basic individual development."

"[K]nowledge-in-practice, constituted in the settings of practice, is the locus of the most powerful knowledgeability of people in the lived-in world," Lave argues. "Practice theory, in short, suggests a different approach to cognition and to schooling than that embodied in . . . cognitive theory" (p. 14).

For experimental psychologists, this view of human learning simply doesn't exist. Researchers must be able to control the phenomena they are studying. Of necessity, the task must be synthetic and artificial; it cannot be embedded in the everyday literate activities of young children because it must be managed, repeated, replicated, given to other children, tested, and evaluated.

"Students were defined as reading disabled if they obtained scores below the 25th percentile on Basic Reading Cluster (Word Identification, Word Attack) of the Woodcock-Johnson-Revised," Foorman and her colleagues tell us, "and were also at least 15 standard score points below intelligence test scores on the Weschsler intelligence tests (WISC-R or WISC-III)"(p. 7).

The task must be isolated so that it can be manipulated.

"The experimenter presented the child with isolated pairs of onsets and rimes at a rate of two per second and asked him or her to 'put these parts together to make a whole word'" (p. 10).

From this perspective learning is not complex, but it is complicated. Once the specific, artificial, and narrowly defined examples of the phenomena have been measured, they must be analyzed, and mathematical models must be constructed. The research becomes more abstract, more distant, and there are only isolated behaviors on batteries of tests, and gobs of numbers. From this perspective, culture becomes an impediment, a nuisance variable. Culture is something outside of children, a problematic overlay, "a risk factor," an obstacle to be overcome. As Foorman and her colleagues wrote in their proposal, their research focused on whether "relevant precursors of reading ability . . . can reduce the morbidity of social and cognitive risk factors." Children were then split into ethnic groups and tested to see if there were any differences between them. Then the researchers took their amalgams of data and wrote about the social and racial differences in their phonemic awareness abilities, which, they argue, are a prerequisite for learning to read and write. Is this research responsive to the social, cultural, and intellectual lives of children?

Is this test relevant to children's everyday lives?

Let's address the next two questions. How was the research conducted? Were the tests and measurements relevant to the stated objectives of the studies? To examine the ways in which the research was conducted, I am going to focus on Foorman's study of children with reading disabilities from which I quoted above. In this study, Foorman and her colleagues write, "13 special education teachers taught 113 second and third graders 60 minutes a day either synthetic phonics, synthetic/analytic phonics, or a sight word program." The children were drawn from 13 of 19 schools in one Houston school district.

I have already shared with you how the students were defined as "reading disabled." Children were reading disabled if they scored below the 25th percentile on the Word Identification, Word Attack subtests of the WJ-R Basic Reading Cluster, and if their WJ-R score was at least 15 standard score points below intelligence tests scores on the WISC-R or WISC-III. The spelling subtest of the Kaufman Test of Educational Achievement (KTEA) and the Formal Reading Inventory (FRI) were also administered. The FRI data were later discarded because of low scores. As will become evident when we discuss the events taking place in California, the fact that the FRI scores were tossed out becomes of critical importance.

Were the measures relevant? Let's take the Word Attack subtest of the WJ-R—which cannot be reproduced without risking a lawsuit. There are three "pseudowords" in the first level of the subtest. If a child can't read *any* of the pseudowords, he gets a raw score of 0, and that gives the child an "age" of 5.8 and a "grade" of K.7; a raw score of 1 results in an age of 6.3 and a grade of 1.1; and a raw score of 5 an age of 7.3 and a grade of 1.8.

"Zoop!" you might say. "What a jox!" and you'd probably be aged 7.9 in grade 2.0.

Seriously, what is this test measuring? In the Biographic Literacy Profiles Project we could never figure it out. Children who scored low on the WJ-R were reading and writing. Is this test relevant to children's everyday lives? Definitely not. Does it take into account the differences in the children's cultural and ethnic experiences? Not at all. Is it relevant to the way in which Foorman and her colleagues were studying phonemic awareness? Tricky. The WJ-R was being used as a measure of "reading ability," but these are pseudowords, and the children had to identify them phonologically—a similar task to the phonological processing tasks used later in the experiment. Except that the experimenters weren't actually expected to read the pseudowords on Foorman's "blending phonemes into nonwords" test. They were provided a pronunciation key of real words, e.g., "F-ir-t-u-s" Circus. I wonder if they know that their paradigm has slipped? But getting back to the WJ-R, which is supposed to be the measure of "reading ability." At the end of the training programs, Foorman used the WJ-R to measure and compare the results of the various training programs. If in this WJ-R subtest children had to use phonological processing, you would expect the children in those training groups to do better than children who were in training programs dealing with "whole words"—don't be confused, this has nothing to do with whole language.

Here's an analogy. Let's assume that in the Foorman kindergarten study, children were trained to pick up raisins with tweezers and put them into bottles with a narrow necks. Now, if these children practiced this every day while other kids were painting pictures, then you would expect that when both groups were later tested at picking up raisins with tweezers, the children who had been practicing this would do better than the children who had been painting. If they didn't all explode.

In addition to the WJ-R tests, the children's memories were tested for recall on the "Recalling Sentences" subtest of the CELF-R, and the "Digits Span Total" from the WISC-R. They were then divided into three intervention groups, and these groups were further divided up by ethnicity—Black, Hispanic, White—and by sex. Each subgroup was taught using one of these different commercial programs: Alphabetic Phonics, an Orton Gillingham Program; Recipe for Reading, another Orton Gillingham Program that was slightly modified; and Edmark, which is described as "a sight word program." Thus Foorman and her colleagues had African American children in each program, Hispanic American children in each program, and European American children in each program so that comparisons could be made.

In October, December, February, and April a "battery"—an apt word—of tests was administered to the children to assess "growth." These tests were as follows: (1) blending onset and rime; (2) blending phonemes into words; (3) blending phonemes into nonwords; (4) first sound comparisons; (5) phoneme elisions; (6) sound categorization; (7) phoneme segmentation; (8) orthographic processing tasks; (9) letter names and sounds; (10) experimental spelling recognition (two alternatives); (11) word reading; (12) verbal fluency (Rapid Automatized Naming); (13) visual-spatial tasks; (14) visual-motor integration; and (15) visual-spatial recognition. The WISC-R, WJ-R, KTEA, and FRI were also administered at the end of the first year of the children's participation. Were the tests relevant?

"Understanding is not cued knowledge," Grant Wiggins writes in *Assessing Student Performance: Exploring the Purpose and Limits of Testing*. "[P]erformance is never the sum of drills; problems are not exercises; mastery is not achieved by the unthinking use of algorithms" (p. 207).

The tests fulfilled the experimenters' simplistic stimulus-response view of learning, and also fulfilled their criteria for what counts as "evidence" of this superficial kind of "learning," but the tests certainly weren't relevant to the lives of the children.

The descriptions of these research studies are extremely complicated

Here are the next two questions. Were the scientific procedures rigorous? Were the hypotheses properly tested? Tough. The descriptions of these research studies are extremely complicated. The only way to address the question is to break the reading disabilities study down into its component parts. Let's begin by examining whether the study (and by extension, all the studies) meets the criteria for using parametric statistics. Remember, one of the requirements of parametric statistics is that the sample be random. In this study the sample of 113 children was drawn from: (1) second- and third-grade children attending 13 of 19 elementary schools; (2) who scored below the 25th percentile on subtests of the WJ-R; and (3) whose WJ-R score was at least 15 standard score points below their intelligence test scores on the WISC-R or WISC-III.

At best, the sample is only random from the children categorized as reading disabled in 13 schools. The sample is not a random sample from any larger population of reading disabled children in the school district, because six of the schools were not included. The sample is not a random sample from any larger population of "reading disabled" children in other school districts in Houston, or in Texas, California, Massachusetts, or any other state in the nation. The sample is not random from any larger group of children outside of the ascribed "reading disabilities" label. It gets worse. The samples were actually very small. In the "synthetic phonics" treatment group there were only 28 children, in the "synthetic/analytic phonics" group there were 46, and in the "sight word" group 30 children.

What about the distribution? Was it normal? Virtually impossible, particularly for the "synthetic phonics" treatment group because of small numbers as seen in Figure 4.1:

Numbers of Children in Four Ethnic Categories for Three Interventions for Students with Reading Disabilities

	BLACK	HISPANIC	WHITE	TOTAL
Synthetic Phonics				
Female	1	2	5	8
Male	4	6	10	20
Total	5	8	15	28
Synthetic/Analytic Phonics				
Female	6	6	6	18
Male	9	9	10	28
Total	15	15	16	46
Sight Word				
Female	4	4	3	11
Male	12	8	8	28
Total	16	12	11	39

Figure 4.1

As you can see, there are only 5 African American children, 8 Hispanic American children, and 15 European American children. The numbers of children in the other treatment groups are also small.

Any statistical significance attached to any comparison of this group with other groups is therefore highly suspect. Foorman and her colleagues actually acknowledge this when they state, "these results must be regarded as preliminary, however, because there were too few minorities in the synthetic phonics group to directly test the interaction of ethnicity and treatment contrasts" (p. 17).

Now for the interval scale, another prerequisite of parametric statistics.

"For each of the scales to be involved in modeling growth," Foorman and her colleagues write in the proposal for the five studies, "we will first conduct IRT analyses to examine the scale's psychometric properties and to develop an interval-based metric" (p. 53).

Although these experimental researchers will strongly disagree, statisticians will tell you that if the variable that you are measuring is fundamentally not measurable on an interval scale, no amount of mathematical manipulation can make it into an interval variable. Nominal and ordinal scales are not absolute measures. Ordinal scales are arbitrary, as we found out when we were examining the Woodcock Johnson. The difference between an IQ of 100 and an IQ of 120 is not the same as the difference between 140 and 160. If psychologists argue, refer them to Ferguson and his book on statistical analysis.[18]

"[S]cores on intelligence tests, scholastic aptitude tests, attitude tests, personality tests, and the like, are in effect ordinal variables, although they are commonly treated as if they were of the interval or ratio type," Ferguson writes. Then he states categorically, "No aspect of the operation of measuring intelligence, let us say, is such as to permit the making of meaningful statements about the equality of intervals or ratios." Finally. "Such statements are without meaning," he concludes (pp. 15–16).

While we can assign "numbers" in order to measure IQ on a numerical scale, the scale and the numbers are quite arbitrary and their only purpose is to allow us to put things in relative order. However, the difference between 5' 6" and 5' 9" is the same as the difference between 5' 9" and 6'. No matter where on the scale measurement occurs, 3" is 3". That's what makes height or weight or temperature measurable on an interval scale. The measures on pyschometric tests are not physical measurements. They are not absolute measures and they can't be turned into interval scales. Period.

Were the scientific procedures rigorous? No, but they were tedious. Were the hypotheses properly tested? Hardly, but if they had been, what would it all mean? Were the theories proved? First we have to suspend judgement on the appropriateness of measuring "reading acquisition" with the WJ-R tests. But if we accept these measures, what are the results? The Foorman reading disabilities study compared three treatments: (a) synthetic phonics using Alphabetic Phonics; (b) synthetic/analytic phonics using Recipe for Reading; and (c) sight words using Edmark. Several statistical contrasts were performed: (1) phonics (a+b) versus sight words(c); (2) phonics (a) versus sight words (c); (3) phonics (b) versus sight words (c); (4) phonics (a) versus phonics (b).

Take a look at the results after the experimenters "controlled" for memory and demographics (read ethnicity):

1. *No significant difference* between phonics (a+b) and sight words (c) treatments on phonemic awareness tests of phonemic analysis and phonemic synthesis.
2. *No significant difference* between phonics (b) and sight words (c) treatments on phonemic awareness tests of phonemic analysis and phonemic synthesis.
3. *Significant difference* between phonics (a) and sight words (c) treatments on the phonemic awareness tests. *Phonics better than sight words.*
4. *No significant difference* between phonics (a+b) and sight words (c) on the orthographic processing and word reading tests.
5. *No significant difference* between phonics (a) and sight words (c) treatments on orthographic processing and word reading tests.
6. *Significant difference* between sight words (c) and phonics (b) treatments on the orthographic processing and word reading tests. *Sight words better than phonics.*
7. *No significant difference* between phonics (a+b), phonics (a), phonics (b), or sight words (c) on the verbal fluency or visual spatial tests.

The bottom line was that after all the tests that the children took, there were no significant differences between the commercial programs, with two exceptions. The first was that the sight word (c) program outperformed phonics (b) on orthographic processing. The second is that phonics (a) outperformed the sight word treatment (c) on phonemic awareness. Not with a bang but with a whimper.

"The percentiles are quite startling," Foorman is quoted as saying "and you usually don't find these effects in social science research very often."[19] But I don't think she can be referring to the results of these tests, and hopefully none of her other studies either.

Now, before your eyes glaze over, what about the key achievement outcomes on the WJ-R (Basic Reading and Broad Reading) and the KTEA

Spelling for these three "treatments" applied to the "reading disabled" "subjects"? This is important because in Grossen's report on NICHD research she states that phonemic awareness tasks have "a positive effect on reading acquisition and spelling for nonreaders" (p. 7). And yet Foorman and her colleagues found no significant difference in reading and spelling achievement between synthetic phonics (a) and sight words (c) or combined phonics (a+b) and sightwords (c). They did however find that for spelling achievement there was a significant difference between sight word (c) and synthetic /analytic phonics (b). The sight words program was significantly better. Interesting, don't you think? But remember we've suspended judgment and in the end the statistics are confounded and the study is totally unscientific.

One final point before we leave these tests. Foorman and her colleagues divide the children into racial groups, but they do not present any data and they comment only briefly on their findings. Remember there were only five African American children and only eight Hispanic American children in the "synthetic phonics" treatment group.

"The Black versus White contrast was significant in the analyses of the phonological ($p < .001$) and visual spatial ($p < .01$) measures," the experimenters write. "The Hispanic versus White contrast was significant in the analyses of orthographic processing ($p < .05$), visual-spatial ability ($p < .01$), and phonological synthesis when contrasting synthetic phonics with sight word ($p < .05$)."

What are the ethical issues?

By now, you know that even within the frameworks of experimental research they are stretching their findings. They admit that results "must be regarded as preliminary" and that "there were too few minorities," but they spin it out anyway.

"What these significant ethnicity contrasts mean," Foorman tells us, "is that associated with the gains demonstrated by synthetic phonics when compared with the other two reading interventions was lower performance of minorities relative to Whites" (p. 17).

The spin continues in the synthesis paper of all five studies in which Foorman and her colleagues state, "African Americans improved in phonological synthesis skills at a faster rate than Whites or Hispanics, starting the year at a much lower level of skill, but ending the year at the same level. The improvement in African American phonological synthesis skill occurred across treatments." "Across treatments" means in the sight word program as well as the phonics program.

Somehow, by the time these findings are reported the spin is out of control. Without any specific reference, Grossen writes, "Significantly more African American children have lower levels of phonemic awareness and respond significantly better to direct instruction in phonemic awareness than other ethnic groups" (p. 16).

Juxtaposition of this statement with the statement which follows is cause for critical concern. Referring to twin studies, Grossen states at the top of the next page that there is "strong evidence for genetic etiology of reading disabilities with deficits in phonemic awareness reflecting the greatest degree of heritability. There is also behavioral genetic evidence for degrees of heritability for letter processing" (p. 17).

More spin doctoring. No data is presented. No theories were proved. Nothing was gained, but children, especially African American children, lose.

What are the ethical issues? I'll respond as a parent as well as a social theorist and ethnographer. As I read the various reports of these experimental studies, I kept thinking about my own children and the children with whom I've worked. I tried to imagine what I would do if my kids were in one of these experimental studies. I don't even have to think about it. I *know* what I'd do. I'd take them out of school. I wondered about the parents of the children in *Family Literacy*. Actually, I know also what they would do. Just before I started the research study in which they participated, some psychologists were conducting a study in the elementary school that the Lindells' children attended. The Lindells and the other parents who were involved in the experiments got the psychologists kicked out of the school, and they worked with the principal to ensure that such a situation didn't happen again.

I also wonder what the families in *Growing Up Literate* would do. Sadly, I think they would have let their children participate, not because they would have agreed with the experimentation, but because there were only so many battles that they could fight, and there were so many injustices to be endured. Even when Danny was beaten by his teacher, it was difficult for Ieshea to get the principal to respond to her, and nothing happened to the teacher.

"The purpose of this study is to test ways of identifying children who may have reading problems, and show that they can be identified early," Foorman writes in a signed letter sent home to parents in September 1993 for an earlier study. "If this work is successful, then your child's participation will help many future generations of Texas school children."[20]

I can imagine Ieshea's response, or Jerry's. They would clutch at straws and do anything to help their children. I can also imagine what they would do if they knew their children were being divided up into racial groups to be tested one group against the other. Their reaction would be quite different. I also think that the parents of the children attending the schools in Houston where these experiments took place would react quite strongly if they knew that the researchers had involved their children in racial experiments, or if they knew the experimenters were using instruments to determine whether or not their children were suffering from "ADHD [Attention Deficit Hyperactivity Disorder]" or some other "behavioral disorder."

Parental consent is not necessary

"Parental consent is not necessary," Foorman and her colleagues write in their proposal, because *there is no random assignment of subjects* to treatment in these studies. The children in participating classrooms are engaged in normal classroom activities and normal evaluation." Then they qualify this statement. "However, if children leave these assigned classrooms we want to continue to assess their progress with our assessment battery and with our academic outcome measures. Therefore, . . . parental consent must be sought before assessments can be administered" (p. 71) (emphasis added).

While I want to focus on the children and their families here, it is important to note that from the perspective of "the true scientific method," if the assignment of "subjects" to "treatments" is *not* random, then the entire statistical analysis is flawed. This is different from the "random sampling" I discussed earlier. This has to do with how randomly the "subjects" were assigned to the three "treatments."

But whether or not the "subjects" were randomly assigned or not, they were being "treated" and the evaluation procedures were *not normal*. In addition, based on the hypotheses of the researchers, they did expect some children to do better than others according to the type of "treatment" they received. Again, the question is, were parents informed about the possible effects of the experiments on their children?

Did the parents know how many tests their children were made to take? Did they know that their children were racially divided so that the experimenters could administer tests to determine whether African American children had deficits in phonological awareness? Did they know their children were tested to determine whether or not they had ADHD?

"Due process is essential in good assessment, just as it is in legal proceedings," Grant Wiggins writes. "What counts as evidence must be acceptable not only to disinterested judges but also to such interested parties as the student and the student's teachers" (p. 24).

I would add that what counts as evidence must also be acceptable to the student's parents or guardians.

"The tester enters into a contract with the person tested," Lee Cronbach states. "In former days the understanding was left vague. The tester is now expected to be frank and explicit . . ." (p. 73–74).

Wiggins responds, "But demanding that the tester be more 'frank and explicit' is not enough. The power is still so unequally distributed and the methods used by the test maker are so arcane that the student (and teacher, when the tests are external) has no real opportunity to understand the proceedings" (p. 25).

Neither has the student's family.

What follows is the list of tests described by Foorman and her colleagues in the NICHD proposal for the five studies, which included the Reading Disabilities Early Intervention Study and the Chapter 1 studies. They proposed that these tests be given in addition to the extensive battery of tests which focused on phonemic awareness and orthographic processing which were used by the experimenters and were administered to the children four times a year.

Intellectual and Achievement Testing

> WISC-III
>> Verbal IQ
>> Performance IQ

> Woodcock-Johnson Revised
>> Decoding Measures
>>> (Subtest 22, Identification of real words)
>>> (Subtest 31, Identification of pseudowords)

> Kaufman Test of Educational Achievement
>> (Spelling subtest)

> Grey Oral Reading Test III
>> (Reading Comprehension)

> Woodcock-Johnson Revised
>> (Reading Comprehension)

> Woodcock-Johnson Revised
>> (Subtest 25, Calculations)

Tests were to be administered at the beginning and end of the first year and where applicable at the end of subsequent years.

Cognitive Skills Assessment

> Torgeson/Wagner
> > (Construct: Phonological Awareness)

> Beery VMI
> > Recognition-Discrimination
> > > (Construct: Visual-Spatial Skills)

> Peabody Picture Vocabulary Test-Revised
> > (Construct: Semantic Language)

> Rapid Automatized Naming
> > (Construct: Rapid Naming)

> Clinical Evaluation of Language Fundamentals-Revised
> > Sentence Structure, Recalling Sentences Subtests
> > > (Construct: Syntactic Language)

> California Verbal Learning Test-Children
> > (Construct: Verbal Short-Term Memory)

> Verbal Cancellation Test
> > (Construct: Attention)

> Dictation/Recognition Test
> > (Construct: Spelling)

> Word Decoding Test
> > (Construct: Decoding)

Foorman and her colleagues refer to these tests as "experimental measures." They state, "Some procedures are repeated to index growth; others are given only once to characterize the child's cognitive profile" (p. 56).[21]

The Behavior and Environmental Information Battery

> Children's Title Recognition Test

(The child's exposure to print. Assessed once a year.)

Henderson Environmental Learning Process Scale (HELPS)
(Measures aspects of the environment related to literacy. Obtained from parent or other informant.)

Family Resource Scale
(Measures child and family resources for daily subsistence, medical care, transportation. Broad measure of SES.)

Yale Children's Inventory (YCI)
(Questionnaire completed by parent. Assesses for ADHD, behavioral problems, e.g., oppositional-defiant disorder.)

Multi-grade Inventory for Teachers (MIT)
(Parallel instrument to the Yale Children's Inventory. Assesses for ADHD and behavioral adjustment.)

Teacher Report Form (TRF)
(TRF included in the Child Behavior Check List. Assesses for ADHD and behavioral adjustment.)

Harter Perceived Competence Scales
(Administered to children. Assesses perception of themselves in the context of home and school.)

Hollingshead Questionnaire
(Administered to parent/guardian. Measures of home environment that encourage academic development.)

Foorman and her colleagues state that the HELPS was to be administered "to ensure that measures of print exposure are not biased by the inclusion of socially disadvantaged families where base rates of literacy are high." It is not clear how the information from this test was used, but again it raises questions about selective sampling and use of data.

Athough Foorman and her colleagues refused to either confirm or deny that the Yale Children's Inventory was used, there is strong documentary evidence that indicates that it was, indeed, sent home to parents and that they were asked to fill it in.[22]

"The Yale Children's Inventory (YCI), a parent-based rating scale, and the scales derived from it, have been developed to identify and measure multiple dimensions of learning disabilities with particular emphasis on attentional deficits," Sally Shaywitz, who receives research funds from NICHD, Carla Schnell, Bennett Shaywitz, and Virginia Towle write in the *Journal of Abnormal Child Psychology*.

"The following are lists of characteristic behaviors," the instructions state on the actual questionnaire. "Indicate which are *never true, rarely true, sometimes true,* or *often true* of this child." Then parents are told, "Even if the particular characteristic mentioned doesn't *fit* your child exactly, *pick* the choice that most closely fits." The last instruction warns, "*Do not omit or leave any responses blank.*"[23]

In the section on "Attention" parents are asked to rate such statements as: "Is easily distracted"; "Asks for things repeated"; "Has difficulty concentrating or paying attention unless in a 1:1 structured situation."

In the section on "Habituation" behaviors include: "Does not adjust to new situations"; "Does not adapt to changes in routine"; and "Has mood fluctuations usually unrelated to situation."

"Impulsivity": "Disrupts other children"; "Talks excessively"; and "Is extremely excitable."

"Tractability": (birth to 6 years) "Needed constant supervision"; "Broke toys and other things; was destructive"; "Couldn't tolerate a noisy or busy place; would go wild in a crowd."

"Behavior I" which is described in the article by Shaywitz and her colleagues as "Conduct disorder-social": "Cheats; has to be a winner"; "Complains of unfair treatment; everyone is against him/her"; "Is a 'sponger' (takes favors with no effort to return them)."

"Behavior II (Conduct disorder-aggressive)." Parents are asked "Did any of the following occur over an extended period of time (6 months or more)?" "Swearing, use of vulgar language"; "Was violent and aggressive, assaulted others, got into fights." The rating scale changes for the next behavior. Parents are asked to choose one of four statements. The first is: "Never steals or breaks the rules." The fourth is: "Even steals or breaks rules while s/he is closely supervised."

This research raises serious questions about the treatment of children in psychological experiments

Let's stop for a moment and think of the children and the long-term effects of their participation in these studies. More than any other research that I have ever read, this research raises the most serious questions about the treatment of children in psychological experiments, and I am at a loss to explain why the educational community has not been more vocal in defending the rights of these children and their families.

In addition to the intolerable amounts of testing and invasive questionnaires, children were switched from one *treatment* curriculum to another. In Foorman's research, children had no rights. They were put under the microscope, shunted around, curriculums were reversed, and treatment interventions crossed-over. What effect did all the testing and the reversals of the treatments have on their learning?

"Every test, every grade affects the learner," Wiggins states. "Every dull test—no matter how technically sound—affects the learner's future initiative and engagement. No, even saying it this way does not do justice to the consequences of our testing practices: every test *teaches* the student." Wiggins argues that tests such as those used by Foorman and her colleagues are "arcane," and that the use of them is "morally problematic."

Patrick taught me years ago that the long-term effects of constant testing can be extremely damaging to a child's sense of well-being; and I know from many years of working with teachers and children in schools that changes from one form of instruction to another are unsettling for many children and have an adverse effect on their academic performance. Learning new ways of approaching assignments takes time, and these effects are particularly difficult when children move from classrooms with restricted, authoritarian, "given-to-them-by-adults" kinds of activities to classrooms in which literacy is deeply embedded in the social, cultural, and intellectual lives of the children.

Look back at Chapter 3, and imagine Patrick in Trevor's or Melanie's classroom, or Melanie or Trevor in Patrick's class. How long would it take Patrick to risk writing his own stories? What would Melanie think if there was no time for her to write about her family because she had to complete the *Cc* page and write a *c* to go with *up*? At this point in time, Foorman and her colleagues have left the school district, so despite the proposal to follow the children for a second year and the claim by Lyon at NICHD that the studies in which the institute engaged were longitudinal, the Foorman studies were not. This is particularly problematic given the research studies in which she and her colleagues were engaged. To put it bluntly, the children were experimented on, the treatments to which they were exposed were switched, and they were tested excessively. But Foorman and her colleagues are no longer in the district, so there is no way for them to monitor the effects of their treatments or the transitions from one treatment to another on the children. This is especially problematic because in the Foorman studies the transitions were from synthetic to analytic phonics, analytic phonics to whole word, or vice versa. None of these "treatments" supported the evolutionary processes and qualitative transformations that are a part of children's early literate histories.

What would happen to Nicola or Bobby in one of these studies? In every school there are many children whose life histories are just as fragile as theirs. Almost 22 percent of U.S. children, over 15 million, live in poverty, and the number of children who are sexually abused each year is thought to be more than 3 million. We know that some of the children in these experiments read a list of words better than some of the other children, but did any of the children, like Nicola, have an opportunity to use print to cope with the difficult circumstances of their everyday lives? Were there children like Patrick who couldn't read in school but read books at home with his family? We don't know, because this research did not consider the effects of the different and changing treatments, and the children's life histories were not of any consequence.

It has again become acceptable to look for linguistic deficits in African American children

I have tried to keep a sense of humor in writing about the phonemic awareness research, but it's difficult to maintain. There is an "underside" to this research that is very serious. As we reach the year 2000, and after years of struggle, we are once again looking for linguistic deficits in children, and it has again become acceptable to look for linguistic deficits in African American children.

"Low-income and slow students appear to benefit especially from phonics instruction," the readers of the *Atlantic Monthly* are told.[24]

But where did the *Atlantic* get this information from? Probably from multiple sources, but here we are concerned about the research. Implicit in many of the studies that I have read, and explicit in the studies of Foorman and her colleagues, in the research of Stanovich, and in the government report written by Adams, are deficit views of children and their families. Let's retrace our steps and return to the "Matthew Effects in Reading." In this article Stanovich discusses what he refers to as "organism-environment effects," and he describes two types of "organisms." The first are "organisms" who select, shape, and evoke their own environments. The second are "organisms" who are passive. In case you haven't realized it yet, "organisms" are children.[25]

"Organisms not only are acted on by their environments; they also select, shape, and evoke their own environments," Stanovich explains. "The differences in volume of reading between readers of differing skill are partly due to these active and evocative organism-environment correlations. Children who become better readers have selected (e.g., by choosing friends who read or choosing reading as a leisure activity rather than sports or video games), shaped (e.g., by asking for books as presents when young), and evoked (e.g., the children's parents noticed that looking at books was enjoyed or perhaps just that it kept the child quiet) an environment that will be conducive to further growth in reading.

"[T]he other side of the coin, . . . may help to explain certain aspects of reading failure . . . there are also *passive* organism-environment correlations that contribute to rich-get-richer and poor-get-poorer effects," Stanovich reasons. "A passive organism-environment correlation is a relationship between the type of organism and environmental quality that is not due to the organism's active selection and shaping of the environment (pp. 382–83).

"The genotypes of a child's parents partially determine both the home environment of the child and the child's genotype. Other passive organism-environment correlations are a function of social structures. Less healthy organisms grow up in impoverished environments. Biologically unlucky individuals are provided with inferior social and educational environments, and the winners of the biological lottery are provided better environments.

"But of course a child of above-average ability is much more likely to reside in a school with a 'concentration of pupils with good cognitive performance,'" Stanovich writes, referencing Jencks. "Such a child is an advantaged organism because of the superior environment and genotype provided by the child's parents. The parents, similarly environmentally and genetically advantaged, are more likely to reside in a community which provides the 'concentration of pupils' that via the independent effects of school composition, will bootstrap the child to further educational advantages. Conversely, disadvantaged children are most often exposed to inferior ability composition in the schools that they attend. Thus, these children are the victims of a particularly perverse 'double whammy'" (p. 383).

As I mentioned in the introduction, this article received the Albert J. Harris Award and is cited frequently by state legislatures and by state boards of education, as well as by researchers in support of training children in phonemic awareness. I can only surmise that many people agree with Stanovich that some children are "genetically advantaged," while other children are "biologically disadvantaged." Perhaps there is something wrong with me because I disagree.

"Thus, because instruction must mediate the initial stages of reading acquisition, it could well interact with the child's initial level of cognitive skill to cause Matthew Effects in reading," Stanovich writes, referencing Rutter and Madge. "Some of these effects will result from passive organism-environment correlations: Biologically disadvantaged children must learn in instructional environments (composed of teachers, schools, parents, etc.) that are inferior to those experienced by advantaged children."

Adams is less blatant, but her message is the same. "Other children enter school with next to no relevant knowledge about print," she explains. "Relative to their well-prepared peers, these children are likely to have less interest in these lessons and less appreciation of their point." Think of Nicola and the children in Texas. "We must therefore expect their learning to be slower and their patience to be slimmer. At the same time, however, mastery of the symbol-sound relations will require more study for these children. After all, some of them may still be having difficulty discriminating the letter shapes; their entering level of phonological awareness will be relatively low; and so, too, will their prior knowledge of letter-sound relationships. Much of the content of these lessons will be new for these children in detail and concept. As a consequence, it will be more confusing and harder to consolidate. Finally, in order for all necessary symbol-sound pairs to be learned well, each must be allowed sufficient practice and opportunity for consolidation." Think of Patrick. "The implication is that the teaching of individual letter-sound correspondences cannot proceed quickly for these children. It must be spread out over time" (pp. 240–41).[26]

The findings are finally considered incontrovertible

Both Adams's *Beginning to Read* and Stanovich's "Matthew Effects in Reading" are referenced in Grossen's synthesis of NICHD research, *30 Years of NICHD Research: What We Now Know About How Children Learn to Read*. Based on "the true scientific model," Grossen writes that the findings are "finally considered incontrovertible." Not so. As I have tried to show, in these studies the researchers have not even established correlation let alone causation, and there are alternative explanations for their findings.

To the "incontrovertible finding" that *phonemic awareness and other important reading skills are learned and do not develop naturally,* I would respond that this is an indefensible and unacceptable view of human learning, and that there is absolutely no research to support this contention. To accept this proposition, we would have to throw out the research of Vygotsky. It is his research that provides the response that "sign-using activity in children is neither simply invented nor passed down by adults: rather it arises from something that is originally not a sign operation and becomes one only after a series of qualitative transformations."[27]

To the "incontrovertible finding" that *of the three cueing systems frequently mentioned in reading (semantic, syntactic, and graphophonemic cues), the semantic and syntactic cueing systems seem to play a minor role*, I can find no evidence for this finding. To accept this proposition we would have to throw out the research of Emilia Ferreiro and Ana Teberosky, thirty years of miscue research, approximately six hundred miscue studies in many different languages conducted by many different researchers, including the longitudinal miscue research of Ken Goodman and Yetta Goodman which has been so maligned by the proponents of the "true scientific model" of reading research. In addition, the research on practical intelligence and everyday cognition, in which I ground my own research, would no longer make sense. If we subsume semantic and syntactic cueing systems, we subsume practical knowledge and thought for action. Human learning is no longer meaning-driven. All we have to do is crack "the code."

To the "incontrovertible finding" that *only decodable text provides children the opportunity to practice their new knowledge of sound-letter relationships*, all I can say, again, is that there is no evidence for this finding. To accept this proposition we would have to throw out much of the teacher-research that has taken place in the last ten years. The children in *Family Literacy* and *Growing Up Literate* should have had difficulty learning to read. The eight years of research of the Biographic Literacy Profiles Project would never have taken place. In thirty years of working with young children learning to read and write, I have never used texts such as those recommended in the Grossen's report on NICHD research. The example "Sam sees a big fist," which apparently is completely decodable, sounds rather offensive to me.

To the "incontrovertible finding" that *the most reliable indicator of a reading problem is an inability to decode single words*, once again, there is no scientific evidence. The studies are flawed. The data is confounded. The statistical results are meaningless. Replicating defective studies doesn't result in proven theories. Longitudinal studies are more than a series of short experiments. The sample sizes are misstated. Studies might have around 200 subjects, but if they are placed in different treatment groups and there are only 5 subjects in a group, then something is wrong. Researcher bias is not reduced by sheer numbers of researchers when they are all wedded to the same narrow and simplistic research paradigm. To return to my original proposition: if A cites B; B cites C; C cites A, B, and D; D cites B; and B then cites them all, including himself, in support of his arguments, and B's research rationale and statistical procedures are fundamentally flawed, then this finding places in jeopardy the research findings of A, C, and D.

Quod erat demonstrandum, Q.E.D.

In which teachers are turned into clerks and we discuss power, privilege, racism, and hegemony

■ ■ ■

"This is truly an incredibly sophisticated and important study," Maggie Bruck of McGill University is reported as saying about the Foorman studies.[1]

And Reid Lyon, acting chief of the child development branch of NICHD, is reported to have called Foorman's work "a tremendous contribution to the scientific evidence on how children learn to read."[2]

Needless to say, by now you know that I disagree.

In a letter to the editor of *Education Week* posted on the TAWL listserv by Marilyn Jager Adams, Lyon writes that studies supported by NICHD "must meet the highest levels of scientific integrity, review and application." To impress the elite of educational decision-makers, he talks of "traditional scientific standards," work that is "theoretically guided" with "robust tests," and he adds that "[t]he measurements used to test the hypotheses must meet established standards of reliability and validity."[3]

Again, if A cites B . . .

Back in the exhibit hall at the International Reading Association's Annual Convention, teachers fill canvas bags emblazoned with publishers' logos with phonemic awareness charts and small brightly packaged samples of decodable books. They do not know that the children they teach have been described as "passive organisms," or that those who teach these children are supposed to have constructed inferior learning environments for them.

"At *Literacy Place* young readers get solid, systematic instruction that emphasizes phonics and phonemic awareness," they read in the Scholastic pamphlet.

Teachers smile as they fill their bags, and the researcher from Laguna Beach who is selling the phonics books and spelling books that he writes and publishes smiles at them benevolently.

When the teacher from Massachusetts returns home, she will be told to choose a phonemic awareness program. She will pick one arbitrarily. Some teachers will try to resist, while others will select one even though they disagree. Either way, it's hegemony.

For years I've heard critical pedagogists use the word "hegemony." It's a Henry Giroux kind of word, but he always seems to use it as if we all understand what it means, and I don't think many of us do. For a long time I tried to figure out how we are, or can be, the victims of hegemony, or how our behavior can be hegemonic. The coal mining villages in South Wales where my parents grew up were segregated communities. Only the poorest of the poor lived in them: the lower working class, the miners who dug coal on the coal face and their families. I spent my summers in my Nan's village, and I grew up with first-hand knowledge of racism, prejudice, and exploitation. I learned what it was like to live in a racist society. But hegemony? It was not until I was in graduate school that I came to see how the miners acquiesced, how my parents deferred to their betters (my mother still does), how we all agreed. This is my personal understanding of hegemony. Perhaps this is why watching publishers sell their programs to teachers in the exhibit hall at IRA had such a profound effect on me. As I walked around I felt that what I was witnessing was a hegemonic situation. There was no visible coercion, but it was clearly a moment of intense political persuasion.

A "hegemonic project" Norman Fairclough might call it. Here's how he explains it: "[I]n education, for example, the dominant groups also appear to exercise power through constituting alliances" (I take this to mean state governments, researchers, and publishers) "integrating rather than merely dominating subordinate groups" (these are, of course, teachers), "winning their consent, achieving a precarious equilibrium which may be undermined by other groups" (p. 94).[4] *That's researchers and teachers who, like me, are not willing to acquiesce to the findings of unscientific studies on phonemic awareness.*

Antonio Gramsci[5] described hegemony in terms of "spontaneous consent." That's what I was observing as teachers moved towards publishers, who, perhaps believing their own lies, smiled and greeted them and filled their bags with their phonemic awareness prize. The hegemonic project *is* persuasive.[6]

"From Alphabet Cards to game mats, the Sounds and Letters Kit contains materials designed to involve children," the Open Court catalog states. "It develops print and phonemic awareness while children are learning letters and sounds and understanding how the alphabet looks" (p. 5).

Gramsci also writes about more direct forms of power that are overtly coercive, and are more typical of state domination which we all imagine has nothing to do with young children learning to read and write. But in the United States, and for that matter in the United Kingdom, governments have become coercive, and many states stand ready to legally enforce direct, systematic instruction in synthetic phonics, and by extension the teaching of phonemic awareness.

As I have worked on *Spin Doctors*, I have talked with teachers, administrators, and college professors in various parts of the country. Teachers living and working 3000 miles apart tell me they are scared, and they make me promise that I will not use their names as they tell me their stories. Teachers who are single mothers ask what can they do. They say they have to work, they have children to support. Administrators tell me they are worried about the "silencing" that will take place if they speak up, speak out, and let their voices be heard. Some administrators tell me that there have already been repercussions, and they tell me of the backlash that has taken place. In a single day, three educators living in three different states describe what is happening as McCarthyism, and on that day I decide that I cannot use the stories I have collected, just in case a teacher is recognized, or an administrator is identified, even though I didn't use their names. I've collected many stories that I cannot tell. The political project is coercive. An educator might be identified, censured, silenced, blacklisted, or fired.

"In reading—and this is stern," remember Garvin Winick, "and I know that, and I mean to be, and I understand this is not the most popular kind of talk—but in reading, too many people seem to ignore what works and to stress dogma rather than data."

For the first time I find it worth the struggle to read Giroux, who writes of right-wing groups and of how conservative political interests work to structure schools.

"(I)ideological tendencies strip literacy from the ethical and political obligations of speculative reason," Giroux writes in his own inimitable style, "and subjugates it to the political and pedagogical imperatives of social conformity and domination" (*Schooling*, p. 149).

Giroux writes of the discourse of "management and control," and of the ways in which teachers are positioned "within pedagogical models that legitimate their role as 'clerks' of the empire." It seems extreme, but "the technocratic interests that embody the notion of teachers as clerks" is right in front of us in newspaper articles, in sound bites on TV, in publishers' basal programs, in letters and transcriptions, in research papers and reports, and in state governments' ratified bills.[7]

In which Governor Bush's Business Council holds a pre-summit meeting in Texas

■ ■ ■

In Texas, the discourse of management and control is readily available for us to read in the transcript of the 1996 pre-summit workshop of Governor Bush's Business Council. In the next few pages I will quote from the document, staying as close to the text as I can, but I encourage every educator to read the original transcription to discover firsthand how the ideological tendencies about which Giroux writes "strip literacy from the ethical and political obligations of speculative reason and subjugate it to the political and pedagogical imperatives of social conformity and domination" (p. 149).[1]

"Lack of educator training in how to teach reading is a hurdle that must be cleared," Governor Bush's Business Council states in the forward to the transcription of the meeting. "Currently, many teacher training programs are not research based. Structured programs that are based on good research offer one solution" (p. 1).

"Most children must be explicitly be [sic] taught to read," the Council continues amorphously. "Teaching and practicing the alphabet, the sounds of letters, decoding and blending are important. Frequent testing of progress is necessary" (p. 1).

Charles Miller, the chairman of Governor Bush's Business Council, opens the meeting. "Good morning. Welcome. . . . I don't want to exaggerate, but I believe the Governor's Reading Initiative could be one of the most important steps towards improving Texas education that we've ever taken. However, it's going to take continued and sustained effort by a large part of the community in Texas to succeed. You could say we're in the beginning skirmishes of a major battle" (p. 2).

Miller talks for a while, and then he thanks the press. "First I want to offer special thanks to the people representing the media. The *Houston Chronicle*, *Dallas Morning News*, and the *Texas Monthly* are with us today. In our efforts to reform education, the support from those three publications has been extremely valuable. They have been positive and constructive. I want to thank them personally and on behalf of the Governor's Business Council" (p. 3).

The press is part of the spin, and part of the pre-summit workshop, together with the government representatives and researchers from the scientific community. Forget neutrality. Forget integrity. Forget accuracy. Ominous news accounts of illiteracy misrepresent reality, present selective information, offer worst-case scenarios, and are used to legitimize the claims of "scientific" studies on phonemic awareness. In 1997 the *Dallas Morning News* published an article called "Sounding Off" with graphs that look remarkably like those generated by Foorman and her colleagues. The article states, "On tests of ability to read words, children with low phonological awareness (PA) scored below their grade levels and below children with normal PA. . . . When given specific instruction in phonological awareness, phonics, and text reading, children who started out with low PA showed dramatic improvement in their ability to read words." There are no alternate perspectives presented. In this article all the "experts" agree, including Lyon of NICHD.

"We're not here for public record in the sense of being newsworthy, but we are going to publish virtually anything that's said today," Miller says as he finishes. "I would just encourage you not to hold back during that process because of that possibility. What we really need is frank, open, clear discussion of the most hard-hitting and constructive type."

The participants of the pre-summit introduce themselves. Patrick Oxford, a lawyer in Houston; Marina Ballyntyne,[2] the founding head of the John Cooper School; Peter O'Donnell, president of the O'Donnell Foundation; Rosie Zamora, on the Board of Regents of Texas Southern University; Henry Tatum, associate editor of the *Dallas Morning News* editorial page; David Langworthy, the opinion page editor for the *Houston Chronicle*; Carolyn Bacon, from the O'Donnell Foundation; Jim Nelson, chair of the new State Board of Educator Certification; Jim Ketelson, retired chairman of Tenneco; Leonel Castillo, assistant to Houston's mayor on educational issues; Beth Ann Bryan, from the Governor's Business Council; Greg Curtis, the editor of the *Texas*

Monthly; Ed Adams, who among his other credentials is the president of Texans for Education; Michelle Tobias, special projects counsel for Governor Bush; Margaret La Montagne, senior advisor to Governor Bush; Wanda Watson, principal of Ryan Elementary School; Lenox Reed, director of the Neuhaus Education Center in Houston (which trains teachers in Alphabetic Phonics); Marsha Sonnenberg, consultant in reading and curriculum alignment in the state of Texas; Sandy Kress, president of the Dallas School Board and a consultant to Governor Bush's Business Council; Carmyn Neely, deputy director for statewide initiatives; Mike Moses, Commissioner of Education; Darvin Winick, who we've met before and who is consultant and advisor to Governor Bush's Business Council; Douglas Carnine, professor at the University of Oregon who has long been associated with DISTAR; Jean Osborn, from the Center for the Study of Reading at the University of Illinois, who is associated with the Reading Mastery program, which is the latest version of DISTAR; Barbara Foorman, from the University of Houston and an author of the Scholastic Spelling program; Johnlyn Mitchell, principal of Kramer Elementary School in Dallas; Alda Benevides, principal of E. B. Reyna Elementary School in La Joya; Suzanne Slevinsky, third-grade teacher at Bowie Elementary School at HISD; Felipe Alanis, Associate Commissioner with the Texas Education Agency; Dub Rider, a businessman; and Jodie Jiles, member of the Governor's Higher Education Coordinating Board.

Back to Charles Miller. He tells the participants at the pre-summit that the Governor said, "If the existing programs don't work, get another program." He talks about statistics. "The National Adult Literacy Survey in 1993 found that nearly half of America's adults are poor readers or functionally illiterate." He mentions another study and then continues arbitrarily using statistics. "The overall literacy rate has gradually eroded from 97 percent in 1950 to less than 80 percent today," Miller states. "More than 3 out of 4 that goes on welfare are illiterate, 85 percent of unwed mothers are illiterate, and 68 percent of those arrested were illiterate." He concludes, "Must be some kind of causal effect there." He continues with his statistics.

"No topics are prohibited, no comments should be off the table," Miller ends by reminding the participants, "and we should try to build a record today that can be used to start discussions across the state."

He turns the meeting over to Winick who talks about microphones and tells the participants to speak up. Then he introduces Mike Moses, the Texas Commissioner of Education, who begins with a story.

"My son came home during the last six weeks and his reading grade was not very good. I said, 'Mason, this reading grade is not acceptable. If you don't do better at the end of this six weeks, somebody is going to get a whipping.'" Moses tells the participants what happened next. "He went to school the next day to see his teacher. He went up to her. He said, 'Mrs Dawkins, I don't want to scare you or anything, but my daddy said if my reading grade doesn't come up, somebody is going to get a whipping.' And I had to call her and explain that it was not she that had anything to worry about."

Moses gets serious. "The fact of the matter is we're not doing it very well. We're not doing anywhere near what we need to be doing in Texas in terms of teaching our children to read." Moses talks about scores on the MAT and the TAAS, then about the Governor, NAEP, and TV. "I think the problem is obvious," he says, and he begins his wrap-up with "I don't know that it needs a great deal more elaboration."

Winick introduces Sandy Kress and tells everyone that he will be wearing his Dallas School Board hat. Kress talks about reform in Dallas, and about increasing test scores. He says he wants to talk about what they did before "the experts in reading " speak. He talks about accountability.

"We need to measure student performance," he says. "And there has to be consequences from the performance, particularly the adult performance." Kress elaborates, "We found, for example, all over our district principals who simply were not paying attention to their mission." He praises the Dallas principal who is at the pre-summit. Then he continues. "A principal who is not focused on the Governor's goal to get the youngsters reading by grade 3 is probably going to be a principal of a school that doesn't make a lot of progress with us." He talks some more about principals and then says, "This is at least what we found in Dallas."

Kress is on a roll. "My bad news for those cities across Texas who just offered the TAAS test as a principal means of testing, if you're not testing youngsters K, 1, and 2, and you don't offer a test until the State requires one, at the end of grade 3, I want to suggest to you that you're going to be operating at a school that does not have the diagnostic tools in order to help youngsters grow and know that accountability is taking place and that teachers are performing."

Kress ends by coming back to accountability. "This can be done. This is not as difficult as a lot of things we do, measuring them and holding adults accountable for their growth," he says. "But it's going to take us, as adults and business leaders in every city across Texas, saying, 'This is our mission,' working with a focus, working with our school districts, and making this kind of change take place."

Winick introduces Carmyn Neely, the deputy director of statewide initiatives, who reads from the McGuffey First Eclectic Reader—"Ned is on the box"—before reading from a book she says her granddaughter might read in school this year—"Once in the deepest ocean there was a little fish." She talks about teachers.

"Teaching students to read continues to be tremendously demanding of our educators," she explains. "It involves constantly unpacking our ideas about reading and instruction."

Neely's presentation is conciliatory, deferential, but at one point there is a bite to what she says. "In the early days of America notions about literacy were rather simple and basic," she says. "One source tells us that in the early 1900s, of the 100 children who would start to school at age 7, only 13 would still be there at age 16. The literacy level at that time [that] came close to being universal was fifth-grade level." She ends this thought by stating, "Only very lately has literacy been addressed in classrooms that included young women, learning-disabled students, those students who are physically challenged, where all students read, not just recite, and all students write, in other words, compose, not just copy."

Neely talks about a report that is being written that came out of a meeting that Moses organized. She explains, "So Dr. Moses' group did not aim toward balance by picking and choosing the best from competing theories and practices. This cafeteria approach would sound like the eclecticism advocated during the sixties and seventies. If balance were achieved simply through a pick-and-choose method, there would cease to be either a definable or defensible position to articulate."

Neely states categorically that "balance" means that "[s]tudents engage in decoding and spelling activities through explicit and implicit instruction in developmentally appropriate skills and strategies."

After Neely finishes speaking, Moses talks about "a student who has a second language" who is exempt for two years but in the third year must take the TAAS in English. The question of Hispanic American children taking the TAAS test has been mentioned several times, and he says that the exemption is a real problem and that he is trying "to have a state Board rule that would tighten that up."

Winick introduces the experts. He talks of their "impressive research credentials" and their "illustrious academic records."

"I would like to comment," Winick states, "that we sought out qualified individuals who were serious about the need to pick reading skill development programs and strategies after careful review of experimental findings."

"Our next presenter is Jean Osborn."

The treacheries of reading education

After a short preamble Osborn states, "Let's just focus on beginning reading, which is probably the most controversial topic in education. Lots of people have belief systems about how to help children learn to read. Teachers have belief systems. Researchers—some of them—have belief systems. Some of them have research. Parents have opinions. Professors—they're among the most questionable." Osborn continues for a while and then says, "The problem is lots of children do not learn to read the words very well, and yet the adults go on in this ideological and often very nasty warring with each other about how children should learn to read."

She talks about points of agreement: "oral language knowledge is related to the understanding of printed language"; "learners need lots of good experiences with print"; "and most everyone in the world agrees reading aloud to young children is good." Osborn lists the controversies. She talks about whole language and gets to phonics.[3]

"Teaching the sounds of letters interferes with reading as meaning," she says, stating the controversy. "Now, for those of you unexposed to the treacheries of reading education, this is a big, big item. There are those who say if you say, 'Look, here's an M and it makes the sound "mmm"' you're abstracting meaning from print, you're making it automatic, and you're going to, the more extreme will say, ruin children for reading."

"There are others," Osborn explains, "who say this is a sensible way to teach children to read. Teach them letter names with the sounds the letters make and some procedures for combining them. That's a big argument right there."

Now to the research.

"Systematic phonics instruction is effective. There happens to be a lot of data that supports that, but there happens to also be a lot of people who say it's not necessary or it's damaging to children."

Osborn talks of other reading methods. Of reading by colors or by drawing boxes around words. No kidding. She says, "There's a current view that says different children learn to read in different ways and all you have to do is to find out if a child likes to read in a hot room or a cold room."

She continues with language experience and "Read Along with Uncle Bob," before returning to whole language.

"I don't know specifically how popular whole language is in Texas classrooms, but if it's like most states, I would assume it's swept the state." Osborn gives her hot room/cold room version of whole language, and then she states, "it also discards any organized and grade-level-calibrated basal reading program."

This is, of course, a big problem for researchers who are authors of basal programs. Osborn herself is an author of the Reading Mastery program.

"There are too many casualties," she says. "Let me tell you what these children do. They look earnestly at the teacher, who will give them some advice. They guess. They look at the pictures. They remember. They have all kinds of strategies, some of them excellent, for not dealing with print."

I am neither a whole language educator nor researcher, but I do support those who are, and this is disinformation, propaganda, not even techo-babble—which would be preferable because at least then we would have to work to deconstruct the spin she's in.

Osborn talks about "research."

"[M]y third caution is that we know something from research and from science about reading," says Osborn, pulling on what Winick called her illustrious academic record. "We have information. We have evidence that has enormous implications toward the teaching of beginning reading." Osborn warms to the hegemonic project. "And I think the time has come in our evolution as reading educators to really take advantage of what science can tell us. So right now I would like to talk about some research-based education for beginning reading. Any questions so far?"

"All right. Let me hold up a couple of things here." Osborn holds up a copy of *Becoming a Nation of Readers*. She encourages everybody to read it. She holds up the summary of Adams's government report, *Beginning to Read*. Osborn calls Adams's book "totally and wonderfully fascinating." Referring to the summary, she says, "We just felt there was such an important message in that book that we wanted to get it out in a form that a lot of people would consider reading." She talks about the reading of isolated words. How adults read, according to Adams. Then she talks about children.

"They have to understand that spoken words can be divided into sounds," she tells the participants in the pre-summit workshop. "Now, a lot of children, young children, do not know that. Study after study can show you that."

Not so.

"There is a high correlation between that kind of knowledge in children coming into kindergarten and ease of learning to read."

That depends on which tests you administer and the synthetic programs you use.

"Because after all, it is the sounds of spoken words that map on to the letter. Right?"

I disagree. Osborn is ignoring linguistic ambiguity. But, even so, in classrooms where children are deeply engaged in developing their own individual and shared literacy configurations, they are continuously engaged in activities that build on their understandings of the relationships between spoken and written language. Remember Martha and Leigh (the teachers in Chapter 3)?

"It's not the meaning that's the first level. It is the sounds."

Throw out Piaget, Vygotsky, and Ferreiro.[4] Scrap the work of Dyson. Forget Yetta Goodman. Tear up Ken Goodman's forty years of research. Toss out *Family Literacy, Growing Up Literate, From the Child's Point of View.* Ignore the research on practical intelligence and everyday cognition by Barbara Rogoff and Jean Lave. Get rid of Michael Halliday and, of course, James Wertsch.

"[I]f you're going to say the word Sam by its sounds, 'sss aaa mmm,' you have to have another set of skills, which is to put it back together again," Osborne says. "A lot of children could go 'sss aaa mmm' and the teacher will say, 'What word is it?' and the children will say 'sss aaa mmm' because they don't know how to blend."

Patrick had to write "sssssssssssss" before "un" when he was "blending" sun—I counted the "s's." But he also had to write "eeeeeeeeee" before "gg" when he was blending "egg." Wouldn't this make it ēgg? You might not agree. But I can document ethnographically that while Patrick was having difficulty blending in school, he was writing stories at home with me. Perhaps it has something to do with the activity?

Osborn is stuck on blending. "Teachable," she says. "It's absolutely teachable."

"Now, all this research that Marilyn and others have pooled together, this should make you believe in the alphabetic principle. So often people say, 'Well, there are so many irregular words in English.'" Osborn contends this fact. "Written English is far more regular than not."

Actually, based on the scientific study in the late 1960s of phoneme–grapheme correspondences to improve spelling conducted by, among others, Paul Hanna, John Carroll, Edgar Dale, Harry Levin, and Ruth Strickland, she's got it wrong. In the conclusions to their study, these researchers and their colleagues state that "About half (49+ percent) of all the words in the 17,000+ word corpus" they studied "can be spelled correctly on phonological bases alone." They then state, "To the extent that the corpus is a representative sample of the entire lexicon, this statement can be generalized to hold for the entire lexicon" (p. 122).[5]

These researchers then emphasize that "No member of the research team would advocate that these rules be memorized and used in a *deductive* manner by elementary school children" (p. 123). Later they state, "Complex, abstract understandings require a great deal of previous concrete, multisensory learning" (p. 128). . . ."[E]xperiences should proceed from the concrete to the abstract" (p. 128). "Furthermore, the lines of evidence that have been presented here suggest that the encoding process of spelling possibly can be learned more readily when children are given the opportunity to discover for themselves that basic structural properties underlie the spellings of many words. Further, children should be given numerous opportunities to apply this knowledge in their writing" (p. 128).

Thus we can state that American English is far more *irregular* than many researchers believe it to be, and we can use this information to ask why they would insist on teaching children to read phonetically.

Back to Osborn.

"So here's a recipe. Learn about teaching sounds and how they relate to symbols. Of course, there's a problem with vowels. Some vowels are, quote, long. Some vowels are short. Some vowels are silent. There are problems with consonant letters that have two sounds. So one of the implications of this is that you don't do it all at once. You have a sequence. You have a plan for teaching this. Blending is essential. Blending is a very important component of beginning reading instruction."

Osborn talks about her experience in a school that was in "big trouble" in Ohio. She says they adopted "a very systematic program of instruction." She tells the pre-summit that in this school they had two language arts sessions in the morning and two in the afternoon.

"They teach reading twice a day. Full reading instruction twice a day," Osborn states. "So two language arts in the morning and two in the afternoon. They gather children with similar needs into groups and classes. They track."

"Book reading is the spare-time activity by design," Osborn states. "I'd walk in last fall, and kids were drawing pictures in their spare time. I said, 'We're not going to have many artists out here. We've got to have readers.'"

If you are like me, reading such statements makes you reach for Maxine Greene. And please excuse the aside if I stop to tell you that one of the teachers with whom I've been talking sent me a short piece by Maxine "to lift my spirits" as I worked on *Spin Doctors*. I cannot call her Greene, because to those she mentors through her writing, she will always be Maxine. In the piece that the teacher sent to me, "What Matters Most," Maxine expresses her concern about the dismissal of the arts by educational reformers. She reminds us that in *Local Cultures* Clifford Geertz writes of "art as a cultural system . . . as wide as social existence and as deep." She also shares a quote from John Dewey. In *The Public and Its Problems*, he writes, "Artists have always been the real purveyors of news, for it is not the outward happening in itself which is new, but the kindling by it of emotion, perception, and appreciation" (p. 35).

"Personal agency, passion, imagination, and a making of meaning: all of these must be part of full engagement with the arts," Maxine tells us, "and it is difficult to accept a call for excellent teaching and 'teaching for America's future' that pays no heed to the awakenings the arts make possible."

The idea that children would be forced to spend most of the morning and most of the afternoon in a direct instruction phonics program and then forced to read is an anathema to me. I think of the five-, six- and seven-year-old children I taught in a "lower working class" community in the East End of London. In our classroom, art was a means of communication, a celebration. We made our own books, wrote stories, and drew pictures. In Spain, where I taught American engineers' children who were too young to be sent away to school, the arts were central to our literate activities. When I was working on my doctorate at Teachers College, a group of kindergarten kids used to come to my house and sit around the kitchen table and paint pictures and write stories. Sometimes their paintings filled the counter tops and spilled onto the floor and stretched out into the front hall, and invariably these paintings were splashed with writing that became integral to the visual composition.

I think of the children in *Family Literacy* and *Growing Up Literate*. I think of Patrick, whose first forays back into the world of print occurred as he tentatively began to draw pictures and then write about what he had drawn. In the Biographic Literacy Profiles Project, we spent years studying what Dyson calls the "symbol weaving" of children. It was impossible for us to interpret their writings without interpreting their drawings. In all of these different settings children learned to read. Irrespective of the social circumstances of their everyday lives, they loved to read stories and they loved to paint pictures. Both were aesthetic and intellectual activities which expanded the boundaries of the children's existence.[6]

Osborn reaches the end of her presentation.

"So I say we get to work on successful research-based and successful practice-based programs," she says. "Thank you."

Just in case the pre-summit participants missed the sales pitch, Margaret La Montagne, senior advisor to Governor Bush asks, "Is that a specific product program, and if so, what is it called?"

"Yes," Osborn replies, unabashedly pushing her own program. "It's Reading Mastery Program, and it goes from first grade."

Other questions follow. "If research is so clearly in favor of things like phonics and clearly not in favor of whole language," an unidentified speaker asks, "why in the world is there such a—"

Osborn interrupts. "It is a mystery to me why we are so reluctant, we as a profession, are so reluctant to take up research."

"Is that a diplomatic answer?" the unidentified speaker queries.

"Well, it's maddening."

"What are you doing about retooling teachers before they become teachers at the university level?" Rosie Zamora asks.

"Good luck."

"Why?"

Osborn hesitates and says she has to be careful. "A lot of professors of education are not really knowledgeable about what goes on in the schools." She talks about professors' romantic notions.

Peter O'Donnell talks about increasing the number of courses in reading at the University of Texas.

Osborn says, "I agree."

The question-and-answer session continues. Winick tries to move the meeting on, but there are more questions. Again it's an unidentified speaker.

"You're not suggesting, are you, it's either-or, either phonics or whole language?" the unidentified speaker asks. "You're not suggesting it's one or the other? Are you?"

"I'm saying at the beginning you'd better be serious about systematic instruction," Osborn responds.

Winick introduces Barbara Foorman, who tells the participants in the pre-summit that her talk follows Osborn's "nicely."

The design of this study is hopelessly complex

Foorman talks about NICHD and the Institute's years of research in literacy, research on the alphabetic code, genetics, attention deficit disorders, the etiology of learning disabilities, early intervention, and epidemiological research that shows that girls have as many reading problems as boys. She discusses the epidemiological study and says that the growth of reading achievement was measured on the Woodcock-Johnson. She says, "it is a very excellent test." She talks some more about girls and boys and then gives her definition of reading disabilities.

"Reading disabilities reflect a persistent deficit rather than a developmental lag," she explains. "You need to intervene early because these are deficits in particular areas, not lags. They don't go away without intervention."

She talks about learning disabilities and says they are "conceptually flawed" and "statistically flawed," and she talks about her preference for mathematical growth modeling.

"There's nothing special about reading disabilities," Foorman explains. "It's a continuous distribution. And where you make the cut mark and decide who you're going to serve is largely just your decision on how much money you have and who you can serve. *There is no statistical basis on which you can make that decision*" (emphasis added).

Isn't that exactly what Foorman and her colleagues did? They defined reading disabilities statistically. Go back and take a look at Chapter 4. Their cut-off was at the 25th percentile on the Woodcock-Johnson.

Foorman then gives an Adams definition of reading. She talks about correlations, growth curves, reading achievement, about her handout and the "powerful effect."

"It shows you the critical performance of early successful rapid decoding," she explains, "and the ability to do that kind of decoding is dependent on the ability to segment words and syllables into phonemes."

"Deficits in phonologic awareness reflect the core deficit in dyslexia," she continues, "and the good news, it's treatable."

"Now, in terms of the NICHD Intervention Findings, disabled readers do not readily acquire the alphabetic code due to deficits in phonological processing." Foorman is focused. "Thus, disabled readers must be provided highly structured, intense programs that explicitly teach the application of phonologic rules to print by well-trained teachers."

Foorman talks about "controlling factors," and here's the critical statement.

"Controlling for socioeconomic status, dialect differences mediate the level at which phonology predicts word reading for disabled readers." Foorman makes the statement and moves on, but we need to pause and think about the implications of her statement.

Dialect was not discussed in any of the Foorman studies that I read, and yet it is presented here as a factor that had to be "controlled." In the Foorman studies there were many children speaking many different "dialects" who had to respond to the experimental tasks phonetically. On the pseudoword tasks, the experimenters were given "real" words to guide them with their pronunciation of the pseudowords. Some of the children in the research were in the process of learning American English. How were their interpretations of pseudowords scored? Who determined the correct pronunciation for the African American children? The Asian American children? Or the children from Michigan? New Jersey? Alabama? Indiana?

"And the ethnicity differences turn out to be all in the phonological area and with African American differences in language." Foorman states later in her presentation. She says "ethnicity differences diminished, disappeared over the course of the year by having a good phonological awareness training program."

Whose phonemes? Did Alphabetic Phonics wash the ethnicity differences out? Did the Northern European nursery rhymes get the children to speak like me? Are we talking about first-language loss phonetically?

"When I came to Texas, I was lost," Foorman says. "I had never heard of 'fixin' to go' and 'might ought to should.' It took me five years and I was right in there being a good Texan with my Southeast Texas dialect. And Houston was an interesting place to study. There were a lot of people from Detroit and New Jersey and all over the place and native Texans, and I always have a native Texan on my research project because they need to tell me that *r-e-a-l* on my word list is pronounced *rill, r-i-l-l.* I need that person to help me."

On blending phonemes into "nonwords," who decides whether a child's response is correct or in error? Who decides on the pronunciation of "y-a-s"? The experimenter's pronunciation key says it rhymes with "gas," that "th-u-ng" rhymes with "rung," and "f-ir-t-u-s" with "circus," and "n-i-s-p-a-t with "mistake." I'm presuming that this last one should be "nispate," and that it was a "mistake."

How do you deal with all this dialectically?

"Dialects differ in all aspects to some degree," Ken Goodman wrote in the early 1970s. "Some aspects, vowels for instance, are easily observed while others are more subtle or lost in misconception. Systematic difference often is treated as isolated error."

"Vowel difference is notable in the way speakers of English dialects would pronounce this list," Goodman states, "been, bean, bin, Ben, being. Any two or more of these will be homophones," he writes, emphasizing that some of them will sound alike.

"Dialects of English vary in the number of vowels they use. Furthermore, there is not a consistent correspondence from one dialect to another. The vowel in the following group may be the same or the group may split in two," Goodman adds, "though not consistently for all dialects," and he presents the list, "*log, dog, fog, hog,* cog, *bog, frog,* smog, flog, grog, jog." Then, always personable, Goodman writes, "Those italicized rhyme for this writer (the vowel is /ə/) while the others rhyme (the vowel is /a/)."

To emphasize that Foorman's "one native Texan" won't do, let's continue.

"/r/ and to a lesser extent /l/, particularly in the final position, vary considerably in English dialects," Goodman explains. "A speaker from

Maine and one from Michigan might hear each other's pronunciation of *media* and *meteor* as exactly opposite."

"Consonants vary less notably than vowels but some variation does exist," he continues. Goodman gives as examples *dis/this* and *nuffin'/nothing*.

My nephews in England say "nuffink."

"Some consonants vary in certain sequences (Etna/Edna) or in clusters (Eas'side/Eastside) or final position (col/cold)."

Goodman then states the problem.

"What complicates dealing with and accepting phonological differences is that there is an artificial phonology, sometimes based on spelling, that confuses many teachers on what is acceptable in any dialect" (pp. 63, 64).

Once again I ask, given this complexity, how do you teach a child to read phonetically? A final quote from Goodman. "No language, and no dialect of any language, is intrinsically superior to any other in coping with any specific area of human knowledge or learning in general" (p. 62). It's important to keep this in mind, especially when we are considering studies that report the elimination of ethnic differences.

Foorman next turns her attention to the Chapter 1 study, the one that has been the center of national attention. She talks about the manipulation of classroom instruction.

"[T]hey either got a direct instruction program which consists of phonological awareness, phonics, and text reading; an embedded phonics program, which practiced phonetic patterns in context. I'll call them spelling patterns from now on. Or, a whole language program, which focused on a print-rich environment."

"The design of this study is hopelessly complex," Foorman says. "If just looking at this gives you a headache, you'll know how I feel every day trying to monitor this."

She gives a definition of whole language.

"Within this whole language philosophy, students are given a wide variety of opportunities to read, write, learn and construct meaning within a meaningful context. In this interactive, student-friendly learning environment, learning is not only active and meaningful, but also fun, with the ultimate goal being to instill the desire for life-long learning."

Then Foorman deftly confounds her own study.

"I don't know what it means," she says. Then she tries to recover what she has just said. "I mean, my project director is a committed whole language person."[7]

By her own admission, Foorman conducted a study comparing training in phonemic awareness and whole language and she doesn't know what whole language means. Problematic? Definitely.

She provides a context for the study.

"When the study started, the superintendent was fired for her whole language belief. The school board took over curriculum decisions and decided in the middle of our study that we should stop the study because in NIH when a drug works, you stop it, and everybody gets the good drug." Foorman then explains, "And they had already decided that phonics worked, so they wanted the whole district to have the phonics program. But we persisted and continued the study, but it's very difficult to do good research in these settings. There are too many stakeholders who know the answers before you start."[8]

Once again the study is confounded and biased. Again, forget neutrality, because the study lacks a key ingredient of experimental research, and that is objectivity. If the superintendent is fired for her whole language philosophy, what chance do the teachers have of dealing with the school board's negativity? How can they participate in a study when the principal researcher doesn't understand the way they teach?

Later in her presentation Foorman talks about the two whole language groups as she shares the results of her study on a graph, and for the sake of making a cohesive presentation let's take a look at what she says.

"There are two groups of whole language. There's the group that we saw and we trained, and then there's a control group from the district that was actually the lowest SES [socioeconomic status] group, which isn't a good control. But the amazing thing is how similar the two bottom lines are."

How can a "control group" be drawn from the lowest SES group? By definition, a "control" group, if you agree with this type of research, must be drawn at random from the entire population, in exactly the same manner as the "treatment group" is drawn. Otherwise you're comparing apples with oranges and any comparative analysis is meaningless.

It's time to turn to Robert Rosenthal and his 1960s research on pygmalion effects. Rosenthal upset experimental researchers by conducting experiments in which he found that students lived up or down to their teacher' expectations. In 1973 Rosenthal presented another series of studies to support his theories. In one he stated, "In spite of the fact that all experimenters read the *same* instructions to their subjects, we found that they still managed to convey their expectations" (p. 56).[9]

Rosenthal writes of one study in which the teachers of Headstart children were told that they could expect poor performance from the "below average children" and exceptional performance from their "bright children." There were in fact no measurable differences between the children. The teachers and children were then observed.

"The teachers worked much harder when they believed they had a bright child," Rosenthal writes. "In a unit on word learning for example, 87 percent of the teachers of the 'bright' children taught eight words or more words." But then making his case he states, "[O]nly 13 percent of the teachers of the 'dull' children tried to teach them that many. Not surprisingly, 77 percent of the 'bright' children learned five or more words, but only 13 percent of the 'dull' children learned that many" (p. 62).

Rosenthal emphasizes, "The expectations may be translated into explicit, overt alterations in teaching style and substance."

"There are very large teacher variability in these studies," Foorman states, "and we are going to average the growth curves for children in each of those methods to answer the question of whether the direct instruction program reduces teacher variability."

"One alternate possibility, *vis-a-vis* teacher knowledge and competence," Lyon writes in his *Education Week* official version of Foorman's study, "that could account for the failure of the whole language approach to enhance reading-skill development in the Houston study is that many College of Education professors may themselves not be fully prepared in their understanding of reading development and reading disorders, and that the information passed on to their students is equally limited and fragmentary in theory, content, and application.

"In short, the conventional wisdom imparted to whole-language teachers during their preparation may not be very wise and is sadly conventional." Lyon is in a tale-spin. "While this may seem to be a harsh interpretation, our studies of teacher-preparation practices indicate that it is accurate."

The tale gets taller and he digs himself in. "It is also important to note that the children in the literature-based groups were taught and assessed according to whole-language philosophy and principles." Apparently Lyon is being disingenuous, because the test reported by Foorman and her colleagues was the Woodcock-Johnson. "Portfolio assessments were carried out frequently during the year, as were continuous observations of oral reading of predictable texts." The children might have been in whole language classrooms and their teachers might have practiced portfolio assessment, but Foorman did not include portfolio assessment in her study. How could she? She is not trained in the disciplined observational techniques used to systematically document children's early literacy learning, and it is highly questionable whether she has the analytic training to interpret the complexities of the children's literacy configurations that are revealed by this approach to instructional assessment.

"Because deficits in phonological skill are prime candidates for what is specific about specific reading disability," Foorman and her colleagues write in the NICHD proposal referring to a1989 paper by Foorman, "measurement of phonological awareness is central to the prediction of growth in reading and spelling skills as well as achievement outcomes" (p. 57).

In the Chapter 1 study, teachers must have been aware that Foorman and her colleagues were advocates of phonemic awareness and phonics. Other studies had already taken place. Foorman and her colleagues appear to genuinely believe that "reading disabilities," as they define them, are caused by deficits in phonemic awareness skills. Consequently, they used the Woodcock-Johnson word and pseudoword tests—which are essentially tests of phonemic awareness—as their measure of "reading achievement." They trained children with synthetic phonemic awareness drills. Four times during the year they tested the children with their own phonemic awareness pseudowords, and as tests teach, when they tested them again on the Woodcock-Johnson, the children were better at decoding a few more pseudowords.

Teachers aren't daft. They understand the old "raisins in a bottle" routine, even if the researchers don't. Already disparaged in the district, the superintendent was sacked, and the pressure was on to include more synthetic phonics and phonemic awareness training in the kindergarten and first-grade classrooms. It's impossible to imagine that the whole language teachers were not mindful of the researchers' bias. They must have been aware of their unfavorable position, and it's entirely possible that they transmitted their response to the situation to their students. Similarly, there is a strong possibility that the expectations of the teachers of the phonological awareness and phonics treatments affected the way in which they worked with the children.

In addition, some of the poorest children in the district were in the whole language "control" group, and Rosenthal emphasizes that the pygmalion dilemma is doubly significant for children who are poor and for African American children.

"Teachers were much less favorable to the lower-class children than they were to middle-class children," Rosenthal states, quoting another study. "[L]ow income children who had *higher* IQ's [than middle income children] tended to have teachers who viewed them *negatively*, and this was especially true for lower-income children who were black" (p. 63).

Once again Foorman's study is confounded. Who knows what Foorman was actually measuring? Maybe what she did just confirms the ways in which we treat children who are poor and African American children. The researchers didn't expect them to achieve, and this was transmitted through the teachers to the children.

"The two whole language groups' growth rates are bunching around zero," Foorman says. "Zero growths."

Under these circumstances we have to ask: What did the researchers do to these children? Zero growth? That's simply not possible unless there was something seriously wrong with the experimental design, with the ways in which the study was conceptualized and organized, with the tests that were administered—what Rosenthal refers to as "the prejudice of stunted expectations."

Let's backtrack for a moment and pick up Foorman's presentation as she talks about the use of Open Court as one of the treatments.

"Just a word why we use that program," she tells the pre-summit participants. "We reviewed the literature. We were going to use the Reading Mastery program many know here as DISTAR because the literature supported that program with children of low socioeconomic status."

Foorman's presentation is disorganized here but I will present it exactly as it appears in the transcript.

"This is a brand new program" (I presume referring to Open Court). "I didn't know about it. But I called my friend, Marilyn Adams, and I said, 'Help. I'm not allowed to use DISTAR,' which is what happened. In the eleventh hour before the grant proposal was signed off the district said I couldn't use it. However, they said I could use Open Court because they were using Open Court math, but I had to pay for it myself.

"Well to equip 18 classrooms and teacher training would have cost me close to $100,000. NIH doesn't have the money. I certainly don't in my checkbook. So I called my friend Marilyn Adams and I said, 'Help. What am I to do?'

"And she said, 'Well I happen to know of a program you might try.'"

The program was Open Court, and of course Marilyn Jager Adams is one of the program's authors.

So, here's the question. Who paid for Open Court? Not the school district. Not NIH. Not Foorman. So, who paid? The basal company that publishes and profits from the adoption of the program?

On the title page of "Early Interventions for Children with Reading Problems," in which they present a synthesis of all five studies, Foorman and her colleagues thank "Open Court Publisher for providing materials and trainers." In the description of the Chapter 1 study the experimenters state, "Open Court trained the teachers delivering the DI curriculum as well as one of our research staff members so that she could monitor the teachers during the year."

Then in the "Research Update" Foorman, writing apparently on her own, states, "The fact that Open Court helps economically disadvantaged, low achieving children to perform near the national average is very impressive."

The Marlboro Man meets Joe Camel. How did reading research become such a corrupt business?

"The results make a strong positive statement for teachers using the Open Court system," Mary Kay Simpson of SRA/McGraw-Hill writes in a letter to the superintendent of the school district in which Foorman's studies took place. She encloses a copy of a memo from Mike Moses, the Commissioner of Education who is at Governor Bush's pre-summit, which announces that "the second year of funding for *Academics 2000: First Things First*, the Texas Goals 2000 initiative, was approved by the U.S. Department of Education." Mary Kay Simpson, representing the publisher of Open Court, reminds the superintendent that government funds "are available."

Winick next introduces Douglas Carnine. I have never heard or read a presentation quite like Carnine's, and I will present excerpts without commentary. Once again I urge you to read the original transcript which was distributed and is a part of the public record.

We've got to get straight and help educators get straight that we're going to build a new culture

Carnine focuses on procedures.

"Educators are hooked on procedures. They're not hooked on results. That's the challenge," Carnine states. "What we have to find are programs that work that produce results with kids."

"We've got to get straight and help educators get straight that we're going to build a new culture that is performance dominated, not philosophies, and not procedures."

He talks about a "billion-dollar study in 1990 dollars" that compared reading methods and of the superior performance of direct instruction.[10] He talks about different methods, then focuses on child-centered approaches to reading instruction.

"When we don't use research and we don't know how to provide services that make a difference, we're going to let the child figure it out," Carnine explains. "This will change, but it will only change with leadership from people such as yourselves that help education become a performance-oriented culture, because it will not change from within. The incentives are not there. And the know-how is not there."

He talks about one method that works. The unnamed program must be DISTAR, with which he is closely associated.

"Now, fortunately, there was one approach included in this massive study that was very structured, very intensive, and very academically oriented, and there were very strong and very positive results."

He talks about the results. He talks about children in first, second, and third grade with low IQs and the gains they made. Then he says that the scores for kids with high IQs also went up.

"We actually don't want to close the learning gap," Carnine explains. "Don't get caught on closing the learning gap or you'll create problems for public education."

"What happened as a basis of this research? Well there were reasonably sized projects in Chicago, Houston, Dallas, San Diego, New York City. But you know what happened? Structured teaching fell out of favor. All programs were closed down."

He tells the pre-summit what happened. He says in California a language arts specialist taught a child with Down Syndrome to read. He explained that a curriculum specialist listened to her read.

"And you know what her response was?" Carnine asks. "The curriculum specialist said, 'Yeah, but you taught her how to read.' That's frightening. That's right."

"Now, there are three things that I think are very important to keep in mind. These are all points that you need to help educators do. First, get it straight. What works? What do we know about effective instruction? The inspiring part of this meeting is you didn't bring in educational innovators. That's why I'm happy to be here. You brought in people who can deliver results. That's the new message. That's the new culture."

"Do not underestimate the difficulties of getting things to work on a broad scale. And, finally, keep it straight. You have to set up a safeguard to prevent the educational establishment from wiping out effective programs and replacing them with new fads, such as happened 20 years ago after the release of the data I described."

"Unfortunately, there's no other field where we do such important work and there are absolutely no safeguards or controls."

This is a point on which Carnine and I agree, even if tangentially.

"There needs to be ways in which the profession figures out what it knows and acts on that knowledge. One thing that most people usually don't realize is that, unlike other professions, teachers cannot be sued for malpractice. And the reason for that is that the courts have ruled that educators don't know anything. That's true. There's no tort claim.

"We've got to recognize that in education it's not simply a won't-do problem. A lot of times it's a can't-do problem. These schools really don't know how to fix themselves. They need help. You've got to give them help that will work. We can't send in any more fads."

He talks about state assessment in Texas.

"Now, here's two pieces of advice. If you want to level the playing field on TAAS. They're not easy to do. First you don't test grade-mates, you test age-mates. Then all advantages of retaining kids to inflate scores are gone.

"Second, you multiply the school score by the percent of kids who took the test. Very simple. Very controversial. But what it does, it excludes all advantages for retaining kids and it excludes all advantages for exempting kids."

He talks about report cards.

"The report card I'm recommending for California is quite simple. You get the scores for your kids, and right above it you get the scores for an average of 15 percent of the highest scores in the state."

He talks about high-performing schools.

"Again, if you look at modern management, the idea is not to punish the employees. The idea is to make those employees as productive, as profitable as they can be.

"Now many educators will object to this notion of copying high-performing schools, but let me tell you an example. Let's say I'm running down the concourse to get a plane. I'm almost late, and I drop. The next thing I know, I wake up and I'm in the operating room and the heart surgeon is there and he's going to open up my heart. And he says, 'I'm not a typical surgeon. I do not copy the open-heart surgery processes that have been validated hundreds and hundreds of times. I am creative. I am going to do something new with you.'

"The hallmark of a profession is knowing when and what to copy. That's it," Carnine says, having made his case. "I want things very routine, professional and routine."

He discusses his credentials.

"My training was not as an educator. I was trained as an experimental psychologist."

He talks about England. Russia. Strategies of infiltration and subversion.

"You have to be very careful in terms of the people you appoint and make sure that they are going to share and value this new culture of results-oriented.

"Just be aware that there is an understandable struggle about what shall prevail in education and what the rules shall be, and that was the choice I had to make—either change the rules or get out of the business.

"I appreciate the opportunity to be here today because you have the influence and the intelligence to understand the need to change the rules and do something about it, and I hope that I can be part of that process. Thank you."

Presentations from three educators followed, but they were not included in the transcript of the pre-summit meeting. No explanation is provided of why their presentations were excluded. We can only surmise the reason.

Miller sums up.

"I'd like the group to know that we didn't, let's say, cherry-pick the experts to lean one way or the other. We did look for research or substantial backing for people's opinions or concepts, in other words, that there was scientific, quantitative or research backing for their opinions. That's why we ended up with the folks we had.

"The encouraging part is we know what needs to be done," Miller tells the group. "The discouraging part is that our school system seems to resist proven practices and ignores the lack of achievement. Most energies are not directed toward improvement. So that's a big problem.

"Challenges that we can hear out of this meeting today is that it's important to build awareness and acceptance. The Governor's initiative seems to be going well, but it's very important that we keep momentum.

"Any of us that have worked in the area of changing education, education reform, whatever you want to call it, know that entrenched interests make that difficult. So we need to move to a research-based, accountability-driven system. That's the way to do it.

"We have to reorient. We have to help reorient a large number of educators who are poorly informed about reading skills development."

Teaching reading has become the task of the United States' conservative generals and their subaltern intellectuals

Gramsci writes about a certain type of "intellectuals" whose fortunes are linked to industry. He calls them "subaltern[11] officers in the army" who carry out the plans of the "industrial general staff." He says "some intellectuals become more and more identified with the industrial general staff," and that sometimes the intellectuals reach a point where they think "they *are* the State." Gramsci writes that when this happens there can be "important consequences" and "unpleasant complications" for those who live in the State.

It's as if Gramsci had just visited Texas.

Teaching children to read has always been a part of the struggle for democracy, a human rights issue. But recently teaching reading has become the task of the United States' right-wing generals, such as those in Governor Bush's Business Council, and their subaltern intellectuals, who, together with the publishers of basal reading programs, are exercising power through constituting alliances and winning consent for their hegemonic project.

First, speaking for Governor Bush as a member of his "general staff," Miller establishes his political authority. "The Governor said, 'If the existing programs don't work, get another program,'" he tells the pre-summit. Then he expresses his concern for the erosion of the national literacy rates from 97 percent in 1950 to less than 80 percent today. Untrue, but a good spin.[12] Moses, another member of the governor's general staff, establishes that there is also a local problem. "The fact of the matter is that we are not doing very well." Kress, a member of the lower echelon, but still in a position of considerable authority, elaborates, "We found, for example, all over our district, principals who simply were not paying attention to their mission." He talks of schools without the diagnostic tools to "help youngsters grow," or for "accountability to take place," or for the general staff to know that teachers "are performing."

Kress talks about holding teachers accountable. The teachers in the hegemonic project are, as Giroux puts it, "the clerks." They are low-paid paper-pushers who "know nothing" according to Carnine, and are "variables" to be "reduced" according to Foorman. But they must nonetheless be held accountable, according to Kress, who states, "It's going to take all of us, as adults and business leaders across Texas, saying, 'this is our mission,' working with our school districts, making this kind of change take place." From this perspective, teachers are not even adults, because it's the "adults" who are going to make the changes and hold the teachers accountable. So the teachers will be damned if they do and damned if they don't. If children don't have high reading scores when the generals test them, it will be the teachers' fault. If the children score well, then it will be in spite of the teachers, because the generals and their subalterns have controlled "teacher effects" and reduced them to a "know-nothing variable."

The subaltern intellectuals then make sure of the teachers' compliance in this impossible situation by stating categorically and with absolute authority that the artificial programs that they are promoting are supported by the indisputable findings of the "true scientific method." In her presentation, Osborn, as a subaltern intellectual, supports the generals by disparaging and distorting more democratic approaches to reading instruction. Then with a one-two punch she KOs more holistic approaches by comparing them with learning to read by colors and with reading in a hot or cold room.

The way is then clear for her to introduce her own "scientific" version of how children should be taught to read. "We know something from research and from the science of reading," she says. "We have information. We have evidence." By using "science," Osborn fulfills her role as subaltern, while at the same time she ensures that the links with the publishers of basal reading programs are maintained as she highlights the four-times-a-day language arts use of Reading Mastery, the reading program of which she is an author. Foorman then adds to the "science" by talking about "deficits," "lags," "controlling factors," and "powerful effects," before she plugs Open Court, the program that Adams, her "good friend," co-authored.

In case there is any dissent, the subaltern intellectual who talks as if he is the state proclaims the new culture. Carnine tells the generals on the Business Council that they have to "get it straight" and "keep it straight." He reminds them that "[w]e actually don't want to close the learning gap." He talks of the "new culture" of "people who can deliver results." He says that's the "new message," and he cautions the generals about educators' "strategies of infiltration," "subversion," and the "understandable struggle about what shall prevail." Carnine cautions the generals as he expounds the virtues of the "new culture of results."

"Just be aware that there is an understandable struggle about what shall prevail in education and what the rules shall be," he says, as he deftly invalidates all other approaches to reading instruction and promotes his own commercial program. Ingratiatingly, he talks about the intelligence of the generals in understanding "the need to change the rules," and presents himself as a willing candidate to assist them in making the necessary changes.

Osborn, Foorman, and Carnine are or have worked as consultants for the state of Texas. However, I've been told that their actual job positions are being "kept anonymous."

Conflicts of interest and ethical problems involved in researchers publishing findings which support commercial programs that provide financial incentives

Make no mistake about it, for many researchers, teaching children to read is a way of making money, a lucrative business, a commercial enterprise. This is fine as long as we know of their affiliations with publishers when we evaluate their research findings. It doesn't necessarily mean that their findings are tainted, but this possibility exists, and educators who read and perhaps use their research findings should be able to make that judgement for themselves. Public disclosure is of critical importance so that research can be reviewed for possible bias, because the financial incentives, which can be enormous, create the potential for serious conflicts of interest.

I suspect that there are very few teachers or members of the general public who are aware of just how much money can be at stake. To give you an example, several years ago a well-known literacy researcher and whole language pedagogist was offered $250,000 to work for a basal publisher. The researcher refused, but as you can imagine, with children in college putting the telephone receiver down was not an easy thing to do.

In years past I've also received calls from publishers of basals, but I've always said no, and no money has ever been mentioned. However, last year I received a call from the Early Childhood Division of Scholastic inviting me to be a guest at their annual advisory board meeting in New York, and as I have been impressed with Scholastic's publication of children's books and by their early childhood magazines, I agreed to go. Unfortunately, it wasn't until I visited the exhibits at the International Reading Association's Annual Convention that I realized that Scholastic is now the publisher of a basal reading program, and also that the company is heavily invested in the publication of synthetic materials to systematically train children in phonemic awareness. My first impulse was to cancel my participation in the meeting, but I decided to go and share my concerns at the meeting about the research on phonemic awareness and to explain why the research is extremely problematic. This I did; however, for ethical reasons, I declined the $3,000 honorarium for my attendance at the meeting. Those at Scholastic who had invited me to participate in the advisory board meeting did not question my decision. They expressed their willingness to work with me to choose books to be paid for with this money to send to Letta Mashishi in South Africa for the parenting center she is trying to establish for families living in Soweto, and to Red River Parish in Louisiana, where the conditions of the schools in which children are educated are, as you will read later in this book, worse than you will find in any other supposedly "enlightened" industrialized nation.

I want to emphasize that, just as I would defend any researcher's right to work with a basal publisher, I would also defend the right of basal publishers to produce these commercial programs. Similarly, I hope researchers and publishers alike will defend my right to dispute the research findings, to raise objections to the manner in which the research was conducted, to question the role of basal publishers, to point out the possible conflicts of interest and ethical problems involved in researchers making claims and publishing findings which support commercial programs in which they or their colleagues have financial interest, and to caution people about making inaccurate references to the indefensibly flawed research findings of some of the studies on phonemic awareness.

If research on reading is to be fairly evaluated, full public disclosure is essential. In the financial community, public disclosure is a legal requirement, and investment bankers and major brokerage houses have to disclose their vested interests when making recommendations, or their licences would be revoked. Similarly, news organizations such as *Time* and *Newsweek* routinely disclose their parent companies' vested interests when the company might stand to gain from the publicity resulting from an article in one of their newsmagazines. If medical researchers are funded by pharmaceutical companies, then professional ethics demand that such funding be disclosed when the research findings are published in the *New England Journal of Medicine* or the *Journal of the American Medical Association*. The *Reading Research Quarterly* has no such requirement, and unfortunately the same standards of professional ethics do not apply.[13] In fact, in the past, editors of the journal have also been paid by publishing companies for their work as basal authors.

Now that we are out of the quagmire of the pre-summit meeting of Governor Bush's Business Council in Texas, let's pull together the various threads of the arguments that I've presented. If you recall, Grossen writes that the usual nature of research in education is to present untested hypotheses as proved theories, but that in a true scientific paradigm, theories are tested by doing everything to try to prove the theory incorrect. The same applies to scientific arguments. Perhaps the events taking place in Texas are anomalous, and maybe there is no hegemonic project. After we've visited the state legislature in North Carolina, where I'll develop the arguments further, I'll let you decide. But first let's tie some of the loose ends together.

In which we have an "If-they-say-it's-so-it-must-be-so" attitude toward experimental research

■ ■ ■

We began in the exhibits hall with basal publishers luring teachers with their colorful packaging and unfounded scientific claims for their synthetic phonemic awareness programs. "Research shows that 11 to 15 hours of training in phonemic awareness is the key to reading success," states a Scholastic pamphlet. At Open Court, the salesperson insists that "the program is based on the latest scientific research." Who can argue with science?

Unfortunately, many teachers and researchers are still intimidated by the results of an experiment.[1] We have an "if-they-say-it's-so-it-must-be-so" attitude toward experimental research. Mention a Spearman-Brown split-half reliability or a correlation with $p < 0.01$ and we all shut up. We don't even balk when Bill Honig in California praises Barbara Foorman's research and says, "It's like in science when you get a theory and you have evidence to back it up and the results are what you predicted, you know you have something." We don't challenge California's Reading Advisory when they reference Stanovich and state that "Research has shown repeatedly that phonemic awareness is a powerful predictor of success in learning to read." We might vent our frustration when Winick tells us that "[t]he rules of engagement are clear" and that "well-defined experiments are expected," but we are cowed-down when he talks about the National Institute of Child Health and Human Development. After all, NICHD is a government-funded agency, so doesn't that ensure its integrity? From what we've seen so far, apparently not, but it does establish the Institute as some sort of authority.

When Reid Lyon makes *ad hominem* attacks stating that "education professors may themselves not be fully prepared in their understanding of reading development and reading disorders and that the information passed on to their students is equally limited and fragmentary in theory, content, and application," there is no response in *Education Week* from either professors of education or their students. Instead, we argue philosophy rather than science, even when we are goaded with claims that we have no research, that we have no science, and that our pedagogies, as Osborn states, are "romantic." Someone needs to plainly point out that NICHD is a "scientific institution" that is waging a political campaign to undermine decades of scientific research on young children learning to read and write, and which is trying to impose its own "true scientific model," which in reality supports the ideologically extreme views of right-wing conservatives.

In the first section of *Spin Doctors*, I responded to these attacks by criticizing the research on phonemic awareness from the perspective of a holistic pedagogy based on a theoretical foundation of practical intelligence and everyday cognition. Here are the major criticisms I presented:

1. Phonemic awareness experimentation rests on the assumption of cultural and social uniformity.
2. There are no children in the phonemic awareness studies, only labels, aggregates, and measures.
3. In phonemic awareness research, there is a complete separation of children's everyday worlds from their performance on certain isolated cognitive tasks.
4. In phonemic awareness research, the form of written language is separated from the meaningful interpretation of the text.
5. Phonemic awareness research is based on the false assumption that children's early cognitive functions work from abstract exercises to meaningful activity.
6. In phonemic awareness research, the tests given to children provide measures which are of no value outside of the testing situation.
7. In phonemic awareness research, there is an underlying assumption that there will be a transfer of learning from isolated exercises to reading texts.

8. The direct application of experimental research on phonemic awareness to classroom situations changes the relationships that exist between teachers and children.

Thirty years of observing human behavior has convinced me that human learning is socially formed and culturally transmitted. Watching very young children as they begin to establish themselves as readers and writers has provided me with countless opportunities to observe their moves back and forth between function and form, meaning and abstraction. For young children, reading and writing are social activities and their interest in the forms of written language is always purposeful. The research on phonemic awareness flies in the face of such observations, and flouts the research of some of this century's greatest educational pedagogists and social theorists.

To accept the notion that human learning moves from abstraction to meaning—in this case from mapping the smallest units of sound onto the smallest units of print, to blending pseudowords, to reading words in a controlled vocabulary—we would have to disregard the work of Vygotsky and Piaget. None of the research on practical intelligence and everyday cognition would make sense. Lave, Rogoff, and Scribner would all find their theories maligned, just as Goodman's theories have been maligned and denigrated because he's a more visible target. We could fill pages with the names of researchers whose work would have to be tossed out. Make a list. Write down some of the names of researchers whose work has informed your teaching. If Dyson is at the top of your list, you'll have to cross her out. The pedagogical implications of the "new" theories of phonemic awareness dismiss everything but studies of phonemic awareness research and the findings of other reductionist experimental studies that push reading theories into progressively narrower areas of expanding complexity.

So what is this research that uses the "true scientific method"? In the second chapter of *Spin Doctors*, I traced some of the most influential studies back to Stanovich. Taking "Matthew Effects in Reading" as the foundational study, I worked back into the literature to review the key studies that are referenced, and although it's tedious I urge you to do the same. What I concluded was that studies were selectively and misleadingly cited out of context to support the arguments (1) that phonological awareness stands out as the most potent predictor of ease of initial reading acquisition, and (2) that explicit training in phonemic awareness is the key to reading success.

Although I reviewed and critiqued a number of the studies referenced by Stanovich, I also focused on the study by Olofsson and Lundberg because Stanovich stated that their results were "most convincing," and because of the forthright way in which these researchers presented their findings. Olofsson and Lundberg included their own critique. They talked about "great variances" and "ceiling effects." They were cautious and there was no talk of causal relationships. But Stanovich was not so cautious. In "Matthew Effects in Reading" he writes of reciprocal causality without actually ever establishing causality. Even in his references to his own work, he neglects to tell the reader that he and his colleagues discarded data and used statistical procedures that are highly questionable when applied to the types of data he generates through his experiments on children. Caveats apply but are not mentioned.

Of course, none of this would be of any consequence except that the article has become a foundational reference on which many phonemic awareness studies rest, and was referenced by Adams in her government report. Adams relied heavily on the work of Stanovich, and as *Beginning to Read* was picked up by conservative state governments across the country, so was the work of Stanovich. NICHD also relies heavily on Stanovich, and his research is part of the foundation for the Foorman studies. Defy gravity for a moment and imagine a house of cards; turn it upside down in your mind so that the broad base is on the top. At the bottom are just a couple of cards precariously leaning against each other holding up the entire stack. Now pull out one of the cards and watch as the whole house shudders and shakes and then caves in. If A cites B . . . if B is Stanovich and the "Matthew Effects in Reading"?

The house that Foorman and her colleagues built was already falling down when they began their research on early interventions for children with reading problems. In their proposal they began with a Stanovich assumption that "measurement of phonological awareness is central to the prediction of growth in reading and spelling as well as achievement outcomes" (p. 57). These early intervention studies are a prime example of the reductionist experimental studies that push reading theories into progressively narrower areas of expanding complexity. As Foorman herself said at the pre-summit meeting, the study was "hopelessly complex," and dealing with all the data gave her a headache.

In the papers I've read by Foorman and her colleagues which describe the early intervention studies, culture is a risk factor, race is an issue, and dialect is ignored. Children with "limited English proficiency" were included in the study. There is a presumption of "reading deficits" which are reminiscent of the "linguistic-cognitive deficits" that Riessman spoke out against in the 1960s and early 1970s. And now, just as then, it is African American children who are most at risk of being ascribed these researchers' deficits.

Children were defined by Foorman and her colleagues as "reading disabled" if they scored below the 25th percentile on the word identification and word attack subtests of the Woodcock-Johnson Revised, and if they were also at least 15 standard score points lower in intelligence tests scores on the WISC-R. Without actually naming the test, Lyon refers to the WJ-R as "a measure reported to have excellent construct validity by the National Academy of Sciences."[2] The scientific truth is that the test is arcane, an embarrassment to the field of special education, and is kept under wraps to preserve the power of the testers, the WJ-R's mystique, or maybe just the commercial worth of the test.

Wiggins writes, "Any use of power and its limits involves moral questions and moral consequences, and testers have extraordinary and often unilateral power."[3] He states, "Each school district ought to, at the very least, state the permissible uses of such morally problematic practices as test security, scoring on a curve, the use of nonarticulated and generic tests. . . ."[4]

Keeping the Woodcock-Johnson off limits to teachers, parents, and children is a political act. Stating that an age equivalent is K.7 means nothing unless the test from which the grade was derived is open to consideration, and compared with other forms of documentation. Go into the special education department at your local elementary school, and ask if you can review the WJ-R, and if you're allowed, check out subtests 22 and 31. To be ascribed a reading disability in the Foorman studies only takes the mispronunciation of a few pseudowords. It would be a joke if the test wasn't used so indiscriminately, and if children's lives weren't so adversely affected by the results.

I won't go into the rigamarole of the statistical procedures again, but I do want to remind you of Olofsson and Lundberg, whose study I discussed in my critique of the research of Stanovich. Olofsson and Lundberg cautioned us that "we must consider the effects of violating the assumptions about normally distributed scores and homogenous error variances. Distributional violations have generally small effects but unequal variances in combination with unequal group sizes may seriously affect the statistical significance tests." In the Foorman studies there were racial subgroups with as few as five children. Even if we ignore the issues of assumption of normal distributions and the inappropriate use of interval scales, even the most liberal interpreter of the use of parametric statistical procedures in the field of education must be concerned about conducting statistical analyses and reaching "significant" conclusions using such small groups of children. If you are, speak out!

Perhaps it is somewhat ironic that in the end, the most damning criticisms of these early intervention studies have come not from me but from Foorman herself when she spoke at the pre-summit meeting. At the Houston pre-summit she gives a definition of whole language but then admits, "I don't know what it means." This would seem to be a bit of a problem when her research involves comparing reading methods. She also admits that the whole language "control group" was "actually the lowest SES group," and that it "wasn't a good control." She tells the participants at the summit that "there are very large teacher variability in these studies," but in her analysis of the data she does not take into consideration any teacher effects. Foorman also relates how Open Court came to be used as the commercial program of choice in the early intervention studies, and from her acknowledgments on the synthesis paper there seems to be little doubt that the publishers of Open Court provided both training and materials.

But most importantly, our concerns about these studies must be for the children and their families. Their rights were violated, and I urge the educational community to address the very serious issues that are raised by this sort of experimental research.

Just as "Matthew Effects in Reading" has, the Foorman studies have become the foundation for state interventions into the ways in which children are taught to read and write. In Chapter 5 on the politics of spin doctoring, I used the work of Gramsci and Giroux to introduce this state intervention as a hegemonic project. I then used the work of Fairclough to demonstrate through my discussion of the pre-summit in Texas (1) how state governments, researchers, and publishers exercise power through constituting alliances, (2) how they work together to persuade and win the cooperation of teachers, and (3) how coercion is used when resistance to the hegemonic project is expected. At stake are power and privilege and commercial profits. Vast sums of money are changing hands as systematic, explicit phonics becomes the lucrative prize. But at what cost to young children who are learning to read? To their families? To their teachers? These are the questions I want to address in my discussion of changes that are in the process of being made, as I write, in North Carolina which are the result of Senate Bill 1139 that was ratified in 1995 by the General Assembly.

In which the kindergarten children in North Carolina are no longer expected to ~~try to read and write~~

■ ■ ■

"This is unbelievable!" says the note from the educator who sent me the documentation from North Carolina.

In the package was a memo dated November 26, 1996, from Michael Frye, Chief Consultant for the North Carolina State Department of Public Instruction. "In response to Senate Bill 1139, the Program Committee of the State Board of Education has been evaluating ways to make phonics more explicit in the *North Carolina Standard Course of Study/ Teacher Handbook for English Language Arts*," Frye writes. "Please feel free to collaborate with your colleagues as you react to the draft."

Included with the draft was a copy of the Senate Bill. Under "School Based Management and Accountability," Section 8 is of particular interest. Here's the gist.

"Section 8.1. The State Board of Education shall develop a comprehensive plan to improve reading achievement in the public schools. . . . The plan shall be based on reading instructional practices for which there is strong evidence of effectiveness in existing empirical scientific research studies on reading development. . . .

"Section 8.2. . . . The General Assembly believes that the first, essential step in the complex process of learning to read is the accurate pronunciation of written words and that phonics, which is the knowledge of relationships of the symbols of the written language and the sounds of the spoken language, is the most reliable approach to arriving at the accurate pronunciation of a printed word. Therefore, these programs shall include early and systematic phonics instruction. . . .

"Section 8.3. In order to reflect changes . . . that include early and systematic phonics instruction, the State Board of Education, in collaboration with the Board of Governors of the University of North Carolina and the North Carolina Association of Independent Colleges and Universities, shall review, evaluate, and revise current teacher certification standards and teacher education programs within the institutions of higher education that provide coursework in reading instruction.

"Section 8.4. Local boards of education are encouraged to review and revise existing board policies, local curricula, and programs of professional development in order to reflect changes to the standard course of study and to emphasize balanced, integrated, and effective programs of reading instruction that include early and systematic phonics instruction."

Educators in universities tell me that the current fetish for phonics will only last a couple of years. Some say five years; others say it will blow over and we must continue with our own literacy research, stay out of the fray, and "show by example" how effective holistic pedagogies can be. Teachers and administrators are perhaps more realistic.

"We've gone back twenty years and it's going to take another twenty years just to regain some of the ground we've lost," one superintendent of schools tells me. "Once a program comes into a school it takes years. A whole generation of children will suffer through this."

The superintendent is correct that the effects of the changes taking place in state legislatures *are* and will be far-reaching. Innocuous as Section 8 might seem, these are systemic changes, a massive lurch to the right that will have far-reaching consequences as we enter the twenty-first century, not only for how young children are taught to read and write but also for our democratic way of life. This is the argument that I am going to make in the next few pages of *Spin Doctors.* See if you agree.

Let's begin by asking why the North Carolina General Assembly decided to make phonics more explicit and revise the *Standard Course of Study* and *Teacher Handbook for English Language Arts.* Our subaltern intellectuals are about to reappear. The document on "Recommendations for Changes to Reflect Research"[1] states as follows:

"Reid Lyon, Marilyn Adams, and others have consulted extensively with the state of California in the development of their documents. The 'Guide to the California Reading Initiative: Definitions and Research Findings, Legislation and Funding Sources' (1996) and the document, 'Implementing the Components of the California Reading Initiative: A

Blueprint for Teachers of Early Reading Intervention' (November, 1996) reflect these changes. The state of North Carolina would be well advised to work from these documents" (p. 8). Clearly, Lyon and Adams are exerting serious influence on state governments in the United States, both directly through consultation and indirectly through the research that they promote, Lyon through NICHD and Adams through *Beginning to Read*.

A few years ago, while Bill Honig was still the Superintendent of Schools for the state of California, I spent a day in Sacramento at the State Department of Education. This was before Honig found phonics, and at that time he was gung-ho to revolutionize special education. Shirley Thornton, who at that time was the Director of Public Education and a strong activist for racial equality, convened the meeting. Over the past few years there had been a series of lawsuits in California challenging the use of IQ tests with African American children, and I was there to talk about student advocacy and instructional assessment. There were several lawyers representing the State Department of Education who seemed to be keeping close tabs on what was said at the meeting, and it was from these lawyers that I first began to understand the influence of powerful mega-states such as California and Texas on other states in the nation.

Educational decision-making in California affects the decision-making process in Texas and New York. It's an extension of if-A-cites-B, then, like lemmings, C and D follow; and once again we have to ask what happens if A or B were mistaken in the direction they had taken?

I have often thought about the meeting in California as I've reviewed the documents that have been sent to me from California and Texas—often via other states. Clearly, events taking place in California and Texas are shaping how children are taught to read and write in the rest of the nation. If North Carolina has the documentation from California, then it seems reasonable to assume that so do the other fifty states. Similarly, what is happening in Texas is also affecting other states. We know that in California, Honig is promoting the Foorman studies, and that in Massachusetts, Silber has sent every superintendent of schools in the state a copy of the document Grossen wrote on NICHD which is based, in part, on Foorman's work. All politics are local, so the saying goes, perhaps more so than any of us realize.

In North Carolina, at least three researchers-who-are-also-authors-of- commercial-reading-programs made presentations to the State Board Reading Committee in response to Senate Bill 1139, including Bonnie Grossen and Marilyn Adams. As you will recall, Grossen wrote the synthesis of 30 years of NICHD research which Lyon has stated is a largely accurate portrayal of NICHD research.[2] Like Carnine, she is also associated with Reading Mastery, a reinvention of DISTAR published by McGraw-Hill, who also publish Open Court, for which Adams is an author.

In the *Summary of Research Findings for Senate Bill 1139*, Grossen and Adams are named as "nationally recognized experts" and their influence on the document is clearly evident in the statements that are made about educational research.

"Empirical scientific research refers to experimental and quasi-experimental designs (where variables are manipulated and their effects upon variables observed) as well as other forms of quantitative research (which systematically analyzes data) and qualitative research (which appropriately and systematically analyzes descriptions and interpretations that are in narrative rather than in numerical form)."[3]

At first glance this seems to be a more inclusive statement than the statement in the document on NICHD written by Grossen. But then comes the slight of hand.

"Empirical scientific research in education should conform to the evaluation standards of the Joint Committee of Standards for Educational Evaluation. The more control that the research design has, the more confidence one can have in the results of the research. Research should:

"Be comprehensive and thorough—"

No problem.

"Test different theories against each other—"

Difficult. Most qualitative studies of early literacy development, certainly ethnographic studies, are not testing theories against each other but are *building* theories based on disciplined and systematic observations of young children learning to read and write. Many studies are comparative but not in the sense of testing one "reading theory"—often a code for a "commercial reading method"—against another. Comparisons might be made between children growing up in very different social situations.

For example, a comparative analysis of the literacy practices of the families in *Family Literacy* and *Growing Up Literate* found that there were many similarities between the kinds of literacy practices in the children's homes, but there were also differences. The children in the African American families were critically affected by the political and economic circumstances of their everyday lives. Neither the children nor their parents had access to the literacies of power. In school, children were "skilled and drilled," and the literacy practices that were deeply embedded in their homes and communities were not recognized. Their parents were similarly cut off. Even when Paula got an associate degree in computer science, she could not find a job, and Jerry, who had educated himself, try as he might, work as hard as he could, always struggled to support his family. In the end Jerry died trying to make sure that his family survived.

"Be longitudinal in order to look at variables over time"

Qualitative research on early literacy development is often longitudinal, but researchers are not usually "looking at variables." Very often, they are observing children and the qualitative transformations that take place as young children learn to read and write.

Maria has been Andrew's classroom teacher for two years, and during that time she has kept detailed notes on his literacy development. The following excerpt is from her notes for October, November, and December.

"Andrew uses print in many ways," Maria writes. "He has submitted weekend news about something he has done, written notes to me, made signs, 'Do Not toch! AndreW,' recorded information in his computer log, and he continues to write in his journal."

"Andrew continues to bring his work to me when he has finished," Maria writes in February. "I now wait and look to him to begin the conversation. He starts with 'I made a book' or 'Want me to read it to you?'"

Later in Andrew's second-grade year, Maria chose to focus on him when she met with an extended student advocacy group of teachers that meets on a regular basis in the school in which she teaches. Maria chose to focus on Andrew because of his shyness and because of his early history in another school, where he was regarded, according to the special education records, as "slow." Based upon their consideration of the information that Maria had collected, the extended student advocacy group helped her formulate instructional strategies that she could use to support Andrew's academic and social development.

In Andrew's third-grade year, Maria focused on documenting the ways in which Andrew uses different symbol systems. She focused on Andrew's development of problem-solving strategies, the important role of literacy technologies in his reading and writing development, his developing understanding of story structure, his writing of narrative descriptions, and his development of conventional spelling patterns.

The documentation over time of Andrew's early literacy development is disciplined and systematic and provides Maria with the detailed information that she needs to develop small instructional interventions to support Andrew's continuing development as a reader and a writer. In classrooms such as Maria's where the pedagogy is emancipatory, children's literacy learning is continually documented, and in ethnographic studies of children's early literacy development researchers can spend many years in one classroom, but in both situations the focus is on children and not on artificially defined reductionist variables.[4]

"Have controlled variables"

Let me be more explicit. Attempting to control variables in human learning is arcane, an anathema, a throwback to behaviorism and to reductionism.

"And be capable of being replicated"

Think back to the phonemic awareness studies that I've described in *Spin Doctors*. Each study, although "carefully controlled" with so-called "replicable variables," was anomalous. Qualitative studies are based on the assumption that no two events, however "controlled," can ever be replicated. We cannot relive experiences. A teacher might teach two classes of children the same lesson but she is changed by the experience of teaching the first group of children. The second time she teaches the lesson, even if she is using a basal and just reading a script, she will read it differently and the children will respond in different ways. It's later in the day; she is tired; the children are hungry; there are announcements coming over the loudspeaker that interrupt the lesson; a child gets up and leaves for a pull-out session.

Drive a car along the same route every day and the road conditions are always different, the driver is different, a headache, a fight with a spouse, an overdue payment, a new boss at work. Routines are always subject to variance, and they are never replicable. Patterns can be detected, but exactly how events will happen cannot be predicted. There are unforeseeable occurrences, and life is mercurial and often capricious. Follow a recipe, measure all the ingredients, but the dish never tastes quite the same. Make love at the same time, in the same place, in the same way . . . and there will always be something new about the experience. Whether in a scientific experiment or in some mundane everyday event, life can never be duplicated. Even though our lives are filled with routines and rituals, culturally patterned and socially systematized, the details of human experience cannot be copied, cloned, reproduced, or replicated.

Findings with a high degree of replicability are considered incontrovertible

In *North Carolina School Improvement Program in Beginning Reading: Recommendations to Reflect Research*, the document which is based on the recommendations presented by the experts, what counts as research is more explicitly stated.

"Research to support the claim that one teaching approach is better than another must compare the recommended approach with the other. Research that does not compare cannot be used to support a teaching recommendation. Therefore, only reading research where one approach was compared with another (intervention research) were included in the following review of research" (p. 8).

In "the true scientific model," Grossen seems to echo through the text, "findings with a high degree of replicability are finally considered incontrovertible."[5]

"Theories must drive hypotheses to be tested." Lyon seems to be between the lines. "The measurements used to test the hypotheses must meet established standards of reliability."[6]

Take another look at the list I asked you to make of researchers whose studies have affected your teaching. Scratch out all those who do not try to pit one theory against another, or attempt to control and replicate human behavior, or use highly questionable tests to artificially measure children's "ability" at some narrowly defined task. Now make a second list of the scientific theoretical orientations that have informed your pedagogy. Some of these theories might be mutually supportive while others might be contradictory, but as they rub against each other each one of them might have deepened your understandings of how young children learn to read and write. Check each theory. Does it conform to the "true scientific method?" Cross out connectionism, which Jim Gee defines very differently than Adams in *Beginning to Read*.[7] Then draw a long line through critical pedagogy, cultural model theories, discourse analysis, ethnomethodology, ethnography, evolutionary approaches to mind and behavior, feminist theory, modern sociological studies, narrative studies, new literacy studies, semiotics, sociohistorical psychology, and situated cognition.[8]

"All these movements were, or have been used as, reactions against the behaviorism of the early part of this century and the 'cognitive revolution' of the sixties and seventies that replaced behaviorism, both of which privileged the individual mind." Again it's Gee, this time discussing the historical foundation of Lyon's true scientific method. "Both behaviorism and cognitivism saw 'higher order thinking' and 'intelligence' as primarily the manipulation of 'information' ('facts') using general ('logical') rules and principles. Fact and 'logic,' not affect, society, and culture, were emphasized. The digital computer stood as the great metaphor for what thought was: 'information processing' (and computers process information based on its form/structure, not its meaning)."[9]

These sociocultural theories are all used by researchers to inform our understandings of children's early literacy development. For example, situated cognition is another way of describing the research on practical intelligence and everyday cognition that I presented at the beginning of this book. But, as Gee makes clear, none of these theoretical orientations and ways of doing science support the in-the-head reductionist "true scientific method" promoted by NICHD and adopted by state governments as the *only* research on which to base teaching young children to read. Thus, social theories have been systematically discredited and discounted. Whatever the theory, so goes the spin, unless it is true to the scientific method then it simply isn't science.

What a *coup*! Decades of research, three-quarters of a century of scientific investigation, have been discredited and rejected. I think we should be concerned about this, and so should North Carolina and the other states which have participated in this dissolution of scientific knowledge.

"Begin teaching phonemic awareness directly at an early age, preschool, kindergarten, and first grade," the *North Carolina School Improvement Program in Beginning Reading* recommends under the subheading, "Brief Synthesis of Relevant Findings from Intervention Research."

The document then provides examples of phonological awareness tasks that were published by Stanovich in 1994, and which also appear in Grossen's position paper, *30 Years of NICHD Research*.

"What word would be left if the /k/ sound were taken away from cat?" Stanovich asks, presenting his "phoneme deletion" task. "What is the first sound in rose?" he asks for his "sound isolation" task. "What sounds do you hear in 'hot'?" "Is there a /k/ in bike?"

Then come the "Technical Notes," which read as if one of our subaltern intellectuals wrote them.

Technical Notes: Teach phonemic awareness directly.

The rationale?

"Recent research on phonemic awareness has found the following types of tasks to have a positive effect on reading acquisition and spelling: rhyming, auditorily discriminating sounds that are different, blending spoken sounds into words, word-to-word matching, isolating sounds in words, counting phonemes, segmenting spoken words into sounds, [and] deleting sounds from words."

Among the references given is one to Foorman and her colleagues. "In a study by Foorman, et al., (in press), 260 children were randomly assigned," you know the spin, "[c]hildren in the revised curriculum made significant gains in phonemic awareness over the year" (p. 9).

What many educators might not know is that this technical note is taken directly from McGraw-Hill's SRA *Mastery Learning* program that we all know as DISTAR. In the *Mastery Learning* Program Overview Guide it states on page 4 "Technical notes: Teach phonemic awareness explicitly," making it clearly evident that there is a strong connection between this commercial reading program and North Carolina's new state standards.

Technical Notes: Each letter-sound correspondence must be taught explicitly.

Explanation?

"Phonemic awareness alone is not sufficient for many children. Explicit instruction in common letter-sound correspondences is also necessary."

Both *Beginning to Read* by Adams and "Matthew Effects in Reading" by Stanovich are referenced to support this proposition. Then, further down the page, North Carolina relies on Carnine to support the statement that "[t]he majority of studies find that explicit phonics achieve better results than implicit phonics."

Again, this technical note is taken directly from SRA *Mastery Learning*. On page 6 of the Program Overview Guide, it states, "Technical notes: Each letter-sound correspondence should be taught explicitly."

Technical Notes: Select high-frequency letter-sound relationships and sequence them carefully.

There is another reference to Carnine. "The rules used to sequence the introduction of letter-sound correspondences have been evaluated in comparative research by Carnine" (p. 10). Examples follow of "the most frequent, highly regular sound-symbol relationships." These include <u>ay</u> as in haul, <u>ou</u> as in cloud, <u>w</u>—"woo"—as in well, and <u>y</u>—"yee"—as in yuk.

SRA *Mastery Learning*? The language is identical. "Technical notes: Select high-frequency letter-sound relationships and sequence them carefully."

Technical Notes: Pupils should be taught how to blend sounds together into words.

Again, Carnine appears among the references. North Carolina states that Carnine reported "teaching letter-sound correspondences and sounding out resulted in students correctly identifying more unfamiliar words than when students were trained on a whole-word strategy."

And again the technical note is lifted directly from SRA *Mastery Learning*. On page 10 of the guide: "Technical notes: Pupils should be taught how to blend sounds together into words."

Technical Notes: Use code-based material rather than reading materials that require pupils to use context to figure out words, such as authentic or predictable texts.

Foorman is quoted to support this statement, with a 1995 reference that is not in the bibliography. It states in the document that "Foorman commented, 'Thus, to the extent that meaning-oriented programs include instruction in phonic principles, there is little opportunity to practice applying these principles in connected reading.'"

An interesting comment from a researcher who admitted at the pre-summit in Texas that she doesn't know what whole language means.

Carnine and his colleagues are also quoted: "Pupils who learn to read with a systematic, explicit phonics approach are able to use context to figure out new vocabulary words just as readily as pupils taught in a meaning-emphasis program."[10]

SRA *Mastery Learning* says it this way: "Technical notes: Use code-based readers rather than reading material that requires pupils to use context to figure out words."

Technical Notes: Build accuracy and fluency with daily performance measures, goals, and decision rules for making instructional changes.

Test the children every day. What else can I say?

SRA *Mastery Learning*: "Technical notes: Build accuracy and fluency with daily performance measures, goals, and decision rules for making instructional changes."

Technical Notes: Every oral reading error should be corrected.

This technical note is almost a sound bite, slipped in without fanfare and accompanied by only a short narrative and one meager reference to a 1988 four-page article by Darlene Pany and Kathleen McCoy.[11] But the effects are far-reaching. In the section on assessment, miscue analysis is summarily discredited.

"[M]iscue analysis will not meet professional standards for technical adequacy because it is not reliable."

Unadulterated propaganda. A four-page paper by Pany and McCoy does not wipe out the findings of the almost six hundred scientific studies that specifically focus on miscue analysis which have been conducted in the last thirty years.[12] In the article the authors state that the study focuses on "corrective feedback."

Sixteen third-grade students, twelve males and four females, in six schools participated in the study. All of the students were labeled learning disabled. There were three treatment conditions: (1) total feedback; (2) meaning change feedback; and (3) no feedback.

"For students with learning disabilities," Pany and McCoy conclude, "provision of corrective feedback appears to be an effective teaching practice to enhance both word accuracy and comprehension" (p. 550). Then they state, "Although three passages were used in all treatment conditions, results of this study may not generalize to reading materials of different lengths or levels of difficulty. All passages in these experiments were relatively short (300 word). Passage difficulty was purposefully selected to produce a 10% word recognition error rate to allow opportunities for feedback. Feedback effects on passages that result in much lower or higher error rates could be quite different."

"As always," Pany and McCoy write in their concluding paragraph, "we urge teachers to routinely assess the effects of any individual instructional procedure on individual students to validate effectiveness in conditions that most certainly will differ from experimental conditions" (p. 550).

With all due respect to Pany and McCoy, their four-page study pales in significance when it is stacked up against the scientific evidence that has been gained from the miscue research. Their study is insufficient to refute the findings of more than a thousand studies in which miscue research has been an integral component of much larger scientific projects. I have been studying miscue analysis for the last five years, and I would conservatively estimate that the scientific evidence to support the use of miscue analysis amounts to more than 50,000 hours of researchers documenting children reading real books.

These are not studies of isolated pseudowords, and bits of children are never thrown away. Miscue analysis gives teachers the opportunity to consider the sociocultural histories of children. Miscue provide insights into the evolutionary processes of mind and behavior, and challenges assumptions of cultural and social uniformity. Miscue does not separate children from their everyday worlds. The forms of the written languages that children use are not separated from their meaningful interpretation of the text. Children are not expected to contend with senseless abstractions. Reading is always a meaningful activity.

The information that miscue provides to both teachers and children is immediately useful and does not assume a transfer of learning from isolated task to reading texts—*because there are no isolated tasks*. Finally, and this is especially the case for retrospective miscue analysis, miscue builds on the relationships that exist between teachers and children, and provides teachers with a disciplined and systematic way of documenting young children's early literacy development.

The kicker, of course, is that this technical note is also taken directly from SRA *Learning Mastery*. The guide states on page 13, "Technical notes: Every oral reading error should be corrected."

Technical Notes: The most effective way to prevent reading problems is to change the regular classroom program to include explicit, systematic instruction in phonics using decodable text.

This final technical note brings us back to Foorman.

"Foorman's research indicates that to prevent reading problems the first thing to do is to replace whole language with explicit, systematic phonics in the classroom. When children do fall behind at these early stages, more intensive work may be necessary."

There is no reference.

The crossing out is no longer hypothetical

What effect will the researchers' technical notes have on teachers' instructional practices in North Carolina? The crossing out is no longer hypothetical. It appears in two of the documents. The first is the document from which I've just been quoting: *North Carolina School Improvement Program in Beginning Reading: Recommendations for Changes to Reflect Research,* and the second is the actual edited version of the *North Carolina Standard Course of Study/Teacher Handbook for English Language Arts.* The section of the "Standards" to which I will be referring is the "Strands in the English Arts Curriculum."

So how are teachers supposed to teach reading? Let's first take a look at the section of "Recommendations for Changes to Reflect Research," which focuses on how teachers should be trained.

"In order for teachers to bring children to achieve the standards, they need to be trained in the important learning steps leading to the achievement of the standard and in the instructional methods that are most likely to help them achieve the standards set by the state."

Somewhat convoluted but I think we get the message. Let's take a look at what teachers are actually supposed to do.

Emphasize the importance of developing phonemic awareness in preschool, K, and 1ˢᵗ grade.

We got that.

Develop the graphophonic cueing system beginning in K and finishing at the end of grade 1 using explicit, systematic instruction in highly regular sound-symbol relationships and provide practice applying this knowledge to reading connected, decodable text.

I can imagine some teachers and teacher educators thinking to themselves, "Okay, that's not so bad. Half an hour of skill and drill and we're back to predictable books and authentic texts."

Forget it.

"Integration of the graphophonic cueing system with the syntactic and semantic cueing systems is impossible if initial texts the children are expected to read use 'predictable' or 'authentic' text."

Wake up! A revolution is taking place, a book-burning of incredible proportions. The books leap and dance like roasting birds, their wings ablaze with red and yellow feathers.[13] Get rid of your text-sets. Purge your personal libraries. Throw out ~~Eric Carle, Lucille Clifton, Joy Cowley, Tomie DePaola, Marjorie Flack, Mem Fox, Ezra Jack Keats, Arnold Lobel, Bill Martin, and Robert Munsch.~~ If a book isn't decodable you can't use it and children can't read it.

Censorship anyone?

"Using predictable or authentic text results in phonics becoming an isolated activity having no relevance to reading connected text. It is impossible to integrate the graphophonic cueing system into reading if any material other than decodable text is used for the children's initial reading practice. Decodable text can be used for both reading and spelling dictation."

Like Patrick in *Learning Denied,* in North Carolina children will now only be allowed to read "Dot and Tom ran to Al. Tom is not mad at Al. Dot is not mad at Al. Is Al bad?"[14]

Delete all references to the use of prediction and guessing to recognize words.

You can't do this without throwing out almost a century of scientific research, including evolutionary approaches to mind and behavior and the more recent research in modern sociological studies, new literacy studies, semiotics, sociohistorical psychology, and studies in practical intelligence and everyday cognition.

"While prediction is a valuable comprehension skill, it does not work for word recognition," the document states. The supporting evidence is provided by Stanovich and Stanovich.[15]

"[R]esearch shows that predicting the next word is not a very successful strategy (the documented success rates range from .10 to .39 and most of the words successfully predicted are simple function words such as 'of,' 'that,' 'if,' 'the,' and so on.)"

If A cites B. There is no evidence, only counterevidence.

"Predicting and guessing are behaviors that describe poor comprehenders, not good comprehenders."

Spin, doctor, spin.

"Good comprehenders rely extensively on the graphophonic cueing system to read."

Go back to Chapter 3. To the "incontrovertible finding" that of the three cueing systems frequently mentioned in reading (semantic, syntactic, and graphophonemic cues), the semantic and syntactic cueing systems seem to play a minor role. I can find no evidence to support this finding.

"Predictable text leads children to rely on syntactic/semantic cueing systems to an extent that does not transfer to authentic text."

Again, Chapter 3. To the "incontrovertible finding" that only decodable text provides children the opportunity to practice their new knowledge of sound-letter relationships. Again, there is no evidence for this finding.

"Predictable texts create a false strategy for reading and undermine the development and use of the graphophonic cueing system in reading and ultimately lead to the behavior characteristic of poor, not good, comprehenders."

Someone needs to ask: who wrote this document for North Carolina? Then there are other questions. Is the North Carolina Senate aware that the "Recommendations for Changes to Reflect the Research" are filled with false assumptions and erroneous presuppositions? Does the Senate know that the research on which they are relying is seriously flawed, that the data are confounded, and that the results of the statistical procedures provide no scientific evidence on how young children learn to read or write? Do they know? Do they care? Or, do they have another agenda? Hegemonic, perhaps?

I am going to switch documents for a moment to quote from the

"Strands in the English Language Arts Curriculum," in particular to the section that deals with reading, so that you can get an idea of the impact of North Carolina's new mandates. As you will see, Yetta Goodman, Dorothy Watson, and Carolyn Burke are quite literally crossed out, and underlined words are added to the text (see Figures 8.1, 8.2, and 8.3).

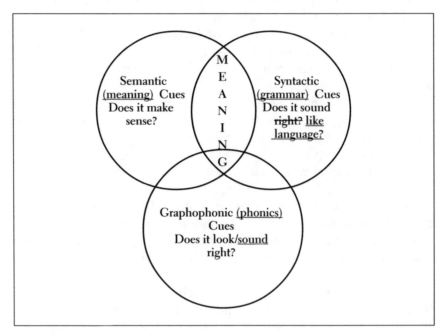

Figure 8.1. Holistic Model of Reading Instruction (Goodman, Watson, and Burke, 1987).

<u>~~Holistic Model of Reading Instruction~~</u>
<u>A Comprehensive Approach to Reading Instruction</u>

<u>A Comprehensive Approach to Reading Instruction</u>
~~This whole to part or holistic model of reading~~ can be depicted as three interacting spheres. These spheres represent the graphophonic, syntactic, and semantic cueing systems. If meaning is to be constructed all cueing systems are employed simultaneously in a social context (~~Goodman, Watson, and Burke, 1987~~).

~~Subskill Model~~

~~The subskill model of reading instruction, like behaviorist learning theory, includes the assumptions~~

that reading must be taught in an explicit way; that reading is learned from parts to whole through a carefully ordered sequential hierarchy of skills; and that each skill must be taught, positively reinforced, mastered, and tested before the next appropriate skill in the hierarchy can be taught. Instruction directed toward the mastery of subskills usually precedes a focus on the meaning of what is being read . . . . Practice leads to mastery of the hierarchically arranged skills (Goodman, Watson, and Burke, 1987, p. 132).

Reading instruction is carefully organized and directed to ensure exact responses, thus following a test teach test model.

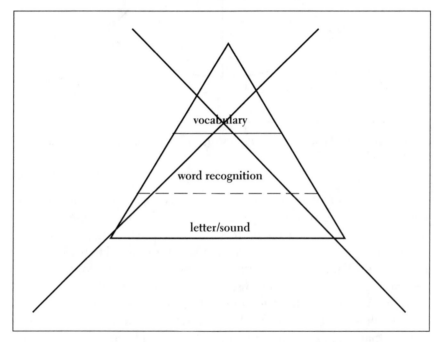

Figure 8.2. Subskills Model of Reading Instruction (Goodman, Watson, and Burke, 1987)

Subskills Model of Reading Instruction
(Goodman, Watson, and Burke, 1987, p.132)

This model of reading can be visualized as a triangle with a foundation of letter sound relationships which supports the next two levels of word recognition and vocabulary.

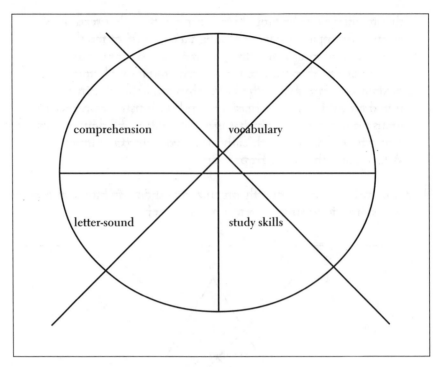

Figure 8.3. Skills Model of Reading Instruction (Goodman, Watson, and Burke, 1987)

If Goodman, Watson, and Burke were on your list of researchers who have affected your pedagogical practices, but whose research is no longer acceptable, you were correct to draw a line through their names. In the hegemonic project there is no place for them. Their work is too democratic. They will not acquiesce. They are too astute for that. Their research has actually been crossed out, because their theories are not reductionist, because they do not practice the "true scientific method," because they do not use artificial measures to test children, because they believe that reading is something more than pseudowords on the Woodcock-Johnson, because their reading theories build on the work of researchers who have also been wiped out.

Let's return to the "Recommendations for Changes to Reflect the Research." In "Appendix C: Benchmarks," the reader is told to delete the words in italics and parentheses and add the bold-faced words.

"Delete the second section, 'Reading Strategies: Uses one or more of the following strategies as appropriate to construct meaning from text.' Replace the it [sic] with the section entitled 'Benchmarks for Kindergarten.'"

"Kindergarten children (*realize*) **should learn** that print conveys meaning (~~and they try to read and write~~) **by listening to stories the teacher reads.**"

Then "Characteristics of a Reader: ~~Perceives self as a reader and writer~~" is also crossed out. If you are wondering why North Carolina does not want children to perceive themselves as readers and writers, in a few pages you will find out.

The "Benchmarks" for kindergarten follow. There are two.

1. By the end of kindergarten, children will demonstrate 90% competence in phonemic awareness tasks.

The teacher is then told that "[t]he following types of tasks represent measures of phonemic awareness."

"Phoneme deletion: What word would be left if the /k/ sound were taken away from cat?" I'm sure I don't have to remind you who wrote that. "What is the first sound in rose?" The phoneme awareness tasks are presented in a neat little box. "How many sounds do you hear in the word cake?" And at the bottom is the usual reference to Stanovich.

2. By the end of kindergarten, children will know 35 (actual number is optional) sound-symbol relationships, be able to read single words composed of these sounds, and read connected phrases and sentences composed of the same sounds with 95% accuracy.

In the section on assessment which accompanies the benchmarks, teachers are told that for kindergarten they should delete "Reads own dictated stories, pretend reads predictable pattern books, and reads environmental print."

First grade also has two benchmarks, but first some text is crossed out and some bold text has been added.

"First graders (~~want to read, listen to and talk~~) **should continue to learn** about a wide range of texts . . . . They **should** expect the text to make sense (~~and if necessary, they make a second attempt and reread. These students take risks when reading and talk about themselves as readers.~~) **They should continue learning the graphophonic cueing system until they have learned all the fundamental sound-symbol relationships. They should be able to blend these sounds in words as they read single words or pseudowords. They should be provided opportunity to practice these skills in connected, decodable text.**

Here are the benchmarks:

1. *By the end of grade 1, children will read pseudowords and single words composed of these highly regular sound-symbol relationships.*

The sound-symbol relationships in the experts' draft are then restated. Remember au as in haul, ou as in cloud, w—"woo"—as in well, and y—"yee"—as in yuk.

2. *By the end of grade 1, children will read novel (unpracticed) text that is at least 85% decodable with 98% accuracy at 60 wpm and answer simple questions about the text with 90% accuracy.*

In the North Carolina documents from which I've been quoting, kindergarten children no longer ~~try to read and write.~~ A child is not expected to ~~perceive self as a reader and writer~~. Children do not join in the ~~refrains in predictable books.~~ They do not ~~read own dictated stories,~~ or ~~pretend to read predictable pattern books.~~ In first grade they are not expected to ~~want to read, listen to, and talk~~ about narrative picture books, poems, short chapter books, and short informational and practical materials. Children are not expected to ~~take risks when reading and talk about themselves as readers.~~ They are no longer expected (allowed?) to respond personally to ~~student-authored texts.~~ If we jump to grade 3, we find that North Carolina no longer expects their students to ~~predict based on semantic, syntactic, and graphophonic cues~~. They are no longer required to ~~search, predict, monitor, and cross check using semantic, syntactic, and graphophonic cues independently.~~ Children do not have to ~~read on and reread to check predictions and clarify meaning.~~ In fourth grade they are not supposed to ~~use strategies of sampling, predicting, confirming, and self correcting quickly, confidently, and independently.~~[16]

Are you growing increasingly uneasy? Even positivists who disagree with everything I've written so far should be a little apprehensive. This was supposed to be about beginning reading, a few highly questionable kindergarten and first-grade studies on phonemic awareness, *not* reading in third and fourth grade. Where are the findings of the "true scientific method" to support the radical pork-barrel changes that are being mandated by the North Carolina Senate? When did the subaltern intellectuals and their generals decide that our children should stop thinking? Why doesn't North Carolina want children who are confident and independent? Be careful. We are deep inside the hegemonic project and all the lights just went out. If you reach out make sure you know who takes your hand.

"The instructional models used in wealthy schools are likely to be too weak to serve the needs of low SES schools," North Carolina pronounces. On the first page of the "Recommendations for Changes to Reflect Research" is the following statement: "Previous research would lead us to predict that more intensive instructional models will be required to bring the performance of children in schools serving low SES communities to read at the same standards achieved in wealthier schools."[17]

Keep your arms by your side, and think it through.

Adams was one of the nationally known experts who testified in North Carolina. "Other children enter school with next to no relevant knowledge about print," Adams explains in *Beginning to Read*. "Relative to their well-prepared peers, these children are likely to have less interest in these lessons and less appreciation of their point."

"We must therefore expect their learning to be slower and their patience to be slimmer. At the same time, however, mastery of the symbol-sound relations will require more study for these children." Again I'm quoting Adams. "After all, some of them may still be having difficulty discriminating the letter shapes; their entering level of phonological awareness will be relatively low; and so, too, will their prior knowledge of letter-sound relationships.

"Much of the content of these lessons will be new for these children in detail and concept. As a consequence, it will be more confusing and harder to consolidate. Finally, in order for all necessary symbol-sound pairs to be learned well, each must be allowed sufficient practice and opportunity for evaluation." You know it's Adams. "The implication, in short, is that the teaching of individual letter-sound correspondences cannot proceed quickly for these children. It must be spread out over time" (pp. 240–41).

We're back at the meeting of the Program Committee of the State Board of Education in North Carolina, and we know that Adams relies heavily on Stanovich for her opinion on beginning to read. Grossen is also at the meeting, and she quotes Stanovich extensively in the document *30 Years of NICHD Research*. Both researchers rely on "Matthew Effects in Reading," and the article is specifically referenced in the North Carolina "Recommendations for Changes to Reflect Research."

"Less healthy organisms grow up in impoverished environments," Stanovich states in his International Reading Association award-winning research. "Biologically unlucky individuals are provided with inferior social and educational environments, and the winners of the biological lottery are provided better environments."

"But of course a child of above-average ability is much more likely to reside in a school with a 'concentration of pupils with good cognitive performance,'" Stanovich writes, referencing Jencks. "Such a child is an advantaged organism because of the superior environment and geno-type provided by the child's parents.

"The parents, similarly environmentally and genetically advantaged, are more likely to reside in a community which provides the 'concentration of pupils' that via the independent effects of school composition, will bootstrap the child to further educational advantages.

"Conversely, disadvantaged children are most often exposed to inferior ability composition in the schools that they attend. Thus, these children are the victims of a particularly perverse 'double whammy'" (p. 383).

"Some of these effects will result from passive organism-environment correlations: Biologically disadvantaged children must learn in instructional environments (composed of teachers, schools, parents, etc.) that are inferior to those experienced by advantaged children."

If we use the "passive organism" language to rephrase the statement made in the North Carolina "Recommendations for Changes to Reflect Research," we would come up with something like this:

The instructional models used (*in wealthy schools*) **in the superior school environments of biologically advantaged children with superior genotype parents** are likely to be (*too weak*) **too richly endowed** to (*serve the needs*) **provide the appropriate phonemic awareness skill and drill instruction** (*of low SES schools*) **for less healthy, environmentally and genetically disadvantaged children, whose parents and teachers are inferior and who attend inferior schools**.

Add Grossen to the mix. With her she brings Foorman and her racially divided experiments and her "significant ethnicity contrasts," which get reinterpreted by Grossen in the *30 Years of NICHD Research* and spun out into "[s]ignificantly more African American children have lower levels of phonemic awareness and respond significantly better to direct instruction in phonemic awareness than other ethnic groups" (p. 16).

Then the *coup de gras* comes when Grossen states that there is "strong evidence for genetic etiology of reading disabilities with deficits in phonemic awareness reflecting the greatest degree of heritability. There is also genetic evidence for degrees of heritability for letter processing" (p. 17).

Power, privilege, racism, and hegemony. We had better tread carefully. How easy it would be for us to contribute unknowingly to the hegemonic project as the MIT linguistics have done, probably inadvertently.[18] In the field of education there are many bitter struggles, and any one of us could unwittingly find ourselves co-opted into inadvertently providing support for statements such as those made by the North Carolina Senate.

We must learn to be vulnerable enough to allow our world to turn upside down

In recent years there has been a backlash against holistic pedagogies in urban schools, and as Gee recently pointed out there are some forms of holistic practice that educators in inner cities refer to as "urban violence."[19] This makes sense to me. Interpretations of holistic pedagogies which do not take into account the social and cultural lives of children and that are insensitive to the adverse economic and political circumstances in which they are forced to live are extremely problematic. But Lisa Delpit, who writes of the cultures of power, would be the first to state that the alternative is not skill and drill in low-level skills.

"I run a great risk in writing this," Delpit tells us, with revealing honesty and obvious concern, "the risk that my purpose will be misunderstood, the risk that those who subject black and other minority children to day after day of isolated, meaningless, drilled 'subskills' will think themselves vindicated." She is sharp: "That is not the point. Were this another paper I would explain what I mean by 'skills'—useful and usable knowledge which contributes to a student's ability to communicate effectively in standard, generally acceptable literary forms."[20]

"I suggest that students must be *taught* the codes needed to participate fully in the mainstream of American life," Delpit states more explicitly in an article that she wrote two years later, "not by being forced to attend to hollow, inane, decontextualized subskills, but rather within the context of meaningful communicative endeavors; that they must be allowed the resource of the teacher's expert knowledge, while being helped to acknowledge their own 'expertness' as well; and that even while students are assisted in learning the culture of power, they must also be helped to learn about the arbitrariness of those codes and about the power relationships they represent."[21]

"Let there be no doubt," states Delpit, again from the first article, "a 'skilled' minority person who is not also capable of critical analysis becomes the trainable, low-level functionary of dominant society, simply the grease that keeps the institutions which orchestrate his or her oppression running smoothly."[22]

"And finally," Delpit writes, "we must learn to be vulnerable enough to allow our world to turn upside down in order to allow the realities of others to edge themselves into our consciousness. In other words, we must become ethnographers in the true sense."

Certainly that has happened to me. Ieshea . . . Tanya . . . Jerry . . . Shauna . . . Gary . . . so many families have touched my life; Patrick . . . Nicola . . . so many children and teachers in schools are in my heart as well as in my head; Cindy . . . Sam . . . Laurie . . . Kathryn . . . so many members of communities have shared their lives with me. They have affected me personally, my feelings, values, and expectations. They have influenced my thinking, the way I position myself as a researcher, and the risks I am willing to take.

In which I become the documentation on which I build my case

∎ ∎ ∎

As you read this text I'm sure you realize that my response to the research articles and official documents that I have critiqued is also deeply personal. Like Ieshea, and Jerry, Patrick, Nicola, Cindy, and Sam, when I was young the pejorative "passive organism" could also have been and in a way was ascribed to me.

Are you smiling? You know from my writing that I am anything but "passive." Last year I was told that someone at a conference said I write with a spray can. Sounds like theoretically grounded graffiti.[1] I like that. I continually try to nudge the boundaries of social science research, exploring emancipatory systems of meaning, to take my literacy studies in new directions, and sometimes, as in *Toxic Literacies*, I try to push my readers out of their comfort zone and over the edge by disembedding the ideologies of social, cultural, and political practices to uncover the hidden assumptions that shape our perceptions. To me the ascription of passivity is a racist activity, and however confrontational my writing, however bitter the clash, I have no alternative but to voice my objection, even if in doing so some may find my analysis objectionable. Again I say, neither I nor any of the people with whom I have worked are "passive organisms." None of us are apathetic or acquiescent, none of us are lazy, lifeless, or listless, none of us are subdued, submissive, or nonresistant, and none of us are biologically disadvantaged or genetically inferior.

In "Facing Myself: The Struggle for Authentic Pedagogy," Michael O'Loughlin writes, "In graduate school in the 1980s the message from most of my professors . . . was to deny myself and my roots. Use the passive voice when writing, I was told. Avoid personal language and anecdotes. Don't use Irish spellings of English words because they are distracting to readers who are used to American English. Be scientific! Be rational! Don't be emotional! Don't be angry! Don't show your passions! Be detached. . . . Be invisible. . . . My journey beyond those crippling messages has been slow and tortuous, a teetering walk between my desire to offer caring and enabling experiences to my students, and a sometimes paralyzing fear of self-disclosure and loss of control" (p. 49).[2]

"Understanding my autobiography is key to understanding my teaching," O'Loughlin goes on to explain. "In teaching, I necessarily teach myself. How else but through engaging my life story can my students or I make sense of my deep belief in the possibility of education as a vehicle of personal transformation and social change?" (p. 49).

Situating our own lives within our teaching, research, and writing, learning to be vulnerable enough to allow our world to be turned upside down and inside out, creates new understandings of the ways in which we teach, do research, and write.[3] Not only my research but my life is wrapped up in *Spin Doctors*. But understanding my life history not only provides you with a more in-depth understanding of why I am willing to risk being severely censured by the proponents of the "true scientific method"; it also provides you with *counterevidence*. I *am* documentation, as Jenny DeGroat taught me; I am the data on which I build my case.[4] So let me switch hats for a moment from social theorist, ethnographer, pedagogist, and social activist to become an informant, and to share with you the experience of a lower-working-class child whose personal story is relevant to the issues of power, privilege, racism, and hegemony which are at the very center of the critical analysis I am presenting in this book.

A couple of weeks ago, while I was looking in one of my mother's cupboards for some wrapping paper to wrap up a birthday present, I found my father's "Soldier's Release Book."

"Before enlisted worked as a rubber worker for 4 years and wishes to go back to this job," his testimonial states. "Has been employed for 6 years as a miner since being in this unit has been generally employed on construction work and has shown himself to be an excellent man and a good worker."

My father was born in Wales, and like my mother he grew up in a segregated coal mining community. When he was fourteen, he was given a pick and a shovel and he joined his father and older brother "down the mine," and the pittance he was paid to dig coal was kept by the colliery to help pay off the money his family owed in rent, for even with his father and brother working down the mine they were unable to keep up with the payments.[5]

"You'd have a coal-mandril which was very light and very sharp with a long—the blade was like a stiletto. You had a shovel, of course, and then you had an axe, a seven-pound axe which was kept like a lance," George Evans writes, quoting a miner in *From the Mouths of Men*. "It could be quite a painful affair. You'd work until the rock would be a kind of plastic layer on you—where the skin had been taken off. And it would get stiff like as if you'd baked it in clay—till you put it into the bath in the night; and it would start to burn."

When my father was twenty, he left Wales and went to Birmingham and got a job in Dunlop's tire factory. He swapped one hell for another, and instead of digging coal he worked with molten rubber. The war started, and he spent six years building bridges in North Africa, which he said was easier than working on the coalface in Wales. After the war he went back to Dunlop's and more rubber. I was born in 1947. My birth was registered, but I never had a birth certificate. It was not until I needed one to apply for permanent residency in the United States that I learned my mother had not obtained one for me. She looked troubled when she told me that my father had been working as a "plumber's mate," and she didn't want that on my birth certificate. I think my mother would have been quite happy if "coal miner" could have been written on my birth certificate, even though she did not want my father to go back down the mines. In Wales, the families of coal miners treated them with immense respect because of the dangerous work that they did. "Hell on earth" they called it. But a plumber's mate? I don't think my mother could find any dignity in that.

By the time I was born, my father was trying to find another way to make a living, and when I was one year old he left my mother and me and went to London to train for a job with the Royal Society of Prevention of Cruelty to Animals. He received a small stipend while he was training, and every week he sent as much money as he could back to my mother. My mother managed the best she could, but by Wednesday we often ran out of food, and if the letter didn't come by Thursday we had nothing to eat. Many times she has told me of taking me for a walk one Thursday because we were hungry and she was trying to pass the time away while she waited for the letter that she hoped would come on Friday, and there by the side of the road she found half a crown and she picked it up and took me straight to a fish and chip shop to eat. Her eyes still look troubled when she talks about having no food, and they always light up when she gets to the part of the story where she found the half crown and we got to eat.

I was three when we moved to Kent and my father became an RSPCA inspector. Just after we arrived, Lady Richie, who was the chair of the local branch of the RSPCA and a benefactor of the society, visited our house to meet my mother. Lady Richie told my mother that my name was too much for a little girl, and she said she thought I should be called "Denny." So from that day on that was what my mother and father called me. It didn't matter that I had been given my grandmother's favorite name or that my mother had promised that she would give the name to her first daughter. Lady Richie had power and privilege and my father was a probationer in the RSPCA. What is perhaps surprising is that I never questioned how I got my name until I was at a conference and we were asked to introduce ourselves by giving the history of our names. My parents treated Lady Richie with great respect and deference, and even today I don't think my mother realizes that Lady Richie had no right to change my name.

Because we are Welsh, music was important. My father had played the tuba in the brass band in his village in Wales and once went with the band to the Crystal Palace in London to take part in a national competition. I was four when he bought an old piano for me to play. I was reading music before I went to school, and I took my first music exam before I could read orthographic texts. There were at least sixty children in my kindergarten class. We were the "infants," and our classroom was bulging with babies born just after the war. I only spent one semester in the entry-level class, because there were too many children coming into the school and I quickly got moved up. We were "streamed," A, B, C, and D. I was always in the "A" class, and in exams when our teacher told us of our relative positions, I was usually somewhere in the top half of the class. But none of this was important to me. My parents told me to be "a good girl" at school, they visited my classroom once a year on "open day," and as long as I didn't "get into trouble" they were happy with me.

At home our lives revolved around the RSPCA and the adventures we had taking care of sick animals. I truly had an idyllic childhood. It wasn't until I was ten and I failed the 11+ exam that I realized the significance of the tests we had been made to take. Out of 120 children only four children were accepted at the grammar school. The rest of us were told that we had to attend the secondary modern school. Even though I spent all my summers in a Welsh coal-mining village where families lived in abject poverty, and even though my parents were extremely poor, this was the first time I am aware of personally suffering from the social injustice of the British class system. I remember thinking that the situation was totally unfair, and while many of my friends accepted this rejection of their intelligence, I did not. I resisted the designation of "failure" which we all wore like the badge on our school uniforms.[6] Rebellion for me was working hard at school. But that was not easy, because as second-class students we received second-class instruction.

In the secondary school I attended we were "tracked"; the "A" students were not encouraged to associate with the "B" students, and the "D" students were totally alien and alienated. We kept our distance and regarded them as if their brains were different. Of course, we learned that from our teachers. They were often derogatory in a "compassionate" sort of way about the "D" children. But they were also derogatory about us, and even in the "A" class we knew that we were different too, otherwise we would have been at the grammar school.

The "A" children at the secondary school did learn French. Our geography teacher had minored in French, which was the only reason we had French lessons, actually French grammar. I remember him telling us that if we had gone to the grammar school we would have learned to speak French and we would also have taken Latin, but as we were not bright enough for that we were learning French to help us understand English grammar. What was the point of that? French was one of the few classes in which I never worked. Who wants to memorize a few French verbs if we were never going to be able to speak the language? None of us worked. Which I suppose just went to prove what our teachers already knew, that students in the secondary school were not capable of learning French like students in the grammar school.

No one took chemistry or physics, and the girls were not allowed to take mathematics. The girls weren't supposed to be good at "maths," so we took arithmetic, and while the boys were spending long hours studying maths we took needlework and domestic science instead. In the end-of-term exams our relative class position in each subject was recorded and appeared on our report cards in blue pen except for the student who came "first." Then the 1 was written with a red pen and surrounded by a red circle. I collected red-penned circles industriously and I was always "top," but I don't think I was obnoxious about it. I never considered myself any brighter than my friends; the only difference was that I worked and they did not. Besides, as our teachers often told us, even though we were in the "A" class at the secondary modern school, we would not have been able to do the work that the "C" students did at the grammar school.

We learned that the intelligence of grammar school students was of mythical proportions, and we really did come to believe that their brains were miraculously different. Of course, most of us had no way of knowing. The class differences meant that we hardly ever spoke to each other, let alone played together. In the five years I was at the secondary modern school, I never said more than "hello" to a grammar school student, except for a few occasions at Sunday school, and that quickly came to an end. When I was about twelve, I took an exam in Bible studies at the church I was attending. Several grammar school students were in my study group, but they rarely spoke to me. Of course I studied, and when the exam results were announced they said there had to be a mistake, because I couldn't possibly have got "higher marks" than they did. I stopped going to church shortly after that, I didn't want to deal with their hostility, but I left with a new revelation. The brains of grammar school students were no different than the brains of secondary modern school students, even though, like our teachers, they thought they were, and that gave me a perverse kind of pleasure.

At thirteen most of my friends had given up. They were all working-class children and they knew the limitations of their possibilities. A good job for a boy was working for the government-run electric company. There were no good jobs for girls, unless you count working in a bakery. One of my friends kept a calendar in her desk, and for several years she crossed off each day as she marked time until she reached the school-leaving age of fifteen. She left at the end of the term in which she celebrated her fifteenth birthday, and I remember trying to persuade her to at least finish the year. I could see her life monotonously stretching out before her, and I was insistent that she was throwing away the only opportunity she had for a better life.[7] But I think she regarded me as something of an oddity. Some boys worked at school because they didn't want to do manual labor, but girls just didn't work at school, and even my teachers seemed to find my behavior peculiar. On one occasion the geography teacher tried to account for my high grades. In front of me he explained to the class that my exam results had nothing to do with intelligence. He said I had "a good memory," that was all. My friends used to remind me of that when I got more than my fair share of red circles, and I didn't mind, because while I was determined to prove my teachers wrong, I didn't want my friends to think that I was "different."

When I was thirteen, my father visited the school to talk with the headmaster about something to do with the RSPCA. When he came home, he told my mother that the headmaster had said I was "doing very well in school." My father said that the headmaster had explained that if I was a boy he would have recommended that I be transferred to the grammar school, but as I was a girl he didn't think it would make any difference. I can see my parents standing in the kitchen, my father so proud that I was doing well, my mother smiling; neither of them was aware that for me this pronouncement was extremely problematic. I was angry with my dad for several weeks, but as I thought about his conversation with the headmaster I rationalized the situation. Somehow being denied the opportunity because I was a girl was less objectionable than being denied the opportunity because I wasn't intelligent.

Later that year the mathematics teacher asked me if I would be interested in taking "maths" with the boys. He had taught at the school for thirty years, and this was the first time he had invited a girl to participate in one of his mathematics classes. I said I would like to take maths but I didn't think I would be allowed to give up needlework or domestic science. He said he didn't think that would be a problem, so I agreed, but he had underestimated how objectionable this arrangement would be to the needlework and domestic science teachers, who petitioned the headmaster to keep me in their classes. But the mathematics teacher was determined, and although it took him over a year, the headmaster did finally agree. Even then there were continual difficulties. I "missed" domestic science one term and then needlework the next term, and both teachers made life difficult for me. I have vivid memories of the needlework teacher storming into the prefabricated hut where we had maths and the mathematics teacher taking her outside as they argued, quite volubly, about whether I should be in maths or needlework for that particular lesson.

By the time I entered the class, the boys had been studying mathematics for three years, and while they were not rude to me, they made it perfectly clear that I had no business in "their" class. I was in their territory and I had no alternative but to prove my right to be there, which I did in the exams at the end of the first term by collecting another red circle. After that my presence seemed less problematic, and mathematics became my favorite class. I enjoyed working with the boys, the joking and the camaraderie, and I didn't even mind when the O level mathematics prize went to a boy even though I had a higher score in the national exams. I made do with the biology prize, if a little begrudgingly.

However, I did mind when I transferred to the grammar school at the age of sixteen, and the two boys who transferred with me were allowed to take mathematics and I was not. On the first day, after the first assembly, we went up on the stage and introduced ourselves to the headmaster, who nodded and looked at his list and told us what subjects we would be allowed to take at A level. He told me I could take English, geography, and biology. I told him I wanted to take mathematics. I had hoped that I would be allowed to take physics and chemistry at O level and take an extra year so that I would have three A levels in the sciences.

The headmaster shook his head. On the first day at grammar school he effectively ended my chances of attending any English university. You needed three A levels in the sciences or three A levels in the arts. You couldn't mix them. All that work and it ended right there on the stage one hour after I had entered the school.

I had always been interested in becoming a teacher, and I did manage to get accepted at a teachers' training college even though the woman who took over as headmistress called me into her office to tell me not to apply because the college wouldn't accept me. I remember taking my acceptance letter to her office. She was gracious, but she obviously didn't agree with the decision. She would have been much happier if I had decided to become a secretary.

Several years later, while I was in college, I visited the town in which I went to school, and a young woman came up to me and said she wanted to thank me. She said that because I had "done well" in mathematics she was going to be allowed to study maths "with the boys." She said she hoped to transfer to the grammar school when she was sixteen and that she wanted to go to college.

It was the first time I realized that I was struggling for others as well as myself. What I accomplished mattered for this other young woman who wanted to change the circumstances of her working-class life. All she needed was the opportunity, a reason to believe in herself, and someone like the mathematics teacher who believed in me. I was the first girl in my school to go to college and probably the only girl to get two Master's degrees and a doctorate. My husband, whose mother worked in a cotton mill, was the first boy to pass the 11+ in his primary school in twenty years. He grew up in public housing, and he says his friends deliberately failed the 11+. Both his parents were upset when he went to the grammar school, and they went to see the headmaster to voice their objection when he was accepted at university. They wanted him to stay at home and learn a trade like other young men and live in the community.

"University isn't for the likes of us," they said, both angry and perplexed.

The hegemonic project. This summer, while we were in London, a taxi driver made a similar statement to my husband. Working-class families in the "United Kingdom" were—*are*—well taught of their inferiority.

"Just as I was seeking to recover my roots I entered an academic community where everybody appeared to masquerade as upper class," O'Loughlin writes. "Was I the only professor of working-class origin? Why was it taboo to speak your mind? Why did people seem uncomfortable when I raised issues of poverty, equity and racial justice?"[8]

We have to stop hiding our life histories. Never has there been a time this century when our voices are needed so urgently.

When eminent researchers with power and privilege write of "above average children" as "advantaged organisms because of the superior environment and genotype provided by the child's parents," and of "biologically disadvantaged children" who are "less healthy organisms" who "grow up in impoverished environments," we have to respond as scientists, but we also have to respond personally, to be angry, as O'Loughlin encourages us, and to show our passions . . . whatever the risk.

When NICHD, a government-financed institute, funds research such as the Foorman studies which separates children by their race and ethnicity, and finds that African American children have lower levels of phonemic awareness and that "deficits in phonological processing are heritable,"[9] we have no alternative but to deconstruct the research and expose the political nature of the "scientific" data.

And when states like California and Texas use these studies to justify a radical shift in the ways in which children are taught to read, we have to ask why the changes are taking place. North Carolina provides the clearest evidence that in the United States, politicians are intent on taking over public schools to create separate educational systems for children who live in affluent, mostly white communities and children who live in lower socioeconomic communities.

England has a long history of separate systems for rich and poor children. The class system ensures that upper-class children—"posh kids"—go to private—paradoxically known as public—schools.[10] Middle-class children, predominantly white, who will enter "the professions," go to grammar schools, which were supposed to be abolished over thirty years ago but are still in existence today. In the *Sunday Times*, which reports on the national ranking of both public and private schools, grammar schools are described as "[t]he elite of the state system" which "provide a quality of education which rivals that offered by the most expensive private schools in the country" (p. 3). The report gives the examination results for the top ranked of these elite state schools and reports on the competition to attend them.

"Over-subscribed, taking top 112 pupils who pass 11-plus examination and name the school as their first choice," the report states for the top-ranked school.

"Substantially over-subscribed with five applicants per place," the report states for the school that ranked second (p. 4).

"Hugely over-subscribed: 850 applications for 93 places."

"More than six applicants per place."

"Nine applicants per place."

"Ten applications for each of 120 places."

"Takes top 10% of ability range. The facilities include 12 laboratories and workshops for science and technology, two computer suites, drama studio, music suite, a ceramics room, library, two large gymnasiums, courts and playing fields."

Needless to say, there are very few working-class children and children of color who attend these schools.

"He's got an athletic scholarship," a mother tells me, talking about her seven-year-old son, "but we can't afford the uniform or all the equipment. And his brother and sister, they won't be able to go, if we can't afford the uniform we certainly can't afford the fees."

Her children will go to comprehensive schools, working-class institutions which prepare children for their place in life, and while some of these institutions are ranked alongside grammar schools, most are much more utilitarian with few opportunities for students to compete with the students of either the elite private schools of the upper class or the grammar schools of the upper-middle professional class.

For many years, even though they remained in existence, there was little talk of grammar schools; the focus was on the comprehensive schools which had replaced the grammar and secondary schools in inner cities and working-class communities. The rhetoric was of equity if not equality, and other noble ideals. So it was interesting to observe a couple of weeks ago that no one seemed to take any notice when the new conservative Labour Party announced that the hegemonic monolith to England's self-aggrandizing class-ridden society was in favor once again.[11]

"LABOUR BACKS ELITE PUPILS," Patrick O'Flynn writes for the *Express*,[12] a working-class newspaper. "The cleverest children will be creamed off to sit exams ahead of their peers." "Streaming," "tracking," "whole class teaching," and "rote learning" are the terms that are used.

"Government to have its hand in every school," Lucy Ward writes in the *Independent*,[13] whose readers are predominantly middle class. "The Government and local authorities will get unprecedented powers to drive out failure in schools under proposals in a White Paper aimed at levering up national educational standards." Then later in the article, "Ministers were quick to stress that new responsibilities for authorities in monitoring and enforcing standards did not detract from the schools' watchdog, Ofsted, which will continue to inspect schools."

"In every cry of every Man," William Blake wrote in his poem "London," "In every Infant's cry of fear,/In every voice, in every ban,/The mind-forg'd manacles I hear."

10

In which we are told that in America we are all equal. Are we or aren't we?

∎ ∎ ∎

In the United States we would all denounce the social selectivity of England's class system if we thought there was even the remotest chance that such a system would be adopted here. After all, we are all equal here. We do believe, don't we, that American society is built on the ideals of equality and opportunity? Regardless of where we come from, however poor our families, whatever our ethnicity, if we work hard, everybody gets a chance. We do believe that, don't we? Don't we?

In *Savage Inequalities*, Jonathan Kozol makes it clear that this is the question we "don't want to ask."[1]

"According to our textbook rhetoric," Kozol writes, "Americans abhor the notion of a social order in which economic privilege and political power are determined by hereditary class. Officially, we have a more enlightened goal in sight: namely, a society in which a family's wealth has no relation to the probability of future educational attainment and the wealth and station it affords. By this standard, education offered to poor children should be at least as good as that which is provided to the children of the upper-middle class" (p. 207).

"All our children ought to be allowed a stake in the enormous richness of America," Kozol writes at the end of his book. "Whether they were born to poor white Appalachians or to wealthy Texans, to poor black people in the Bronx or to rich people in Manhasset or Winnetka, they are all quite wonderful and innocent when they are small. We soil them needlessly" (p. 233).[2]

Power, privilege, racism, and hegemony. In the United States the rhetoric is more carefully constructed. We find other reasons for the disparities. In North Carolina "instructional models" for children in "wealthy schools" are described as "too weak" for low SES children. Politicians, with the assistance of their subaltern intellectuals, have come up with ways to convince the educational community and members of the public that poor children learn differently than rich children and that some of them need more intensive methods of instruction. They have accomplished this aim by using the fundamentally flawed research of scientists who have found "cognitive deficits" in children by totally disregarding the highly problematic social and economic circumstances in which they are forced to live their everyday lives.

Let me be even more explicit about what has happened within the scientific community that studies reading. There is no doubt that a small cadre of researchers, many of whom are in the payment of basal publishing companies and who are working closely with state governments, have conducted a campaign for public opinion in which the information provided to the public has been manipulated to such an extent that it is nothing more than spin doctoring. In the process, many educators, both university professors and classroom teachers, have been bullied and silenced if they have expressed different points of view. As you will find out when we reach California, their research teaching practices are vilified, and any protests that they might make are described with self-righteous indignation as unwarranted ad hominem attacks lacking any scientific justification. The arrogance of power creates a paranoia that equates all criticism with disloyalty, and so educators who do not support the positivistic, in-the-head reductionist findings of the "true scientific method" are vilified.

The irony, of course, is that the war that is being fought in the schools in the United States has nothing to do with improving reading instruction. If that were the case, then politicians would be concerned about the conditions in which many children receive a public education. In Texas, where the struggle for equalization of funding began in 1968 with *Rodriguez v. San Antonio* and continued more recently in 1989 with *Edgewood ISD v. Kirby*, Carol Ascher writes that the differences in school spending remain extremely high.[3]

Ascher writes in a discussion of efficiency, equity, and local control in the state, "In 1985–1986, the wealthiest district in Texas had over $14,000,000 of assessed valuation per child, while the poorest district had only $20,000," which as Ascher points out is "a ratio of 700 to 1" (p. 4).

"Even in the 100 wealthiest districts, property wealth is 20 times greater than in the 100 poorest districts," Ascher continues. "And in the two neighboring districts," which were represented in *Edgewood ISD v. Kirby*, "per pupil wealth in Edgewood is $39,000, compared to $570,000 in Alamo Heights." [4]

"Because of the vast differences in property values, wealthy districts have characteristically raised much more for their students' education even while taxing themselves at a far lower rate," Ascher explains. "For example, because Alamo Heights, one of the 12 school districts in San Antonio, has so much property wealth, its residents pay taxes at the lowest rate in the county and still generate the highest revenue of any of the San Antonio school districts." [5]

"During the past years of controversy, wealthy districts in Texas have often argued that poorer districts should be 'leveled up' to their standard of spending," Ascher states in a discussion of strategies to equalize resources among districts. "Yet the *per annum* cost of bringing all school systems in Texas to the level of the highest spending district would be approximately four times the annual operating budget of the entire state government." [6]

"Some hope of change was briefly awakened in the fall of 1989," Jonathan Kozol writes in *Savage Inequalities*, "when front-page headlines in the *New York Times* and other leading papers heralded the news that the school funding system in the state of Texas had been found unconstitutional under state law."

"In a nine-to-zero decision," Kozol writes, "the state supreme court, citing what it termed 'glaring disparities' in spending between wealthy and poor districts, said that the funding system was in violation of the passage in the Texas constitution that required Texas to maintain an education system for 'the general diffusion of knowledge' in the state."

"The court's decision summarized some of the most extreme inequities," Kozol writes. "District spending ranged from $2,112 to $19,333. The richest district drew on property wealth of $14 million for each student while the poorest district drew on property worth only $20,000 for each student."

"Let there be no misunderstanding," the court said. "A remedy is long overdue" (p. 225).

But Kozol is skeptical. "Predictions were heard that, after legislative red tape and political delays, a revised state formula would be developed," he writes, with resignation. "The court would look it over, voice some doubts, but finally accept it as a reasonable effort" (p. 227).

"It is now the spring of 1991," Kozol continues. "A year and a half has passed since these events took place. The Texas legislature has at last, and with much rhetoric about what many legislators call 'a Robin Hood approach,' enacted a new equalizing formula but left a number of loop-holes that perpetuate the fiscal edge enjoyed by very wealthy districts. Plaintiffs' attorneys are guarded in their expectations. If the experience of other states holds true in Texas, there will be a series of delays and challenges and, doubtless, further litigation. The implementation of the newest plan, in any case, will not be immediate. Twenty-three years after Demetrio Rodriguez went to court, the children of the poorest people in the state of Texas still are waiting for an equal chance at education" (p. 229).

We are back to the hegemonic project, and the perpetuation of the myth of universal education and of equal opportunity. The United States has never had any intention of educating all its children. If you are poor, if your name is Rodriguez, if you are of African descent, you already know that. For the most part, the American education system ensures that the poor children and children of color become what Delpit calls "the trainable, low-level functionaries."[7] They are fodder for subaltern intellectuals.

If you are well-off and born with opportunity, you might not agree. But let me present my argument and then you decide if I made the statement erroneously. I want to take you to Louisiana, to the Mississippi Delta, to visit some school children who live there, and then to Washington, D.C., to a share with you the testimony of educational researchers before the Committee on Education and the Workforce of the United States House of Representatives, and then finally to California, which is where we began our journey. Then see if you disagree.

But before we go to Louisiana, let's consider some political realities that directly affect public education across the country and have particular relevance for how children are taught to read. For those with power and privilege, American schools face two major demographic difficulties, the first being the declining revenues available for public education, and the second the substantial increases in the numbers of "minority" children receiving public education.

"Texas was experiencing a 20 percent increase in the number of school children," Ascher states, writing of the 1980s, "with Hispanic students comprising the largest, and African American students the second-largest, increase. Moreover, a similar growth in the number of students, largely caused by minority population growth, has been projected for the 1990s. Thus, an aging white population with fewer children has seen itself as paying for a growing minority population."[8]

In California, where "minorities" are now the majority, 25 percent of the population are new immigrants and the first language of most of these new immigrants is Spanish. The backlash in California against immigration is frequently discussed by politicians on Sunday morning TV shows, and national attention was given to the implications of Proposition 187 and more recently on the abandonment of affirmative action in California colleges and universities. In California, as in Texas, an affluent, aging white population is increasingly disgruntled at the thought of paying for the education of a rapidly increasing poor minority population.

Texas, California, Florida, North Carolina—what's the difference? States across the nation have rapidly increasing poor and minority populations and tremendous inequities in the funding of public schools, and politicians who wish to stay in public office have no interest in equalizing resources between poor and rich schools. The problem is that they have to look as if they are doing something while maintaining the status quo. So what better way than to pronounce the educational programs in wealthy schools "too weak" for poor children and children of color? There are certainly enough researchers who are willing to support them by stating that some poor children and children of color have biological or genetic difficulties learning to read or that they learn to read "differently." Publishers can also be counted on to supply "more intensive instructional" basals which are much cheaper than equalizing the educational disparities which exist between rich and poor schools. The press then recycles the spin and the government appears to be actively addressing the inequities.

But as Gee points out, there are other reasons for the lack of interest in providing an adequate education for poor children and children of color. There is no place for them in society except in McDonald's-type service industries.

"The New Capitalism is the product of massive global and technological changes that made competition global and hyper-intense," Gee writes. "Under these conditions, businesses need to out-compete their competition by producing the highest quality product or service as quickly as possible at the lowest price. This means, in turn, no 'fat,' no excess: no person, practice, or thing that does not directly 'add value' to the final service or product."[9]

"The highest and most important form of knowledge and skill in the new capitalism is what I will call *sociotechnical designing*," Gee explains; "that is designing products and services so that they create or 'speak to' specific consumer identities and values."[10] Gee calls these "niches" and he gives a list: "designing better ways to organize the production and delivery of products and services; designing ways to shape consumer identities and values through advertising and marketing; and designing ways to transform products and markets based on consumer identities and values. All this design work is heavily social and contextual and semiotic," Gee concludes, "that is, it often involves manipulating symbols of identity."

In another presentation Gee states that in the New Capitalism there will be a two-fifths–three-fifths split. Only two-fifths of the workforce will find a "niche." So what happens to the other three-fifths? It's another indication that the United States is in the process of building a two-tier public education system.[11] Paradoxically, at a time when the federal and state governments are providing vast sums of money to bring advanced science and technology into schools, and when there is an emphasis on highly contextualized problem solving and creative thinking and what Gee calls "cutting edge pedagogies," federal and state agencies are also providing financial support for research which mandates low-level literacy skills.

But this is too abstract for me. I want to describe the inequities. Whatever challenges I faced as a child are nothing compared with the challenges many children face today in the United States. Kozol has tried to raise our consciousness, but few of us have come to grips with the deprivations that poor children and children of color experience on a daily basis when they go to school.

In which we find the desks and chairs are broken and the toilets don't work

■ ■ ■

I want you to meet some of the three-fifths of our children who will get the skill and drill and who have no science and technology in their schools. Come with me to Louisiana where children are left to fester in the Delta heat.[1]

"Court rejects lawsuit to force more funding for schools," Doug Myers announces in the *Baton Rouge State Times/Morning Advocate*. It's Saturday, March 8, 1997, and Myers tells his readers that "A state appeals court Friday threw out a lawsuit filed by 31 school districts and the American Civil Liberties Union to force the state to pump more money into Louisiana's 1,400 public schools."[2]

The defendants in the case are the Governor of Louisiana, Murphy J. "Mike" Foster, the Legislature of the State of Louisiana, the Louisiana Board of Elementary and Secondary Education (BESE), and the State Superintendent of Education.

"A panel of the 1st Circuit Court of Appeal voted 3–2 to grant the state's motion for summary judgement," Myers tells his readers, "meaning it ruled in the state's favor to dismiss the lawsuit without a trial."

Myers quotes Lewis Unglesby, the lead counsel for the state. "The winning of the case does not diminish the desire of the governor, the Legislature, state Superintendent of Education Cecil Picard, and BESE to finding solutions to the problems that this case has pointed out,"

Unglesby declares. "It's just how we're going to do it that we're fighting over."

Governor Mike Foster is quoted in a prepared statement. "The duty to provide adequate funding for K–12 (kindergarten–12th grade) education falls within the responsibility of the governor, the Legislature, and the Board of Elementary and Secondary Education—not the courts."

Martha Kegal, a staff council for the Louisiana ACLU, is also quoted as stating that the appalling conditions in many of Louisiana's public schools are "the direct result of the state's failure to comply with its constitutional duty to supply local school boards with adequate funding."

"Many children are going to schools so poorly funded that the children don't have pencils, paper, and textbooks," Kegal relayed by Myers. "The buildings are so badly in need of repair that roofs are falling down, ceilings are leaking, and walls are crumbling."

"The schools catch on fire because of old and faulty wiring. Desks and chairs are broken, playground equipment is broken or nonexistent. The bathrooms are unusable." Again it's Kegal via Myers.

On the same day, in the *New Orleans Times-Picayune*, Governor Foster is quoted by staff and wire reports as stating, "I made it clear at the outset that this lawsuit was the wrong way to try to take care of the educational needs of this state."

The ACLU disagreed and an appeal has been made to the Louisiana Supreme Court. The following statements are from the ACLU's *Application for Supervisory Writs of Certiorari and Review*.[3]

"The applicants seek the 'minimum foundation of education' that the children of Louisiana are promised by this State's Constitution," the lawyers, representing the Louisiana schoolchildren and their parents, the Orleans Parish School Board, and fourteen plaintiff-intervenor school districts, write in the statement of the case. "Their lawsuit, filed in 1992, contends that the State has failed to provide a constitutionally sufficient education, as required by Article VIII, Section 1, 13(A) and 13(B) of the Louisiana Constitution, and, as a direct result, the schoolchildren in East Feliciana, Madison, Orleans, Pointe Coupee, Red River, and St. Helena parishes are denied their right to an adequate education."[4]

"In this case, applicants desire," the lawyers write, "a declaration that Article VIII of the Louisiana Constitution grants every child in this state the right to receive an adequate education and imposes an affirmative duty on the State to provide funds sufficient to ensure that such an education is provided." In addition, the lawyers state that the applicants desire "a declaration that the State has failed to carry out that constitutional mandate in at least the six parishes where applicants attend public school" (p. 3).

"The State's contention that the judiciary should be precluded from interpreting the Louisiana Constitution to determine the duties and limits it imposes upon the State with respect to education is inconsistent with the fundamental principle of judicial review and is insupportable as a matter of law," the lawyers argue, in a response to the First Circuit Court of Appeal's dismissal of the case without a trial and a presentation of the facts. Categorically, they state, "The judicial branch unquestionably has both the power and the duty to determine whether the legislature has acted within its constitutional authority."

"At no point in this action has the State attempted to deny the existence of the deplorable conditions," the lawyers assert, "[the] severely dilapidated facilities, outdated and insufficient textbooks and materials, uncertified teachers and unsatisfactory student performance." And then they emphasize that these conditions "plainly evidence that the education provided by the State falls short of any conceivable standard of adequacy" (pp. 5–6).

The facts in the Louisiana Supreme Court writ are presented in the original 1992 Charlet Plaintiff's Petition for a Declaratory Judgement. The applicants and defendants are the same. What follows are excerpts from statements taken verbatim from this original document.[5] Let's pick it up at the point at which the discussion is about school funding and the local support for education.

"The State's inadequate support for the provision of even a minimum foundation of education means that the parishes must rely heavily on local revenues to fund their public school systems," the lawyers representing the plaintiffs write. "Local parishes contribute over one billion dollars annually to the cost of public education. Local revenues are principally derived from property and sales taxes. In virtually every parish, the local contribution must far exceed the revenues that can be generated by the constitutionally-mandated five mill property tax in order for schools to attempt to meet the minimum standards of adequacy that the State has established."

"Many parishes are unable to raise sufficient local funds to insure a minimum foundation of education for their students," the lawyers stress. "Although taxpayers in parishes with small tax bases generally are taxed at higher rates than taxpayers in wealthier parishes, the poorer parishes nevertheless generate substantially less local revenue. Even some parishes with large tax bases are unable to raise sufficient local funds, because of the considerable needs of their children and their schools. As a result, these parishes do not have sufficient resources to provide their schoolchildren with the minimum foundation of education that the Constitution mandates. Neither can they provide an education comparable to that offered by some of their wealthier neighbors" (pp. 16–17).

"State support for public education in Louisiana is not only inadequate, it is also inequitable," the lawyers write, shifting their focus from inadequacies to inequities. "It fails to provide greater funds to those parishes which are least capable of raising local revenues to support education or to those whose students have the greatest educational needs" (pp. 17–18).

"Overall, state education funding has virtually no equalizing effect. A recent study commissioned by BESE concluded that in 1987–88, the MFP[6] formula provided an average of $1,348 per student to the wealthiest parishes and $1,384, only thirty-six dollars more, to the poorest parishes. In fact, when other sources of state funding were included, the study found that the wealthiest parishes actually received more state funds per student, $1,819 to $1,796" (p. 19).[7]

Methodically the lawyers present the resulting deficiencies in the schools in the poor parishes that they represent, and they contrast these deficiencies with the minimum standards required for public education as set forth in *The Louisiana Handbook for School Administrators*.

Standard 2.008.00: The learning environment shall be conducive to the educational and overall well-being of students.

Standard 2.065.00: The school site and building shall include appropriate physical facilities and custodial services to meet the needs of the educational program and to safeguard the health and safety of the pupils.

Standard 2.065.01: Sufficient classroom, laboratory, shop, office, storage, and meeting room space shall be provided for the number of students served and the activities conducted in assigned places.

Standard 2.065.02: Adequate facilities shall be provided for specialized services such as food, guidance, library, and physical education.

Standard 2.065.09: Sufficient comfort in school facilities shall be provided through adequate ventilation, cooling, heating, and lighting.

"The MFP provides no money to parish school districts for school construction or for adapting existing facilities to meet changing needs of the student population," the lawyers state as they stress that none of these standards are met. "The MFP also provides no money for essential classroom furniture, such as desks and chairs" (p. 21).

"Children attend schools that are old, badly maintained, in need of immediate repair, and unsuited to fulfilling their educational mission. Many of the schools do not even comply with fire, health, and safety codes." The lawyers follow these general statements with specific examples.

"Clinton Middle School is the oldest school in East Feliciana Parish. It has suffered from a major fire, and is now in terrible, rundown condition. The student restrooms are located outside the main building in a small brick enclosure. In heavy rains, the restrooms flood and the plumbing backs up. In fact, flooding is a problem throughout the school. On occasion, the administration has had to close the school due to flooding.

"The school cafeteria is too small for the student population, necessitating five lunch periods. The roof in the cafeteria leaks. Because of the inadequate restroom facilities, students must wash their hands at a long water trough in the middle of the cafeteria before lunch.

"In Madison Parish, Tallulah High School, constructed in 1928, does not have central air-conditioning and the school system has no funds for window units. In order to air-condition their classrooms, some teachers have used their own money to buy window unit air-conditioners and to pay for rewiring their classrooms. This building still relies on the original steam boiler heating system, which is prone to breaking down.

"In the science labs at Tallulah High School, the old water pipes are clogged with sediment and corrosion products, so there is no water available for experiments. The roof leaks in classrooms, in the cafeteria, and in the library. When it rains, water drips through these holes onto the tables in the library. Some shelves in the library are not sturdy enough to hold the books. The gymnasium does not have working showers and the drains in the bathrooms are often clogged" (p. 23).

"Tallulah Elementary School in Madison Parish uses eight temporary buildings, none of which has bathrooms. Inside the school, the bathrooms are unsanitary and in a state of disrepair because there is no money to repair them. The health inspector has issued warnings about the inadequate number of restroom facilities. As a result, students are now assigned to go to the bathroom at certain times.

"The cafeteria at Tallulah Elementary School is so small that the school must schedule its first lunch period at 10:00 a.m. As a result, teachers request that parents provide their children with afternoon snacks, because the children often become hungry before the school day ends.

"Wright Elementary School has sewage back-up problems. There are exposed pipes in the classrooms. There is asbestos in the building that needs to be removed. The school does not have a gymnasium or an auditorium. There are no facilities for physical education during the rainy season which runs from November through March.

"The Thomastown School has exposed pipes and heating ducts in classrooms and bathrooms. The roof leaks in several rooms throughout the building. The cafeteria's ventilation system is inadequate; as a result, the cafeteria becomes far too hot during warm weather. The cafeteria has holes in the ceilings and walls and a number of floor tiles are missing.

"The majority of students in Orleans Parish attend schools in buildings that were built before 1940. Out of 123 schools, only two comply fully with all applicable health, safety and fire codes. The city fire chief recently cited fifteen elementary schools for 'serious' fire code violations and insisted on expedited corrections. As of 1989, over one hundred school buildings required immediate asbestos removal.

"Seventy-one Orleans Parish schools are overcrowded. Three hundred and ninety-one classes of students are taught in temporary classrooms. Students in 234 other classes must try to learn in halls, closets, and similar inappropriate spaces. Due to space shortages, classes have been held in stairwells and in restrooms" (p. 25).

"At least forty-three New Orleans schools have become infested with Formosan termites, which cause considerable damage to the structures. They are much more difficult and expensive to control than normal termites. One school, Abrams Elementary, has been ordered closed due to extensive termite damage that the school system cannot afford to repair.

"When this school year began, Orleans Parish had no desks for more than 2,000 students. Students had to stand during class or sit on the floor.

"At Upper Pointe Coupee Elementary School one wing of the school is unsafe and had to be closed down. There are leaks in the gymnasium and the floor is in need of repair. Throughout the school, bathrooms are in terrible condition. They suffer from leaks and inadequate drainage. As a result, floors in the bathrooms are often wet. Many of the stalls have no doors. Because the school was originally a high school, the toilets are too large for the younger children.

"Throughout Pointe Coupee Parish, student desks are old and in bad condition. One kindergarten class at Upper Pointe Coupee Elementary has no desks, so students must sit on the floor.

"Most of the school buildings in Red River Parish were projects of the federal Works Progress Administration, built during the 1930s and 1940s.

"Bathroom facilities at Coushatta Elementary are old and inadequate. The main building has only one bathroom for boys and one for girls. These bathrooms have seven to nine stalls in each and must serve the needs of almost 500 students. The trailers have no running water or bathroom facilities, so the children must walk to the main building to go to the bathroom, without the benefit of a covered walkway to protect them in inclement weather.

"Water damage at Coushatta Elementary has caused plaster to peel from the walls in the stairwells. The radiators are old and often leak. Some leak so badly that moisture drips down the walls of the classroom beneath the leaking radiator. A leaking radiator also leaves puddles of hot water on the floor, causing damage and presenting a threat to the children.

"Coushatta High School is old and decaying. A number of classroom roofs leak and walls are crumbling. The floor in the gymnasium has partly buckled. Heating is a major problem in the main building. Many restrooms are unsanitary, have broken plumbing, and are missing stall doors. In the gymnasium locker rooms only two toilets and no showers are in working order.

"Even though Coushatta High School serves more than three hundred students, there is only one small classroom equipped for laboratory experiments. No more than fifteen to seventeen students can use the laboratory classroom at the same time. The science teachers must coordinate to schedule its use.

"Martin High School is a kindergarten through twelfth-grade school with over 350 students, yet it has only one restroom for the girls and one restroom for boys, with four commodes in each. The school has no separate facilities for the elementary and high school students, so five-year-olds must share the bathroom with high school seniors.

"The cafeteria at Martin is made of wood and at one time was infested with termites. The termites have been exterminated, but the damage is extensive and visible. The gymnasium at Martin is threatening to collapse.

"The middle school in St. Helena Parish is only twenty-seven years old, but the building has not been maintained properly. The fire marshal had to condemn two rooms. The library, located in the former shop area, floods when it rains.

"The middle school does not have enough bathrooms and the showers in the gymnasium do not work. Because of the lack of bathrooms, some of the boys use the showers to relieve themselves.

"The elementary school building was built in the 1940s. It is grossly overcrowded. Before consolidation, the school never had a student population over four hundred. St. Helena Central Elementary School now has over eight hundred students. Kindergarten classes must double up in a single room with forty-five to fifty students.

"The elementary school cafeteria is in a converted gymnasium; there are exposed wires on the walls. Children must sit in the center of many classrooms on rainy days, because water pours in through the walls. Rats have chewed holes through some of the temporary classrooms.

"The bathrooms in the elementary school are in decrepit condition. On a recent visit, the toilets were filthy and did not flush properly. The doors to the stalls were broken and there were holes in the walls. Light bulbs were missing and pools of leaking water had collected on the floor. A bad stench pervaded the room."

In an affidavit signed December 11, 1996, Richard Fossey, who teaches at Louisiana State University, swears that he observed "unsafe conditions" in many of the schools. The affidavit states that he observed "that guard rails had been constructed inside the classrooms of Hall Summit School in Red River Parish to prevent badly decayed window casings from falling on and injuring students."

Fossey also observed the "unsanitary conditions" at many of the school facilities. In the affidavit Fossey states that the bathrooms in some schools are "grossly unsanitary, lacking privacy doors, soap, hot water, and toilet paper," and that "the gym showers at a number of schools were dilapidated and vile."

The schools violate every state standard which focuses on the educational environment and the well-being of students. Cross out ~~Standard 2.008.00~~, the conditions in which children are supposed to learn violate the health and safety regulations. Strike out ~~Standard 2.065.01~~, students are being taught in bathrooms, kindergarten children are learning to read standing up. Draw a heavy line through ~~Standard 2.065.02~~, lunch starts at ten and children wash their hands in a communal trough; the libraries are grossly inadequate and in some schools there are very few books. Another line, ~~Standard 2.065.09~~, the ventilation and cooling are totally inadequate to cope with the water-saturated air and oppressive heat of the Mississippi Delta.

But none of these facts are new to us; few if any of us can claim that we do not know of the deplorable conditions in which many poor children and children of color are schooled. Kozol made sure of that when he wrote *Savage Inequalities*.

Go and look into a toilet here if you would like to know what life is like for students in this city

"In East St Louis," Kozol writes, "as in every city that I visit, I am forced to ask myself if what I've seen may be atypical. One would like to think that this might be the case in East St. Louis, but it would not be the truth."

"'Go and look into a toilet here if you would like to know what life is like for students in this city,'" a student named Christopher tells Kozol when he visits his school in East St. Louis.

"Before I leave, I do as Christopher asked," Kozol writes, "and enter a boy's bathroom. Four of the six toilets do not work. The toilet stalls, which are eaten away by red and brown corrosion, have no doors. The toilets have no seats. One has a rotted wooden stump. There are no paper towels and no soap. Near the door there is a loop of wire with an empty toilet-paper roll" (p. 36).

"Critics," Kozol argues effectively, "also willfully ignore the health conditions and the psychological disarray of children growing up in burnt-out housing, playing on contaminated land, and walking past acres of smoldering garbage on their way to school."

"In view of the extraordinary miseries of life for children in the district, East St. Louis should be spending far more than is spent in wealthy suburbs," Kozol argues. "As things stand, the city spends approximately half as much each year on every pupil as the state's top-spending districts" (pp. 37, 38).

"So there is, in fact, no exit for these children," Kozol writes at the end of the chapter. "East St. Louis will likely be left as it is for a good many years to come; a scar of sorts, an ugly metaphor of filth and overspill and chemical effusions, a place for blacks to live and die within, a place for other people to avoid when they are heading for St. Louis" (p. 39).

The schools in Louisiana will also be left. The difficulties that the schools face are politically organized and systemic, and the miseries of the children's lives are endemic, given to them because of their "place" of birth. Power, privilege, racism, and hegemony; some children are poisoned by this caustic mix, the drug of choice of politics. The Charlet Plaintiff's Petition for a Declaratory Judgement was filed on March 24, 1992. Governor "Mike" Foster, and the Louisiana State Legislature, and the State Department of Education, the co-defendants in the case, were made aware at that time—if they didn't know before—that the conditions in the schools violate state and federal health and safety regulations. For at least five years they've known that children attend crumbling and decaying schools with vile, foul-smelling bathrooms, and that they stand in their classrooms because their desks are falling apart and they have no place to sit. But on March 7, 1997, the state appeals court threw out the lawsuit.

In the Charlet Plaintiff's Petition for a Declaratory Judgement, which attached to the Louisiana Supreme Court writ, the ACLU lawyers focus next on the availability of textbooks. They begin by stating that the Louisiana Constitution requires that the Legislature "appropriate sufficient funds to supply all schoolchildren in the state with free school books necessary for instruction and learning." The lawyers also note that the Legislature passed a law in 1991 requiring BESE "to promulgate a regulation to ensure that all public school students are able to take books used to teach reading home with them after school and on weekends."

They add to the constitutional requirements and state law the standards as they are set forth in the *Louisiana Handbook for School Administrators.*

Standard 1.070.03: Each school system shall make a formal adoption of textbooks within 12 months from the date of their approval by the State Board of Elementary and Secondary Education (BESE).

Standard 2.070.02: Each school shall provide textbook materials for each student and shall have proper procedures for selection, storage, and preservation of textbooks.

Once again the lawyers make it clear that the money available is totally inadequate to fulfill the requirements of the Louisiana State Legislature and BESE. "The current MFP formula allots each parish school district only twenty-seven dollars per student for the purchase of textbooks, library books, and school supplies." They emphasize that "[t]he twenty-seven dollars supplied by the MFP is not enough for parish school systems to purchase new textbooks adopted by BESE, even if those dollars are used to purchase only textbooks, to the exclusion of library books or school supplies." The lawyers then provide "just a few examples" of the textbook problems that have resulted from the unavailability of sufficient funds.

"Schools throughout East Feliciana Parish must rely on out-of-date books. At Clinton Middle School, one set of math textbooks was thirteen years old. Only last year, the school had replaced science textbooks that predicted that man would someday go to the moon. Other textbooks were so old they were literally falling apart. Clinton High School students are using a World History text copyrighted in 1966 and, at Clinton Elementary, some books date from 1978.

"At several schools, students must make do with a 'class set' of text books, which are left behind in the classroom for use by students in other periods. 'Homework' must be done during class time.

"To cope with budgetary shortfalls, the East Feliciana school system has obtained some used textbooks for free that had been retired by East Baton Rouge Parish. Also, students are required to pay for workbooks.

"Madison Parish has overspent its textbook allocation by several thousand dollars, but still cannot provide all books mandated by BESE.

"Some students at Tallulah High have no textbooks in certain subjects and some classes share textbooks because the parish cannot afford to purchase an entire series; some of the textbooks that students do have are in terrible condition.

"At the Thomastown School and Tallulah High, English teachers are unable to provide their students with novels. Ninth- and tenth-grade students at the Thomastown School also do not have math workbooks.

"At McCall Junior High School in Madison Parish, there is a constant shortage of textbooks. The shortage is so acute that students in the same algebra class were using two sets of textbooks, one of which was nearly two decades old.

"In the environmental science classes at McCall Senior High, 85 students must share only 29 books."

"Many courses in Orleans Parish must be taught with outdated textbooks or with none at all. For example, the vocational education books used in the parish were copyrighted 1975.

"Apart from a few outdated middle-school Spanish books, the Orleans Parish Public Schools have no foreign language textbooks at all. Teachers must teach everything off the chalkboard and this substantially limits their ability to assign meaningful homework in these foreign language courses.

"The twenty-seven dollars provided by the MFP falls far short of meeting Orleans Parish's textbook needs. This year, the state curriculum development cycle required local school districts to adopt new texts in mathematics, music, foreign languages, business, distributive education, and home economics. Orleans Parish could only afford to adopt new mathematics books with its MFP money.

"Although Red River Parish expends its entire twenty-seven dollar state allotment, plus some local funds, on textbooks, school administrators do not have sufficient funds to provide all prescribed textbooks to the students. Either classes do not have enough textbooks for the number of students in the class, or the textbooks are outdated and in poor condition.

"Currently, Martin High School's seventh-grade social studies class is using a textbook edition copyrighted in 1968. It thus fails to inform students about the last twenty-four years of United States history. The books are so old that pages are missing in almost all of the volumes. Because Red River Parish could not afford to buy new books on the State adoption list, the school administration had to order additional outdated books so that students would at least have books that they could read and use.

"The earth science book in use at Coushatta High School dates from about 1972 and is written at a fifth-grade level. Another math book has not been updated since 1978. At least one English class last year did not have any textbooks at all.

"Coushatta High School was able to buy some new algebra books last year, but Martin was not. Therefore, Coushatta High School gave Martin its old algebra books so that Martin would have enough books for its students. Martin, in turn, shared some of its excess books that Coushatta was lacking. However, like the social studies books, these textbooks are old and missing pages."

Once again I question whether the United States is interested in educating all its children

Submitted with the 1997 Louisiana Supreme Court writ are excerpts from the deposition of Jay Frank Norris, Director of the Bureau of Special Projects that is responsible for the adoption of textbooks and materials in instruction for the schools of Louisiana.

The Louisiana Constitution requires that the Legislature "appropriate sufficient funds to supply all schoolchildren in the state with free school books necessary for instruction and learning." But Norris, who is in charge of textbooks, doesn't know if the children have books.

The Legislature passed a law in 1991 requiring BESE "to promulgate a regulation to ensure that all public school students are able to take books used to teach reading home with them after school and on weekends." Norris testifies that children in the plaintiff's schools do not take books home because of the philosophy of the teacher, because they don't want them to have book bags, because the schools want to eliminate lockers.

"Have you ever heard of a situation within any given system, where for the same grade level," Mr. Shields, the lawyer who is examining Norris asks, "two or more different copyrights, I'm using that term as you used it earlier, in a given subject, are used?"

"I don't know specifically, no, of any schools," Norris answers. "I don't know specifically of that. In the same school, in the same grade?"

Norris doesn't know, doesn't have an opinion. He is in charge of textbooks, but he knows nothing about whether or not children have access to them. Presumably this is the official position of the Louisiana State Department of Education. The Governor and the State Legislature don't give any indication that they want to know. I've heard people say what you don't know can't hurt you, and once again I question whether the United States is interested in educating all its children.

Strike out ~~Standard 1.070.03~~. The school districts represented in the Louisiana Supreme Court writ cannot afford to fully participate in the formal adoption of textbooks within the date of their approval by the State Board of Elementary and Secondary Education (BESE). But what little money they have you can be sure will be spent on basal readers and other textbooks. Whatever money there is the publisher will take, and whatever else the children need they will be forced to go without. In Orleans Parish the entire allotment is spent on the purchase of basal texts. Cross out ~~Standard 2.070.02~~. There is no money to follow the "proper procedure" and nowhere to "store and preserve" the books. School libraries are a luxury that children have to do without.

The lawyers move on to essential instructional materials and they point out that the Louisiana Constitution and Revised Statutes guarantee more than adequate textbooks and obligate the Governor and the State Legislature, together with the State Department of Education, to ensure that every child in Louisiana has the "appropriate materials of instruction to further their education." Excerpts from just a few of the relevant standards in the *Louisiana Handbook for School Administrators,* including the standards for libraries and media, are presented below.

Standard 1.070.00: Instruction shall be supported with adequate and appropriate instructional materials, equipment, and available community resources.

Standard 2.070.01: Instructional materials and equipment shall be in a good state of repair, and provisions shall be made to replace outdated instructional materials and worn out equipment.

Standard 2.0701.06: Each school shall have library or media services appropriate to the instructional levels and exceptionalities of its students.

Standard 2.0701.01: The library shall be the major instructional resource center of the school and shall offer varied services and activities for students.

Standard 2.071.04: Each school shall have in its library center a collection of print and non-print media and equipment in sufficient number and quality to meet instructional needs of teachers and students.

The lawyers state again that there are no monies for either instructional materials or library books. What money the schools have is spent on textbooks.

"The MFP provides no other funds for instructional materials or equipment," they write. "Neither does it provide any funds for school librarians."

"As a result of inadequate funding, schools in the plaintiffs' parishes, and throughout the State, lack essential instructional materials, equipment and supplies," the lawyers state. Then they focus on what is left once the publishers have taken whatever money the schools get. "Because virtually the entire twenty-seven dollar MFP allotment must be spent on textbooks, many of the schools in the plaintiffs' parishes cannot afford to buy basic school supplies, library books and other instructional materials necessary for a minimum foundation of education."

"In many cases, teachers have to spend their own money to purchase supplies that the school should be providing," the lawyers emphasize. "Schools are certainly not able to afford computers and up-to-date audio-visual equipment. Library resources are outdated and inadequate. The following are just a few examples of the consequences of inadequate funding.

"Instructional equipment and materials are in short supply in East Feliciana Parish. Teachers receive no funds to purchase instructional supplies. At Clinton High, teachers had to buy their own paper in order to give tests. The school cannot afford the materials needed to conduct science experiments. Students in one recent chemistry class went through an entire year without a single experiment. A recent biology class was only able to perform dissections because the biology teacher went out and caught the frogs himself.

"Madison Parish lacks critical instructional materials, equipment and supplies. The inadequate science laboratories are symptomatic of the problem. The Tallulah High School science laboratories do not have properly working water and gas outlets. The venting in the laboratories is insufficient for some of the required experiments. Poor sink drainage prevents students from using sections of the laboratory. The school lacks laboratory equipment, such as chemicals, microscopes, and beakers.

"Tallulah Elementary School is lacking instructional materials. Teachers often have to pay for materials out of their own pockets because most parents cannot afford to buy them. One teacher spent $1,200 of her own money for supplemental materials last year. Through February of this year she has spent $500. In fact, the school is so short of funds that when the cafeteria ran out of paper supplies and straws in the middle of the school year, there was no money available to restock them.

"In Orleans Parish, the twenty-seven dollar MFP allotment is used primarily for the purchase of basal texts in required courses, to the virtual exclusion of all other covered items.

"As a result, most Orleans Parish schools have virtually no supplementary teaching materials, such as globes, maps, audio-visual equipment. In fact, at many schools, teachers go out and spend their own money to buy more basic school supplies like ditto paper, pencils, and chalk.

"Science laboratory facilities and equipment are virtually nonexistent in many Orleans Parish middle and high schools. Many science teachers are forced to spend their own money to buy equipment and supplies to demonstrate science experiments. Science laboratories in fifteen of New Orleans' seventeen high schools do not meet safety requirements.

"Red River Parish is unable to provide any funds for instructional materials and supplies. Maps, globes, workbooks, pencils, pens, glue, and any other supplies needed for the classroom are often purchased by teachers with their own money. On other occasions, the teachers give parents a list of materials to purchase for their child. However, if some families cannot afford the materials, either the teacher will be forced to buy them or the child will have to do without.

"The science laboratories in Red River Parish schools are all badly antiquated and some lack necessary safety equipment. As a result, science classes perform few or no scientific experiments, an essential part of the science curriculum.

"Coushatta Elementary School has no library. According to State guidelines, a school the size of Coushatta Elementary should have a full-time librarian and a clerk, but the school cannot afford either.

"At St. Helena Central High School, the three science rooms are not equipped for laboratory experiments. The school's portable biology laboratory does not work. There are no other facilities for student experiments. There is very little equipment, mainly some graduated cylinders, some measuring tools, and a few microscopes.

"In the middle school, only three of thirteen computers are functioning. . . . There are only two overhead projectors in the school for over six hundred students and only one of them works properly. There are no film strip machines.

"Other basic equipment is also missing. Some of the social studies classes do not have maps or globes. The physical education department has no equipment. There are not even mats in the gymnasium. The school has too few desks and many of these are broken. The health class has no desks at all; the students must stand up for the duration of the instructional period.

"St. Helena Central Elementary School lacks overhead projectors, record players and filmstrip machines. It has only two televisions with VCRs for over 800 students. The elementary school library has fewer than two books per student. The school cannot afford enough instructional supplies. Teachers are allocated only two pieces of chalk each semester."

If these descriptions are true—and there is no reason to believe that they are not—then the Governor of the State of Louisiana, the State Legislature, and the State Department of Education are in violation of the Louisiana Constitution and Revised Statutes which guarantee that more than adequate textbooks and the appropriate materials of instruction be provided to every child living in the state.

Cross out ~~Standard 1.070.00.~~ Put a line through ~~Standard 2.070.01~~, all the children have are instructional materials that are obsolete and equipment that is worn out and broken. Scribble through ~~Standard 2.0701.60~~, the idea that every school should have a school library is nothing more than a cruel joke, the stacks are empty except for a few dog-eared out-of-date texts. Continue to scribble, through ~~Standard 2.0701.01~~, and ~~Standard 2.071.04~~, as well as ~~Standard 2.071.08~~, ~~Standard 2.00701.02~~, ~~Standard 2.071.03~~, ~~Standard 2.071.05~~, and ~~Standard 1.07700.00~~, the criteria for these standards have not been met and the Governor and the Louisiana State Legislature don't seem to be inclined to meet them.

Let's return to the deposition of Norris to see what a spin he is in. Once again it's Shields who is examining him.

"Have you ever visited, for instance, a classroom that had a map or a globe that was out of date according to the politics which had occurred after that globe or map was made?" Shields asks.

"No," Norris replies.

"Have you ever visited a math classroom that had an insufficient number or insufficient type of other instructional materials to use for that?"

"No."

"Have you ever visited a classroom, a science classroom, that had an insufficient number or an out-of-date type of equipment?"

"No."

"You know that these three types of things which I have just mentioned do exist today in Louisiana classrooms, don't you?"

"I don't have personal knowledge."

"Have you heard?"

"I've heard probably in passing that that probably exists."

"You certainly wouldn't doubt that there were maps and globes out there that had the USSR on there?"

"Probably, yes, there are."

"Do you think that there are maps and globes that have the Belgian Congo and Rhodesia on them still in use?"

"I object to these questions!" Mr. Hrdlicka, who represents the Governor and the Louisiana State Legislature, interjects. "He testified he doesn't have any personal experience."

"You don't have any reason to doubt that?" Shields persists.

"I doubt a lot of stuff," Norris replies, spun out and wrung out. "But

I don't have any opinion one way or the other."

Let's move on. Norris is a quintessential official in a hegemonic display of non-committal.

The lawyers discuss teachers. They quote the state law that requires all public school teachers to be certified to teach the subjects and grades in which they offer instruction, and then they focus on the standards in the handbook for administrators.

Standard 1.016.00: To be legally eligible for teaching, administrative, supervisory, or other professional services in the schools of this State, personnel shall hold a valid Louisiana certificate, appropriate to the services rendered.

Then they refer to the Louisiana Standards for State Certification of School Personnel and the requirements for certification, including the requirements of the college curriculum.

"Parishes that are unable to hire sufficient numbers of teachers with regular certifications are permitted," the lawyers note, "under certain circumstances, to hire teachers with temporary certificates." They define a temporary certificate as a bachelor's degree and a passing score on the National Teachers Examination (NTE), but inadequate teacher education.

The lawyers discuss the hiring procedures and the payment of teachers. In Louisiana a teacher with a bachelor's degree and no experience is paid $14,631, and a teacher with a doctorate and twenty-five years of experience is paid $26,020.[8]

They note that parishes use local funds to supplement teachers' salaries and that the supplements that wealthier parishes pay exacerbate the difficulties of poorer parishes in attracting qualified teachers and that the MFP provides no funds for teacher inservice training or other staff development programs.

"As a result of inadequate funding, many students attending public schools in the plaintiffs' parishes, and throughout the State, are not taught by fully certified teachers.

"Many of the best teachers leave for more attractive jobs in neighboring parishes. As a result, underfunded school districts must hire many uncertified or provisionally certified teachers.

"Overall, the public schools of Louisiana currently employ more than 5,800 teachers who are not fully certified in the subjects they teach. Over 2,000 of these teachers are uncertified.

The lawyers then provide "a few examples of the deficiencies" from which I have taken the following excerpts.

"Because of low salaries East Feliciana cannot fill its teaching positions with certified teachers.

"Madison Parish faces serious financial barriers in attracting certified teachers. Generally, in Madison Parish, the teachers move on to Monroe or Vicksburg, Mississippi, in order to earn higher salaries.

"Orleans Parish has difficulty attracting and retaining qualified teachers. Many teachers leave the Orleans Parish Public Schools for positions in nearby jurisdictions, resulting in high teacher turnover. The parish had to hire approximately nine hundred new teachers last year.

"More than nine percent of all elementary and secondary school classes in Orleans Parish this school year are taught by teachers who are not fully certified. One of every six non-certified teachers in the state teaches in Orleans Parish.

"Point Coupee Parish employs only the number of teachers authorized and compensated by MFP or through other outside funds. The parish cannot afford to hire any additional teachers with local funds.

"In Red River Parish, the school system used to provide a small local supplement to the state salary schedule, averaging $800 per year. Now it cannot afford to pay any.

"Out of approximately one hundred teachers in the parish, thirty-three have not passed the National Teachers Examination and are uncertified. An additional ten to twelve teachers either do not have a degree in education or are teaching out of their area, and thus have only temporary certification.

"There are only three certified teachers of mathematics in Red River Parish and only two certified science teachers. Martin High School has no certified teachers in either subject.

Twenty-nine of St. Helena Parish's 113 teachers are uncertified, over 25 percent. Another five have only temporary certification. The problems are even more severe in particular subject areas. For example, St. Helena Central High School has only one certified science teacher.

Attached to the Louisiana Supreme Court writ is the affidavit of Judith Greer, which was notarized on December 11, 1996. Greer works as the Personnel Coordinator for the New Orleans Public School System in its Personnel Department. During the 1996–1997 school year, the New Orleans School Board hired 242 uncertified teachers and 456 teachers on temporary teaching assignments outside the field of certification. The parish employs a total of 4,400 classroom teachers.

With Greer's affidavit is the 1995 ranking of the uncertified teachers in Louisiana schools which was compiled by the *Baton Rouge Advocate*. Red River Parish is at the top of the list with 50.7 percent of the teachers in the parish uncertified. Madison Parish is next with 28.2 percent, and St. Helena Parish follows with 28.0 percent. East Feliciana Parish comes next with 25.2 percent.[9]

However serious the difficulties caused by the shortage of certified teachers, it is important that we do not denigrate the uncertified teachers who are working in the schools. Throughout the original 1992 Charlet Petition for Declaratory Judgement, there are references to the teachers and to the fact that many of them spend substantial amounts of their own money to buy books and materials for their students.

We cannot assume that the teachers in these schools do not take extraordinary measures to provide whatever opportunities they can to support their students' learning.

"Have you ever heard of situations," Shields asks Norris at his deposition, "where teachers or other administrators at a given school in a given school system used their own money to pay for ancillary or supplementary curriculum materials?"

"I don't have specific knowledge in terms of a school, a teacher, or a system. But I hear that they do that," Norris replies.

"Have you ever visited a classroom in any school?" Shields asks.

"Yes," Norris states.

"Which classroom and which school, please?"

"I visited Caddo Parish, Calcasieu Parish, Orleans Parish. There is probably others. Those are the ones that come out."

"What was the purpose of your visiting the classrooms in those parishes?"

"The supervisor wanted me to see some of the things that were happening in the classrooms with the instructional materials."

"The textbook supervisors?"

"Yes."

"What was happening in those classrooms?"

"Well, some of them had developed computer labs, alternative, non-traditional-type programs."

"So they were showing you what they were proud of, in other words?"

"Yes."

"Not what was wrong?"

Norris says, "Right."

Given the conditions in the schools, the lack of textbooks and instructional materials, it isn't very difficult to guess what is meant by an alternative, non-traditional-type computer lab and computer program.

"Schools are certainly not able to afford computers and up-to-date audio-visual equipment," the lawyers state in the 1992 Charlet Petition.

In St. Helena Central Middle School only three of thirteen computers are functioning, and there are over 600 students. In discussing the curriculum, the lawyers for the plaintiffs present as a matter of fact that many schools must teach their students computer literacy without access to a working computer. So, don't underestimate the teachers in Louisiana.

There is no doubt that the children represented in the Louisiana Supreme Court writ are politically and economically disadvantaged and actively discriminated against, but their teachers are not inferior. Most Ph.Ds, whatever their "scientific knowledge," would be lost in the classrooms of New Orleans. No, given the extraordinary hardships that both teachers and children are forced to endure, the efforts of the teachers cannot be overestimated, but neither can the impact of their intellectual and moral abandonment by the state, by the academic community, and by the United States.

In which we ask:
Do you think America
likes children?

■ ■ ■

"Welcome to America!" a woman's voice on the telephone says when I try to help Tanya find a place to live. I am working in Newark with Cathé Dorsey Gaines studying the lives of poor, urban, African American children and their families. Tanya has been told to get out of the abandoned building in which she has made a home for herself and her two young children. I am in a panic and Cathé smiles sadly at me and shakes her head. But, I am still naive enough to think that there must be some official agency that will help Tanya find an apartment, a room, some place, *any* place where she and her two children can live.

"Welcome to America!" the woman says, again, then she laughs and says, "Nobody cares about poor people here!"

Not true; of course we care. We care enough to spend millions of dollars on phonemic awareness research to alleviate the problem. We care enough to talk at conferences about our research. We care enough to write books, to get tenure, to win awards, to become intellectuals who are known for their erudition, to get lost in our own abstractions and the rigamarole of academia, to become caught up in our own importance, and in protecting our turf. Of course we care.

"Of course *I* care," I say, in a conversation with myself. "But not enough," I answer back, disgusted with myself. Whether you call the children in New Orleans "passive organisms" who are "biologically disadvantaged" or whether you protest the use of these terms and the implications of the language, it is still an academic exercise. We are still talking to ourselves. It won't make a difference to the kids that we pass by on Canal Street when the International Reading Association holds its annual convention in New Orleans.

"'Do you think America likes children?'" Jonathan Kozol recounts that Mrs. Washington asks him, in *Amazing Grace*. They are sitting together in her kitchen after they have eaten dinner.[1]

"What do you think?" Kozol turns her question around and sends it back to her.

"I don't think so," Mrs. Washington replies, and she hands Kozol a clipping she had saved.

"The story," Kozol tells his readers, "which is from *Newsday*, is about an abandoned steel plant that is going to be used this fall as a school building. The factory, which is next to a cemetery and beside a pipeline that carries 'combustible fuel,' is in an area, according to the Board of Education engineer, that 'appears to be a dumping ground' for 'tires, rugs and parts of bodies.' Because of unexpected overcrowding, some 500 children will be forced to go to school there."

"In the margin, next to a sentence that says the site of the building is 'a haven' for rats," Kozol notes that Mrs. Washington has written, "'this is the rock-bottom. So what else is new?'"

Mrs. Washington gives Kozol a second clipping that she had saved for him. He writes that the clipping "describes a school in which another group of children will be having classes in a bathroom next to the urinals."

"That ain't new either," Mrs. Washington tells Kozol as he folds up the clipping and puts it in his pocket.

We have to become more critical, not only of others but also of ourselves. We cannot be immune to self-scrutiny. Willingly or unwillingly, whatever our scientific orientation or political persuasion, we are all a part of the hegemonic project. We are part of the spin. We get caught up in philosophical debates and argue about the "true scientific method," while children in every state—New Orleans, Louisiana; San Antonio, Texas; East Los Angeles, California; East St. Louis, Missouri; Chicago, Illinois; Newark, New Jersey; Cincinnati, Ohio; the Bronx, New York— fight for the right to be intelligent, either in school or in their own way on the streets, sometimes violently, with hostility, as their lives are slowly diminished through publicly sanctioned human rights violations that few public officials are willing to admit.

"I won't defend it any more," Cecil Picard, the Louisiana State Superintendent of Public Schools, is quoted as saying in the *Times-Pica-*

yune, on March 11, 1997, after the state appeals court threw out the lawsuit to force the Governor of Louisiana and the State Legislature to provide Louisiana children living in poverty with a public education. "I won't defend a system that isn't working," Picard said, in an unprecedented statement by a public official.[2]

We have got to find new ways to respond, to write back, to increase our activity, to become activists, to advocate, with spray cans if necessary. We have got to resist.

"And so politicians acting correctly," my son writes in a poem, "dangle the child over the garbage can and cut the strings."[3]

Children who are poor and children of color who attend schools in poor urban and rural communities have been officially abandoned, and many of them are psychologically abused and emotionally battered when they go to school. Read Kozol's *Savage Inequalities* and *Amazing Grace*, request the Louisiana Supreme Court writ from the ACLU, and then tell me that in the United States we educate all our children. Tell me I'm wrong. Tell me that children are not psychologically abused and emotionally battered by the conditions of their schooling and that their academic lives are not discarded state by state.

How can we expect children to learn to read and write and become scholars in schools where there are no working toilets? Try going to the toilet in a room full of shit, and if this suggestion offends you, try to imagine how offensive it must be to the young child who has no other choice but to use the bathroom. Imagine that it is your daughter. How would you feel if nobody cared enough about her to provide her with clean facilities that have toilets that flush, and wash basins with clean running water, and soap to wash and paper towels to dry her hands? Does it make a difference that the little girl is someone else's child? Does it matter that it is someone else's son who is forced to turn the shower into a urinal? How can children learn when we think so little of them? When we treat them so despicably?

How do we expect children to learn to read and write when there are guard rails in their classrooms to stop the window casings from falling on top of them? How do we expect children to learn to read and write when there are holes in the ceiling of their classroom and the rain is coming in? How do we expect children to learn to read and write when their desks are falling apart and they have no chairs on which to sit? How do we expect children to learn to read and write when there are not enough books for them to read? When their books are out of date? When there is not enough paper for them to write? When they are treated as if they are less than human? When animals are treated better than children? Tell me. How do we expect them to learn?

Stand up. Don't sit. Write a story. Read a book. Wash your hands in a trough. Eat your lunch at ten o'clock. Turn off the air conditioner or the heat. Sit on the floor and try and complete a phonics worksheet. Now tell me about your self-worth. Ask the children in Red River Parish in Louisiana what society thinks about them. They know. I knew. Even though the conditions of my childhood were far less extreme, I knew that I was not supposed to be intelligent, that menial work was what society had planned for me.

"It all comes of being poor, you see," my cousin, who still lives in the four-room house in Wales in which she was born, tells me this summer, when I talk with her on the telephone. "Like the third world, we were. And people are still getting sick."

"Poverty, not a lack of ambition, precludes them," another of my cousins writes about children in South Wales who want to go to the grammar school.

"Biologically disadvantaged children must learn in instructional environments (composed of teachers, schools, parents etc.), that are inferior to those experienced by advantaged children." [4]

Remember Stanovich? Are you willing to accept that the two thousand children who don't have chairs in Orleans Parish are biologically disadvantaged if they have difficulty learning to read? Take the children with you as you travel back through the pages and read again what Stanovich has to say. Then read Grossen and her statement based on NICHD research that significantly more African American children have lower levels of phonemic awareness.

Make your way to Texas and ask yourself what does it *really* mean when Foorman writes, "What these significant ethnicity contrasts mean, is that associated with the gains demonstrated by synthetic phonics when compared with the other two reading interventions was lower performance of minorities relative to Whites"?

Travel on to North Carolina and bring your own interpretation of what the state means when it argues that the instructional models used with children in wealthy schools are likely to be too weak to serve the needs of children in low SES schools. Ask the children from Louisiana what difference it would make if their classrooms were light and airy and filled with books and computers for them to use. Ask them what difference it would make if their schools had libraries and clean bathrooms and safe places to play. Would it make any difference? What do you think they would say?

Now come with me to Washington, D.C., where we are going to stop for the Hearing on Literacy and Why Children Can't Read held by the Committee of Education and the Workforce of the House of Representatives. Then we'll travel on to California, our final destination, and there, at last, we'll expose the hegemonic project and how it works.

In which we consider if we are comfortable mandating reading programs based on neuroimaging research and genetic studies of reading disabilities

■ ■ ■

At the Hearing on Literacy which took place on Thursday, July 10, 1997, Rich Long, representative for the International Reading Association and the National Council of Teachers of English, says Reid Lyon "really moved the debate." Long explains to me that Lyon's phonemic awareness research is "the real stuff" and that the committee was impressed by what he had to say. But then he tells me Lyon mixes rigorous work with less scientific data. Long tells me that while he does not question the phonemic awareness research of NICHD, he does have reservations about Lyon's research on teachers.

"Not all of his conclusions are based on the same kind of data," he says.

I ask him if I can quote him and he agrees. I tell him I have serious reservations about NICHD's phonemic awareness research, but he glosses over what I say and tells me that he is the president of his local PTA.

"The government is just reflecting my PTA," he says.

Knowing that he lives in an affluent community, I smile to myself, and agree. Once again he tells me what an effect the presentation Lyon made had on the committee, and then agrees to overnight the presentations of the experts to me.

Richard Venesky, Catherine Snow, Bob Slavin, and Vivian Gadsden, who are all college professors, spoke, and I urge you to send for their presentations. But here in *Spin Doctors* I'm going to focus on Lyon's presentation before heading to California to a meeting of the Education Committee of the State Assembly, which is where our story ends.

Lyon's presentation is well written, and to anyone who has not studied the research his arguments are convincing.

"The psychological, social, and economic consequences of reading failure are legion," Lyon states. "It is for this reason that NICHD considers reading failure to reflect not only an educational problem, but a significant public health problem as well."

Lyon talks about NICHD and the research of the institution on the critical environmental, experiential, cognitive, genetic, neurobiological, and instructional conditions that foster strong reading development and the risk factors that predispose youngsters to reading failure.

Speaking of "alarming trends," Lyon uses NAEP to his own advantage, and in ways which contradict statements made by Venesky.[1] Lyon tells the committee, "These data underscore the fact that reading failure is a serious national problem and can not simply be attributed to poverty, immigration, or learning English as a second language."

Are you thinking about the children in Louisiana or the children in Kozol's books *Amazing Grace* and *Savage Inequalities*? Are you also beginning to question whether the war that is taking place is really about teaching children to read? As you study the experimental research on phonemic awareness and examine the official documentation from state legislatures and state departments of education, are you also concerned about the frequency with which poverty is discounted, and the focus shifted to genetic etiology?

Lyon talks about the ease with which the brains of some children process information that allows them to link the discrete sounds C/A/T with the word *cat*. He then asserts that "in many children that skill is only learned with difficulty."

"Does this mean that children who have difficulty understanding that spoken words are composed of discrete individual sounds that can be linked to letters suffer from brain dysfunction or damage?" he asks the committee. "Not at all. It simply means that the neural systems that *perceive*[2] the phonemes in our language are less efficient in these children than in other children."

"In some cases," Lyon states, "our NICHD studies have taught us that the phonological differences we see in good and poor readers have a genetic basis, although it is important to note that genetic influences in reading can be modified significantly by environmental factors" (p. 5).

"Children raised in poverty, youngsters with limited proficiency in English, children with speech and hearing impairments, and children from homes where the parent's reading levels are low are clearly at increased risk of reading failure" (p. 8).

This begins to sound like a sociopolitical argument, but Lyon quickly moves back inside children's heads and blames them for their deficiencies.

"[R]ecent research has been able to identify and replicate findings which point to at least four factors that hinder reading development among children irrespective of their environmental, socioeconomic, ethnic, and biological factors," Lyon states categorically, wiping out the effects of learning in classrooms where children's desks are falling apart and they do not have enough chairs to sit on, where there are no computers and the only books that they have are old and torn through years of use.

"These four factors include deficits in phoneme awareness and developing the alphabetic principle, deficits in acquiring reading comprehension strategies and applying them to the reading of text, deficits in developing and maintaining the motivation to learn to read, and limitations in effectively preparing teachers"(p. 8).

"In fact," Lyon states, narrowing his focus two paragraphs later, "difficulties in decoding and word recognition are at the core of most reading difficulties."[3]

"In contrast to good readers who understand that segmented units of speech can be linked to letters and letter patterns," Lyon states definitively, "poor readers have substantial difficulty in developing this 'alphabetic principle.' The culprit appears to be a deficit in phoneme awareness," which he defines for the committee as "the understanding that words are made up of sound segments called phonemes."

"Difficulties in developing phoneme awareness can have genetic and neurobiological origins or can be attributable to a lack of exposure to language patterns and usage during infancy and the preschool years. The end result is the same, however. Children who lack phoneme awareness have difficulties linking speech sounds to letters," Lyon explains, "their decoding skills are labored and weak, resulting in extremely slow reading. As mentioned, this labored access to print renders comprehension nearly impossible. Thus the purpose for reading is nullified because the children are often too dysfluent to make sense out of what they read" (p. 9).

Lyon moved the committee, Long said. This is unfortunate, as the research on phonemic awareness does not support Lyon's proposition that phonemic awareness is the primary area in which children with reading difficulties differ from other children.

In an article entitled "NICHD Research Program in Learning Disabilities," which Lyon gave to the members of the House of Representatives Committee in Washington, along with the written version of his speech, Lyon and Duane Alexander discuss how the research of NICHD differs from other research on learning disabilities. "Studies were typically conducted on biased samples, obviously leading to biased results," Lyon and Alexander state. My response to this statement is that the studies conducted by NICHD are also conducted on biased samples, and the results of the institutes' studies are equally biased.

Lyon and Alexander then talk about haphazard research strategies which lead to "predictable difficulties in replicating and generalizing research findings." Based on my analysis of Foorman's research, it is clear that NICHD suffers from the same inherent difficulties, and that the problems the institution faces undermine any statements that Lyon makes about phonemic awareness and how young children learn to read.

Let me be specific about the serious inadequacies of Foorman's research. In addition to the fact that, from a sociocultural perspective, the research has no scientific merit, the research is also defective from the perspective of empirical, experimental science. Her methodology is critically flawed. To be even more explicit, the statistical modeling of individual growth rates, the statistical methods, the statistical assumptions, and the statistical analyses are variously dubious, unverifiable, false, or inappropriate, as well as simplistic and biased. The numerous defects in her study and the resulting statistical uncertainties make any correlations and conclusions that she presents little more than complicated guesses based upon the biases with which she began the research.

In addition, Lyon must also address the added difficulties that in other studies funded by NICHD, the arguments are tautological and misleading. Furthermore, other independent research is selectively and misleadingly reported out of context to support the argument that phonemic awareness training must take place explicitly.

If A cites B . . .

Indeed, Lyon's own work suffers from the same difficulties. In a research article that Lyon wrote with Vinita Chhabra on the current state of science, which was also given to the members of the committee in Washington, Lyon and Chhabra list the NICHD research sites and include in the list the University of Houston.

"The comprehensive multidisciplinary longitudinal investigations undertaken at these sites," they state, noting the exclusion of NICHD's animal studies at Beth Israel, "have obtained converging data indicating that deficits in phonological processing reflect a core cognitive deficit in reading disability; that illuminate the neurobiological and genetic underpinnings of phonological deficits; that provide a map of the developmental trajectory of reading disability; and that show, for the first time, how different treatments can alter the course of the disorder" (p. 4).

Spin doctors, spin.

"Data derived from a number of well-designed studies indicates that reading disability typically reflects insufficient phonological processing abilities," Lyon and Chhabra state, referencing among others Adams and Stanovich (p. 4). "[A] number of well-designed longitudinal treatment or intervention studies have been conducted," Lyon and Chhabra write, and among the citations is a reference to Foorman's research.[4] "The data from these studies indicates that children with phonologically based reading disability require treatment programs composed of direct and explicit instruction in phonemic awareness combined with instruction to develop sound-symbol relationships via synthetic phonics instructional methods" (p. 6).

When does the spin stop and the lying begin?

Lyon and his colleagues at NICHD are building theories of how children read based on their study of pathology. They write of cormorbidity and co-morbidity, decreased activation of the left temporoparietal and superior temporal cortex, autosomal dominant transmission, effects of major genetic loci on the transmission of phonological deficits and subsequent reading problems.[5]

At the University of Colorado, NICHD supports research to elucidate "the genetic aspects of reading development and disorders."[6]

At Johns Hopkins Research Center, NICHD researchers are exploring "the genetic and neurobiological underpinnings of both disorders of attention and language-based reading disorders."

At the University of Washington, the NICHD researchers are engaged in "a range of basic neurobiological and genetic studies."

At the Children's Hospital in Boston, NICHD researchers from Harvard are "testing hypotheses related to temporal processing and reading development and disorders. In addition, functional MRI studies are being conducted with both normal reading children and youngsters with reading difficulties to better understand the neural basis of language and reading behaviors."

At Beth Israel Hospital, NICHD researchers, also from Harvard, are conducting studies "devoted specifically to identifying neuroanatomical and neurophysiological models of reading disorders."

In the Bowman Gray Reading Research Project, NICHD researchers are studying "the linguistic basis of reading development and disorders and the genetic and neurobiological correlates of reading development and difficulties."

Researchers for NICHD are engaged in studies which focus on "children at risk of reading failure" at Florida State University, the University of Texas Medical Center (that's Foorman and her co-researchers), and Georgia State University.

In NICHD's Washington, D.C., Early Reading Intervention Project, Lyon has brought together Adams, Carnine, and Foorman to use commercial reading to "better understand which components of reading instruction are most beneficial for well-defined children at different stages of reading development."

At Syracuse University, NICHD researchers are using neuroimaging to study children who are considered at-risk for reading failure. They are "studied first with neuroimaging technology and then reading intervention is initiated. Neuroimaging is repeated during and after intervention trials."

Put a child in a gantry, the mind-forg'd manacles of modern science, and take pictures to determine which areas of his brain become engorged with blood as he is told to read the words that are flashed on a TV screen.

"Deficits in phonological processing appear to be heritable, as shown in both behavioral and molecular genetic studies," Lyon and Alexander state. "Likewise, language-based reading disabilities are highly related to significant differences in neural processing" (p. 15). Lyon and Alexander also argue that, "[I]t is important for us to know how neurophysiological and neuroanatomical differences are related to genetic factors and to environmental influences" (p. 15).

In a paper published in the *New England Journal of Medicine*, Sally Shaywitz, whose research is supported by NICHD, echoes Lyon and Alexander in presenting as science a view of phonologic deficits as the primary cause of reading difficulties.

"A range of neurobiologic investigations using post-mortem brain specimens, brain morphometry, functional brain imaging, and electrophysiology suggests that there are differences in the temporo-parieto-occipital brain regions between people with dyslexia and those who are not reading-impaired," Shaywitz writes. Later, in a tautological argument, she states, "[t]he application of what has been learned about the acquisition of reading and the availability of tests of phonologic skills now make it possible, first, to identify children with dyslexia even before they fail in reading, and then, to provide appropriate early interventions" (pp. 307, 309).

Lyon, Alexander, and Shaywitz remind me of something Stephen J. Gould said about science being a socially conditioned enterprise filled with bias. But the point is this: even if you forget my analysis of the empirical research; if you put aside my social and economic arguments, do you think children should be taught to read based on NICHD's deficit-driven analysis of cormorbidity and co-morbidity? Are you comfortable mandating state-by-state reading programs based on neuroimaging research and genetic studies of reading disabilities?

Where is the research on how children become literate? How they use written language? How they learn about written language?[7] Where are the longitudinal studies, the years of systematic observations, of young children who are learning to read? Program evaluation studies don't count. Where are the longitudinal studies of children's writing? Where are the descriptions of the sociohistorical evolution of children's graphophonemic awareness? Where is the research on reading which informs us of the ways in which children cope with the inherent ambiguity in even the simplest of English texts? Where are the studies of the development of such important concepts as the spaces between words? Punctuation? Spelling? The research on children's early lexico-grammatical knowledge? Where are the studies which help us understand how even very young children use print, as Nicola did, to cope with the difficulties that they experience in their everyday lives?

As you will see when we reach our next destination, these studies are officially censured, politically embargoed; to put it bluntly, they are banned. Decades of scientific documentation have been replaced by isolationist, *in vacuo* theories of the neurophysiological and neuroanatomical differences related to genetic factors which, it is claimed, determine whether or not young children will have difficulties learning to read—replaced by, in other words, the research of NICHD.

In which California politically reinvents how young children learn to read

■ ■ ■

At last we have reached California to witness the end of social science, the death of emergent literacy research, and burial of all approaches to scientific inquiry that do not conform to the "true scientific method." Forget the free and open debate of the issues, forget civil rights, forget civil liberties, forget democracy.

In *Toxic Literacies* I wrote about the ways in which the lives of men and women who live in poverty are reinvented in official texts. I wrote about how Cindy, who was chronically abused as a child, was reinvented by the criminal justice system in the official documentation that controlled her life. About how Sam, who was homeless, had his story rewritten in the paperwork of the state and local welfare agencies. How Laurie, who was a mother with three young children, was harassed by social agencies, denied adequate medical treatment for the cancer from which she was suffering, and eventually died. How Kathryn, who was homeless and pregnant, was vilified by those in authority and then totally reconstructed in the documentation that framed her life.

The official texts and the political rhetoric that I deconstructed in *Toxic Literacies* are in many ways similar to the political rhetoric of official texts that I have encountered in *Spin Doctors*. Professors in universities, teachers in schools, and even children in kindergarten and first-grade classrooms have all been vilified and their lives reconstructed in official texts. The paper trail makes it clear that the scientific study of reading is being politically reinvented, but for reasons that go far beyond teaching young children to read.

In her Nobel lecture, Toni Morrison writes of oppressive language. "It is the language that drinks blood," she states, "laps vulnerabilities, tucks its fascist boots under crinolines of respectability and patriotism as it moves relentlessly towards the bottom line and the bottomed-out mind."

"The official text cannot tolerate new ideas. It represents truth," I write back to Morrison in *Toxic Literacies*. "Or so we are led to believe. We are enculturated into the dominant ideology."

Power, privilege, racism, and hegemony.

"Official language smitheried to sanction ignorance and preserve privilege is a suit of armor, polished to shocking glitter, a husk from which the knight departed long ago," Morrison writes, calling official language "dumb," "predatory," and "sentimental."

"'Dumb,'" I write back, "because it is ideological. In real terms, in the reality of people's everyday lives it is *il*-logical. 'Predatory,' because it preys on people. Official texts are self-perpetuating, self-originating, pathological in construction, people-violating, bureaucrat-generating, and open to corruption. 'Sentimental,' because we believe that the worn-out texts that control our lives represent the core values of society."

"Oppressive language does more than represent violence, it is violence; does more than represent the limits of knowledge; it limits knowledge," Morrison writes. "Whether it is obscuring state language or the *faux* language of mindless media; whether it is the proud but calcified language of the academy or the commodity-driven language of science; whether it is the malign language of law-without-ethics, or language designed for the estrangement of minorities, hiding its racist plunder in its literary cheek—it must be rejected, altered, exposed."

"Question," I write in *Toxic Literacies*, "but we don't question. We acquiesce. We are insignificant. We believe that official texts are 'factual.' When in 'fact' such texts are political constructions that do not represent reality. They are no one's actuality."

Prepare yourself. We are going to attend the Informational Hearing of the Education Committee of the California State Assembly that took place on May 8, 1996. It is a pivotal meeting in the takeover of public education in the United States. You will witness the violence of official rhetoric, and the hegemonic project will be exposed when the "dominant groups," as Norman Fairclough describes them, exercise their power through constituting alliances and by integrating rather than just dominating subordinate groups. Together, Gramsci's generals with their subaltern intellectuals, and the various like-minded factions who attend the meeting will try to kill science as many of us know it. Researchers will be maligned and teachers discredited. Children's books will banned and children's writing denigrated.

Even the lies have been distorted

As there are no counterarguments or alternative positions allowed at the meeting, before we go in, let's stop and read what Gary Ravani, president of the Petaluma Federation of Teachers, writes in an article published on Sunday, June 22, 1997, in the *Press Democrat*.

"[T]he public needs to realize that when it comes to public education," Ravani writes, "it has been bombarded with apocryphal hyperbole to the point where even the lies have been distorted."

"The point is, if we base our reform efforts on faulty assumptions," Ravani says, "we are unlikely to be successful." Ravani then debunks the myths about public schools. The first myth is that "*[e]verybody knows that compared to other countries U.S. kids are basically 'illiterate.'*"

"The International Association for Evaluation of Educational Achievement," Ravani states, "in a study released last summer, looked at reading comprehension of fourth- and ninth-graders in 32 developed nations. Students in the United States ranked second in the world on this test. In fact top U.S. readers—above the 90th percentile—were the best in the world."

"'The average American student today can read, write, and solve problems better than ever,'" Ravani then writes, quoting a study done in 1995 by the Rand Corporation. Ravani focuses on the next myth, "*[e]verybody knows that California schools rank near the bottom in national assessments of reading,*" which, he states, is based on the results of the National Assessment of Educational Progress.

"There is an element of truth buried here that is very significant, but not in the way that is commonly discussed," Ravani explains, as he brings to the attention of his readers the findings of a study, known as the California K–12 Report Card, conducted by the nonpartisan Legislative Analyst's Office.

"[B]ased on 1992 data," Ravani states that the study "shows a shocking 150-point gap," which he emphasizes is nearly 10 grade levels, "between the NAEP scores of high-achieving suburban students and low-achieving urban students."

"According to the director of the education unit in the analyst's office," Ravani hits home, "'the data suggest a very divided student population in California. On average, California's students score somewhat lower than the comparison states. Much of that difference, however, stems from the relatively low scores of California's low performing students and students from low-income urban areas.'"

"News flash to the officials and groups at the state level," Ravani again, as he debunks the myth that *the problem lies with the curriculum.* "It's not the curriculum's fault," he argues, as if the curriculum that has been so demonized has suddenly come alive. "The fault lies with the decades of underfunding of the schools, huge class sizes—the latest class size reduction has moved us from 50th of 50 states to 49th—and the systematic dismantling of the social safety net, leaving schools trying to deal with the consequences of children living in conditions of grinding poverty."

"The absolute number and percentage of school-age children in poverty has increased dramatically in California," Steve Krashen states. "California ranks 41st out of 50 in terms of the percentage of children living in poverty, and there was a 25 percent increase from 1989 to 1993 in the number of children in poverty in California. The NAEP reported that California ranks near the bottom of the country in the percentage of homes with more than 25 books."[1]

In California, as in other states, poverty is politically organized and inequities are officially sanctioned.

"California children experience amazing disparities in their print environments," Krashen writes in another article. "The average child in Beverly Hills has more age-appropriate books at home than the average child in Watts and Compton has in his or her classroom library," Krashen writes, citing Smith et al., 1997. "Privileged children," he continues, "also have far better school libraries, and greater access to bookstores."[2]

"Beyond the quality of library collections themselves," Krashen continues, "additional barriers deprive children of the rich reading they need to develop literacy. While students in low-poverty schools usually have relatively open access to school libraries, children in high-poverty schools often face severely restricted access to the few services their school libraries offer. Some schools even bar children from taking library books out of the building, despite the print-poor environment many of these children face at home. Affluent schools place no such restrictions on their students" (p. 20).[3]

In *Education Week*'s "Quality Counts: A Report Card On the Condition of Public Education in the 50 States," there is a short article by Lyn Olson on race and demography.[4] "Quality Counts," she states, "focuses on what states can do to raise the achievement of all students." "Stress the word all," Olson says, and she refers to a report published by the Education Trust. "The fact that progress in minority achievement has stopped at a time when minorities comprise a growing portion of the student population should sound a wake-up call to the whole country."

"[W]e have constructed an educational system so full of inequities," says Olson, again quoting from the Education Trust report, "that it actually exacerbates the challenges of race and poverty, rather than ameliorates them. Simply put, we take students who have less to begin with and give them less in school, too."

In "The Report Card on California" published by *Education Week*, California gets a D for equity, a D for school climate, and a D- for adequacy. Only the teachers get a B-, which is ironic as it is the teachers who are being blamed for California's educational difficulties. "A once world-class system is now third-rate," the Report Card states in a cryptic commentary. "Can it be rebuilt? State has enormous resources with problems to match. Pays a high price for rule by referendum." Then the final comment: "Pace-setting reforms derailed by politics and conservative resistance."

Let's go into the meeting and observe the derailment by California's conservative right of any attempts by teachers to support the literacy development of the diverse student population which attends California's public schools. But before we go in, let there be no doubt that what happens in this room will critically affect what happens in public education across the nation. What you will read is of necessity a much-shortened version of the ten-hour hearing, which I have annotated and presented with counterarguments.[5]

The cycle of the locusts: the meeting of the Education Committee of the California Assembly, May 8, 1996

The hearing takes place in a small room which quickly fills up with the people who are going to testify, the reading "experts," the officials from the state government, and the representatives of the far right. There are too many people. Overflow rooms have been set up, and relegated to these rooms are the teachers who have come, some hoping to testify, to speak of their personal experiences as teachers of reading and to present an alternative view of reading pedagogy. But there will be no debate or discussion. Unreceptive to interrogation, only the proponents of explicit systematic phonics get to speak.

"Politics moves the game to a whole new level," P. David Pearson writes in the *Council Chronicle*; "Indeed, it may change it to a whole new game."[6]

The members of the Education Committee take their places. Steve

Baldwin, the chair of the committee and a former aide to Newt Gingrich, opens the meeting.

"Today is the day of the teacher," Baldwin begins, "and I would like to take time to acknowledge the vital role that teachers play in our society and culture. They are one of our most valuable resources." Paradoxically, during the meeting teachers will be portrayed as know-nothings who are out to hurt kids. Baldwin smiles and claps and the audience claps with him, then they lift their crinolines and pull on their boots.

"I think everyone here is in agreement that there is a reading crisis in California," Baldwin states. "The last few years have revealed test scores, declining test scores, to the point that we are now considered last in the country."

"The legislature has intervened on behalf of California's children to try to curb this alarming rate of failure," Baldwin says, lapping the vulnerabilities of those who listen to him speak.

"Last year AB 170 by D. D. Alpert and AB 1504 by John Burton, also known as the ABC legislation, passed unanimously in the House and were signed by the governor," Baldwin continues reading from a prepared script. "These bills collectively mandated a return to phonics, a return to, to, um—books that emphasize spelling."

"Also last year the State Board of Education and the State Superintendent adopted a Reading Task Force report which recommends direct and organized instruction in phonemic awareness and systematic explicit phonics instruction." Baldwin looks at Ruth McKenna who is representing Delaine Easton, California's Superintendent of Schools. "I understand that the Department of Education is now in the process of preparing a Program Advisory which will directly influence how the districts carry out the Task Force recommendations." It is not a question. He is not asking; he is telling. He continues without stopping, "In addition, the governor has set aside over 100 million dollars in his budget proposal to help improve reading instruction."

"I am also carrying legislation AB 3075, co-authored by Assemblyman Willard Murray, that would give the commission on teacher credentialing greater authority in establishing standards for schools of education as they develop their reading courses for prospective teachers.

"The committee chose to call this hearing to assess the status of the state's implementation of AB 170[7] and AB 1504[8] and to assess the implementation of the recommendations of the Reading Task Force as they relate to phonics.

"It is the opinion of this committee that the research is very sound and overwhelming and that phonics is a superior system of instruction, and it's already clear that the intent of the legislature and all the different agencies involved in education that we head back in that direction," Baldwin states.

Wait a minute. What research are you referring to? Who reviewed the research for the committee? Were any contrary opinions considered? Explain what you mean by "sound and overwhelming." Are you talking about the research of NICHD? The studies of Foorman? If so, you'd better stop the meeting now.

"So what we are trying to establish here today is how do we go back, returning to direct systematic instruction, and phonics, and what needs to be done to accelerate this process." Baldwin gets apocalyptic. "I don't think we can afford to have another generation of children who are unable to read."

The word system is an automatic unconscious rapid process

Baldwin introduces Bill Honig, the former Superintendent of Public Instruction. The last time I saw Honig was at the State Department of Education in Sacramento, at the meeting on special education that I mentioned earlier in the book. Late in the morning Honig came into the meeting. I remember Honig as tall and angular, a pale, stone-faced, authoritative figure. All conversation stopped, and some of the participants in the meeting looked down at the table. Honig was a general then, and everyone was deferential. He spoke briefly, issued directives, and then left, but it took several minutes before everyone relaxed enough to continue the meeting.

At the May 8 hearing, Honig is no longer a general. Instead he has assumed the role of a subaltern intellectual, even though many would argue that he has no particular expertise in reading. He is deferential and at times almost obsequious as he makes his presentation to the Education Committee.

"Thank you Mr. Chairman, members of the committee, members of the State Board." Honig holds up two pieces of paper and summarizes a book he has written which, he says, "backs up what the chairman was saying."

Honig talks about "a convergence of both research and best practice" on how young children should be taught to read. He says, "We have a good theory and we have evidence that backs it up," as he begins to lay out the official reconstruction of how young children learn to read.

Show us your evidence. Let us review your data. Don't talk as if it is a fait accompli. There are many educational researchers and classroom teachers who disagree with the "theories" and "evidence" you are about to describe.[9]

"[O]nce again some folks are overstating, exaggerating, and maybe even creating evidence to support the effectiveness of code-oriented, or phonics, materials and methods," Richard Allington writes in a commentary in *Reading Today*. "[T]here is no convergence in the research indicating just how school programs might best foster development of such strategies and what types of phonics instruction, of what intensity, over what duration will produce the largest number of children who read well and willingly."

"But this lack of evidence seems not to much matter to many proponents of a pro-phonics agenda," Allington states, and then as an aside he writes, "and I include here some researchers, publishers, legislators, lobbyists, journalists, and others."

"Lobbyists' materials, state education agency documents, product advertisements, legislative testimonies, and other materials, have recently begun to contain a set of strikingly similar assertions about phonics teaching and learning," Allington writes, which he describes as "assertions that are simply distortions of the available research even though often couched in terms such as 'scientifically rigorous research.'"

Honig talks about the 1986 framework and says he takes "some personal responsibility" as he was superintendent at the time. He rambles disjointedly through what sounds like a confessional, at times appearing conscience-stricken, and at other times defensive and unapologetic.

"Okay," Honig says, switching gears. "I'm going to spend my time talking about what it is we mean specifically when we say systematic explicit phonics and why that is important and what the theory is and why that makes sense and why that has been backed up by evidence."

"Number one. When you look at a good proficient reader, what do they actually do?" he asks, engaging the committee in his presentation, "And it turns out a good reader gets reading from two places." He has his elbows on the table and his fists are clenched. He moves one fist as he says, "They get it from the word. " He moves his other fist, "And they get it from the passage." He drops his passage fist and moves his word fist. "The word system is an automatic," Honig searches for the politically correct definition. "Um, er," he hesitates, "automatic," he moves his fist, "um," he's forgotten the definition.

"[U]nconscious and rapid process," Honig writes in an article entitled "Reading the Right Way" in the *School Administrator*.

Honig improvises, "quick, immediate, effortless system in a good reader."

"You don't think about the words you're reading," Honig explains.

"And they have good evidence from computer eye research now and several other major inquiries and it turns out that a good reader will look at the word and scan the letters and the patterns of letters, basically that starts retrieval in the mind."

Again, show us your data. Does the reader look at the word or scan the letters? Which? How does this start the retrieval in the mind? In the seventies this approach to reading was called "informational processing approaches to cognition." The research was simplistic and yet overly complicated, a meaningless robotic that displayed all the trappings of science but in the end was shown to be fundamentally flawed.

Honig points a finger at the side of his head, "And that letter pops into consciousness. If you can't do that automatically, if you are not automatic with a word, you basically don't have enough mental energy to think about what you're reading."[10]

Honig waves his hands in the air and points his word finger at the committee. "They now know what it takes to become automatic," he says, giving his newly revised, conservative learning theory. "Number one. You have to read the word successfully a bunch of times, sort of like your phone number till it gets automatic."

Wait! What do you mean you have to read the word successfully a bunch of times till it gets automatic? Isn't this what used to be called "whole word"? I thought we were talking about phonemic awareness and systematic explicit phonics. I thought once you learned the sounds you just decode the word. Which is it? This is important. What you say makes a difference to how California's children are taught to read. Please, be more specific.

"When you first read it," Honig states, "you have to encode, you have to store it in your mind with the letters and the letter patterns, and the sounds, and that's a key point, if you try to look at the letters without the sounds, without phonology, it doesn't work, you can never find it."

Your theory must take into consideration special situations. If sounds are so important, how does a deaf child learn to read?[11]

Honig talks rapidly. "If you store it by the first letter only, you're not going to find it quickly enough. If you store it by all the letters and patterns like horse and house, you will never find it if you don't get the whole word."

Let's be quite clear. There is not a shred of scientific evidence to support Honig's description of how young children learn to read. At the end of the second chapter I quoted Oliver Sacks, who says the brain is not a library, nor a granary, nor a computer.

Sacks also says, "There is no snapshot of how things are. Whatever comes into the mind always comes in a new context and in some sense colored by the present. This doesn't mean that it is distorted but it is against any mechanical reproduction."[12]

"So the secret is," Honig states, "can a youngster learn the technique of looking at a word, seeing the letters, generate the sounds from that word, and then put that together and say 'oh, that word is cake?'" According to Honig it's a piece of cake. "If they can do that, they are going to learn to read; if they can't do that, they are not going to read."

Honig speaks directly to the committee. "And that's where you are going to have to make a decision," he says. "Early in first grade there are simple diagnostics which you are going to hear about, decoding tests, assessments that teachers can give that don't take much time," he tells the committee, but no such tests are ever presented at this hearing, "and if you get 19 out of 20 on these simple things right, like v-i-m or b-i-m, sometimes they're real words, sometimes they're not, you can read those, it means you have the idea of the alphabetic system, how print matches sound. If you can't you're going to have major problems, and the reason we're having problems is that a large number of kids are not taught it, and are not checked on it, and get through the system."

If less than half of the words in the English language are spelled phonetically, how do children learn to read all the other words?

Honig says Reid Lyon will talk about the importance of phonemic awareness. "It's crucial," Honig states. "It's probably one of the major findings in the last ten years that they found over and over again. Many of our youngsters do not have, just are wired just a little bit differently, essentially, on hearing sounds."

I don't think anyone would contest that phonemic awareness is important, but many educational researchers and classroom teachers would take exception to the statement that some children do not have phonemic awareness because they are "wired just a little bit differently." There is no scientific evidence to support this proposition. Empirically it has no validity, no replicability. If this is what we call science at the end of the twentieth century, then the social science journals should indeed be empty.

Honig's arms are in the air, and he waves his hands on either side of his head. "On the natural," he says. "They cannot hear let's say the *ssss* in *sat, sss*, they can't hear the *sss* sound properly without some interventions. Luckily, it's about one out of six kids."

Show us your data! If children are not aware of the sounds of language how do they learn to speak?

"Luckily with the proper interventions and with about twenty hours, err, excuse me, about fourteen hours, twenty minutes a day for a third of the year, you can get 90 percent of those kids up to where they can learn the phonics."

Baldwin said, "The research is very sound and overwhelming," but this is a joke. Is this the information that colleges of education are supposed to give to teachers?[13]

"We used to think some kids couldn't learn phonics and therefore we didn't teach it and it turns out we haven't prepared them properly early on so kindergarten is a crucial place to find out who's getting it and who's not."

Honig says that "special ed youngsters may take two years because they may not need to read the word twelve or fourteen times, but may need to practice the word fifty times or a hundred times." He talks about grouping for skills. "That's not tracking," he says, "that's grouping for skills."

It's tracking, and some kids in the lowest groups will be skilled and drilled and never get to read because they are turned off by the mindlessness of all that skill and drill.

He moves on to "implementation" and California's master plan.

"Number one: the message has to be clear from the State Board, from the Department, from the Legislature, from the Governor, from the educators. This is what we want. I think we are very close to that. A lot of hard work has gone into fashioning a message like that and there is that potential.

"Two: the training that's out there and both in the universities and in the school districts has to reflect this. The governor's budget reflects that, but there's a lot of sponsored training that has a different message. A guess message, or a skip message. These eclectic messages or, the statement, is that they can learn to read this way or learn to read this way. You don't learn to walk or ski or read in different ways. If you don't know phonics, and you're not automatic with words, and you don't know how to tackle a new word, if you haven't figured that out, you're going to be relegated to being a weak reader. Every kid has to learn that."

So there you have it. There is only *one* way to learn to read. Honig goes on to describe the way in which he was taught to ski and then says he never became a good skier. If children are only taught one way to learn to read, will they ever become good readers? Honig says there is no compromise.

In *Reading Today*, Allington calls the assertion that direct systematic phonics is the only way to go "unscientific."

"There is suddenly much ado about the need to ensure that 'direct, systematic, and sequential' phonics instruction is offered," says Allington.

"Often, 'incidental, opportunistic' phonics instruction is contrasted negatively against the 'scientific' assertions for 'direct, systematic, and sequential' phonics."

"The problem," Allington explains, "is that the available studies of exemplary teachers portray powerful phonics instruction that is 'direct and opportunistic.'" Then he states as an aside that this approach to phonics instruction may also seem to be "systematic and sequential," before asking, "[b]ut exactly what sort of 'direct, systematic, and sequential' phonics instruction does the research endorse? Simply said, there is no convergence of research on just what sort of phonics instruction should be offered."

Honig talks in the same disorganized way for a while about special education and then about the materials that have been put into place.

"Fifthly," Honig says after a few rambling statements about special education and materials, "I think each district has got to take on the responsibility, and school, and teacher, to make sure that they thoroughly look at their programs, to make sure this comprehensive approach is in place, and that they have read and connected to this research that you're about to hear. It's very powerful stuff. I think it backs up this consensus position. It shouldn't be a right or left or moderate."

"Mr. Honig, thank you very much for your testimony," Baldwin says when Honig finishes speaking. "What is your opinion as to why some of the more militant advocates of whole language refuse to, um, acknowledge the massive amount of research demonstrating that phonics is a superior form of teaching?"

Phonics don't teach, teachers do, and you haven't presented them with any scientific evidence that demonstrates that explicit, systematic, explicit phonics is a superior form of instruction. However, many teachers do have counterevidence.

"He had all this backlog of phonics papers in his folder," Marge Knox says in a published interview that follows her ethnographic study of a boy called Tom who couldn't read when he came to her class. "When he started to read, it was not through phonics, he used many different strategies."

"You were dealing with meaningful texts?" I ask.

"His only success with reading, initially, did not come from knowing sounds," Knox explains. "It came from a book that he really wanted to read. And if we helped him, he wouldn't want to bother with the sounds. He wanted to read the book."

She talks about California. "I just can't believe what's happening," she says. "I just can't."

"What is it," Baldwin asks, "120 separate studies now that validate phonics? And yet it seems that the more research we have on it, the more willing they are to fight us. And I get the sense that large elements in the educational establishment are going to fight us all the way, err, when it comes to implementing phonics."

Name the studies. I don't know of any research that shows that systematic explicit phonics is a superior form of instruction. But I do know of studies which show that direct instruction programs can have a deleterious effect on young children's sociomoral development. I do know of studies which show that direct instruction increases the stress factors in young children's lives. And, I do know of research which shows that direct instruction alone cannot enable young children who are economically disadvantaged to catch up academically with children who attend rich schools in affluent communities.[14]

Baldwin talks of "plots" and of "conspiracy theories" and he jokes that Honig must be the leader of the Christian Right. The room is filled with laughter, and then Baldwin says, "I mean some of these plots and conspiracies that are being disseminated by our tax dollars against phonics are beyond belief."

The reality is that teachers, who are just trying to teach children to read, have been under assault for years by well-organized conservative right-wing ideologues and fundamentalist Christian organizations. Visit their Web sites. Take a look at the literature of the Eagle Forum and read the *Blumenfeld Education Letter*. The rhetoric is hateful, and there is talk of the devil. The National Right to Read Foundation refer to themselves as "reading reform activists," and the rhetoric of literature produced by the organization is confrontational. See if you can find the right-wing Web sites that are particular to your state.

"Nothing short of parental revolt will stop what is happening," the organization known as the Arizona Parents for Traditional Education writes in the documents I pulled off the Web. "If we win, we will have successfully stopped an insidious plan for the hearts and minds of our children. If we lose, we will be plunged into a nightmare of plummeting test scores, privacy invasive tests, politically correct, culturally diverse curriculum and children who will not be able to read or write."

The reading resources on this Web site include references to articles which are described as "More whole language bunk!", "Extremist educational reform. LUNACY!", "Whole language: An explanation of what it is and why we don't want it in our schools." The language is aggressive, there is talk of "major insanity," and teachers are referred to as the "thugs" of the National Education Association. One section has the heading "ANTI-AMERICAN, EXTREME LEFT WING, AND ANTI-FAMILY ORGANIZATIONS." These organizations are described as "organizations whose agenda destroys our country." There are links to the Eagle Forum homepage and the list of reading resources includes Grossen's synthesis of NICHD research *30 Years of NICHD Research: What We Know About How Children Learn to Read.* Under the listing of another article by Grossen entitled "What Does It Mean to be a Research-Based Profession?" is a listing of a "Proclamation for the Separation of School and State."[15]

"In a pluralistic society, we must undo government compulsion in school funding and attendance," the proclamation states, "By my signature below I proclaim publically that I favor the Separation of School and State."

Conspiracy? No. Hegemony.

Hegemony in which the hegemonic project takes on the form of a labyrinth in which there are many different factions and organizations that exercise power by not only forming alliances by integrating, but also by dominating subordinate groups.

"Everyone is jumping ship," a teacher tells me in California. "I think they're scared."

Labyrinthian hegemony builds on the description of the different kinds of labyrinth described by Umberto Eco in his essay on the writing of *The Name of the Rose.* Eco writes of traditional labyrinths, the kind that do not let you get lost but where the Minotaur in the center lies in wait.[16]

"Terror is born, if it is born, from the fact that you do not know where you will arrive or what the Minotaur will do" (p. 524).

At the end of the twentieth century, the Minotaur is the end of civil liberties, education dictated by the state, and the belief that some poor children who are Black or Hispanic learn differently than some rich children who are European American. But the hegemonic labyrinth is more than a Minotaur lurking at the center of the maze. The last labyrinth described by Eco "is so constructed that every path can be connected with every other one."

"It has no center, no periphery, no exit, because it is potentially infinite," Eco writes, then later explains, "it can be structured but is never structured definitively" (p. 526).

"I don't know how to explain it," a teacher from Texas says to me. "It's like an ant hill with lots of narrow twisting tunnels, and if you go down one tunnel all you find are more tunnels, and you have this feeling that you don't know what's really going on but it's dark and dangerous in there."

"Let's forget about the paranoia," Honig says. "Let's forget about the politics of it. Let's just look to the facts and I think there is enough evidence here that if people will just open their minds. I'm really not in the position to judge why they do crazy things. Part of it is resistance. Because people have to change their minds. Because I believed one thing and now I have to change my mind. I would have sworn a year ago that I skimmed when I read, and I start being confronted with this research which says, no, computers show you look at every word, virtually every word and you don't skip."[17]

How do we forget politics when you tell us we have to change our minds? That there is only one way to think? That we are crazy if we disagree?

"Educators are going to have to be open enough to look at the facts," Honig continues. "There is some very strong research on these issues. You could say twenty years ago, yes, you could substitute context or meaning to decode a word and that would work. They didn't have the details of it, now they know that only works 10 percent of the time and that's not a good strategy to teach kids if you are going to get an automatic fast strategy, it's a second-rate strategy that will mean they are slow readers for the rest of their lives."

There is absolutely no evidence that demonstrates that context is not important when young children are learning to read. Even the most extremist anti-context experimentalist makes that clear. Tom Nicholson, who seems to have spent most of his academic career trying unsuccessfully to undermine the findings of Ken Goodman's 1965 study on context, makes that clear. Nicholson asks if the use of context leads to reading failure in an article entitled "The Case Against Context."

"In other words," Nicholson writes at the end of the article, "reliance on context can have a positive effect on learning to read if, in the process, children learn to decode. However, if learning to decode does not happen, then children will not learn to read" (p. 103).[18]

More compelling evidence that counters Honig's testimony comes from the many ethnographic studies that have taken place in the last thirty years which provide fine-tuned systematic observations of young children learning to read. For example, Nadeen Ruiz conducted an ethnographic investigation of children who had been identified as language-learning-disabled and who were bilingual. As in the study conducted by Foorman, the basal of choice was Open Court. Ruiz found that in the use of this program there were certain textual features that were associated with communicative breakdowns and problems with literacy tasks.[19]

Ruiz found that the tightly scripted lexical and syntactic restraints and the phonological and grammatical accuracy had a negative effect on the children's ability to produce meaningful interpretations of the Open Court materials that they were using. She presents lessons based on Open Court which illustrate the difficulties the children were experiencing and then draws some conclusions.

"Children," Ruiz writes, "learn the primacy of the written word, especially as it arises from curricular materials. Their own words and the meaning that they wish to express are secondary to the form and meaning of the materials. Only when their own words and meanings coincide with the latter are their verbal and written responses accepted."

"This view [of reading] stresses the importance of linguistic form over meaning," Ruiz goes on to state. "Linguistic forms become the object in these lessons. They are broken down, separated from contexts with real communicative intent. They are practiced until the children's 'bad' or deficient language habits become 'good' language habits."

Ruiz provides the following example of a student's difficulty comprehending, or decoding, meaning from restricted lexical and syntactic sets. The teacher is using Open Court.

"Nelly struggles first to decode then comprehend a sentence written on the board by Mrs. Dixon," Ruiz writes. The sentence is: *My wife flies.*

"My wife?" Nelly reads, as if asking if that is correct, "Smiles."

"Nelly," Mrs. Dixon says. "Look at that."

Nelly doesn't say anything for twelve seconds.

"I?" Nelly asks.

"Mhm?"

"Flies?" Nelly reads. "Flies?"

"Flies," Mrs. Dixon says. "Mhm."

"My wife," Nelly speaks softly, "haves?"

"No."

"My? My wife?" Nelly tries, "Flies."

"My wife flies," Mrs. Dixon says, "good." She starts to say, "We had never seen" —

"Flies?" Hector says.

"—that sentence," Mrs Dixon finishes what she was going to say.

"Flies?" Nelly says again.

"I don't know," Mrs. Dixon says, "how could my wife fly?"

"Lies," Nelly says. "Lies. She lies."

"When she manages to read 'flies' correctly," Ruiz writes, "Nelly immediately tries to change the sentence to make more sense to her." She then explains, "Contextualizing, or making meaning of such skeletal and vague texts are difficult for all children, but much more so for children whose background experiences are quite different from those supposed by text developers' children whose experiences include family members that use air transportation as a matter of course."

"I think that part of it is they have not examined some of the statements they are making," Honig continues, and he gives as an example the statement "You don't need to read words." He says it just doesn't check out and then adds, "For some reason they have a problem with the power of words."

"Have you signed up to be on a team for our annual school-community celebration of words and spelling?" the notice reads from a school where there are no basals, and where synthetic phonemic awareness and phonics programs are never used.

"This is how 'Spell Your Heart Out!' will work. Classrooms, parents, neighborhoods, community groups and organizations will each create their own teams of 4–5 individuals to participate in the Spell-A-Thon. Every student and staff member will be involved. Each team will present itself before a pair of judges who will give the team 25 words to spell. Students' words will be derived from their classroom work and adults' words will be taken from a variety of resources, including lists of the most frequently misspelled words.[20]

"Recognizing that many adults are self-conscious about their spelling skills, we'd like to emphasize that one does not need to be a proficient speller in order to participate. Unlike a spelling bee, individuals will not be singled out to spell words. All spellings will be by decision of the team. There are many ways to contribute to a team, so we hope all the members of your group will consider joining us. We want this to be a fun experience for everyone. Towards that end we invite teams to create for themselves, if they choose, a logo, a costume, anything to capture the spirit of the event and the pleasure of using and studying words."

One year, among the names of teams were "CONSONANTINOPLE," "LETTERMANIA," "SOUTH SPELLOPIA," "SPELLICAN ISLANDS," and "UNITED SPELLING STATES."

"The performance will end," a spell-a-gram announces another year, "when the FAIRY GODMOTHER does her final little speech and proclaims: '"They spelled happily ever after."'"

It is precisely because teachers care about words that they are resistant to political mandates to teach systematic explicit phonics. Words are lost in meaningless exercises. Language is lost. It's the California Education Committee and the hearing presenters who have a problem with the power of words. They *are* powerful. Children love them.

"One berry. Two berry. Pick me a blueberry," children read in Bruce Degen's *Jamberry*.[21]

"I've got two fat little piggies," children read in Audrey and Don Wood's *Piggies*. "Two smart little piggies, two long little piggies, two silly little piggies, and two wee little piggies."[22]

But these books will no longer be available to many children. Little books with beautiful language are not politically acceptable; instead, children will have to read "Dad sat," in John Shefelbine's dumbed-down, word-deadening, monotonous, decodable books. "Dad and Sam sat and sat."

Honig is still talking about why those whom Baldwin labels "militant advocates" have a problem with the power of words. "You are going to have to ask them," Honig tells the committee, sounding perplexed. "Part of where they go off is that they will discount and discredit, they will discredit scientific evidence," he says. "In other words to them teaching is an art, it's a theory, its an ideology, don't confuse me with evidence or facts."

There isn't any scientific evidence to discount. What you count as science is just political reconstruction of how young children learn to read. The language of science has been officially co-opted, but that doesn't make it science.

"There is a sucker born every minute," Allington writes, and then as if responding to Honig, "[t]his is my assertion, and it is unscientific but long-lived in American folklore. It is based on the premise that Americans are often easily misled into parting with their money."

"I will suggest," he continues, "that evidence for this assertion may be gathered in various legislative venues, school district board meeting rooms, and editorial offices. All it seems to take is for someone to tout the message, and lots of folks can be convinced that 'research says . . .' even when research says nothing of the sort. Perhaps this means that all of us should be more concerned with developing critical readers rather than just focusing on developing rapid decoders" (p. 15).

Honig likens educators to doctors bleeding patients a hundred years ago. He continues his talk disjointedly, as if he is rapidly decoding. He says educators are "stubbornly ignoring evidence and theory that now makes sense."

"This makes sense, it proves out," he says and then, sounding like a party pamphlet, he urges the committee, "if you don't adopt it, to me then you're basically hurting kids. Large numbers of youngsters are being hurt by the failure to adapt to this knowledge quickly enough to change what is going on in classrooms."

"We've wasted a year in this state even after this report came out because we didn't act quickly enough," Honig continues, "and we didn't get the word out fast enough, and there is still training going on with tax dollars, as you said, that has got the wrong message at these early grades and that's got to be stopped."

Forget about living in a democracy. If you are a teacher in California, there is only one official way in which you are allowed to teach. If you are a parent, there is only one politically correct way in which your child can learn. Local control has been given up for the mind-bending, mind-shaping, central control of the state.

Bruce Thompson, an assemblyman and committee member, talks about his anger at the educational establishment.

"Mr. Honig, you need to understand that I am furious over our education system," he says, staring venomously at Honig. "I am going to try to hold back my anger towards you because you were at the helm when all this nonsense was going on."

"I can appreciate your position, sir," Honig says, his demeanor acknowledging that he has been censured.

"I'm glad you've found religion, as Mr. Baldwin would say," Thompson tells Honig, "because we have been ridiculed as conservatives for many years by you and your colleagues and even the current superintendent." He says educators who he refers to as "educats" respond as if "we don't know what we are talking about."

Honig is contrite when he answers and tries to separate himself from other educators. Then he talks about Adams's book and calls it "the Bible" as if to make sure that the committee knows that he has found religion, and that he believes that there is only one true scientific method and only one way to teach children to read.[23]

The language interactions of inner-city children are nil. They've never even heard these sound systems

Baldwin introduces Lyon as the NICHD Director of Research Programs in Learning Disabilities, Language Disorders, and Disorders of Attention.

"Because I was cross-trained," Lyon explains, "I am a neurobiologist and a neurophysiologist as well as someone who has expertise in language and reading, I was recruited by the NIH which is the biomedical research arm to develop a research program in this area so that we could understand issues about child development and how they learn, as well as the genetics and neurobiology."

In the biographical sketch that accompanied his testimony to the House of Representatives Committee on Education and the Workforce, Lyon describes himself as a "research psychologist" with a doctorate "with concentrations in neuropsychology and special education." The title page of his doctoral dissertation states that he fulfilled the requirements for the degree of Doctor of Philosophy in Pupil Personnel Services from the Department of Special Education at the University of New Mexico in Albuquerque.[24]

"So would it be accurate to say that you are probably the lead person in the federal government when it comes to research on reading issues," Baldwin asks, as if in a courtroom establishing the unimpeachable expertise of his star witness.

Lyon does not acknowledge that there are other prominent reading experts and specialists working for the government. He smiles, "By way of the time I spend in it, maybe more than my knowledge but yes."

"Great! Great!" Baldwin is ecstatic with the credentials of his witness.

"Last week I was speaking with Senator Hatfield's committee," Lyon states, demonstrating that he is indeed the main man, "the Senate Appropriations Committee, and they are aware of the work that California is doing. And looking at this particular question, I think at the national level, I think there are many people who are impressed by a state that is willing to look at research issues to guide policy, sometimes it's the other way around."

Lyon gives the history of NICHD's research on reading. He says the "compelling issue" was "what is it that goes wrong when kids do not learn to read?"

"Of all of the academic skills that kids bring to bear in school, if you don't learn to read you simply don't make it in life." He talks quickly, as if it is a speech he has made many times before. He is fluent, and some might describe his presentation as slick. "And at the same time if you don't learn to read, and we follow youngsters over time who do not learn to read well, a substantial proportion of them don't finish school, a substantial proportion of these kids get into trouble with the juvenile justice system or in prisons later on, a substantial number of our young female students are unwed mothers and that seems to be related to the lack of success in school and so forth."

Political rhetoric, not scientific fact. Lyon should read Harvey Graff. Even though we struggle for universal literacy, there are still inequities. I have worked with young people who "drop out" of school, with young men and women who "get into trouble" with the juvenile justice system, and with some who have gone to jail. I have helped "unwed mothers" find places to live, and I have tutored them[25] as they have studied for a GED. I have worked with men and women suffering from drug addiction, and I have worked with men and women who are homeless, and every last one of them knew how to read.[26]

"Who is served by this seamless rhetoric of dropouts as losers?" Michelle Fine asks in her book *Framing Dropouts*. "What is obscured by a portrayal of dropouts as deficient in a fair system?" Then on the next page, challenging the fairness of the educational system in the United

States, she writes, "The issue of who is officially in and out, who is the dropout, will surely be retained as a metaphor for a system constantly negotiating inclusion and exclusion. This is the fetish of public education."

Many of the men and women with whom I worked in *Growing Up Literate* had "dropped out" of high school, but all of them could read and write, and some of them were highly literate. Some of them had taken college courses, and some of them had degrees. Their poverty was caused by racism and prejudice, by the lack of access to advanced education, and the denial of economic opportunity, and not illiteracy.

"It's hard finding people who will really help you without exploitin' you," says Jerry, who had read more books than many university professors, and, in fact, had many literacies. "Without really exploitin' you and using you," he tells us, a few months before he died of poverty and neglect, leaving behind him the two young children who were the center of his existence. "And I'm tired of being used. I'm tired of it." Jerry gets up. "I'm sorry. Book is closed. I'm sorry. The book is closed."

In *Toxic Literacies* I wrote about Cindy, who dropped out of school and who is a heroin addict. But she is a reader and a writer, and for years she kept a journal as she tried to overcome her addiction.

"Drugs overpower you," she writes. "I've grown up using drugs to survive. I don't know how to live without them. I was so depressed last night I wanted to die. If I had a gun I would have blown my head off just to be at peace. Or, if I had enough pills to die I would have. No one can imagine what I've been going through. No one. It's so much pain."

"Why does anyone try to commit suicide?" she asks in her journal. "Well I can answer that. Why should anyone live through a life of hell and torment? They say change, well if you are right-handed for twenty years try to write with your left hand. You always go back. I really tried. I just go back. I'm set in my ways. I go through hell every day wondering am I going to make it through another day."

"Among the papers that Kathryn keeps in her briefcase is a play that she wrote in 1982," I write in *Toxic Literacies*. "At the top of the first page is a circled A and beneath it is written 'Well-done.'"

Kathryn is a poet and she writes every day. "Your little face comes to pass over the pages of my mind—the smile of someone young, seeking knowledge, trying to ease the pain." She tries to get help but is continually turned away.

"She knows that she is in a double bind," I write. "She is criticized for being on welfare but the system has no intention of helping her find a job or go to college. It is all a sham. There is no way out—it was never intended that there should be."

Most of the men and women with whom I have worked would like to "get a better education." Many of them are, indeed, "undereducated," and some of them I have helped to obtain a GED.

One of the men with whom I worked, who had been incarcerated and had been a hard-core addict for over twenty-nine years, had dropped out of school in seventh grade. I helped him get a GED and then go on to college to get an associate degree. I met him several years later and we shared some memories of working together. He had worked as a community researcher in the storefront literacy center that I established in a small northeastern city.[27] He used to joke that he got his Ph.D. before he got his GED.

"Do you know Oliver Sacks?" he asked me. "Have you read *Awakenings*?"

"And seen the movie," I said as I nodded my head.

"That's how I feel," he said, "about working on the project with you." He laughed. "It was like you gave me L-DOPA and I woke up."

I knew things weren't going well, but stupidly I said, "But you have your degree."

"I'm in a coma," he said, with a look of pain etched on his face. "For a short while I woke up, but now I'm back where I started. I'm still just a convicted felon and a drug addict. Nobody cares that I've got a degree."[28]

Someone should tell Lyon that he can't use "dropouts" and pregnant teenagers as a justification for his deficit-driven experimental studies of how young children learn to read.

Lyon talks about research and once again discredits the work that is done by the educational community. Science is defined the way he defined it in Washington, deficiently, and reading is parsimoniously nothing more than the automatic, accurate decoding of words.

Alan Flurkey, in a doctoral dissertation of rare erudition, knocks out the cornerstone of Lyon's "research" by deconstructing the notion of "fluency" and presenting it as a flawed metaphor.[29]

"Why," Flurkey asks, "has a segment of the field of reading embraced the notion that one of the most complex of all human acts can be explained in terms of the rapid matching of visual input to internal templates?"

Flurkey responds to the question that he has posed by the mathematical modeling of the time relationships in children's authentic oral reading.

"[W]hat counts as science?" Flurkey asks at the end of the dissertation in which he challenges empiricists such as Lyon as he discusses the nature of science and scientific research.

"Many researchers in the field subscribe to a narrow view. In this view, scientific research is equated with empiricism and knowledge derived from careful experimentation is prized. Among those who hold to this narrow view, knowledge derived by other means is discounted." Flurkey is assertive. "But I argue for a broader view. Ultimately, science is what scientists do. If science was confined to experimental research, then Darwin's studies as he voyaged on the Beagle would not be recognized as science. Nor would be Einstein's ruminations when he emerged from three days in his upstairs study to remark to his wife, 'I have a marvelous idea.' In a broader view, science proceeds in a cycle of observation, theory generation, hypothesis refinement, testing, more observation, theory refinement and so on. Sometimes serendipity plays a part and sometimes it is just hard work" (p. 417).

Lyon is talking about funding. "The annual budget for NICHD reading research is 14 million dollars," Lyon tells Baldwin and the Education committee, "and since 1983 the cummulative budget looking at these issues that I will talk to you about today is 104 million dollars that has gone into this work."[30]

"What does a human being have to do to be able to read?" Lyon asks, as if NICHD was the first organization to ask that question. He talks for a while, as he did in Washington, about disabled readers, and he makes references to Honig's presentation, supporting what Honig said and expanding on the reading disabilities that NICHD has ascribed to young children.

"So the children we are looking at, that we study in the main, that have reading difficulties in our country, at each of the twelve sites, that certainly replicate one another, are first of all slow, labored decoders and word recognizers, and in the words of Jeannie Chall, years ago, they are youngsters that bark at the print."

"Their reading is halting and hesitant and nonautomatic and it's extremely effortful," he says. "And in fact the research evidence replicates well on this point, that if you are a slow, labored reader in reading single words on a page, the chances are about 98 percent of the time that you are not going to get a thing out of what you've read."

"The theory of reading as rapid and accurate word identification can't be supported," (p. 398) Flurkey states in his study, which included some children who Lyon would consider "slow, labored readers," but who in fact comprehended what they had read.

"Of course," Flurkey writes, "the failure of reading-as-word-identification to explain either the production of miscues or the phenomenon of reading rate variability stems from two assumptions. The first is that instead of treating the text as language, it treats text as a sequence of items, each with equal value. The second assumption is that instead of viewing the reader as a thoughtful and tentative maker of meaning, it views the reader as an automatic processor of text. In this view, the non-proficient reader is a faulty processor" (p. 392).

"Clearly one simple straightforward finding that the research replicates on," Lyon states, "and one critical condition that has to be in place to be a good hefty reader is that you've got to automatically and fluently and accurately read words."

In studies such as Flurkey's of children reading authentic texts, this "finding" simply does not replicate, and even in experimental studies in which reading is defined as rapid and accurate word identification, there are in fact no empirically acceptable replications.

Lyon talks of the conditions for reading.

"Again what are the conditions?" he asks, engaging the committee. "Fast accurate decoding of single words. If children have difficulties doing that, what is it in their system that predisposes them to be a lousy reader, to bark at this print?"

I have worked with many children who have been in intensive programs of explicit systematic phonics who try to decode every word. They are Lyon's "lousy readers." It is as if they have been taught the purpose of every muscle in their legs and to walk they have to consciously control each individual muscle involved in walking. Like Tom, who Marge Knox wrote about, sometimes it takes years for these children to develop other important strategies that they need as well as an understanding of graphophonemic relationships in order to read connected text and become readers.[31]

"Mr. Honig talked about an issue, a language issue called phonological or phonemic awareness," Lyon states, "and Dr. Foorman will address this to some degree, and there's some technical issues associated with this, and I don't want to belabor or bore you with it. But to learn to read the English language, to learn to read words quickly and accurately, you have to understand that words have sounds to them, that words are actually made up of teeny sounds, because all of you on the panel know that whenever you come across a word you've never seen before what you do is chop that word into pieces, and bring sound to each of those pieces."

Think for a moment. Do you always break words you haven't read before into their constituent sounds? Are you conscious of the process? If you were reading a page-turning novel, might you possibly just skip the odd unknown word? Or would you visualize the word and get some idea of what it means from the way it is used in the text? Is it possible that you would only "sound-out" the word if you wanted to use it to tell a friend about the book? Have you ever run around trying to find someone to help you pronounce a word that you have read for years but now you have to use it in an oral presentation and you don't want to make a fool of yourself? Have you ever heard someone say "para-didge-um" instead of paradigm? Or, hear someone, as I did at an airport, tell her friend that she read in a book something about a para-digm. "I can't remember," she said, "if it was about one dime or two dimes." Reflect on your own reading process. Does Lyon's description of the process fit?

"And the only way you can bring sound to each of those pieces, is in fact to know that words are made up of sound," Lyon explains, "so phonological awareness or phonemic awareness which, by the way, is not phonics, is not phonics." He gives a definition, "It's the auditory issue that allows us to speak the English language, to understand that words are made up of tiny sound pieces. And the hard thing is that a lot of kids who do not learn to read don't understand, for example, that the word *cat* has three sounds to it *kuh-ah-tuh*, but they don't know that, why, because something in the nervous system doesn't apprehend or parse those sounds out of running speech. In fact, none of us in this room, none of us that speak the English language, hear the sounds in words. If I say the word *cat* to a normal reader, the normal reader doesn't hear three sounds, it's the brain that hears it, because nature has given us this linguistic ability when we talk to be able to jumble all the sounds together."

Lyon is beginning to sound a bit like Honig.

"For example, if I say the word *cat* out loud, the minute I start to say *cat* and I say *kuh*, the *ah*, and *tuh* fold up into the *kuh* sound. If it didn't we would be here until Christmas, and I would be going *kuh-ah-tuh*, and so forth, and so on. So even good readers have language coming by the ear in large pulses of sound, not teeny sounds, and the brain's job is to recover these sounds, and a lot of these kids' brains can recover these sounds, but a lot can't, and don't do it well, and a lot of our research is trying to figure that out. A lot of our research is neurobiological," and then he overstates his case. "And all of the children we study, or the majority of them, have brain images taken so we can understand what's moving there."[32]

"If I can interrupt you," Baldwin leans forward and looks intently at Lyon. "Exactly how are you able to track a child's neurology as they go through different reading processes? What kind of equipment exactly are you using to do this with?"

"It's expensive equipment, I'll tell you that," Lyon responds with a laugh. "What we use with children has to be noninvasive with respect to looking at the nervous system. There are some ways you can look at the brain by injecting a radioactive isotope and allowing it to flow to the brain and then taking pictures. Let me give you a picture of what it looks like. When your brain is working to perform a behavior, it requires more blood, because blood brings glucose and oxygen, so when you're performing behaviors, and you are interested in which areas of the brain that are responsible for those behaviors, you'll see those areas being inundated, if you will, or engorged with greater degrees of blood volume and blood flow. The task is to figure out how to track that blood flow without sticking something radioactive in the system. So we have developed ways whereby we use the physics of blood flow very noninvasively. We can ask kids to read or write or spell or sing or listen and we can actually track those regions of the brain that are activated to do that. They're generally in a large gantry, and inside the gantry is a TV screen, and we ask them to read the words, or try to read the words that come up, or we can pump sound to them, and so forth and so on. And the point is, that it's now getting, it's easy to do, it's extremely complex to figure out how to design the work, and so forth, but we have nice replication on the fact that lousy readers, these slow, labored readers who are having difficulties getting the print off the page, because not understanding that the sounds exist in words, show us a different neurophysiological signature in the brain and it is highly replicable."

"Lousy readers . . . show us a different neurophysiological signature in the brain and it is highly replicable." This is quite an extraordinarily definitive statement, at a time when many researchers of neuroscience are still trying to figure out how memory works.

"The obstacle to our thinking about this process," Steven Rose, the internationally recognized neurobiologist, explains in *The Making of Memory: From Molecules to Mind*, "lies in our reliance on technological metaphors of office management as if thinking about biological memory." The argument that Rose makes is in many ways similar to the argument made by Flurkey.

"Our imagination is dominated by computers and filing systems," Rose complains. "Memories become items of 'information' to be 'stored,' 'classified,' brought out of store on demand and later refiled. Thinking about memory in this way, instead of in terms of human or biological meaning, has come as a result of the marriage of the neurobiologist's enthusiasm for hebbian synaptic models and the 'bottom-up' school of neural modelling" (p. 316–17).[33]

"Whilst the information-processing metaphor dominates the language and thinking of much of present-day neuroscience—typified by the manifesto for a theoretically committed reductionist 'computational neuroscience' by philosophers like Patricia Churchland—such enthusiasm is not universally shared, even within neuroscience, still much less outside it."

Clearly, there are many questions that need to be asked about the scientific evidence on the different neurophysiological signatures in the brains of the children that Lyon calls "lousy readers." But whatever questions we ask are overshadowed by the questions that Lyon raises himself about neuroimaging research that he presents in his testimony to the California Assembly Education Committee.

A year after the May 8, 1996, hearing in California, Gerry Coles sent an e-mail to Lyon to ask him for his appraisal of Grossen's synthesis of thirty years of NICHD research. In the copy of the Grossen paper that was sent by Silber to every school superintendent in the state of Massachusetts, and that was later circulated in California by the State Department of Education, Grossen writes that "modern neuroimaging technology" has "identified a unique signature on the brain scans of persons with reading problems." Grossen goes on to state that "[t]hese unique brain scans seem to reflect an inability to work with phonemes in the language." In his response to Coles, which was officially circulated throughout the State of California by Alice Furry of the Comprehensive Reading Leadership Center of the Sacramento County Office of Education, Lyon is supportive of Grossen's synthesis of NICHD research except for her interpretation of the neuroimaging research.

"I think that her comment regarding the state of the science in our neuroimaging studies is premature," Lyon tells Coles. "I have attempted to provide the field with information regarding the difficulties we face in conducting and interpreting neuroimaging data," Lyon says, and he notes that he has sent two books to Coles that focus on the difficulties. He then continues by stating, "No *statement about neurological correlates should be trusted unless there is an extraordinarily precise description of WHO is being studied. Again, if differences in neural activation patterns between well-defined good and not so good readers are replicated, I would venture that the relationship only holds for some children and not others—common sense.*" He adds, "I, for one, am constantly at odds with those who wish to overinterpret very basic findings from neuroimaging studies until the replications are in."

Read again the testimony of Lyon to the committee about this research and its replication.

"And the point is, that it's now getting, it's easy to do, it's extremely complex to figure out how to design the work, and so forth, but we have nice replication on the fact that lousy readers, these slow, labored readers who are having difficulties getting the print off the page, because of not understanding that the sounds exist in words, show us a different neurophysiological signature in the brain and it is highly replicable."

"When I discuss our neuroimaging data," he tells Coles in the officially circulated e-mail, "either in person or in my writings, I try very hard to be extremely cautious and indicate where my analysis represents speculation, but I probably fall down a bit at times in this regard."[34]

Ask yourself if you consider the testimony of Lyon to the California State Assembly Education Committee just "spin doctoring," or did he, quite literally, and possibly deliberately, provide false information? Either way, the contradictory statements he has made have serious implications for the scientific veracity of the research generated by NICHD, for the ways in which it is being reported, and for its legitimacy as the "scientific" basis of how young children are taught to read.

After Lyon finishes his testimony, Brooks Firestone, a member of the Education Committee, asks him about the role of family. Lyon says, "when children are in utero you might want to talk with them a little bit," and there are chuckles from the committee.

"The issue is again," Lyon responds more seriously, "there are a number of ways to come to these reading difficulties, and because our samples are mirrors or mosaics of the population, we look at every type, we look at every type of child that comes into this world, or his or her representative. You can come to be a lousy reader in a number of ways. You can come to reading and be lousy from a white middle-class, upper-middle-class home, where your parents talked to you in utero, where they did grocery lists, where they did magnetic letters, where they did Dr. Seuss, and in fact we have a lot of children who come to us who still cannot read. There is a genetic predisposition in that regard that bumps the physiology that produces the poor reader."

"On the other hand, we look at a lot of kids in inner cities who haven't even seen a book by the time they come to kindergarten, and you give them one and they hold it upside down and the wrong way," Lyon says. "The language interactions that they've had at home are nil. They've never even heard these sound systems. Are they lousy readers? A lot of them are. Are they genetically predisposed? Some of them are, making that combination a tough one to treat. But you can come to be a lousy reader in this country because you're predisposed for it. It's something you trade wise. Or you can be non-exposed to the language foundation that we've been talking about. That puts you at high risk what the heck it is, the job is in reading and applying sounds to print."

Lyon stops me in my tracks and I keep replaying the tape in the hope that I've misunderstood what he just said about inner-city kids.

"The language interactions that they've had at home are nil," Lyon said, in his official presentation to the Education Committee of the California State Assembly. *"They've never even heard these sound systems. Are they lousy readers? A lot of them are. Are they genetically predisposed?*

Some of them are, making that combination a tough one to treat."

Forget science, forget objectivity, forget replicability. The man that the federal government has provided 104 million dollars of taxpayers' money to study how young children learn to read has just made what sounds to me like a racist statement, and no one at the hearing has said a word.

"Be angry," O'Loughlin encourages, "Show your passions!"

The statement that Lyon made sickens me, and I keep wondering why members of the California State Assembly, some of whom represent parents and children who live in inner-city poverty, do not express their concern.

When Fuzzy Zoeller made a racially derogatory comment about Tiger Woods, it was front-page news, and it was replayed endlessly on CNN Headline News. The golfer lost his contract for a professional endorsement, and he had to make a public apology. But when a powerful, government-funded scientist makes a racist statement, there is no one around to rush to the defense of the children of Compton and Watts, and the scientist does not lose his endorsement from the federal government. Instead, he becomes even more powerful and his research, which is racially indefensible, becomes even more "scientifically" acceptable to those who want to change the way in which young children learn to read—especially the children in our inner cities.

"Like many children I have come to know in the South Bronx," Kozol writes in *Amazing Grace*, "Jeremiah and his friends do not speak during our meeting in the jargon that some middle-class Americans identify with inner-city kids. There's no obscenity in their speech, nor are there any of those flip code-phrases that are almost always placed within the mouths of poor black children in the movies—a style of speech, I sometimes think, that may be exaggerated by the media to lend a heightened sense of 'differentness' to children in the ghetto" (p. 134).

"Imposed language disadvantages are accompanied by imposed cultural disadvantages," Ken Goodman wrote in the early 1970s when he was at Wayne State. "Materials and lessons often are built around experiences not common in the urban culture of the learners. Urban children, however poor, are not deprived of experience" (p. 69).

Lyon should take note. Perhaps we should just play him a few CDs so he can hear the sound systems of the language that we have inherited from those who have been systematically and disproportionately denied the opportunity of formal education. Maybe we should all listen to the sound of Duke Ellington, Scott Joplin, W. C. Handy, Louis Armstrong, Charlie Parker, Bessie Smith, Dizzy Gillespie, John Coltrane, Otis Redding, John Lee Hooker, Pee Wee Crayton, Memphis Slim. Without the sounds of African Americans, there would be no jazz, no blues, no soul, no rock 'n' roll, no funk, no rock fusion. I wouldn't be able to listen to Herbie Hancock play "Watermelon Man" as I sit writing this book. I wouldn't be able to attend Hancock's *1+1* concert in which Hancock played with Wayne Shorter.

"Herbie wrote this first tune when he was in Head Start," Shorter tells the audience, as he looks at Herbie, who shakes his head and laughs.

At the concert Hancock and Shorter play for two hours straight, and I close my eyes and I listen to them play and get lost in the music, and I wonder what each of them hears as they play. Hancock's piano and Shorter's clarinet become one as they blend together and communicate with each other using sound systems that I have never even heard before and in which my language interactions are nil.

"I was struck by the idea of each composition as a story, not a soundtrack per se, but more like the movie itself," Hancock is quoted as saying about the recording *1+1* he has just made with Shorter. "Wayne described it later as the notes being the actors," Hancock continues. "We kind of planted this idea in our heads and then forgot about it. But the album did come out as though the pieces are miniature stories."

Without artists like Hancock and Shorter, American culture as we know it would cease to exist. We would be deprived of the music and lyrics that define us, White as well as Black, and our lives would be phonemically flat. But I'm not just talking historically; without children who have grown up in inner cities there would be no hip-hop, there would be no rap.

"'Common' who was formerly known as 'Common Sense,' in my opinion as well as many others, is one of the most well spoken lyricists in Hip Hop today," writes Brandon Ward, a young performance poet, who I telephoned to ask for help. He had read sections of *Spin Doctors* when he was staying with my family a few weeks ago, including Lyon's negative comments about inner-city kids, so when I telephoned he quickly sent me a fax with hip-hop lyrics and some personal notes.

"Common actually was born and raised three blocks from where I grew up on the South side of Chicago," Ward writes. "I chose this quote because many people don't realize that hip-hop isn't all sex, money, and violence. There are responsible artists out there who use their talent and popularity to spread a message. In this quote from the song, 'Retrospect for Life,' Common addresses the issue of abortion in a 'conversation' with his unborn [aborted] child. It's from the album *One Day It'll All Make Sense.*"

"The next song 'Pain' is on the album *No Way Out*," Ward writes. "Sean 'Puffy' Combs is the owner of Bad Boys Entertainment, and producer and friend of Christopher 'Notorious B.I.G.' Wallace who was gunned down in Los Angeles earlier this year." Ward has transcribed the lyrics for me, and he writes, "This quote is a good example of how not all young black males are completely desensitized to the senseless violence that plagues our society."

"In 1993 hip-hop saw a great change," he tells me. "Jazz and poetry, which I believe to be the essence of hip-hop, suddenly started becoming more prominent in the art form. A trio called 'Digable Planets' emerged upon the scene with an album entitled *Reachin' [A New Refutation of Time and Space]*." Ward continues with his narrative and lyrics, sharing tunes that push the boundaries of our existence, that change us and introduce us to sound systems that are new to us, and even if we don't listen to them, our children do.

If Lyon listened to music, or heard Ward read his poetry, or read Derrick Bell, he'd know that there are voices as well as faces at the bottom of the well.[35] Would Lyon have made such a racist statement if Bell had been sitting in front of him in Baldwin's chair? What would have happened if William Labov had been there? If Lisa Delpit, Fred Erickson, Michele Foster, Catherine Dorsey-Gaines, Yetta Goodman, bell hooks, John Ogbu, Luis Moll, or Robert Rueda were on the committee? If Stanley Aronowitz, Anne Haas Dyson, Lily Wong Fillmore, Vivian Gadsden, Ken Goodman, Jim Gee, Jeanne Henry, Dan Madigan, or David Schaafsma were sitting in the room?

We might ask why there was no one in attendance who could respond to Lyon. We might ask why Ray McDermott was not invited to speak.

"At first, they were deprived," McDermott says, referring to children in the sixties. "[T]hen, they were curiously different in language, skills, attitudes, and overall culture," he states, referring to the seventies. "[A]nd more recently, they have been understood as passively reproduced, put through the mills of inequality, and shaped into a pap form marked only by cross-generational failure," McDermott concludes, talking about the period from the mid-seventies to the present.

But now we are back before the sixties, before most of us became teachers, before many of us were born. Without language, children have no culture, without culture they are less than human, without their humanity they have no life. They are dead at an early age.[36] The coded framework of the hegemonic project, the reactionary semantics of "scientific correctness," the ideological mapping of rich and poor has been abandoned, and we are left with a large, thirties-era, Aryan sore.

"I wanna say I am somebody," Precious Jones says in Sapphire's first novel *Push*. "I wanna say it on subway, TV, movie, LOUD. I see pink faces in suits look over top of my head. I watch myself disappear in their eyes, their tesses. I talk loud but still I don't exist." Then later, Precious Jones asks, "Why can't I see myself, *feel* where I end and where I begin."[37]

"The language interactions that [inner-city kids have] had at home are nil," Lyon said. "They've never even heard these sound systems. Are they lousy readers? A lot of them are. Are they genetically predisposed? Some of them are, making that combination a tough one to treat."

Perhaps Sapphire should have been at the meeting to shout "Look at me. I use language! I hear sounds! I begin! I end! I exist!"

Willard Murray asks the last question.

"If a child comes to school speaking a different language, a language other than English, does that affect them?"

"It depends on what the language is," Lyon responds, "some languages are pretty close to ours in terms of the sound structure. Spanish being one. Probably, here's, I think, a finding replicated-wise that I am comfortable sharing with you. If you just look at dialect whether that dialect is a function of a second language or the dialect is a function of a regional dialect, that dialect is going to get in the way of learning to read when the child has a phonemic sound difference and when the teaching method is very broad and not explicit as is whole language."

Lyon gets in a "replicated-wise," but he's evasive and vague.

"Let me give you an example. In Winston-Salem, North Carolina, we're following the population there which is 51 percent African American. Now quite a few of those youngsters have dialectical differences. We study some kids in Georgia whether they're Caucasian or African American with dialectical differences. The only time we see those dialectical differences interfering with learning to read is when they are combined with this sound system difficulty, and the teaching is too broad to go after the kids, not enough phonics, not enough phonemic awareness, so these interactions come together—."

Murray interrupts. "But speaking Spanish would not be a handicap?"

Lyon jumps back in. "Not in and of itself, and the reason I can be clear on that is that we have a lot of people, second- , first- , excuse me, second-language speakers who do learn to read English quite well. We have a lot of kids who are dialectically different whether or not they're Hispanic or from Georgia or from whatever," there is laughter at the back of the room, "and they learn to read quite well."

Lyon should read the work of Tomas Enguidanos, Richard Figueroa, Margie Gallego, Eminda Garcia, Kris Gutierrez, Norma Lopez-Reyna, Luis Moll, Pedro Pedrasa, Klaudia Rivera, Robert Rueda, Elvira Sousa Lima, Henry Trueba. He might have begun by talking about the importance of knowing a child's place of birth and, if the child was born in another country, how old the child was on arrival in the United States. He might have focused on the importance of understanding the language background of the child, if Spanish is spoken in the home or if there is dual (L1+L2) proficiency at home. But Lyon fudges his answer. He forgets the importance of basing his answers on the "scientific evidence" and equates speaking a dialect with speaking a language other than English.

Whatever. Who cares. A phoneme is a phoneme. Second-language speakers do learn to read English quite well, so they can't have any difficulty reading phonetically.

In Mrs. Dixon's class her Spanish-speaking children are struggling to learn to read in English using Open Court.

"Working together," Ruiz writes, "the two features of fixed lexical sets and restriction of syntactic form set up a way of using language that is difficult for many of Mrs. Dixon's students. In essence, the children in this context are asked to make meaning given a limited set of grammatical and lexical tools. The process entails the teacher first giving the *form* in which the students' response is to be fashioned, and then asking them to construct meaning using that form. Many of the children's struggles with language emerge when these features co-occur."

Victor, who works with Mrs. Dixon at the same time as Nelly, is trying to formulate a sentence using "mine."

"Um, I'll say," Victor begins, "That's is my recorder."

"No," Mrs. Dixon says. "The word is *mine*, Victor."

"Look at mine," Nelly volunteers.

Mrs. Dixon ignores Nelly's suggestion. She focuses on Victor. "Can't say, 'That is my,'" she tells him. Then, "Nelly," she says, "hold your feet still."

"That book is mine?" Victor asks.

"That book is mine, sure," Mrs. Dixon says, accepting Victor's answer. "That book is mine. Uh-huh."

Ruiz writes, "At the end of this lesson Mrs. Dixon attempts to protect Victor from similar problems with the seatwork task she will assign—writing sentences with their reading words."

"The words in 3 and 4," Mrs. Dixon explains, "you need to write sentences for." She makes sure she has his attention, "Victor, you be careful," she says, "with words like 'sneeze' and 'please,' that you don't use 'he' with these words, or 'she.' Okay?"

"Using 'sneeze' with 'he' results in the ungrammatical 'He sneeze,'" Ruiz explains. "In this lesson and others revolving around reading words, it is not an option to add an 's' to (make) 'sneezes'; the word is 'sneeze' and that is the word form that must be used in the sentence." Ruiz then says, "As it happens, I collected Victor's sentences the following week and found that he had written 'He's sneeze.'"

Lyon should read the research of Norma Lopez-Reyna, who conducted a longitudinal study which she has published in an article entitled "The Importance of Meaningful Contexts in Bilingual Special Education: Moving to Whole Language."[38]

"Children not only need to receive comprehensible input in their native language," Lopez-Reyna writes, "they must also be engaged in activities that require them to perform at higher cognitive levels. Without comprehensible language or assistance to link their prior knowledge to new knowledge, it is unlikely that these children will learn or be able to recall the lesson's content on the following day. It is even more unlikely that higher level thinking will occur. The active participation of the students and high level of first-language dialogue in the whole language setting we observed support the importance of meaningful first-language experiences" (p. 128).

"But speaking Spanish would not be a handicap?" Murray asks.

"Not in and of itself, and the reason I can be clear on that is that we have a lot of people, second-, first-, excuse me, second-language speakers who do learn to read English quite well. We have a lot of kids who are dialectically different whether or not they're Hispanic or from Georgia or from whatever, and they learn to read quite well."

Lyon tells the Education Committee of the California Assembly what he thinks they want to hear. What he says is neither reliable nor replicable. When he talks in San Francisco to administrators, who have children who speak many languages in their schools, he expresses a different opinion.

"What we do know about ESL youngsters," he tells the administrators, "and we don't know much." He refers to a professor at UCLA, then he states, "Kids who learn to read in their native language probably do better moving to the English language than to pushing them to English initially. We have fallen down dramatically in terms of understanding the conditions that need to be in place for a couple of languages like Spanish. We haven't studied them well enough. It's taken us a long time to figure out the English part of it. And all I can do is to apologize for you."

"The NIH is only just now in Texas moving to Spanish-speaking, Hispanic kids in trying to figure that out," Lyon tells the administrators, "so I think it is going to be cleverly done. I think the research says that kids, at least at early ages, learn if they have an alphabetic language, like Spanish, learn that quite—are better able to learn in their native language before they move to English."

The meeting with the San Francisco administrators takes place in August, 1997, well over a year after Lyon testifies before the Education Committee of the California Assembly. But this is not the information that he provides in his "whatever" testimony.

As Lyon sits down, Douglas Carnine, whom you met in Texas, acknowledges him and tells him his presentation was "great."

You've got to ask yourself, is this a curriculum disability we're creating?

Baldwin introduces Barbara Foorman.

"She is going to use the hearing here to present some new research," Baldwin announces to the Education Committee.

A year later he will write to the San Diego School Board, presumably referring to Foorman's NICHD research on systematic, explicit phonics instruction. "The approach has also been vindicated," Baldwin will erroneously state, "by the recent results of a ten-million-dollar federal study that determined that a child's brain responds most favorably to a systematic phonics approach."

"I don't know that it has been presented anywhere else," Baldwin tells those attending the hearing. "Is that right, doctor?"

"That's correct," Foorman responds, even though she already presented most of the data in April at the pre-summit meeting in Texas.

Foorman stands near an overhead projector and starts her presentation without using a microphone. Baldwin encourages her to use the mike. There is some confusion over the handouts which she has left outside the room, but once that is sorted out, and members of the committee have copies of her graphs and charts, she begins her presentation.

She tells the committee that the study has been picked up in the press and will be discussed on TV with Dan Rather later in the week.

"We are doing these intervention projects in Houston," Foorman states, "in a school district of about 38,000 that's about 20 percent Asian, 25 percent African American, 25 percent Hispanic, and 30 percent White."[39]

This might be true, but it gives a false impression. According to one of Foorman's own overheads, there were 375 children who actually participated in the study, 209 first graders and 166 second graders, and in fact 57.9 percent of the children were African American.[40]

"I'm going to talk about spelling," Foorman states. "The children read or spelled words on a word list, and these words are matched for consistency and frequency, and they're words the children hadn't been exposed to in their reading list. And these are very good measures of the single-word decoding that is highly predictive of children's reading success."

I probably don't have to say it again, but there is no scientific evidence to support the contention that single-word decoding is highly predictive of children's reading success. In Foorman's case, as we have already seen, it is a totally useless measure, because she equates reading words on a list matched for consistency and frequency with "reading." As Flurkey points out, reading is not merely "decoding" a list of words.

"In certain types of rationalistic/experimental research," Flurkey writes, "researchers record readers' responses," which he refers to as an output constraint, "to the identification of words in a list," which he calls an input constraint, "and then call the act 'reading.' From a linguistic perspective, this represents a reduction in information. We don't know how readers respond to 'untreated' texts and we don't know what their full range of responses to the word list might be" (p. 410).

Foorman talks about phonological processing. "And an interesting comment is that I teach a course in assessment at the University of Houston, and the people in my course work on my project and we have a number of adults each year that we dismiss," she hesitates, gives a little laugh and rephrases what she has just said, "or we remediate, because they cannot do these tasks. It's very important to appreciate that we as adults focus on meaning and we don't stop and think about the structure of our language."

If adults focus on meaning and don't stop to think about the structure of the language, then why would we expect children to learn any differently?

Foorman talks about the different treatments and the kinds of lessons the children received in her Houston study. Using the overhead projector, she makes a product-endorsing presentation of the Open Court first- and second-grade curriculum as she talks about her direct instruction treatment group.

"Use of Open Court's 1995 Collections for Young Scholars," Foorman has written on the direct instruction transparency. The first thirty lessons are listed as phonemic awareness activities, followed by phonics with forty-two sound/spellings being introduced at the rate of one a day, and then until lesson 30 thereafter sound/spellings are introduced at a slower pace.

"Is *phonemics* the adjective form of *phonics*?" Willard Murray asks.

"No. No," Foorman responds. She smiles and looks surprised at the question.

"What is it the adjective form of?"

"Phonemic?"

"Yes."

"Phoneme," Foorman says, perhaps realizing for the first time how little the members of the Education Committee understand about phonemic awareness or what Foorman is talking about. "Phoneme is the minimal unit of sound in the speech stream."

"Just out of curiosity, what is the adjective form of *phonics*?"

"*Phonic* is the term a lot of people use," she says, still smiling and looking a little bemused. "A phonic rule or sometimes you'll hear phonics rules."

Sounds like a political statement. "Phonics Rules!" In California it *is* a political statement.

Foorman talks about teacher training and then gets to her data. But she does not mention the great teacher variability of which she spoke a month before at the Texas pre-summit meeting.

"Okay. What happened here?" She puts a graph on the overhead projector. "This is a graph of the growth in word reading for the children who never got tutorials," she says. "They were on the wait list. These were children who were in the bottom third of their class. The children who got tutorials were in the bottom 20 percent. But this was the group between 20 percent and 30 percent. The top line is Open Court or direct instruction group, the next line is embedded phonics, then our whole language group that we trained, and then finally the district control unseen whole language."

Do you remember how Foorman described the "control group"— the children in the "unseen" whole language group at the pre-summit meeting in Texas?

"There are two groups of whole language," she said at the pre-summit meeting. "There's the group that we saw and we trained, and then there's a control group from the district that was actually the lowest SES group, which isn't a good control group."

Foorman focuses on the "growth in predicted word reading."

"The top line is the Open Court or direct instruction group," she explains, "the next line is embedded phonics, and next the whole language group that we trained, and finally the district control unseen whole language group."

"This is a significant difference in growth," she says, pointing to the rising diagonal line that she has drawn for Open Court, then pointing at the bottom two lines which do not rise much above the horizontal, "which is the rate of acceleration and the outcome in April," she explains, "between the direct instruction group and the two whole language groups."

She points at the line just below Open Court. "This difference with the embedded phonics is not significant," she says dismissively.

Taken at face value, the fact that Foorman's presentation indicates there is *no* significant difference between the performance of the embedded phonics and the direct instructional group *is* significant. At a time when the California Assembly is insisting that reading instruction must be "research based" and that teachers must be trained to teach explicit, systematic phonics, the lack of significant difference between the two phonics groups is significant.

New laws have been passed based on Foorman's research finding that children who receive explicit phonics instruction "outperform" children who receive embedded phonics instruction, and educators providing inservice workshops for teachers will have to be certified and submit the content of their programs to the California State Board of Education to ensure that the phonics is explicit and systematic.

"I picked away at the sequential issue until he finally admitted that they don't want any teachers to be trained to teach phonics in context," an educator who gives inservice workshops says about a telephone conversation she had with an official of the state government. "We discussed sequential and ad hoc and embedded."

"So what if I want to teach teachers to teach phonics explicitly and systematically in the context of meaningful literature?" she asks the official. "Will I be blacklisted?"

"You won't be certified," the state official tells her, before he abruptly ends the conversation.

"I know I'm going to be blacklisted," she says, "there is no way they are going to certify me."[41]

Foorman changes the graph on the overhead.

"This graph looks almost identical," Foorman comments, "for the children who were, um, who had no intervention, it's the same ordered effects, same findings, these are the children." She has been talking about the wrong graph. The second graph went with the first part of her presentation. "Excuse me, the first graph I showed you were the bottom 20 percent, these are the children between the 21st and 30th percentile, who never got a tutorial because they were not as bad off."

Foorman carries on, one graph is much like the other; intervention, no intervention, what's the difference?

"This is the same result in terms of the direct instruction outperforming the whole language groups," she says. "This is growth in word reading on our word list. The results are identical in growth of phonological awareness, the ability to blend sounds in the speech stream and analyze sounds in the speech stream. The results are also identical with spelling. These growth-curve analyses are very complex analyses. I'm showing you the mean line for the group. I have the growth curves for all 375 children."

The straight-line graphs that Foorman presents to the Education Committee show the scores on her "word reading test," but the relationship between scores on this test and actual reading ability is neither defined nor explained. There are no children represented. The graphs are nothing more than some meaningless statistical average.

Foorman presents these two straight-line graphs, which are labeled "Growth in Predicted Word Reading by Curriculum," as if they represent actual scores on her word reading test, glossing over the term "predicted" in the figure titles. "Predicted" refers to the fact that on each graph, the four straight lines, one for each curriculum group, are some kind of average of the measured improvements on her "word reading test" over the course of a year for all of the children in each group.

In other words, each of the four lines is the "average" result for all the first- and second-grade children in each group—109 for Open Court, 108 for the Embedded Phonics and Whole Language, and 48 for the "Control Group." So this type of presentation collapses all 48 to 109 children in the group into one "average" child, so that individual differences in scores, and the possible reasons for such differences, are simply lost or discarded.[42]

In Figure 14.1, just one of Foorman's four straight lines—the one for the Open Court group—is shown. In addition, the figure shows the mean scores for the first and second graders in the Open Court group. The figure underscores the fact that Foorman's straight line not only fails to reflect the mean scores of either the first- or second-grade children in the Open Court group, but also provides no information about the wide range of test scores actually measured.

Foorman's straight-line research tells us nothing about individual children's scores, and nothing about the range of scores on the test for the first- and second-grade children in each group. In fact, the data presented by Foorman show that the spread of scores around the "average" line is significant. For example, for the April scores, while the "average" scores for the intervention group were 16, 11, 9, and 7 for the Open Court, Whole Language, Embedded Phonics, and Control groups respectively, the *range* of scores for all four groups was at least from 2.5 to 25.[43] This type of important information is simply removed from Foorman's charts, and is not discussed.

It is highly unlikely that the four "average" data points in October, December, February, and April would lie exactly on the four lines for the four curriculum groups, and no explanation is offered for this seem-

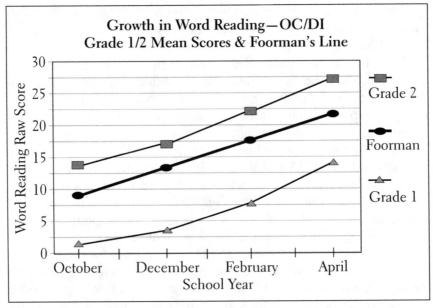

Figure 14.1: Growth in word reading for the Open Court/Direct Instruction group showing mean scores for first and second grades not shown by Foorman's straight-line graph. Foorman's straight line is supposed to predict the growth in word reading for each one of the 109 first- and second-grade children.

ingly artificial result. Foorman changes the transparency.

"The most alarming picture of all of this," she sighs audibly, "is that this is a histogram of the growth estimates, and it is meant to really show you that in the unseen control group of whole language, the embedded phonics group, and the seen whole language group, the bunching of growth estimates around zero is very noticeable."

The histograms are on different scales, which accentuates the differences between the four groups, and the terminology Foorman has chosen to use—"density" and "word reading slope"—makes the "findings" she presents totally incomprehensible.

"The majority of the children are not growing at all in the classroom even with a year of instruction," Foorman says. "The direct instruction growth estimates are almost normally distributed, just what you'd expect."

"A child who comes into the direct instruction group has the opportunity to grow," she says, "that's not the case in these other groups, to the same extent. That's an alarming picture. You'd expect to see improvement, and when you don't see improvement you've got to ask yourself is this a curriculum disability that we are creating?"[44]

It's a good question. Let's return to Nelly, whom you first met when

Honig made his presentation, learning to read using Open Court. Ruiz tells us that Mrs. Dixon is going to work with Nelly and Victor and that she has written words from an Open Court lesson on the board:

I'll	fry	the seal
We'll	fly	the meat
I	sees	me

Ruiz explains that Mrs. Dixon first provides the example "I'll fly." She then asks Nelly and Victor to write sentences. There are a series of interactions between Nelly and Mrs. Dixon.

"Tell me what you're doing," Mrs. Dixon says.

When Nelly doesn't answer, Mrs. Dixon shows her how to start with the left column. Nelly erases her last sentences. She writes, "We'll the seal." Mrs. Dixon asks her to read the first word. Nelly guesses "wagon" and "lamp." Mrs. Dixon tells her to stop guessing.

"Wag"—Nelly begins.

"Get wagon out of your mind," Mrs. Dixon says, snapping her fingers. "Okay?"

"We'll," Nelly reads.

There are other similar interactions, and then Mrs. Dixon notices that the children have not used "the meat" or "fry."

"She asks for a sentence with these words," Ruiz writes, "and Nelly excitedly suggests 'fry the egg' and 'I'll fry eggs.'"

But Mrs. Dixon rejects these sentences.

"I'll fry eggs," Nelly says.

"No," Mrs. Dixon says, "use one of the words that are here."

" 'Kay," Nelly says, and then does not say anything for eight seconds. "Fry the eggs?" She asks, trying again.

"I don't see eggs here," Mrs. Dixon says, and then she is silent for four seconds. "Nelly," she says, snapping her fingers in Nelly's face, "get eggs out of your mind."

Victor goes to speak, but Mrs. Dixon continues.

"Nelly," she says. "I fry, what?"

"Eggs," Nelly says again.

"Nelly."

"The meat," Nelly says.

"The meat," Mrs. Dixon says. "Okay."

At the end of the lesson, Mrs. Dixon tries to explain to the children how learning to read works.

"This is how we can use, in sentences, the words that we've already had, in reading," she says. "In our reading book, okay? So, we usually don't need to look for words that we don't know how to spell. We can just use all the words, the pages we've already had in our reading lessons, and use them to make the sentences 'cause you already know how to spell all those words."[45]

I think about ethical hearings. I try to imagine what it would mean for a child to experience "zero growth" in reading over the period of a whole year. I spend a day going through the biographic profiles of the children whose literacy development we documented when I worked with teachers on the Biographic Literacy Profiles Project. I have file cabinets filled with their systematic observations of the young children in their classrooms. I look for profiles of the most vulnerable children. One of the teachers with whom I worked had a classroom in which there was almost total inclusion, and even the most medically fragile children were welcome members in her classroom. I read her notes of their early literacy behaviors, and there isn't a single child in her room that had "zero growth" and, in fact, I still don't know what "zero growth" means.

But remember Nicola? I think Nicola would have demonstrated "zero growth" if Foorman had got the chance to test her with her artificial "word reading" tests. But it wouldn't mean anything. Her biographic literacy configuration was highly complex, and the progress that she made during her kindergarten year was truly remarkable. Her teacher, Sharron, shared her progress with us throughout the year, and teachers who had never met her came to know her through Sharron's fine-tuned observations and detailed notes. At the end of the year, Nicola had made so much progress that some of the teachers cried.

In all my files, on all those children, in all those years, I do not have a single file on a child whose literacy configuration did not become more complexly structured and whose reading did not become more effective and efficient during the period of an academic year. There are hundreds of thousands of children in our schools who, like Nicola, would not score very well on Foorman's word lists, but who have complex biographic literacy profiles and who are already successfully reading or do become successful readers with the help of knowledgeable teachers who know how to support their learning.

"Dr. Foorman," it's Baldwin, sounding irritated. "Which graph is which? I can't tell from the handout."

"OC, sorry, on the top right stands for Open Court," Foorman tells Baldwin, plugging the publishing company and adding to her ethical difficulties.

"That's Open Court, okay," Baldwin writes it down, as representatives of the SRA/McGraw-Hill, who must be somewhere in the room, rub their hands appreciatively, if only metaphorically.

"CT stands for control," Foorman continues, "which is the district's whole language. This is the standard curriculum. This is a whole language district, this is curriculum as usual, the way they train their teachers. The embedded phonics on the bottom left, EP, embedded phonics, is the phonics in context, and then the bottom right is the whole language group that we trained."

"The main message of this," Foorman concludes after discussing the histogram, "is that there is very little growth in any of these programs except for the direct instruction group in the upper-right-hand corner."

Murray asks what the axis measures.

"Density is a measure of relative frequency along the vertical axis along the right; WR is word reading slope," Foorman says, even though she must know that her explanation is incomprehensible to the committee. "The slope is the estimate of growth rate improvement across the year in—actually it's the number of words on our word list across a year's time."

"I also have these graphs on a metric that is a little bit easier," she says, sounding a little apologetic, "but I don't have them all on one page. This is sort of a default vertical and horizontal axis, but it gives you the main message of this is that there is very little growth in any of these programs except for the direct instruction group in the upper-right-hand corner."

This stuff is complicated. Let's see if we can unravel some of it. First, according to one of her overheads, Foorman and her co-researchers used an "experimental word list" where "words were checked for frequency and consistency and for representativeness of orthographic domain" as one measure of "growth." We don't know and we aren't told if this is an experimental word list developed specifically for Foorman's project. We know nothing about these words except that there were fifty which were presented one at a time on 4 x 6 flash cards to "assess changes in reading skills."[46] There are no norms or other points of reference.

Second, in the histograms of the "Word Reading (WR) Slope" that Foorman presents to the Education Committee of the California Assembly, the vertical scales are labeled "density." But density is not defined, and Foorman is unable to explain what it means to the committee. Moreover, the vertical "density" scales on the four graphs are different —0 to 0.02 for Open Court, 0 to 0.06 for Embedded Phonics and for the "Control," and 0 to 0.04 for Whole Language. For these reasons direct comparisons between the four groups are difficult if not impossible to make.

Third, the histograms using Foorman's "different metric" use a vertical axis labeled "percent of group." The histogram bars for the Open Court group only add up to about 85 percent, whereas the other two histograms both add up to 100 percent. The 85-percent total implies that the scores of approximately sixteen children from the 109 in the Open Court group were not included in the histogram presentation. We don't know and aren't told what the test results were for these sixteen children, so we don't know how they would affect the histogram results for the Open Court group.[47]

Fourth, the two sets of histograms present "WR Slope" and "Words per School Year," which presumably both refer to the same result, namely the slope of the straight line fitted to the word-reading raw score data versus time for each individual child. We don't know and aren't told how well the data for each child are represented by straight lines throughout the year. Since this is highly unlikely, it is impossible to tell how accurately the histograms reflect the actual data for each child in the four study groups.

Fifth, Foorman doesn't say if the histograms include data for both the first and second graders in the study, but the available reports of this study show that the second graders received an accelerated program of first-grade Open Court materials for six months, followed by the second-grade Open Court materials for six months. Although we don't know and aren't told what the relationship is between the "word reading" test and the Open Court training, it's perhaps not surprising that this group scored well on Foorman's "word reading" test but not on the Formal Reading Inventory Test.

"What is the axis?" Murray asks again, as if he is trying to figure out what on earth she is talking about. "What are these measures?" he asks, sounding exasperated.

"These are density," Foorman tries again but ends up just repeating herself. "Density is a measure of relative frequency along the vertical axis. Along the right, WR, is word reading slope. The slope is the estimate of growth rate improvement across the year in, err, actually, it's a number of words on our word list across a year's time."

"Barbara," Lyon interjects, "can I just mention as an NIH project, Open Court, as a methodology, is not being endorsed. Open Court is a methodology that contains those conditions that we were talking about. I want to make that clear."

A year later, in August 1997, Lyon will make a presentation in San Francisco to school administrators.

"Guess what transparency he used," a teacher asks me in a letter. "The one showing that 'phonics alone' was the most effective reading program."

"By the end of the day, several S. F. schools had called the central office asking to change their literacy materials over to Open Court," she writes. "The featured reading program in his presentation."[48]

"Right," Foorman responds to Lyon at the hearing. "In fact next year we hope to look at a number of different direct instruction programs," she says, but then she continues her unabashed advertisement for Open Court.

"Let me mention one other thing that follows up on Dr. Lyon's point," she says to the Education Committee. "We took the growth in phonological progress across the year, and the growth in word reading that I showed you a minute ago with this graph, and we put the phonological growth into this growth in word reading as a covariate, because they are both measured four times across the year, at the same time point."

"And it explains the treatment effect, suggesting that the reason that this particular direct instruction program is effective is that it encourages growth in phonological awareness," Foorman states, as if on-camera to plug Coke but not Pepsi.

"That's enormously important," she says, "another direct instruction program may not have that same component part. And that needs to be studied. In fact I would suggest that what we need to do is look at curriculum in terms of the components that research shows help children learn to read. And there also needs to be objective evaluation of these curricula to see if indeed children are learning to read."

An excellent idea which, as Foorman reveals with the next transparency, is highly problematic for her Open Court treatment group.

"Finally," Foorman changes the transparency to an overhead that is not in the package of handouts which she has given the committee, "the standardized achievement results at the end of the year. The Woodcock-Johnson, the Basic Reading is a decoding measure. The Broad Reading is a comprehension measure, but the passages are really just sentences, so we also include the Formal Reading Inventory, which is a text measure."[49]

Foorman points at the Formal Reading Inventory which is at the bottom of the transparency. "You'll see on the text measure that they're all almost at floor." She wants to get to the word reading scores and so she speaks dismissively, "although even here the direct instruction group is doing better than the whole language group, but it is not significant because it interacts with whether they get the tutorial. You need to be an automatized decoder—"

Wait! Let's take a look at the scores on the Formal Reading Inventory (Figure 14.2):

Approximate Percentile Rankings of Mean Scores on the FRI				
	OC/DI	EP	WL "seen"	SC "unseen"
No Tutorial	17%	22%	6%	10%
Tutorial	10%	11%	10%	13%

Figure 14.2

How would you interpret these scores? On the Formal Reading Inventory, for the children who received no tutorials, the embedded phonics group received the highest ranking of mean scores. The children in the "seen" whole language group that Foorman and her colleagues trained did the poorest, but since Foorman herself admitted she knows nothing about whole language, we can only imagine the kind of instruction these children received.

Whatever misgivings we might have about the "seen" whole language group are compounded when we see that the "unseen" children, the very poorest children in the district who received no special materials and whose whole language teachers received no special training or support throughout the year, actually had higher scores whether or not they had tutorials than the Foorman trained "seen" whole language children.

But what is particularly remarkable is that the children in the "unseen" whole language group, the lowest of the lowest socioeconomic children who were in the bottom twentieth percentile and who received Title 1 tutorials, actually scored higher on the Formal Reading Inventory than the children in Foorman's Open Court group who had tutorials. Foorman herself at the Texas pre-summit stated that implementing the Open Court curriculum cost $100,000, but in the final analysis, at the end of the year, the children in her study who received Open Court instruction in explicit systematic phonics were not reading connected text any better than the poorest of the poor children in the district, the "unseen" children who received no extra help, like the invisible children in Kozol's books.

"You need to be an automatized decoder before you can read long passages of texts," Foorman states, dismissing the most significant finding of her study, "so this is a common finding with our very early readers."

I telephone a teacher who worked with me on the Biographic Literacy Profiles Project. I have called her several times as I have been writing *Spin Doctors*, so she is prepared for unexpected and often incomprehensible questions.

"How many children in your school can't read connected texts at the end of first grade?" I ask.

She is silent and I wait.

"What do you mean?" she asks. "What else would they be reading?"

"Words on lists," I say. "Decoding? Blending?"

She laughs, dismissing my suggestion, and says she is trying to think of any children in her school in the last few years who were not reading books at the end of their first-grade year. She names one child with whom we both worked in 1991 and 1992 who had considerable difficulty reading connected text at the end of first grade. Then we talk for a while about the books that the young children in her school are reading, and she tells me that while they use many predictable books, they are trying to find more books that reflect the speech patterns of young children.

I telephone a teacher in California, with whom I have spoken a few times on the telephone as I have collected documentation for this book, and I ask her the same question.

"How many children in your school can't read connected texts at the end of first grade?"

"What kind of texts?" she asks, sounding puzzled.

"Stories," I say, "little books."

"They all are," she says, still sounding unsure of the question.

I explain why I am asking.

"The way we teach everybody in kindergarten and first grade has predictable books," she says. "By the end of first grade they can all read the simple stories in predictable books. Some of the books are really simple, but there isn't anybody who isn't reading connected text." She is aware of the research that is being foisted on teachers in California, and her voice rises. "How can you learn to read without reading connected text?" she asks, and then she tells me it is becoming more difficult to buy predictable books because they can no longer be bought with state funds. "It's become very difficult to get the books we need," she says. "They've been replaced by those dumb decodable books."

When I hang up the telephone, I rewind the videotape and play again Foorman's explanation of the low scores on the Formal Reading Inventory.

"You need to be an automatized decoder before you can read long passages of texts," Foorman says, "so this is a common finding with our very early readers."

What she has said is anathema to me. I think about Patrick, who was supposed to be learning-disabled. Let me share with you what I wrote in

Learning Denied about the books he read at the end of his first-grade year.

"In July 1987, Patrick read *Ask Mr. Bear* by Marjorie Flack. When he finished the book, he was smiling. He asked me to drive him home to tell his mother how well he had read the book.

"That summer we also read *Funnybones* by Janet and Allan Ahlberg, *Little Bear* by Else Holmelund Minarik, and *The Little Red Hen* retold by Margot Zemach. Patrick found a copy of *Old Mother West Wind*, by Thornton W. Burgess, in my office. He struggled to read the story and then asked if he could take the book home. My husband, David, recorded some of the stories, and Patrick read a few of the tales.

"On one occasion, we visited the town library, and Patrick chose ten books that he would like to read. One of them was *Emmett's Pig* by Mary Stolz. The next time Patrick visited my home, he brought *Emmett's Pig* with him. He sat at the table and talked about the book.

"You read all that yourself?"

"Yes."

"To yourself, or to your mom and dad?"

"To myself."

"That's terrific. So you've been doing some silent reading. Put the book on the table so I can see it too, and you can pull your chair up a bit. So this book is—what's it called? *Emmett's Pig*? Okay. Where are you going to start? Do you want to tell me the story so far?"

Patrick turned back to the beginning of the book. "I want to read it. Okay. I want to read this book until I can read it so well that" he pauses, "that I can read it so well that I can read it any time that I want."

"I think that's terrific."

Patrick turned the pages. "I read it until there and I said, 'Should I keep going or not?'and I said, 'Okay, I'll go.' But I read it until there and then started to read here."

Patrick read. After a few pages he stopped. "Now this is a real tough page," he said.

"That's a lot of words, Patrick!"

"I want to read it."

"You can do it."

"I can read until here," he said, turning the pages. "I'm going to read this whole book!" (p. 42).

I can imagine that some of you might think that Patrick's reading has no relevance to the presentation that Foorman is making, but it is highly relevant. Patrick was reading. He enjoyed books. The summer at the end of his disastrous first-grade year was a celebration. But when he went back to school in the fall at the beginning of his second-grade year, he was referred by his teacher. Let's pick up what happened as it appears in *Learning Denied*.

"On September 25, 1987, the referral was written. The reason for the referral was given as follows:

'Lack of phonetic attack skills:

—can not sound out the appropriate letter sounds and blend together to form a word.

Patrick therefore can not read ["phonetically" is inserted in the text] which further leads [*sic*] that he cannot comprehend what he is reading. Patrick can comprehend what is read to him.

Patrick is placed in the lowest reading group however his group is now up to a new level. Patrick is not able to keep up in this new level.'"

Patrick did indeed have difficulty reading "phonetically." He had received intensive instruction in DISTAR in first grade, and his reading had become slow and labored and extremely effortful. It was only when he moderated his overreliance on decoding and expanded his repertoire of reading strategies to include all of the cueing systems available to him that he was able to learn to read.

"On the decoding measure," Foorman tells the committee, "the direct instruction children are at the 44th percentile; that's close to national average. These children started the year all of them at the same low level. There were no differences in their reading level at the beginning of the year, importantly. And they were also at the rock-bottom lowest level of reading at the beginning of the year. So the 44th percentile on basic and 46th percentile on broad reading are impressive gains."

Once again Foorman equates decoding words on the Woodcock-Johnson with reading. In fact the scores are arcane and meaningless, but not the way Foorman presents them to the committee.

"To get children up to close to national average with a program is very exciting news," she says, "and it suggests to me that prevention in first grade is what we ought to be about." Then she adds, "We also have some evidence that we can create a curricular disability by poor instruction and we need to do something about that."

Foorman has just made a product endorsement that is scientifically indefensible and ethically reprehensible. She has stated categorically that she knows nothing about whole language, and she makes it clear that she hasn't a clue about other progressive pedagogies, including the emancipatory pedagogy which evolved from the work the teachers did who participated with me in the Biographic Literacy Profiles Project.[50] For Foorman to suggest that teachers who do not endorse commercially packaged reductionist approaches to beginning reading like Open Court create a "curricular disability" by poor instruction is an unwarranted and insupportable indictment of thousands of teachers who are highly trained, dedicated professionals who care deeply about the children they teach. Foorman has no knowledge of either their work or their success in teaching children to read. Parenthetically, it would seem that neither does the Education Committee of the California State Assembly.

To accept Foorman's statement we would have to ignore the high achievement of many schools in the United States that have a clearly articulated holistic philosophy, and whose teachers base instruction on their systematic observations of the children that they teach, and not on generic, scripted, cookbook lesson plans which do not take into account the ways in which reading and writing are situated socially, culturally, economically, and politically in the lives of the young children who are learning to read.

Let me give you an example.

The principal in one of the schools in the Biographic Literacy Profiles Project has been following the progress of his students for over seventeen years. Quietly, without national attention, without commercial programs, and without explicit synthetic instruction in phonics or phonemic awareness, the teachers and children have produced results which put into perspective the findings of the Foorman studies. Like many schools in the United States, in the school in which the principal has been monitoring the progress of his children, the pedagogy is socially and culturally responsive, children's everyday lives are not separated from the reading and writing activities in which they participate, they are not forced to learn unnecessary abstractions, and the relationships between teachers and children are warm and respectful.

When the principal began monitoring the progress of his students, he focused on tracking how many students who attended his elementary school went on to complete four years in high school. Between 1985 and 1990, 98 percent of his students who attended six different regional high schools graduated with their high school diplomas, and only 2 percent of his students dropped out of school. What is more remarkable is that for the students who attended his school for five years or more, there were no dropouts, and 100 percent of the students graduated from high school.

At the beginning of the 1990s, as pressure increased both nationally and locally to move away from more holistic pedagogies to reductionist skill and drill instructional approaches, the principal felt that it was necessary to report on the academic successes of his students. In the 1993–94 school year, his school spent $3,824 per pupil, and financially they were at the bottom of the school state rankings. 96 percent of the schools in the state had more money to spend on each pupil than he had to spend on the pupils in his school. But despite this lack of resources and without the use of any commercial reading programs or skill and drill exercises in phonics or phonemic awareness, his school performed well above the state average on the third-grade standardized tests in language arts and mathematics (see Figure 14.3).[51]

In addition, in 1995, 59 percent of his school's graduates who were then freshmen in high school were on the honor roll, as compared with only 44 percent of freshmen students who came from the surrounding elementary schools (see Figure 14.4).

Finally, in a comparison of the ranking of high school seniors at five of the six high schools, students who had attended his school outperformed students who were high school seniors and who had attended the surrounding elementary schools (see Figure 14.5).

The principal and the teachers at the school have developed a clearly articulated school philosophy and curriculum. As the documentation that Foorman presents to the California Committee focuses on spelling, and as many policymakers have difficulty conceptualizing a school curriculum without commercial programs, let me share with you the Word Study Guide from the school to which I have been referring. First the philosophy:

1. Learning to spell is important because it enables writers to communicate with clarity and effectiveness so that readers may reconstruct the meaning in a written message.
2. Learning to spell is a developmental process with predictable stages through which children progress, moving from simple to more complex understandings of written language.
3. Learning to spell involves the effective use of multiple strategies.
4. Learning to spell is a multi-sensory process that involves visual, auditory, and kinesthetic/tactile mechanisms that individuals employ when they see, hear, and write language.
5. Learning to spell is a process of understanding increasingly more complex concepts of pattern, structure, and meaning, and goes beyond simple rote memorization.
6. Learning to spell is a holistic, not a linear or decontextualized process.
7. Learning to spell should focus on the meaning relations of words rather than merely on their sounds in speech.
8. Learning to spell cannot be separated from either reading or writing and should not be taught in isolation from these processes.

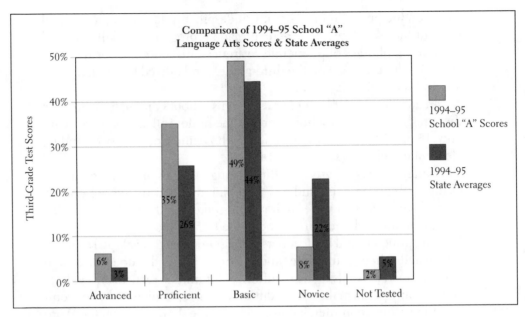

Figure 14.3

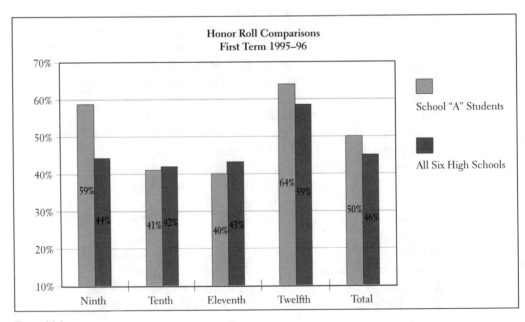

Figure 14.4

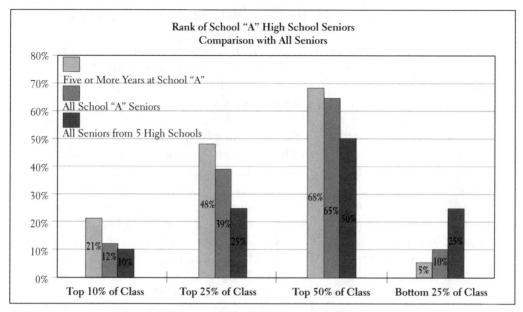

Figure 14.5

The Objectives of the Word Study Guide are as follows:

1. To help the faculty, students, and parents to understand the natural stages of developmental spelling.
2. To create in students an awareness of the importance of spelling as a component of effective written communication.
3. To emphasize the connections between writing and spelling.
4. To help students learn to spell in a variety of ways and to use different strategies so that they can approach new words with confidence.
5. To encourage students to develop a "spelling conscience"—an awareness of misspelled words and a sense of responsibility for their own spelling.
6. To develop in students a sense of the regularities and irregularities of English spelling.
7. To present opportunities for students to acquire a spelling vocabulary of high-frequency and content-related words.
8. To promote the study of words and word relationships.
9. To serve as a resource for activities and techniques that help meet the spelling needs of individual students.

The fetish for explicit systematic phonics seems somewhat absurd when it is compared with the philosophy, goals, and instructional practices of a principal and teachers whose holistic pedagogy creates opportunities for every child to be successful in school.

Kerry Mazzoni, a member of the Education Committee, asks Foorman about the cost of the direct instruction program which she claims is so successful. Foorman talks about basal reading programs and then focuses on a Mary Kay presentation of what is included in Open Court.

"You get materials that practice the principles that are being taught," she tells Mazzoni. "In the case of this program they also have some cards that you can put around the room that actually have the spelling sounds on them."

"Reading is one area in the curriculum where education meets politics and money," Miles Myers, former Executive Director of NCTE, is quoted as saying in an article by Joan Montgomery Halford, which appeared in an *Infobrief* from ASCD.[52] "The publishers have everything in the world riding on this," Myers states. "There's lots of money here."

"Large states, including California and Texas, drive the reading textbook market in the United States and beyond," Halford writes as if in a conversation with Myers. "And the nature of the education field is such that many leading education researchers have some connection, either through endorsement or authorship, to commercial materials."

"The FDA makes certain its pharmaceutical review teams don't have commercial interests in the drugs being reviewed," Myers says. "This doesn't happen in the textbook area. People aren't even required to state conflict of interest" (p. 7).

"What about staff development?" Mazzoni asks Foorman.

"Well, staff development is going to be expensive up front," Foorman says. "Teachers need to be trained in the context of materials, I feel."

"I do workshops with teachers in the summer, and you've got to go back in with them in the fall because they've forgotten it," Foorman explains, giving her "dumbed-down" version of classroom teachers. "And it needs to be in the context of what I am going to do tomorrow for my lesson. So it has to be staff development and not just a quick inservice training, so it has to be thought about as information in the summer and then monitoring a teacher in the classroom and following her through enough so that she is on her own."

At this point in the hearing there is a shift away from the subaltern intellectuals to the corps of engineers. The ground work is done. An explanation of the right-wing coup by Honig, a presentation of "scientific" deception by Lyon, and an official endorsement of a lucrative commercial enterprise by Foorman.

"You have to encode," Honig states, "you have to store it in your mind with the letters and the letter patterns, and the sounds," in a political reinvention of how young children learn to read. "If you try to look at the letters without the sounds, without phonology it doesn't work, you can never find it."

"Lousy readers," Lyon tells the committee as he fabricates the evidence, "show us a different neurophysiological signature in the brain and it is highly replicable."

"A child who comes into the direct instruction group has the opportunity to grow," Foorman states, in support of Open Court, "that's not the case in these other groups, to the same extent. That's an alarming picture. You'd expect to see improvement, and when you don't see improvement, you've got to ask yourself is this a curriculum disability that we are creating."

Without any critical questioning of the "expert witnesses," without listening to any counterarguments or disputation, without allowing any presentation of opposing evidence or contrasting viewpoints, without allowing for any rebuttal, willfully ignoring or in willful ignorance of the last thirty years of scientific documentation on how young children learn to read, the Education Committee of the California Assembly moves the hearing to the implementation of their master plan by the chief tacticians in California's hegemonic corps of engineers.

The key words: systematic, explicit phonics instruction, phonemic awareness, sound-symbol relationships, and decoding

"I'm Bill Furry with the Office of Child Development and Education," Furry states without waiting for an introduction from Baldwin. Furry, who is listed as being from the "Governor's Office," creates a context for his testimony by making clear to the committee that Governor Wilson is a powerful player in the labyrinth. "Let me just say as a preface, to establish the premises here, that the governor's proposal is research based and it's based on the research conducted and reported by Reid Lyon and Marilyn Adams and Barbara Foorman and many others."

"The Governor's proposal addresses such things as what needs to be included in staff development for practicing teachers, what school board members should be aware of, what teacher candidates should know and what teacher-training institutions should include in their credential programs," Furry tells the committee. "So we have proposals in all of these areas and in each of our proposals there is a key set of language, and these are the key words that are in these proposals. And the key words are: Systematic, Explicit Phonics Instruction; Phonemic Awareness; Sound-Symbol Relationships; Decoding; Word Attack Skills; Spelling Instruction; Diagnosis of Reading Deficiencies; Research on How Children Learn to Read; Research on How Proficient Readers Read; Relationships between Reading, Writing, and Spelling; Planning and Delivery of Appropriate Reading Instruction Based on Assessment and Evaluation; and Pupil Independent Reading of Good Books and Its Relationship to Improved Reading Performance."

Furry talks about staff development and what teacher candidates need to know. Then he moves on to what teacher-training institutions need to include. The strategic plan is carefully thought out and reflects Honig's overview.

"Things we have not invested in are additional library books, use of technology, reduction of class size, the hiring of tutors and so forth and so on," Furry informs the committee, dismissing some of the major inequities and social injustices in California schools.[53]

"The cornerstone of this whole proposal is the 146 million dollars to provide every pupil in K–3 with a full set of core reading materials; we think this costs eighty dollars per pupil," Furry states. "The reading materials drive the curriculum in the classroom. They drive what teachers do. They get into the classroom on Monday morning the first day of the school year, they open the book, and that's where they start from."

One of the cornerstones of the hegemonic project is the hundreds of millions of dollars state-approved publishers stand to gain from the biggest textbook scam of this century. Think about this: $146 million in California; a similar amount in Texas, plus the rest of the states, and you have the biggest textbook deal of the century.

No publisher who pays any attention at all, and they all pay attention, could have developed materials for this adoption and not been aware that there needed to be explicit, systematic phonics

Jerry Treadway is the next speaker. Treadway teaches at San Diego State University, and because he often presents with Marilyn Adams, some teachers with whom I have spoken also associate him with Open Court. Treadway says he became a member of the curriculum commission early in 1993. He talks of the blue-ribbon panel from the curriculum commission that looked at reading.

"Basically we have three roles," Treadway tells the committee. "The first is to establish frameworks, and remember we are an advisory group to the State Board so everything that we do goes to the State Board for final adoption, so we develop and we recommend to the State Board."

"Basically what we do is to develop frameworks," he explains, "and from those we develop what we call evaluation criteria. That evaluation criteria goes two places. First it goes to the publishers, and the publishers use that, and that's the basis on which they develop materials. And it also goes to the evaluators. It is the evaluation criteria by which the publishers' materials are later judged."

"There is a thirty-month gap between the time that the evaluation criteria is developed and the time of the adoption, that gives the publishers time to develop materials." Treadway makes clear the tremendous power of the blue-ribbon panel. Hundreds of millions of dollars in textbook sales depend on the recommendations of the panel. The panel quite literally has the power to change how children are taught to read, not only in California but in every state where basals are purchased and used.

"In 1993 we developed new evaluation criteria, and based on the blue-ribbon panel and some other things we changed the criteria to put in more explicit systematic phonics," he tells the committee. "We talked about skills in context and explicit, systematic phonics. And we also extended the framework, had said phonics should be taught in K–2, but we have so many students entering into the system after grade 2, we asked that the publishers, for this adoption, develop phonic and direct skills instruction through grade 8."

We are told reading instruction must be research based. Where is the research to support phonics instruction through grade 8?

"That went to the publishers, then the Superintendent of Public Instruction, Delaine Eastin, and the Board sent a letter to the publishers May 11, 1995, that reinforced phonics as being very important, and then the Reading Task Force in the summer of 1995 also reinforced that that would happen."

This is like ETS giving the test questions and the criteria for scoring the test to candidates and then having them take the test.

"No publisher who pays any attention at all, and they all pay attention," Treadway states, "could have developed materials for this adoption and not been aware that there needed to be explicit, systematic phonics. And as we peruse the programs, we think that there will be many programs like that for school districts."

Treadway seems pleased with the publishers' texts, but he sounds concerned that there might not be enough decodable texts and says that publishers have included "greater and lesser amounts in terms of what we call decodeable texts."

"We'll just have to see how that shakes out," he says. "Basically we think the materials that will be going to the schools will be a vast improvement over what was there."

Treadway talks about developing the new framework and making sure it has a solid research base. "When this group comes to write this project or this framework, they will not have the freedom that most framework committees have," Treadway states, exposing the underbelly of the hegemonic project. "They will be constrained by the language of the Task Force report, and they will be constrained by the language of the Advisory, and they will be constrained by the ABC laws." He adds, "So this will be a different type of framework than we have had in the past."

The hegemonic project is "ruthless in its policing duties," "unreceptive to interrogation," "sanctioned to preserve ignorance and preserve privilege," and "limits knowledge" "as it moves relentlessly towards the bottom line and the bottomed-out mind."[54]

I would recommend that you also adopt legislation that will require the schools of education teach explicit phonics

Jerry Hume, who is a member of the California State Board of Education, also speaks. "The Advisory that comes out will be a good advisory," Hume states. "It will reflect the Department, the CTC, the Reading Task Force, and very gratefully experts in the field. We have Doug Carnine here in the audience; we have Jerry Treadway, John Shefelbine, Marilyn Adams. We are most fortunate to be able to have them developing and making sure that the advisory is right and signing off on the advisory that it is right, so I feel very fortunate there."

Hume talks about the ABC bills and says it "helped us a lot."

"I would recommend that you also adopt legislation which will require the schools of education teach explicit phonics because that is not happening right now." Hume tells the committee, "There is nothing like a unanimous bill by the legislature signed by the governor to cause something to happen."

"We've got legislation on that," Baldwin tells Hume.

"Would the Department of Education oppose legislation to do what this man is suggesting, to require the teaching of explicit direct phonics?" Howard Kaloogian, another member of the Education Committee, asks Ruth McKenna, Chief Deputy Superintendent for the Department of Education, who is at the hearing to represent Delaine Eastin, the noticeably absent California Superintendent of Schools.

"You already have that legislation in the ABC bills," McKenna tells Kaloogian.

"And do you oppose that?" Kaloogian asks McKenna, making sure the troops are lined up.

"No," McKenna is quick. "We have never opposed the ABC bills."

"No," Hume interjects, "I was talking about in the schools of education, that's where I want it to be taught."

"Schools of education?" Brooks Firestone says, as if it is a question.

"Schools of education," Hume reiterates.

"Teaching colleges," Baldwin clarifies, sounding like the White Rabbit who is late.

"Teaching colleges, in other words," Firestone states, as if he had just thought of it himself, "and the Department wouldn't oppose that either?"

"No. We are working closely with the CTC and the Governor's office," McKenna responds. "You'll notice in the Reading Task Force report it does recommend a significant change in teacher preparation."[55]

If you don't figure out a way to institutionalize the findings of experimental research, what's being built today will be wiped out in five to seven years

After almost eight hours of testimony to the Education Committee, and after the labyrinthians have constructed every path so it is connected to every other path, Carnine testifies. But Carnine makes it clear that the Minotaur is real and that the labyrinth has no center, no periphery, no exit, that it can never be structured definitively, and that it is potentially infinite.

"I'm Douglas Carnine. I appreciate the opportunity to be able to comment." Carnine focuses his attention on the Committee. "The sense we're getting today is that there has been a mistake and that it's an anomaly and everything is in line to fix it up." He pauses, "I wish it were true."

"The research on beginning reading in the late eighties indicated that the language arts framework would create many reading failures," Carnine states. "I testified to that to the state board in the late 1980s, and I am going to make a new prediction today."

He leans back in his chair and looks at the Education Committee, and then he comes forward and speaks into the microphone.

"If you don't figure out a way to institutionalize the findings of experimental research, what's being built today will be wiped out in five to seven years, " Carnine stares intently at the Education Committee. "The battle between phonics and whole language has not happened once, and it's not new. It's been going back and forth for years and years and years, and unless there is some way that a bipartisan effort can really find out what the research says, because we are hearing different versions of research from nearly every presenter, you are going to have a very difficult time in seven or eight years, when another group comes back, when phonics is out of fashion, and tells you, 'we have a new answer and the research supports it.'"

"Education does not use research knowledge," Carnine moves back and forth in his chair, and he repeats what he said at the pre-summit meeting of Governor Bush's Texas Business Council. "In fact the courts have ruled that education is not a profession because teachers don't know anything. Teachers cannot be sued for malpractice because they don't know anything."

Carnine talks about California's test scores and then tells phonics stories. He sighs and clasps his hands in front of him and tells the committee about "the second-grade girl who asked to be labeled mentally retarded so she could get into a special ed. room that would teach her to read. The principals who went around and took all the phonics materials and burned them to make sure they would never be used again. The principal who begged and screamed at a teacher because she refused to pretend to use whole language when the superintendent was going to visit."

"In summary," Carnine says, without presenting any research and as if he is near the end of his testimony, "there are many important research studies, what I've said so far, about beginning reading, including a billion-dollar Follow Through Study that was conducted almost twenty years ago.

"Now, I hope this will be seen as a bipartisan issue. The Governor's plan is trying to put money into dealing with this. You're hearing a lot of ideas and things that may be done. I hope that people will recognize that this is a critical bipartisan issue and whatever is needed to bring things to bear so that it will work will be done," his voice deepens, "because I am telling you, the cycles in reading, it's like the curse of the locusts. They come and go every seven years. I'm not kidding. I wish I were."

"I'm going to give you one example of the implications for this," Carnine continues. "If you look at teacher education, you've got to have a knowledge base, that's the core of teacher education, that's the core of professional development, that is the core of the instructional materials that you adopt in the state of California. You're on the verge of an adoption right now. My prediction is that you are going to exclude some of the most effective programs that are available. That's my prediction."[56]

"If you do not establish a knowledge base you can trust," Carnine continues, "and act from that, and institutionalize policy based on that, we will continue in the pendulum swings that we have experienced. You will not be here, you will all be term-limited out, and I won't be here because I'm sure if it happens again in California, I won't set foot in the state. But there is a great likelihood that this will all be revisited on the children of California and their families."

"So I'm urging you that while you're hearing good words about what's happening, I think it was well stated by the previous person who said 'The motto is that phonics is in.'" Carnine speaks directly into the microphone. "'The motto.'"

"If you can't turn this into action where teachers learn how to teach, where higher ed. people really learn how to teach in ways in which students are going to benefit. If you deal on the level of rhetoric you will get results accordingly."

"I really hope that you can set the standard for the country." Again Carnine looks intently at the committee, "Because if you don't have knowledge to make decisions, what's left other than fads?"

At the back of the room, the crinolines clap.

"I see you have a fan club here," Baldwin says to Carnine.

Firestone asks him about Reading Recovery.

Carnine answers negatively and then he seizes the opportunity.

"This is why you need somebody you can trust to put this together," he says, "because my definition of educational research is anything that's ever been said or heard. Everybody in education who has a new idea will tell you it's research based. You can count on it."

The irony that this is exactly what Honig, Lyon, Foorman, and others have just done apparently escapes Carnine.

"And you have to find somebody you can trust." He talks about an advisory of doctors and engineers and then again states that the legislature needs "somebody they can trust."

"It doesn't have to be a lot of money, but if you don't have this how do you know?" Carnine says, as if interviewing for the job.

Murray asks about the research on whole language and phonics.

"The research that I have looked at is very consistent, and has been given in great detail by Bill Honig, and Barbara Foorman, and Reid Lyon, that what they have portrayed is my understanding of what the research shows." Carnine tells Murray and then he adds, "Completely."

All that has been presented is a couple of charts from Foorman's preliminary study and Honig and Lyon talking in generalities and stating that the research replicates nicely.

"This is research just recently," Murray states. "What did it say in the past? Where did we get this whole language from?"

"I think," Carnine replies, "there is a strong element in education and there has been for a long time that education should be fun and easy and natural."

"For teachers or for students?" Murray asks.

"Both," Carnine says. "There's been a lot of additional research in the last five years. Barbara's research just in the last year is extremely important. But it points in the same direction as research that existed ten, fifteen years ago. We're just learning more."

"So why did they push ahead with it?" Murray continues with his questions.

"Because people who make policy decisions are deceived," Carnine tells Murray. "Because people come in and say they have a new theory and it's research based, and people like yourselves assume that what they are saying is true, and you believe them and you give money and judicial or legislative sanction to it." Again he leans forward, "That's why. But ultimately, you're responsible. It's your responsibility to get trustworthy information."

"Are there certain kids with either learning disabilities or reading disabilities who work best with contextual approach in learning to read than kids with phonics," Tom Woods, who is also on the committee, asks, "or is phonics the way to teach in a ubiquitous fashion?"

"In my opinion," Carnine does not hesitate, "it's the way to teach in an ubiquitous fashion."

There is some discussion about the issue and then Carnine adds his weight to Foorman's attack on teachers who don't buy into their ubiquitous, explicit, systematic phonics approach to beginning to read.

"Barbara Foorman's data showed earlier there are so many students who are curriculum disabled," Carnine states. "And what that means is we teach them so poorly that we turn them into illiterates, that until we, on a wide scale, teach students properly, we won't know if there is a very, very tiny fraction that some other approach might work. We have such a huge problem created by professional failure that we can't even begin to answer your question, which is a legitimate one.

"There is so much failure that we create in schools, we can't get to the point of those individuals who have truly unique needs and may need to be treated in different ways."

I talk with Brian Husby, who trained in Oregon to teach DISTAR.[57]

"It became very clear to me in the work that I have done," Husby says, "and certainly in the direct instruction schools I taught in that the model of power is that I have it, you don't. I'll decide when you have it and you will do exactly what I say, *exactly* what I say."

"To the letter," I interject.

"To the letter," Husby replies with a smile. "Literally."

"We had to memorize scripts and we had to do check-outs before we went in to teach," Husby says, talking about his experience many years ago of teaching DISTAR. "The summer school was for kids who weren't reading for whatever reason, who weren't reading at grade level, whatever that meant. And that was determined based on the Woodcock-Johnson. That was it. That was the test of choice." He raises his eyebrows and pulls a face. "Then folks were in my class taking data every day, and I would have to verify how I followed the script. If I deviated from the script then I had to go back and rehearse and demonstrate competence."

"I remember being at a presentation with Ziggy [Engelmann] one time and him saying that he could teach an ape to teach," again Husby smiles. "Teaching was a series of stimulus-response bonds, and you didn't leave it to chance. It was absolutely Skinnerian."

"Why were your scripts checked?" I ask.

"I was being checked because the theory is if you have a consistent stimulus, then you're going to get a consistent response," Husby explains. "And so if I was consistent in this, then the students would have a high rate of success in their response. If I was inconsistent, it's based on behavioral theory, you manipulate the antecedent, well you go back, fix the script, and then you'll get the response."

"I was supposed to simultaneously take data on the number of correct responses that kids made versus the kind of errors they made and then do an error analysis and then do fix-ups." Husby laughs, reminding me what happened that morning when he modeled a DISTAR stimulus-response sequence for some students. "You know this morning when one of the students said, 'Well my students wouldn't sit still'? I just wanted to laugh. You had no choice. You had *no* choice. And I remember this, you know it is kind of like working in an institution twenty years ago, and you say 'I was really sorry that I did that electric shock therapy,' and this is exactly the same kind of thing." Husby shakes his head. "Some of my kids were truly hyperactive, not like the in-vogue ADHD kids now, but they really couldn't sit still. And a kid was allowed four movements and when he had passed four movements it was 'Stand up!' 'Sit down!' 'Look at me!' 'Touch your nose!' 'This is letter A!' 'What's this?' 'A.' I mean it was like this." He bangs his hand on the table four times. "It was based on really sound behavioral theory. Any time a child went off task you did a change-up, *now*. You moved from a motor skill to an auditory skill, visual skill, verbal skill."

"I kept saying 'when will kids play?' 'Kids don't play at school.' 'But isn't play child's work?' 'No. Kids need to learn that this is about stimulus control.'" He looks serious. "I kept thinking to myself, there is a whole child here, there is so much more to learning."

I say to Husby that it is difficult for me to figure out Carnine's perspective.

"From Doug's perspective," he says, "I would bet from a behaviorist's perspective, when I look through those glasses and those lenses, what he's saying makes absolute sense. Absolute sense. Of course, you wouldn't recognize something that wasn't replicable. You would have to have the right number, if you come from that core behaviorist perspective."

"Doug," it's Hume of the State School Board, "would it be possible for you to give a brief synopsis of Project Follow Through and direct instruction and the implications of that for California at this time?"

"The Follow Through Study in 1990 dollars cost about a billion dollars," Carnine states, as he did in Texas at the pre-summit meeting, "and it involved 167 school districts across the United States. And one of the things it did that was critical was the data was collected by independent outside agencies and analyzed by independent outside agencies. What you'll see in most of the reports about educational achievement from different approaches today is that the advocates collect the data so you have a bias problem."

Again it is ironic that it escapes Carnine that this is exactly what Honig, Lyon, and Foorman have just done.

"At that time, which was almost twenty years ago, it compared a whole language approach," Carnine states categorically, despite the fact that whole language was *not* one of the pedagogical approaches in the study, "It compared all the approaches that have been promulgated and spread like wildfire throughout California and the United States."

"And twenty years ago it found out that with disadvantaged students these programs were a total failure."

What Carnine tells the committee is, in fact, not true.

"Not only were they a total failure in academics, you found that students in those programs had a significantly lower self-esteem because they had been mis-educated."

Not true. Carnine is in the labyrinth, in a spin.

"You found that the parents of students in a direct instruction program, you go out and do parents' interviews, these parents felt that their kids were getting a good education, not the parents in these other programs, so everywhere you turn academics, self-esteem, parental perception, it was the same story."

Not true again. Get the documentation. Check it out. Do lies count as spin doctoring?

Let's begin by giving credit. W. Ray Rhine in *Making Schools More Effective: New Directions from Follow Through* states, "If the intent of Follow Through had been to improve children's achievement test scores on the Metropolitan Achievement Test, the results of the national longitudinal evaluation would have established unequivocally that the Direct Instruction Model and Behavior Analysis Model were the 'winners'" (p. 304).[58]

Rhine then goes on to state that increasing test scores on the MAT was not a priority for many of the program sponsors participating in Project Follow Through, and that in fact there were "many winners." This is especially important because the purpose of Project Follow Through was, as Rhine states, "to identify educational approaches that 'work best' with low-income children and their families" (p. 304).

In *Making Schools More Effective*, Rhine presents five of the winning pedagogical models, and I am going to focus on two of them here to underscore the problems with Carnine's testimony to the California Education Committee, and to also shed light on some of the problems inherent in direct instruction approaches to early reading instruction.

The first is the Bank Street Model, which builds on the work of Lucy Sprague Mitchell, and which is a developmental-interactional approach which Elizabeth Gilkeson, Lorraine Smithberg, and Garda Bowman together with Rhine define in terms of goals for children.[59]

"The primary goal for children is to help them develop into adults who can maintain and enhance a free, democratic society," the authors write. "Thus, it is essential in the early years of schooling to establish the foundations that enable individuals to become *confident, inventive, responsive,* and *productive* human beings who can both adapt to and shape their society in meaningful ways. Such individuals possess a mastery of academic skills, but even more importantly, they are competent in the following broad intellectual, affective, social, and physical areas."

"*Intellectual competence,*" Gilkeson and her colleagues state, "includes developing interest and ability in inquiry, investigation, and problem solving; increasing capacity to employ rational and logical processes for organizing meaning; achieving mastery of academic skills in reading, writing, mathematics, and communication; using imagination and symbols to express thought and feelings."

"*Affective competence,*" they state, "includes developing self-awareness and self-esteem as a person and as a learner; acquiring knowledge about and identification with one's own cultural heritage; actively participating in one's own learning process; demonstrating ego strength to cope with emotional stress; and responding to the beauty of life in its artistic, aesthetic interpretation.

"*Social competence* includes communicating effectively with one's peers; empathizing and becoming involved with individuals of different social, economic, ethnic, religious, and age groups; interacting with others in the spirit of understanding, respect, trust, and cooperation; growing in awareness of and ability to enact ethical values in day-to-day living.

"*Physical competence* includes becoming aware of one's physical strengths and needs; demonstrating sequential development of motor skills in age-appropriate activities; and experiencing pleasure in exercising one's physical capabilities as a living person" (p. 225).

In the Direct Instruction Model, no goals for children are presented. Instead, Wesley Becker, Siegfried Engelmann, Douglas Carnine, and W. Ray Rhine focus on "empirical behavior theory."

"The designers of the Direct Instruction Model followed behavioral principles in three major areas of development," these authors explain. "First, they used techniques such as prompts, fades, corrections, discrimination training, and chaining verbal responses in constructing the DISTAR programs. Second, behavioral principles were employed in developing teaching procedures for eliciting and maintaining students' attention, securing their responses, dispensing reinforcers, and so forth. Third, those individuals who designed the model were guided by behavioral principles in activities and organizing classrooms and prescribing management procedures for regulating the verbal behavior of teachers and students, monitoring students' academic progress, and using praise and other reinforcers to encourage students to acquire desirable behaviors" (p. 99).

The authors state that in the DISTAR reading program the teacher focuses first on decoding and then comprehension.

"Students learn decoding skills by advancing through the following program steps: (a) reading individual sounds; (b) blending those sounds into words; (c) reading regular sound words; (d) reading common irregular words (e.g., is, said, was); (e) reading sentences; (f) reading irregular word families (e.g., hop-hope, bit-bite, rat-rate, hopping-hoping, and so forth); and (g) reading less common irregular words" (p. 108).

"The printed instructions in each DISTAR program indicate exactly what the teacher will say and do during classroom instruction," the authors explain, calling this a "scripted presentation" (p. 111).

In *Forces for Change in the Primary Schools*, Walter Hodges and ten other authors analyze the findings of Project Follow Through and make recommendations based on their findings.[60]

"*Instructional models alone cannot and should not be expected to enable economically disadvantaged children to catch up with more advantaged peers,*" the authors write in italic, and then they discuss such critical variables as housing, access to jobs, and family income.

It's the unconnected tunnel in the Education Committee's direct instruction master plan. Clearly the authoritarian, scripted, behavioral modification approach of DISTAR, the direct instruction model that Carnine tells the committee about, did have immediate effects on test scores as is demonstrated by the findings of Project Follow Through. But what are the long-term effects?

Do children develop interests and abilities that enable them to participate in intellectual inquiries? Participate in scientific investigations? Academic problem solving? Use their imagination and use symbols to express thoughts and feelings? Are there lasting differences and benefits for children who participate in classrooms based on models such as the one developed by Bank Street? Or other models that participated in Project Follow Through, such as High/Scope, which seeks "to develop a broad range of skills in conceptual problem solving and interpersonal communication that are essential to successful living in school and later in adult life"?[61]

Rheta DeVries, Halcyon Reese-Learned, and Pamela Morgan conducted an exploratory study to describe the sociomoral atmosphere in three kindergarten classrooms, using DISTAR (DI), Constructivist (CON), and Eclectic (ECL) programs. This research raises serious questions about the long-term effects of direct instruction programs such as DISTAR on the lives of young children. Don't forget as you read the findings of this study that Open Court is also a direct instruction program.

"The results of this study cannot be generalized to all DI and CON classrooms," DeVries, Reese-Learned, and Morgan state in the first of two articles which focus on the research. "However, the results suggest that we must seriously consider the possibility that heavily academic, teacher-centered programs may hinder children's development of interpersonal understanding and their broader social-cognitive and moral development."

"In light of the fact that no differences are found between DI and CON groups on school achievement tests by third grade," the researchers add, "it seems legitimate to suggest that temporary benefits of authoritarian DI programs not only cannot be justified but must be criticized because of possible damage to children's sociomoral development."[62]

In the companion article, DeVries, John Haney, and Betty Zan focus on a microanalytic analysis of the teachers' interactions with children in the three classrooms.

"The children in the direct-instruction classroom experience an almost totally unilateral relationship with the teacher," DeVries and her colleagues state. Then they explain that the children "experience school as a place where the teacher acts to control them according to her desires and expresses little consideration for their feelings."

"This leaves little opportunity for shared experiences or for construction of higher-level negotiation strategies," these authors write.

"The DI teacher's interactions reflect a predominant authoritarian focus on regulating children's behavior," they explain. "The single category most frequently used by the DI teacher was Level 1 Demanding, unilaterally commanding without giving explanation or reason" (p. 463).

It comes as no surprise that the problems of direct instruction are compounded in studies which explore the frequency of stress behaviors in young children. Diane Burts, Craig Hart, Rosalind Charlesworth, and Lisa Kirk highlight the problem in a study that explores the differences in stress behaviors in classrooms with developmentally appropriate and inappropriate instructional practices.[63]

"For organizational purposes and ease of use," these researchers write, "the stress behaviors were grouped into four major categories labeled passive, self-with-self, self-with-others, and self-with-object.

"Examples of passive stress included behaviors such as daydreaming, withdrawing, and ignoring friendly overtures from adults/children. Self-with-self stress included behaviors such as mouth manipulation (e.g., grinding teeth, fingernail biting), ear pulling, and rocking. Behaviors such as physical hostility/fights, stutters, and nervous inappropriate laughter were included under self-with-others stress. The category labeled self-with-object stress included playing with toy/object at inappropriate time/way, pencil tapping, and destroys worksheet/workbook page" (p. 413).

Noting that the study is an initial step in early childhood classroom stress research, the researchers state that children "in the more developmentally inappropriate classroom exhibited significantly more stress behaviors than children in the more developmentally appropriate classroom."

"Initial support has been obtained documenting that developmentally inappropriate educational programs," which Burt and her colleagues describe as emphasizing the use of workbooks, ditto sheets, and whole group instruction, "are potentially harmful to young children." They add, "Such a program produced significantly more stress behaviors in kindergarten children than did a more developmentally appropriate program" (p. 419).

In a follow-up study Burt and her colleagues replicated the findings with a sample of 204 kindergarten children, and they also found that the effects of developmentally inappropriate educational programs were more pronounced for boys and for African American children.

"Empirical evidence is mounting to support the contention that developmentally inappropriate curricula are potentially harmful to young children," these researchers state. "The finding of main effect for SES and race are particularly disturbing in that children who may be more likely to lack foundational experiences are having fewer opportunities to build necessary skills through appropriate experiences provided in the classroom" (p. 314).

Let's take this discussion one step further before we return to the California hearing. As I mentioned, High/Scope was one of the educational curriculum models that was represented in Project Follow Through. What is of interest to us is that a comparison study has been conducted in Ypsilanti, Michigan, which has followed the preschool children who participated in the High/Scope, Direct Instruction (DISTAR), and Nursery School curriculum models studied in Project Follow Through to the age of twenty-three.

In *Lasting Differences*, Lawrence Schweinhart and David Weikart present the findings of the comparative study which they describe at the beginning of the book.[64]

"At the outset of the study, 68 three- and four-year-old children who were living in poverty and at risk of school failure were each randomly assigned to one of three groups."

As you know, in the Direct Instruction model, the teacher initiates activities and sticks to a script with clearly defined academic objectives. In the Nursery School model, the teacher responds to the children with the minimum of structure. And, in the High/Scope model, both the teacher and the children initiate activities. Schweinhart and Weikart state that the High/Scope teachers arrange the classroom and the daily routines so that children can plan, do, and review their own activities, and so that teachers can support them as they are engaged in key learning activities.

Schweinhart and Weikart report that "the three groups differed little from one another on a variety of tests used in the various follow-ups through age ten." However, when the children who participated in these three curriculum models were fifteen years of age, Schweinhart and Weikart conducted surveys which revealed disturbing differences between the sociomoral development and antisocial behavior of the children in the different groups.

"At the age-15 follow-up," Schweinhart and Wiekart write, in *Lasting Differences*, "when the measurement of outcomes was expanded beyond intellectual and academic tests to include examining community behavior, the Direct Instruction group reported committing significantly more acts of misconduct than the High/Scope group, indeed, 2 times as many" (p. xi).

Criticisms were made of the comparison study by Bereiter and Gersten, who suggested that the interviewer knew in which curriculum model the fifteen-year-olds had participated. Schweinhart and Weikart state that the interviewer had no knowledge of which curriculum group the respondents belonged to, and they make a strong case for the internal validity of the study.

For the survey that was conducted at age twenty-three, the young men and women, most of whom still lived in and around Ypsilanti, Michigan, were located and interviewed by Van Loggins, a well-known African American resident, who had been the coach at Ypsilanti High School when the participants in the project were attending high school. Loggins was not informed about which curriculum group each of the participants in the preschool programs had attended.

The young men and women gave their permission for the researchers to obtain copies of their school, police, and social services records, and these data, along with the interviews, were analyzed by Schweinhart and Weikart.

"There is no variable on which the Direct Instruction group had a statistically significant advantage over either or both of the other curriculum groups," Schweinhart and Weikart report.

In fact, the Direct Instruction group had more felony arrests at age twenty-two and over; more property-type felonies; more assaults with a dangerous weapon; and more years of special education for emotional impairment or disturbance than either of the other groups (see Figures 14.6 and 14.7).

"[T]he strongest conclusion from this study is that the Nursery School group and especially the High/Scope group had significant advantages over the Direct Instruction group at age 23," Schweinhart and Weikart write (p. 61).

"Direct Instruction children learned that they had little control over their lives," Schweinhart and Weikart state. "Direct Instruction during their early childhood years did nothing to dispel the lesson that many children living in poverty learn, that they are not in charge of their lives, others are" (p. 66).

"Like all teacher-directed instruction, Direct Instruction places the teacher in control of learning activities in the classroom, but Direct Instruction is more intense and tightly scripted," Schweinhart and Weikart stress. "For this reason, we believe that Direct Instruction techniques should be used sparingly if at all with children who have disabilities; while such techniques may lead to success on short-term objectives, they

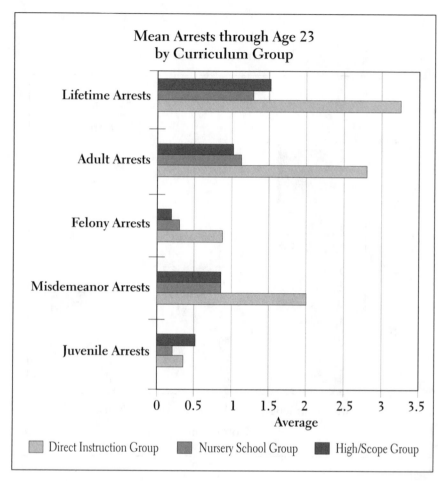

Figure 14.6

do not help children to develop a sense of control of their lives," and then they add, "something that is especially important for children with disabilities" (p. 67).

The possible negative impact of Direct Instruction on children's sociomoral development needs to be seriously considered, but there is no one at the hearing held by the California Education Committee to address this issue or to challenge Carnine's presentation. A discussion should also take place in which consideration is given to the long-term academic effects of commercial, direct instruction programs such as DISTAR and Open Court. But once again no one has been invited to the California Hearing to discuss the issue.

Remember what Carnine said about the programs that did not use direct instruction methods. "Not only were they a total failure in aca-

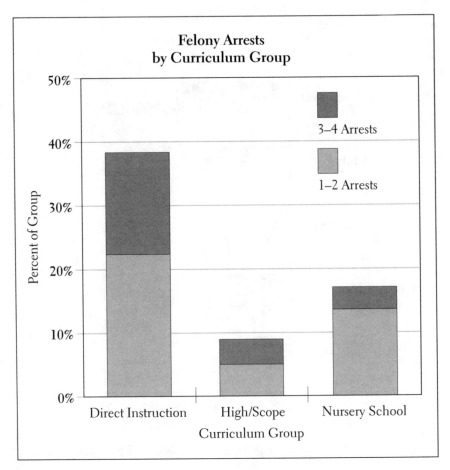

Figure 14.7

demics," Carnine said, "you found that students in those programs had a significantly lower self-esteem because they had been mis-educated."

On the contrary. It would appear from the scientific evidence that it is DISTAR and other authoritarian, scripted, direct instruction programs that mis-educate. In my discussions with educators in school districts in which DISTAR or similar programs are currently used, they tell me that they are concerned by the passivity of the children and by the high incidence of stress-induced behaviors.

"Some of the children are rocking," an educator says. "They sit for ninety minutes every day. They sit with their feet flat on the floor, their arms on the desk, listening to the teacher."

"I watch their mouths," the educator explains, "some of them are not getting it. The kids who need the most help are not getting it. They know all the rules but they can't use them. They can't pick up a book and read. Their teacher said if the kids are moving anything their brains aren't working."

An educator from another state expresses similar concern, specifically about the use of DISTAR. The educator talks about what happens when children are "narrowed into one way of learning."

"When you walk in it sounds like everyone is on task," the educator says, "but little Mary is climbing up the wall and another child is just mouthing it. They are spending four-and-a-half hours every day in DISTAR and it doesn't meet the needs of all the children."

Here are the results of the Grade 5 Stanford Achievement Test for the district which is referred to by this second educator. The chart shows the test data for the elementary school in which DISTAR has been used exclusively for the last four years (see Figure 14.8). The Stanford Achievement Test scores obtained by children in the school in which DISTAR is used exclusively do not support Carnine's testimony.

"Define Direct Instruction," Murray asks Carnine at the Hearing.

"Direct Instruction, Follow Through was, err, all the research here on beginning reading," Carnine tells Murray, "phonemic awareness, the explicit phonics, the blending, making sure that kids are reading passages where they are reading words that they have the phonics skills to decode them. It also includes oral language, it includes spelling, it includes composition, so it's a broad curricular program, highly structured, highly intensive."[65]

"What's the opposite of direct instruction?" Murray asks.

"It's where you kind of expect kids to figure it out on their own and create a stimulating environment and get them excited about learning," Carnine responds.

"Like whole language?" Murray asks.

"Yes."

There is crinoline laughter at the back of the room.

"How powerful in teaching reading is the number of students in a classroom as a variable?" someone asks.

Carnine leans forward.

"Follow Through Study, that cost a billion dollars, the failed approaches had quite small class sizes," he says. "They would have three adults with twenty-five kids."

"Something like eight-to-one?"

"Yes, that's correct. I'm not saying that doesn't help, but this Follow Through Study, from kindergarten to fourth grade, each classroom got a hundred and eighty thousand dollars in additional money," Carnine leans back in his chair, is still for a moment, and then he comes forward to the

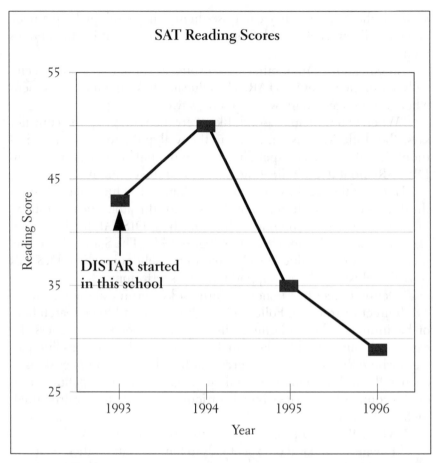

Figure 14.8. Decline of SAT scores from 1993 to 1996 in one school which used DISTAR exclusively.

mike, "and the kids in the whole language and the whole math programs were worse than the control kids who did not get the money."

Carnine leans back and looks intently at the committee.

"Any other questions as we sit here in shock?" Baldwin asks.

More laughter.

"Any other countries adopted the whole language approach that you know of?" Firestone asks.

"Yes, it's been prevalent in all English-speaking countries," Carnine states, "and it runs, like I say, in the cycle of the locusts. It has in the past and I am telling you it will in the future. I'm warning you, I really am, I'm genuinely concerned you have the power, if you treat this seriously, to stop that, and it's not whole language or phonics, it's faddism versus science, make no mistake. Education is not a science."

In Halford's article in *Infobrief* she quotes Carnine.

"It's very important that the education community work together on this issue," he states. "This political divisiveness is not healthy for the profession" (p. 6).

It's an interesting statement, given Carnine's testimony to the California Committee. While the public discourse is conciliatory, "Let's work together"; "Why are educators so hostile and uncooperative?", don't be fooled. There is nothing conciliatory about the hegemonic project. As you will find out at the end of our journey, Carnine has a national agenda that is not only politically divisive but places in jeopardy some of this country's most vulnerable children.

It's been a terrible, horrible, Sam sat, Dad sat, boot-polishing, crinoline-clapping, no good, very bad day

John Shefelbine from the Sacramento campus of California State University testifies after Carnine, and somehow manages to bring some light relief. As I stated earlier, Shefelbine writes the decodable books for Scholastic which children will "read" instead of ~~Bill Martin's *Brown Bear, Brown Bear, or Chicka Chicka Boom Boom*~~. Shefelbine complains to the committee that he was denied a position at a college because of his views on systematic, explicit phonics, and then he speaks of the resistance of teachers to his direct instruction ideas. Do you think it's because they have observed children reading ~~Mem Fox, Arnold Lobel, and Laura Numeroff~~?[66]

I think, instead of listening to Shefelbine explain to the committee how he has been vindicated by the legislature's new laws on systematic, explicit phonics, it would be more appropriate to bring to the hearing some of the children's authors whose books the California Education Committee is determined to replace with Sam sat, Dad sat, totally artificial, linguistically restricted, theoretically indefensible, incredibly boring, decodable books.[67]

Join me. Add to the list books that you know young children love to read in kindergarten and first grade when they are emergent readers.

~~Tomie DePaola. *Mary Had a Little Lamb, Pancakes For Breakfast, and Teeny Tiny*. Byron Barton. *Airplanes, Airport, The Little Red Hen, Trains, The Wee Little Woman*. Donald Crewes. *Freight Train*. Robert Munsch. *Angela's Airplane, Mortimer, Mud Puddle, Love You Forever*. Mem Fox. *Guess What?, Tough Boris*.~~

~~Syd Hoff. *Danny and the Dinosaur, Julius, Little Chief, Who Will Be My Friend?* Ruth Krauss. *The Carrot Seed, Is This You?* Crockett~~

Johnson. ~~Harold and the Purple Crayon, The Little Fish That Got Away.~~
~~Eloise Greenfield. Honey I Love, On My Horse, Sweet Baby Coming.~~

~~Maurice Sendak. Where the Wild Things Are. Mercer Mayer. All the~~
~~Little Critters books. Jack Prelutsky. Ride a Purple Pelican. Robert Kraus.~~
~~Milton the Early Riser. Jane Yolen. Owl Moon, Dinosaur Dances, Com-~~
~~mander Toad. Gerald McDermott. Coyote, Raven. Lucille Clifton. Ed-~~
~~ward Anderson's Goodbye.~~

~~Arnold Lobel. Frog and Toad Are Friends, Frog and Toad Together~~
~~Again, Ming Lo Moves the Mountain, Mouse Soup. Thacher Hurd.~~
~~Mama Don't Allow, Pea Patch Jig. Margaret Wise Brown. Goodnight~~
~~Moon, The Runaway Bunny. Marjorie Flack. The Story of Ping, Ask Mr.~~
~~Bear. Eric Carle. The Very Hungry Caterpillar, The Mixed Up Chame-~~
~~leon. Michael Rosen. Going On a Bear Hunt. Joy Cowley. Greedy Cat,~~
~~I'm the King of the Mountain. Steven Kellog. Chicken Little. Ezra Jack~~
~~Keats. The Snowy Day. Leo Lionni. Swimmy, Little Blue & Little Yellow.~~
~~Paul Galdone. Gingerbread Boy, The Three Billy Goats Gruff, Enormous~~
~~Turnip. Frank Asch. MoonCake, Just Like Daddy. Mike Thayer. Teacher~~
~~from the Black Lagoon. Pat Mora. Pablo's Tree. Tana Hoban. Little El-~~
~~ephant. Eric Hill. Where's Spot? Judith Viorst. Alexander and the Ter-~~
~~rible, Horrible, No Good, Very Bad Day.~~

It's getting late and it has been a terrible, horrible, Sam sat, Dad sat,
boot-polishing, crinoline-clapping, no good, very bad day. Shefelbine
finishes his self-congratulatory-I-told-them-so-presentation.

State legislature, after state legislature, after state legislature is going through exactly the same process that you are here

Robert Sweet, the president of the National Right to Read Foundation
(NRRF), and a general from an allied camp, is one of the last speakers,
and he tells the Education Committee that for him it is ten minutes to
one in the morning, which would make it 9:50 p.m. in California. Sweet
thanks the committee for what it is doing for not only California, but the
entire nation.

"What I have heard today I hear replicated daily with hundreds and
hundreds of people, parents," Sweet tells the Education Committee.
"We're a volunteer organization, we have people in every state in the
union, and I can tell you that state legislature, after state legislature,
after state legislature is going through exactly the same process that you
are here."

He shares some books on explicit, systematic phonics approaches to beginning reading, but he doesn't mention that the Right to Read Foundation sells an at-home phonics test to parents for $10, or that the Right to Read Foundation has officially endorsed Open Court.

"This is a century-old problem at a minimum," Sweet says as he holds up an old basal reader and discusses the problems that NRRF has with the lack of phonics in commercial reading programs. He shares some books on explicit, systematic phonics approaches to beginning reading. "I would just encourage you," he tells the committee, "as you consider the actual text selection of material, that you make sure, if you can, that all of the products that teach explicit systematic phonics that are on the market today are included."

"You're working on the framework here in California," Sweet says, "and what you do here in California is going to affect all the states in the union. You and Texas, I might add, are in a race for who can get the framework in place quick enough so that the textbook companies will follow your lead because you both buy textbooks by, you know, the millions."

"If the framework reflects what I saw in the document just passed out here from, the State Board is going to get a copy tomorrow, temporary spelling is included," Sweet says, making clear to the committee that the NRRF does not think the framework goes far enough. "Yes, they say explicit, systematic phonics, but I can tell you that the way they describe it, it is one of four quote 'cueing systems.'"

"I hear this until I want to," he hesitates and says, "I don't want to hear it anymore. It's a regurgitation, if you will, about the very stuff that has been around this country for the last century."

"Now we have a very serious situation and the reason why I think it's important," he smiles, "for us to stay as late as need be here. We are dividing people up into those who can read and those who cannot."

Sweet talks about prisons and illiteracy.

"And I commissioned, by the way, *Becoming a Nation of Readers* that my good friend Bill Honig said he didn't understand. Well, Rudolph Flesch called me, after that publication was issued back in 1985, and shortly before he passed away, and he told me that it was the first time that the federal government did anything worthwhile in presenting direct systematic phonics.

"In summary, I would suggest that if there is any way that our organization or myself can help in making sure that we lock this down in California, that we don't go on into the twenty-first century with simply redefining the thing that was at one time look and say, then became whole word, then psycholinguistics, then whole language, and now it will be systematic, explicit phonics and it's all going to be the same stuff."

Sweet does not tell Baldwin or the other members of the Education Committee that the National Right to Read Foundation is conducting its own hegemonic campaign in California.

He does not discuss the newsletters that are being distributed in California and in every other state, but as the propaganda produced by NRRF is so readily available it seems reasonable to assume that Baldwin and the other committee members have read many of the documents which are being distributed.

Sweet does not mention that a newsletter from the California Division of NRRF on the "Principles of Reading Instruction" begins "Teach phonemic awareness directly in kindergarten," or that it states, "these skills do not develop naturally and must be taught directly." Nor does he mention, as it does in this particular document, that the NRRF has connected some of the tunnels in the labyrinth and is using the research supported by Reid Lyon and NICHD to support the organization's own right-wing agenda.

"These research findings have been distilled from $200 million in research, conducted over thirty years," states the NRRF newsletter under the principles for reading instruction, "under the direction of the National Institute of Child Health and Human Development. Application of these findings in the classroom is critical if illiteracy in America is to be reduced."

Sweet does not tell the California Education Committee of the California House Assembly that NRRF is monitoring their activities. He doesn't mention that one NRRF newsletter produced in Virginia alerts school boards across the country about the new textbook adoptions that are taking place in California.

"In the past two years, the California state legislature passed laws that require, in grades K–3 of its public schools, reading instruction that emphasizes 'systematic, explicit' (i.e., prearranged, well-ordered, and direct) teaching of phonics information and of spelling," states the NRRF newsletter. "The legislature also mandated that reading instruction programs provide children in these grades 'decodable' stories, that is, ones that afford practice for them in decoding words by using phonics skills that they previously taught."

Sweet does not tell the committee that NRRF has officially endorsed Open Court.

"It is the considered judgement of the National Right to Read Foundation however, that only one of the several reading instruction textbook programs noted below, that the state board approved for use henceforward in California, satisfactorily meets the stipulations of the new reading laws of this state," the NRRF newsletter states. "That one is the program published by Open Court."

Sweet does not tell the Education Committee that the NRRF is distributing "Briefings" which warn parents that the textbook adoptions in California include textbooks which do not "teach phonics properly."

"The warning to parents and other concerned citizens from the current selection of reading instruction texts is evident. Unless you convince them otherwise, schools in the future likely will adopt textbooks that do not provide children full opportunity to learn to read. This need not be the case, however. As noted, there are approved textbooks that do conform to the new reading instruction laws. Also, a school district may gain permission to use its state textbook money for books not approved by the state Board of Education."

In this briefing, the NRRF once again makes an endorsement.

"In our judgment, only one of the grades K–6 reading textbook series approved by the Board meet the new legal criteria. It is published by Open Court."

Sweet does not tell Baldwin that NRRF is also monitoring what happens in California to make sure that the California State Department of Education and the California State Board of Education "does its duty" and "faithfully follows" the new state laws.

"Now you've got chapters in every single state, the National Right to Read Foundation, and you've seen this battle in all fifty states," Baldwin says to Sweet after he finishes speaking. "Where are we compared to other states? Are there any states focusing on systematic, explicit phonics as the main method of reading right now?"

"I would say probably Virginia," Sweet responds, "and it just so happens I served on the commission."

"The standards commission?" Baldwin asks.

"Yes."

"Great standards!" Baldwin is enthusiastic. "I saw the standards produced in Virginia. Excellent standards."

"That's one example," Sweet continues. "In Massachusetts forty linguists recommended that the state framework committee go back to explicit, systematic phonics. I haven't seen the final version; I've seen a draft of it." Sweet expresses reservations about the final version of the document in Massachusetts, and then he says that with Foorman's influence Houston is getting explicit phonics.

If Sweet gets his way, so will the nation.

15

In which California ends local control and the State Board of Education leads the jihad

■ ■ ■

In California the new ABC laws raise serious constitutional questions regarding issues of civil rights as well as civil liberties. Local communities no longer have the right to choose how their children learn to read. Parents and teachers cannot work together to decide what form of instruction best suits the needs of individual children. Even though there is extensive scientific evidence which demonstrates that direct instruction and intensive, explicit, systematic phonics can in fact be deleterious to the health and well-being of many children and can have a negative effect on their ability to learn to read, systematic, explicit phonics is now taught ubiquitously.[1]

"Whole language was never mentioned in the 1987 framework," says Sharon Zinke, a California teacher who was denied the opportunity to testify at the May 1996 Hearing on Reading held by the Education Committee of the California Assembly. "Whole language was not even happening in California. Instead, what we had were teachers scrambling to implement the framework without any training and without the materials necessary to implement it. We were not allowed to use state money to buy appropriate books even though the framework said that our students should be reading trade books at their instructional and independent level. Even though teachers spend their own personal income on books, they do not have enough appropriate books in their classrooms so that students can raise their reading levels."

In one document I read, the writer states, "Just about every paper in the state, including the *LA Weekly*, has done extensive articles on the 'failure of whole language' and no major education related interest group in the state, including teachers, will go on record in support of whole language."

"The battle now seems to be whether you are sufficiently anti-whole language enough," the author writes. "The Wilson-dominated State Board of Education leads the jihad, and has trashed the current Superintendent of Public Instruction, Delaine Eastin." The writer goes on to state, "My guess is that reversing this near consensus is going to be pretty difficult. This 'debate' was over two years ago. I say 'debate' because there really was no whole language side to the controversy. No one defended it."

"Can you be a critical pedagogist if you are not involved in the political process?" I ask Ken Goodman, as I try to figure out why so many of the leading researchers in the field of literacy continue to remain silent as emancipatory pedagogical practices are attacked and as researchers and teachers are denigrated.

"I don't think so," Goodman says with a smile, knowing it's a rhetorical question.

"Critical pedagogy is about action," O'Loughlin says in another conversation.

But where are the researchers in the reading field who study emergent literacy? Where are the researchers who study early literacy development as social and cultural practice? Where are the sociolinguists who study discourse analysis? Where are the researchers who participate in teacher-research? Where are the researchers who develop cultural models of children's early literacy practices? Where are the researchers who write of building a pedagogy of multiliteracies? How can we build pedagogies which are sensitive to the plurality of literacies that are a part of young children's lives if we are reduced to the word level? How can we remain silent when we know that literacy is embedded in different ideologies, with different political perspectives and with different political agendas? How can we abandon the teachers with whom we have worked for so many years and leave them to fight alone? Do we ditch them when they are told that they must abandon their emancipatory pedagogies? Do we desert them when they are told they must forget they are professionals? Do we stand by, mute, when they are told they must return to their role as technical aides and use methods of instruction that "anaesthetize" the children they teach "and leaves them a-critical and naïve in the face of the world"?[2]

"We're Balkanized," I say. "We vie for academic recognition, tenure, and publications, while the rights of teachers and children are taken away from them in a right-wing political coup that is intent on destroying public education."

"It is time for language educators to enter the political fracas," P. David Pearson writes. "Dissemination, the marketplace of ideas, and professional support groups are conspicuously absent from the back-to-the-basics counter-movement. The strategy of the movement is simpler and more direct: work through legislative and policymaking bodies to mandate the changes deemed necessary. Prey on the crisis mentality that policymakers find so appealing as a motivation for their personal attempts to create a better America. Most disturbing about this new game is how ill-suited language educators seem to be at playing it. We may be skilled at turning a phrase in our academic milieu, but we are not so skilled at turning heads in the political fray" (p. 8).[3]

Drop the touchy-feely psychobabble from our schools!

On January 19, 1997, Assemblyman Steve Baldwin testifies in San Fernando, California, at the Field Hearing held by the United States House of Representatives Committee on Education and the Workforce.

Baldwin begins with what's not the problem.

"It is not the lack of money."[4]

"It is not teacher quality."

"It is not for the lack of quality school facilities."

"It is not the lack of federal involvement."

"It is not because of a diverse student body."

"It is not class size."

"It is not the lack of technology."

Baldwin says the problems are with a lack of phonics and the use of cooperative learning. He talks about math. Group methods. Inventive spelling. The personal questions that are asked about students' families. Questions that undermine students' values. Overregulation. *Overregulation?* Yes, overregulation. He talks about Project Follow Through.

"We need to focus on individual accountability," Baldwin tells the House Committee. "Drop cooperative learning and hold kids accountable for what they do on their own. After all, that is how the real world operates."

"Drop the touchy-feely psychobabble from our schools!" Baldwin declares. "If a child really is in need of psychiatric help, then he should be referred to a psychologist or psychiatrist outside the classroom. It's time for teachers to quit playing Freud and focus on academics!"

At the end of his speech Baldwin states, "I do condemn, and do so publically, an educational establishment that for a generation has used political power at the expense of parental control and continues to focus on political matters rather than on teaching our children."

Exquisite politics! Baldwin has it down pat. He is totally political. I don't think it's an act.[5]

"The law states that at least 95 percent of the allocated funds are to be used to purchase core reading program materials," reads the notice from the California Department of Education which focuses on AB 3482 that was sent out to elementary schools across the state. The materials must include "phonemic awareness, systematic phonics, and spelling patterns, accompanied by reading material that provides practice in the lesson being taught."

In case there is any doubt, teachers are told that "systematic, explicit phonics" refers to "an organized program where letter-sound correspondences for letters and letter clusters are directly taught; blended; practiced in words, word lists, and word families; and practiced initially in texts with a high percentage of decodable words linked to the phonics lesson." Teachers are reminded that "[t]he most effective phonics instruction is explicit—that is, taking care to clarify key points and principles to students. In addition, it is systematic—that is, it gradually builds from basic elements to more subtle and complex patterns."

The 1997 California textbook adoption is the largest textbook adoption that has ever occurred anywhere in the world, and in terms of dollars is of enormous commercial value. Of course, as you would expect, on the Reading/Language List adopted by the California State Board of Education is the Open Court program, co-authored by Adams, promoted by Foorman, and recommended by Sweet, creating a right-wing coup d'état of unprecedented commercial worth. But the crinolines are still ruffled at the thought that some schools might not be willing to comply, so they stamp their boots, threatening to audit schools and force them to return their state money if they don't obey the law.

"There should not be some children who by the luck of the draw do not get phonics," says Kathryn Dronenburg, a member of the State Board, who is quoted by Daniel Weintraub, in the *Orange County Register* on April 11, 1997. "I want to have this information out there," Dronenburg declares, "so that people know that this is not a matter of opinion. It's what the law says, and we have to follow the law."

Weintraub follows up by clarifying for the readers of the *Register* the meaning of the new state laws. "For one thing," he writes, "it is now against the law to use state or federal funds for programs that use certain whole language techniques. Those funds no longer can be used for programs that encourage children to use the story's context to figure out unfamiliar words or that encourage 'inventive spelling.'"

"Further," Weintraub states, "the law requires not just phonics but 'explicit, systematic phonics.'" He then adds, "Unfamiliar words must be sounded out, not skipped or guessed at."[6]

Educators are in violation of California law if state or federal money is used for children's literature instead of basal texts. If a teacher looks at a picture with a child or rereads part of a story to help a child figure out a word, the teacher will have performed an illegal act. For the first time in United States history a teacher can break the law just by reading with a child, or just by sitting with a group of children and talking with them about the graphophonic relationships they are reinventing as they write their own stories. If Martha and Leigh, whom you met at the beginning of *Spin Doctors*, lived in California, they would be breaking the law, and Sharron would be engaging in an illegal activity if she supported Nicola, who learned to use her understandings of literacy to express her anger and her grief. Although it is hard to believe, teachers have not only lost their professional status, but can now be accused of breaking the law if they do not embrace the cant, right-wing, political ideology which has replaced their emancipatory pedagogies.

Baldwin makes this clear in a letter that he writes to Yvonne Larsen, the President of the California State Board of Education, which was circulated on the Internet. Baldwin states that he believes some schools are in violation of the law, and he urges Larsen and the state board to investigate. He argues that even if school districts are not using AB 3482 funds, they might still be in violation of the law because of the language set out in the state budget which outlaws any program that "emphasizes contextual clues in lieu of fluent decoding or systematically uses or encourages inventive spelling techniques in the teaching of writing."[7]

Nothing that we say counts because according to them the research is in and teachers know nothing

Nervous about the consequences of their efforts to teach children to read, teachers in the state now talk of the "phonics police," and while some teachers hold fast to their pedagogical practices, others, frightened by the possible consequences, are coerced and quietly acquiesce.

But don't forget the "we all agree" basis of hegemony, for while the politicians establish a totalitarian educational regime, their subaltern intellectuals soothe teachers with the "findings" of their so-called "reliable and replicable research." At the Leadership Conference of the California Reading and Literature Project which was held in Los Angeles the last week in April 1997, Treadway uses the work of Stanovich, Adams, and Foorman to support the proposition that phonemic awareness and phonics must be taught explicitly.

"You do believe in phonics don't you?"[8]

In case there are any nonbelievers at the Leadership Conference, Treadway provides them with documentation to ensure their indoctrination. With a few carefully selected quotes he distorts the theories of Frank Smith and Ken Goodman and portrays them both as nonbelievers.

"Smith and Goodman's theories created great interest," Treadway writes. "Psychologists and educators began an immediate attempt to replicate their studies and substantiate their claims." He then states, "[T]heir notions about decoding and the orthographic processor were proven wholly wrong"(p. 4).

But neither Smith nor Goodman conducted any research on the "orthogaphic processor."

"All nonsense, of course," Goodman says when I read the paragraph to him on the telephone. "Treadway is rewriting history and misrepresenting research."

Indeed, Treadway, like Lyon, Foorman, Honig, Carnine, and Grossen, is in the business of knowledge fabrication and disinformation. Smith has long been a synthesizer of educational research, but he has done very little primary research, so it would be difficult for anyone to replicate studies that he never did. As for Goodman, his two principal antagonists are Nicholson and Stanovich. Nicholson seems to be permanently fixated on the only experimental study Goodman conducted in the early sixties, a study which in fact preceded his classic research on miscue analysis; while Stanovich, who has also consistently criticized Goodman, has not attempted to replicate any of Goodman's studies. Moreover, Stanovich's research practices and the conclusions of his studies have been seriously questioned in this book. But no matter, to fulfill the objectives of the hegemonic project, the work of Smith and Goodman must be discounted, and in print, Treadway's criticisms are authoritative and appear to be authentic.

"They're everywhere," a teacher tells me, referring to Treadway, Lyon, Adams, and Shefelbine, who are making presentations around the state. "Nothing that we say counts because according to them the research is in and teachers know nothing."

To ensure that teachers get the message, the Comprehensive Reading Leadership Program [AB 3482] publishes a book of articles on beginning reading instruction which is distributed to California's county offices of education. The project director of CRLP at the California State Department of Eduation is Alice Furry, the wife of Bill Furry, who works for Wilson and who testified before the Education Committee of the State Assembly.

The first article in the collection is by Elizabeth McPike and was published by the American Federation of Teachers. McPike begins with Stanovich, whom she describes as "one of the world's leading reading researchers," and—you've guessed—the "Matthew Effects in Reading." Adams follows. Writing with Maggie Bruck, Adams criticizes Goodman for an article he published in 1967, but ignores the decades of research on miscue analysis which he has accomplished since that date. Adams and Bruck then attack Frank Smith for the synthesis of reading research that he published in 1971, while at the same time they laud the research of Stanovich and of course reference his article on "Matthew Effects in Reading."

Adams and Bruck then provide weapons to the conservative right by stating that there "exists an anti-research spirit within the whole language movement." Winick grabs at this idea and Honig uses it in his personal battle to re-establish himself as a dominant force in California public education. "Many leaders of this movement actively discredit traditional scientific research approaches to the study of reading development," Adams and Bruck write, and Carnine is back in the battle and Sweet gets his day. "The movement's anti-scientific attitude forces research findings into the backroom, making them socially and, thereby, intellectually unavailable to many educators," Adams and Bruck state. It's the message that drives Wilson, and the message that will give George Bush Jr. the presidency if right-wing conservatives and big business have their way.

The next paper in the collection is by Isabel Beck and Connie Juel, and again the arguments that they present are based on "Matthew Effects in Reading" by Stanovich. Grossen follows. You can read what she has to say on the Web pages of the far right. Next comes Stanovich with his A-cites-B perspective on reality in which he cites Adams repeatedly. With a plea that researchers look "at points of agreement between opposing positions," Stanovich lambastes the "melange" called "constructivism," and states that "[t]hese ideas have unfortunately come into education half baked and twice distorted."

Children learn to read phonetically. We'd all agree if you'd just believe like me.

Perfetti follows with references to Stanovich. Then Grossen again with a fixed-up version of 30 *Years of Research* with references to Adams,

Foorman, and five references to Stanovich, including "Matthew Effects in Reading." The next to last article is "Skills and Other Dilemmas" by Lisa Delpit, and its inclusion in the collection is highly problematic. Delpit is out of the hegemonic loop. She is a strong, deeply committed African American scholar who speaks her mind and is unlikely to be persuaded by the "we-all-agree" mindless conformism of hegemony.

"No," Delpit tells me, when I call her to ask her if she knows her article has been republished by the state of California. We talk for a while, and then she says, "Well, whatever they're doing with the paper I'm sure they're not using it to help black kids."

"I run a great risk in writing this," Delpit states in the paper that the California State Department of Education has republished without her permission, "the risk that my purpose will be misunderstood; the risk that those who subject black and other minority children to day after day of isolated, meaningless, drilled 'subskills' will think themselves vindicated. That is not the point. Were this another article, I would explain what I mean by 'skills.'" Delpit then gives her personal definition, "useful and usable knowledge," she says, "that contributes to a student's ability to communicate effectively in standard, generally acceptable literary forms." She continues, "And I would explain that I believe that skills are best taught through meaningful communication, best learned in meaningful contexts." She ends these thoughts by stating that black and minority students "need to be able to think critically and creatively to participate in meaningful and potentially liberating work inside those doors" (p. 48).

"Skills in meaningful contexts" can hardly be used to support "explicit, systematic phonics" without the use of contextual cues, but I know Delpit will forgive me for saying that's not the point. In California where the "minority" is the "majority," the state needs the endorsement of an African American scholar, and with any luck her name will be enough and few people will actually read Delpit's paper and realize that her views are being misrepresented.

In addition to the book of readings, the Comprehensive Reading Leadership Center sends monthly bulletins called "CRLP Trainers" out across the state.[9] The May-June 1997 package contains seventeen separate documents including: a resolution from the Maryland State PTA Convention on phonics; an article on phonics from the *Dallas Morning News*; an article entitled "The Lone Star Lesson for California" published in the *Orange County Register*; a copy of *The Texas Reading Initiative*; and the e-mail letter from Lyon to Coles from which I quoted in my discussion of Lyon's testimony before the Education Committee of the California State Assembly.

Nothing is left to chance. To ensure the hegemonic reconstruction of how young children learn to read, CRLP also has "Tips for Parents"; a "Read All About It" video; a "2-Day Workshop" video; "2-Day Workshop" modules; "A Blueprint for Professional Development"; and a "Questions and Answers Brochure."

In these packages, which are being distributed throughout the state of California, there is no mention of the problematic statements that Lyon made to the Education Committee of the California Assembly. Nor is any attention paid to the contradictory statements made by Lyon which undermine the scientific veracity of his presentation. No reference is made to the misrepresentation of data or to the numerous defects in Foorman's research which result in statistical uncertainties that invalidate the studies. No copies are provided of the reliable and replicated research on the negative impact of direct instruction on the sociomoral development of young children. Reports from High/Scope on direct instruction and the high incidence of criminal activity are not included in the package. Also missing are the negative test scores of children who are currently in direct instruction programs which teach intensive systematic, explicit phonics. And there is no mention, not even a whisper, about the success of reading instruction in the many schools across the country which do not include systematic, explicit phonics instruction or use commercial reading programs. The documentation is hegemonic.[10]

"You do believe in phonics, don't you?"

"You know I do. I believe phonics should be taught ubiquitously, you know I do."

The f-word. It's not negotiable, by the way

On May 15, 1997, the final draft of the California Framework is sent to the members of the Literacy Team for review. The published document is due in December. By now some of the content will be familiar to you. In the section on phonemic awareness, the key findings of the research are given.

"Phonemic awareness has emerged as one of the best predictors of early reading success, and is the key to subsequent development of decoding skills."

Perhaps the next research finding will be less familiar.

"Children can be helped to recognize and produce phonemes in syllables, or words through direct instruction with reference to place (position of lips, tongue, teeth, where in the mouth etc.) and manner (stop, fricative, nasal, glide etc.) of articulation."

"Chu, chu, chu, is a sound that if you put your hand here," the teacher says, in a film Lyon is showing to San Francisco administrators. The teacher puts her fingers on her neck. "If you put your hand here where your vocal cords are and your voice box you're not using it."

"Chu, chu, chu, chu," the children repeat.

"Because it is made in your mouth. There is a sound that sounds a lot like 'chu' and that's the sound 'sh' and the reason that they sound the same is because you put your mouth the same way to make them. But the difference is that 'sh' sounds like a hot shower."

The teacher asks for foods beginning with /ch/.

"Cherry pie," a child says.

"Cherry pie," says the teacher.

"Jacket," says another child.

"Say it again," says the teacher.

"I don't know what that kid eats at home," Lyon jokes as he stops the video tape and takes a moment to talk about the next segment of the film that the administrators will see.

"'Chu' is a very special sound," the teacher tells the children. "It's not made with just one letter. It's made with two letters. Now they're together. Two letters making one sound. Chu, chu, chu, chu. So now we can read and say the sound."

"Chu, chu, chu, chu," the children repeat.

"When two letters come together and make one sound, that sound, and those letters together are called a digraph. Can you say digraph?"

"Di-graph," the children repeat in a sing-song voice.

"'Di' means two letters," the teacher tells them. "'Graph' means something you write down, or the letters. So, two letters, digraph, one sound. It's a very special sound, 'chu,' and we are going to be using it for the rest of the day."[11]

"You have to be able to develop phonics," Lyon tells San Francisco's administrators. "The f-word. It's not negotiable, by the way." [12]

"A lot of these different philosophical ideas about teaching of reading emerge from the arrogance of adults."

He talks about "major errors in thinking" and he says "we've known it for a long time, but it's the arrogance and ignorance of a lot of college of education professors, because there's no accountability by the way for stupid ideas. There's no accountability yet."

"If you are a phonicator, then you visit Jesse Helms on Wednesday," Lyon says, "and if you are a whole language type, you're with Ken Goodman in Arizona on Thursday."

"California has some guts," Lyon tells the administrators, with

Foorman's Open Court graph on the screen behind him. "Now people may not agree with what California has done, but California is the first state that has said we will use research to try to drive reading practices. Of course people are going to say, 'Whose research are you looking at?' 'What do you mean that's research?' You know all that kind of stuff. Research has to be replicable, it has to be reliable, and it has to be hypothesis-driven."

At the time of Lyon's speech, reforms are taking place in teacher preparation for reading instruction. In the recommended revisions for teachers' credentials, emphasis is again placed on the findings of experimental research. The draft document is similar to the ones we analyzed in North Carolina with some new text underlined and some of the exisitng text crossed out.[13]

"Each credential candidate participates in intensive instruction in reading and language arts methods that is grounded in ~~recent~~ highly replicated, scientifically sound research and exposed to well designed programs that enable her/him to provide a balanced, comprehensive program that includes explicit and meaningfully applied instruction in reading, writing, and related language arts skills and strategies for speakers of English and English language learners. ~~for native English speakers and English language learners, including those in bilingual programs.~~[14]

The first commandment of politics is secure your base

Do you remember the list I asked you to make when we visited North Carolina, of the researchers who have most influenced your pedagogy? If you can find the list, you might want to add the names of a few more researchers even though you will probably have to cross their names out. If Jean Lave and Barbara Rogoff, whose work I referenced at the beginning of *Spin Doctors*, were on your list, you might want to gently cross them off, for Stanovich's preemptive strike on the "melange" of "constructivism" only serves as a warning for what is now happening to constructivist math, which has also come under fire from the far right. Start another list. Write down the names of researchers who study reading pathologies, who do quick-fix experimental studies, who fudge their data, who do clinical trials for basal publishing companies, who are endorsed by the National Right to Read Foundation, or by the Eagle Forum and the Heritage Foundation.

Most of the rooms in the labyrinth are now connected, but the generals and their subaltern intellectuals are determined not to leave any aspect of their hegemonic project to chance.

"The first commandment of politics," Madeleine Albright says, "is secure your base."[15]

But teachers in California who have no political acumen are beginning to understand the behind-the-scenes maneuvering of the generals and their subaltern intellectuals, and for the first time their voices are beginning to be heard.[16]

The California Assembly must act swiftly to silence them and to secure their base with AB 1086. Members Mazzoni, Baldwin, and Pacheco introduce the bill to control the information that can be presented by providers of professional development in reading to elementary school teachers, creating an orthodoxy of instructional practices.

The bill states which instructional methods and topics can be presented to K–3 teachers. Phonemic awareness is an approved topic for instruction and so is systematic, explicit phonics. In addition, providers will be allowed to instruct teachers on how to diagnose children's ability to decode and learn how to instruct them in word attack skills.

"Communication with the senators representing us is now more important than ever," Margaret Moustafa writes to members of the listserv that has been established to help teachers respond to the efforts of the legislature to take away local control and to turn California into a fascist state. "Please get your friends, your local superintendents, your reading specialist friends, your teaching colleagues, and, yes, your grandparents who live in California to fax or phone their senator opposing AB 1086."

"It is undemocratic," Moustafa writes. "It takes control away from local school districts and communities, and is opposed by professional organizations who represent literacy professionals." She ends with, "This is incredibly serious."

On another listserv, Sharon Zinke interacts with Greg Geeting, who is at the State Department of Education. Geeting likens AB 1086 to laws such as the one regulating motorcycle helmets. If you want to ride a motorcycle and the law states that you must wear a helmet, then you wear a helmet. Geeting states that if providers of professional development want to receive funds from the state, they will have to stick to the reading instruction content specified by the law.

Zinke agrees that we benefit from some government regulation and then fights back. "If we are to have our reading instruction rigidly circumscribed by state law, then why were the decisions about the philosophical direction made without consulting experts?" Zinke asks. "Why was the California Reading Association not consulted? Why were teacher educators not consulted? Why were reading specialists not consulted? The criteria for teaching delineated in 1086 are the lopsided result of a small group of nonprofessionals and other interested parties."

"As far as I can tell, the people who were consulted were people who have never taught reading," Zinke continues, "and people who have a conflict of interest and are connected to publishing companies such as DISTAR and Open Court. I have yet to find one single literacy expert who believes in teaching children to develop a balanced way of dealing with print who was consulted or who back the bill."

"It has come to my attention," Zinke states at the end of her response to Geeting, "that Assemblywoman Kerry Mazzoni, author of AB 1086, stated in a news article that local control hasn't worked, so the state needs to intervene. My question is: who decided this? And why did legislators not bother to get both sides of a very old story? A lot has been learned about literacy since Rudolph Flesch, but you would never know it from reading AB 1086."

Despite the efforts of teachers, AB 1086 is passed unanimously by the California Assembly. It is now the law in California that any educator—often master teachers who want to provide professional development—must submit all the materials that they will use to the State Board of Education for their approval.[17] This encompasses all written materials, including those that will be given to teachers, all videos, and all other technology-based resources that will be used during the proposed instruction. Applicants must also sign a statement of assurance that the training will comply with the law. It is anti-democratic and political censorship of the very worst kind.

Here's the oath: *The training provider will comply with all applicable provisions of law, including Section 24.03 of the 1997–98 Budget Act (Chapter 282, Statutes of 1998) which prohibits the use of the Goals 2000 funds appropriated for this training for any program that promotes or uses reading instruction methodologies that emphasize contextual clues in lieu of fluent decoding, or systematically uses or encourages inventive spelling techniques in the teaching of writing.*[18]

"The climate of intimidation that began with the loyalty oath in 1947 remains with us," Gore Vidal writes in an article entitled "The Last Empire" published by *Vanity Fair*, "even though two American generations have been born with no particular knowledge of what the weather was like before the great freeze and the dramatic change in our form of government" (p. 255).

"Sharon Zinke remembers when she started teaching in California in the 1960's," Kathleen Kennedy Manzo writes in the November 5 issue of *Education Week*, "and was asked to swear that she was not a Communist. Some 30 years later, Ms. Zinke," Manzo states, "must once again convince state officials of her adherence to approved doctrine, or suffer the consequences."[19]

"I pledge allegiance."

"Phonics rules!"

You do believe in a democracy? Don't you?

16

In which we enter the central chamber of the hegemonic labyrinth

■ ■ ■

"Deals are being cut every which way but loose," Rich Long tells me.

It's late September and I'm talking to Long on the telephone. You remember I mentioned Long before. He's the representative for the International Reading Association as well as the National Council of Teachers of English. I am trying to get some information about events that are taking place in Washington. I know. California was our final destination, and I had no intention of going back to Washington. But Carnine and Hans Meeder have published an article in *Education Week*. They've put the hegemonic project on the national agenda. The crinolines are off. We have to go back to Washington. The U.S. Congress is about to take direct control of public education.

"There is nothing new about politicians aching to stick their noses into the management of education," Conrad Russell writes, tracing the power struggle back in Europe as far as Pope Gregory VII and William the Conqueror in the tenth century, "nor about their belief that because they have received education, they know all about it"[1] (p. 16).

"In the Army," Russell writes, "accountability stops short of operational judgements taken in the field. In medicine, it stops short of intervention in clinical judgements. Universities and schools need an equivalent form of protection."

But there is no protection. Teachers are vulnerable. First at the state and now at the national level, teachers are being told how to teach. The "reading wars," as they have been dubbed in the press, are not wars between teachers who "believe" in phonics or in whole language. The war is political and ideological, a product of the new capitalism. It is racist and hegemonic, and teachers are the foot soldiers who are supposed to do as they are told, without rights or privilege or professional status. The battle is for power, for control, and of course for profit. Enormous sums of money are at stake. It is about forging alliances with groups across the political spectrum, behind-the-scenes maneuvering, and securing dominance. A profound political shift is taking place, a historic cultural shift which has nothing, and perhaps everything, to do with how young children are taught to read. Either way it is a threat to democracy.

"Under the show, the struggle for power," Francis Urquhart says in *To Play the King*, as he looks directly into the eyes of those who watch him, "deep down, below it all, deeper than honor, deeper than pride, deeper than lust, and deeper than love, is the getting of it all, the seizing and holding on, the jaws locked, biting into power and hanging on, biting and hanging on."[2]

Check out the connections in the labyrinth. You know who Carnine is, but you might not have heard of Meeder. He was a staffer for the House Committee on Education and the Workforce. Remember that Lyon testified before the Committee in Washington, and Baldwin testified at the Field Hearing in San Fernando, California. I've been told that Meeder is so far to the right that even the right-wing conservatives on the House Committee had problems with him. But now he is the president of Horizon Consulting Services, a policy-research firm in Columbia, Maryland, and he is working with Carnine.

"Douglas Carnine and Hans Meeder have put the nation and the education community on notice," Goodman writes in a sharp reply to their article in *Education Week*, "having captured literacy education in California, they intend to use the same blueprint to capture the nation by taking over the America Reads initiative.

"In California," Goodman says, "Mr. Carnine and others have succeeded in convincing key decision makers that there is only one kind of reading research. It is the kind that tests published programs on learners and it has shown beyond a doubt that commercial programs based on direct instruction of explicit synthetic phonics are the necessary and only way to teach reading. Mr. Carnine's Commentary is already law in California."

"It is certainly a bold push that Mr. Carnine and his co-author propose." Goodman continues, "They would hijack America Reads and all its funding in the service of a 'research-based approach.' Then they would, by early 1998, have a national 'expert panel' announce a synthesis of research knowledge about reading (direct synthetic phonics). Reid Lyon, the head of the National Institute for Child Health and Human Development, would become the reading czar with authority to order two Cabinet members, the U.S. Secretaries of Education and of Health and Human Services, to disseminate the knowledge about reading research by imposing it on Head Start, Even Start, and Title I.

"Lest anyone think this plan is too preposterous to be taken seriously," Goodman cautions at the end of his letter, "consider that two key parts are well underway. Messrs. Carnine and Meeder know that a report under the financial sponsorship of Reid Lyon, using NICHD money, will soon be issued which has been produced by a group who largely share the Carnine view of science and research. And the U.S. House of Representatives Committee on Education and the Workforce, on which Mr. Meeder formerly served as director of planning and policy development, has been holding hearings all over the country and recently in Washington with carefully selected testimony supporting just the view of reading research and practice that is the keystone of the Carnine-Meeder plan."

Goodman and I talk on the telephone. In their article, Carnine and Meeder state that according to their plan there would be a "product recall" of all research on reading that is "not scientifically valid" by the narrow set of criteria that they have established.

"Consider yourself recalled," I say to Goodman.

"And you, and you," he says. "We've all been recalled."

Men in Washington make lousy lovers

"They've gotta deal," Long tells me on the telephone. "It suits the purposes of the conservative right. This is a political ideological debate," he sounds slightly disparaging, as if I don't get it, "not a professional debate."

Long talks in innuendos, hints, gives me clues so veiled and deep or trivial and superfluous that I don't know what he is talking about. I have no doubt that he is playing with me. He talks of "good guys" and being "on the side of the angels," but he won't name names. Nothing he says makes sense and I have difficulty taking notes. He's gone political. He's inside the Beltway, in the labyrinth. I ask him about Lyon, and he tells me there's a saying that men in Washington make lousy lovers. He says they make lousy lovers because they are in love with power. He laughs and says Lyon has become a very powerful man.

"He's still enjoying the prominent position he's gained," Long tells me. He says he doesn't think Lyon has reached the point that he realizes he's being used. "It's not about reading," he says. "Lyon suits the purposes of the right. He will get a better job," Long says. "Unless he makes a mistake. Then they will drop him and get a doctor or a judge to take his place. His political support will slip away."

"Is anyone questioning the empirical base of the NICHD research?" I ask. It's the second time I've asked him this question. The first time Long told me that as president of the PTA of the district in which his children went to school, he had given his okay for the funding of a phonemic awareness program. He wasn't interested in anything I had to say about the inherent flaws in NICHD's "reliable and replicable research."

"No," he says, as he did the first time, dismissing the possibility. He explains that there is general agreement on the House Committee that the NICHD research should be the basis of instruction for young children learning to read but the big problem is how to get the research "out there."

On October 2, I telephone Alan Farstrup, who is the executive director of the International Reading Association (IRA). I tell him that Long was not very forthcoming with information about the upcoming bill. Farstrup is protective. He says the "good guys" were probably the staff members who are working with Long and that it was probably their names that he would not divulge. He promises to send me the names of the members of Congress who are members of the House Committee on Education and the Workforce.

"It's a very political process," Farstrup explains, sounding resigned. "The big issue for us is that schooling should be locally controlled." Then he adds, "The most we expect to accomplish is to water down the final version of the bill."

"Have you seen the bill?" I ask him.

"No," he says. "We don't seem to be able to get a hold of it."

Farstrup e-mails the list of the members of the House Education and the Workforce Committee to me with instructions from P. David Pearson on how to address letters to them. He also sends the "Legislative Alert" that Long had sent out to the Board of the IRA.

Long explains that the legislation provides money to support professional development. He writes that it "defines what reading is," and "what reading readiness is," and that all the programs that are funded "must be based on 'reliable and replicable research.'"

"IRA has been and continues to be against the federal government deciding on what must be used in classrooms," Long writes. "IRA believes that this program will reduce the ability of local educators, school-board leaders and others to create innovative programs to meet the unique needs of their students."

We have become part of the book that I am writing and you are reading. It is October 3, 1997. The House Committee on Education and the Workforce was supposed to meet again on the 6th, but rumor has it that the meeting has been postponed until October 8. That gives us time. I've decided to send the Committee some of the documentation that I have gathered together in *Spin Doctors*.

"You're no longer writing the book," O'Loughlin laughs when I speak to him on the telephone, "the book is writing you."

I try to get the bill, but no one has a copy. I'm stuck. Unable to write to the House Committee and unable to write to you. Across the United States, and particularly in Texas, California, Georgia, Indiana, Michigan, Missouri, New York, and Arizona, educators are trying to respond to the bill by calling members of the House Education and Workforce Committee, but once again we are locked out of the process. Our one hope is Long.

"I don't want to divert the conversation," Coles writes in an e-mail to the listserv for California Literacy Educators (CLEers), "but I do have to say publicly that I found his minimalist general information unsatisfactory, his replies to my questions disappointing, the latest round of our uncovering bill information that he should have provided exasperating."

I start sifting through the pages of *Spin Doctors* wondering what to send. What would you send? You would participate, wouldn't you? I spend the weekend drafting a letter.

The U.S. government's official definition of reading creates a mindless conformism to a single political perspective

On Monday, October 6, I receive a fax of the first twelve pages of the bill from Karen Smith at NCTE, and I am told that the complete bill has been mailed overnight and will arrive the following morning. The bill, which still doesn't have a number, is being introduced by Goodling of Pennsylvania and is referred to as the "Reading Excellence Act."

The purpose of the bill is clearly stated. "To improve the reading skills of students and the in-service instructional practices for teachers who teach reading, through the use of findings from reliable, replicable research on reading, including phonics."[3]

The U.S. Government's proposed official definition of "READING" is vintage Lyon. "The term reading," the House Committee on Education and the Workforce states, "means the process of comprehending the meaning of written text by (A)(i) using the knowledge of the relationships between letters and sounds to accurately and fluently identify printed words, both silently and aloud; and (ii) establishing the ability to quickly and accurately apply decoding skills to automatically recognize words; and (B) critical thinking about written materials based on understanding the meaning of the text."

So what's the problem? Who cares if the federal government defines reading?

We live in a democracy. That's the problem. The federal government should not be establishing official definitions of reading. What if the federal government passed a law that created an official definition of thinking?[4] Whose thoughts would be acceptable? Anti-Semites? Homophobics? What if it was of intelligence? Whose gifts and talents would be recognized? European Americans who speak English?

You're in the labyrinth. In California the same arguments that were used to pass the ABC Laws are now being used to establish laws on English Language Education for immigrant children. Take away their language and you take away their culture. Make the connections. The bill establishes an official orthodoxy. If my questions are making you uncomfortable, let's take a look at the proposed U.S. government's definition of "READING READINESS."

"The term 'reading readiness,'" Goodling's committee states in their Lyonized definition, "means skills that (A) build vocabulary; (B) teach the relationships between sounds and the alphabet; and (C) increase phonemic awareness."

What if you were the parent of a deaf child and the teacher tells you that there is an official definition of reading readiness, and that the only reading programs she can receive funds to use focuses on the relationships between letters and sounds?

According to Carnine teaching phonics is ubiquitous, and Lyon says the "f-word" is "non-negotiable."

What if you were Nicola's teacher and you knew she had been sexually abused and that she was using her own interpretations of written language to express her anger and her grief? Would you make Nicola focus on meaningless exercises in phonics when you know that these mindless exercises will interfere with the evolution of the form of her own primitive script? What would you do if you were observing the progress Nicola was making and you were systematically documenting the transformations that were taking place as she moved closer to recognizable interpretations of traditional orthography? If you were teaching her, helping her understand the graphophonemic connections she was making, would you stop her reading because the ways in which she was learning the relationships between sounds and symbols violated the U.S. government's official definition of reading readiness?

"Nicola is a special case."

Every child is a special case.

"[S]ign-using activity in children is neither simply invented nor passed down by adults," Vygotsky states, "rather it arises from something that is originally not a sign operation and becomes one only after a series of qualitative transformations."

For the U.S. Government to have official definitions of reading and reading readiness creates a mindless conformism to a single political perspective. It forces educators into opposing camps. Many educators, including myself, have no alternative but to resist. The bill puts us in an untenable position. It establishes an orthodoxy which is simplistic and ideological. It violates democratic principles of intellectual freedom and controls scientific thought. It is positivist, mechanistic, and it officially sanctions reductionist views on human learning, while at the same time it subjugates the work of scholars whose research focuses on the scientific study of pedagogical practices, and whose disciplined, systematic observations of children's learning have informed our understandings of how young children learn to read and write.

Finally, here is the U.S. government's proposed official definition of "READING RESEARCH." "The term 'reliable, replicable research,'" Goodling writes as Lyon practices ventriloquy, "means prospective experimental, longitudinal studies that (A) include large samples of subjects; (B) rely on measurements that meet established standards of reliability and validity; (C) test competing theories, where multiple theories exist; and (D) are subjected to peer review before their results are published."

Go back to the beginning of *Spin Doctors*. Experimental research on beginning to read assumes cultural uniformity; focuses on aggregates of children; separates children's everyday lives from their performance on isolated cognitive tasks; artificially disconnects the forms of written language from the functional meanings of print; assumes that children's early cognitive functions work from abstract exercises to reading as meaningful activity; depends on cognitive tests that have no value outside the testing situation; assumes the transference of learning; and totally disregards the critical relationships that exist between teachers and children.

Reliable, replicable experimental research is often nothing more than junk science. In the phonemic awareness studies that I reviewed there are a few exceptions. The studies of Bradley and Bryant provide useful information within a reductionist frame, and the Olofsson and

Lundberg work, with the researchers' thoughtful discussions about the limitations of their studies, provides an important contribution to our understandings of phonemic awareness. I would combine this research with the empirical studies of Burts and her colleagues on the social and moral development of children. After that there are many researchers and scholars who inform my pedagogy on how young children learn to read. Among them are ~~educational anthropologists, biographers, constructivists, critical pedagogists, cultural theorists, discourse analysts, ethnographers, ethnomethodologists, feminist theorists, researchers in modern sociological studies, researchers in new literacy studies, semioticians, sociolinguists, social psychologists, and last but not least, teacher-researchers~~. None of their work can be used to support the programs that the U.S. Government is proposing to fund to teach young children to read.

If the Reading Excellence Act becomes law, programs cannot be based on the work of ~~JoBeth Allen, Sylvia Ashton Warner, Nancy Atwell, David Barton, Glenda Bissex, David Bloome, Deborah Brandt, James Britton, Roger Brown, Carolyn Burke, Andrea Butler, Brian Cambourne, Pat Carini, Courtney Cazden, Noam Chomsky, Marie Clay, Bee Cullinan, Estaban Diaz, Margaret Donaldson, Eleanor Duckwork, Anne Haas Dyson, Carol Edelsky, Elliot Eisener, Peter Elbow, Fred Erikson, Janet Emig, Paulo Freire, Emilia Ferreiro, Richard Figueroa, Lily Wong Fillmore, Michele Foster, Catherine Dorsey Gaines, Margie Gallego, Eminda Garcia, James Gee, Clifford Geertz, Celia Genishi, Yetta Goodman, Ken Goodman, Don Graves, Judith Green, Kris Gutierrez, Michael Halliday, Jane Hansen, Jerome Harste, Shelly Harwayne, Shirley Brice Heath, Don Holdaway, bell hooks, Edmund Huey, Peter Johnston, Jonathan Kozol, Stephen Krashen, William Labov, Judith Langer, Jean Lave, Hope Jensen Leichter, Judith Lindfors, Elvira Sousa Lima, Norma Lopez-Reyna, Susan Lytle, Herb Kohl, Ray McDermott, Dan Madigan, Margaret Meek, Hugh Mehan, James Moffett, Luis Moll, Elinor Ochs, Walter Ong, Vivian Gussin Paley, Jean Piaget, Ralph Peterson, Michael Polanyi, Mary Poplin, Gordon Pradl, Linda Reif, Jay Robinson, Barbara Rogoff, Harold Rosen, Louise Rosenblatt, Regie Routman, Nadeen Ruiz, Robert Rueda, David Schaafsma, Bambi Scheffelin, Sylvia Scribner, Kathy Short, Thomas Skrtic, E. Brooks Smith, Frank Smith, Karen Smith, Geneva Smitherman, Brian Street, Denny Taylor, Jan Turbill, Lev Vygotsky, Dorothy Watson, Connie Weaver, Gordon Wells, or James Wertsch~~.[5]

If the Reading Excellence Act becomes law, Carnine will get his product recall, and the official U.S. definition of "READING RESEARCH" will effectively wipe us all out. The work of the teachers in the Biographic Literacy Profiles Project could not be used as a basis of programs to improve teachers' instructional practices, even though all the schools received awards from the National Council of Teachers of English for the work the teachers did with children who were having difficulties learning to read. None of it will count. It will be gone. If the bill passes, programs will have to be built on research which experiments on large numbers of anonymous children.

Russell writes that politicians need "some badly needed humility" and I agree, but I can't help wondering to what extent the legislative process is being manipulated by the power groups who operate behind the scenes. Lyon is the front man whose definitions of "reading" and "research" are written into the bill, but who pulls his strings? Carnine? Meeder? Sweet? And who pulls their strings? Nothing is what it seems.

Literacy is not a commodity to be bought and sold, researched for profit, prescribed medicinally, or doled out for punishment

The kicker for me comes when I realize that Goodling's bill also has a strong family literacy component. I began my work in family literacy in 1977, and the concept of family literacy was introduced in my doctoral dissertation in 1980.[6] The original conceptualization of the term was *descriptive*, but by 1985 it had become *prescriptive* and family literacy programs became deficit-driven. The National Center for Family Literacy (NCFL), a private organization whose "national" status is self-bestowed, turned family literacy into a commercial enterprise, an industry which thrives on educational inequities. Then in 1994 NCFL announced the development of family literacy "standards and rating scales" to be used to evaluate Even Start and Head Start and other government-funded family literacy programs. The operative words appeared to be "intake," "induction," and "retention" and many educators, including myself, became so concerned that we decided to speak out.

In response to NFCL's inappropriate development of "national" standards and rating scales, I organized an International Forum of Family Literacy which took place in Tucson, Arizona, in October 1994. The forum was followed by a series of conferences and seminars which brought together university teachers with elementary school teachers and family literacy practitioners, librarians, and policymakers. Educators from many different countries worked together, and eventually their efforts led to the publication of *Many Families, Many Literacies: An International Declaration of Principles.*[7]

Many Families includes a preamble and then seven sets of principles which are accompanied by articles by leading scholars from the field of family literacy as well as articles by family literacy practitioners and participants in family literacy programs. The entire premise of the declaration and principles is that "[n]o single, narrow definition of 'family literacy' can do justice to the richness and complexity of families, and the multiple literacies, including the often unrecognized local literacies, that are part of their everyday lives."[8]

"Literacy is a universal right," we state. "It is not a commodity to be bought and sold, researched for profit, prescribed medicinally, or doled out for punishment.

"The voices of family members are important. 'Experts' should not speak for them, own the talk, or write family literacy programs in which their voices are not heard.

"Literacy is not a neutral technology. The notion of 'functional literacy' is frequently artificially defined to support political and ideological agendas.

"Literacy is often erroneously equated with intelligence, and charges of 'illiteracy' are used to attack the poor and cultural groups who are marginalized.

"Literacy is commercialized by those working within the dominant ideological and political frameworks and sold in aberrant forms to families who are often struggling to feed and clothe their children.

"Blaming the lack of literacy skills for the ills of society is a national and international form of political propaganda. Multinational corporations profit directly when literacy is packaged and marketed both nationally and internationally."

Sound familiar? We could be talking about events taking place in Texas or California, or the House of Representatives of the United States, or about basal publishers, such as SRA/McGraw-Hill and Reading Mastery and Open Court.

"The NCFL is quite explicit about its goal of shaping public opinion and public policy," Elsa Auerbach states in her article in *Many Families, Many Literacies*. "It has orchestrated a sophisticated campaign of marketing family literacy that includes tailoring its message to particular audiences, from policy makers and funders to academics and the general public."[9]

"Family literacy has become a product to be packaged, marketed, and sold as a panacea for family and national problems," Auerbach writes, and in a recent conversation with me, she says that she has just attended a conference in Massachusetts and heard Sharon Darling, the president of NCFL, extol the virtues of Goodling's new bill.

I go back to reading the bill. I try to imagine deficit-driven family literacy programs teaching parents to use DISTAR's stimulus-response scripted phonics. This couldn't happen, could it? But then a few days later I am told that in Utah family literacy programs are already using DISTAR. It's absurd, but it is already happening.

"The model of power is that I have it. You don't." Husby says, "I'll decide when you have it and you will do exactly what I say. Exactly what I say."

"Stand up! Sit down! Look at me! Touch your nose!"

"This letter is 'A.' What's this?"

"A."

These narrow definitions violate basic principles of local control and democratic decision-making

The telephone rings. A teacher who has been helping me says she just phoned the House Committee on Education and the Workforce.

"Sweet is taking the calls," she says. "He said the bill will be marked up by the 8th and that they hope to have it through by Columbus Day."

"He said they are using the research of NICHD and Grossen's paper on *30 Years of Research*." She is on a car phone and the line crackles. "I asked him if they were using any other research and he said, 'no.'" Her voice rises, "He said they were using the research of Reid Lyon and Barbara Foorman. He said the Houston research is the only research that holds up to scientific rigor."

The phone continues to ring, and I am told the Reading Excellence Act now has a number. It's H.R. 2614.

I fax the draft of the letter I have written to the House Committee to Karen Smith at NCTE. I'm nervous about sending it to Washington. It seems such a radical step, and I'm irritated with myself for wanting someone to hold my hand. But Smith and Faith Schullstrom, the new executive director of NCTE, have their own battle to fight. They are working with Jerome Harste, the incoming vice president, and NCTE leadership to develop an official position statement against the bill that would be sent to the House Committee on Education and the Workforce from NCTE and any other professional organization that will join them. While it is difficult for me as an individual, it must be even more difficult for the executive boards of the professional organizations. NCTE is in uncharted territory. Pearson is right when he says that the political game has changed and in the end we are all inept. Academics are ill-equipped for the new political imperatives.

Late on Monday, October 6, Harste e-mails the document that he has developed with Schullstrom and Smith to the National Council of Research on Language and Literacy (NCRLL), the National Reading Conference (NRC), and the International Reading Association (IRA). He also sends it to the government-financed national centers for literacy research.

"Here are the two documents that we wish to have your boards approve," Harste writes. "We need as quick a turn-around time as possible. There is a real sense of urgency about this as it is rumored that they hope to have everything pass this week."

The heat is on. Can these academic organizations reach consensus within such a short period of time? What do you think? The e-mail discussion reflects the nervousness of the governing boards. While right-wing conservative groups are highly organized and coordinated, and use the Internet to spread their political ideology and further their national agenda, academics, whose universities have historically remained removed from any political activity, lead more insulated lives, and their discussions on the Net are usually only relevant to other academics who share their research interests and pedagogical concerns.

"The bill as currently written uses irresponsibly a review of research that focused on children who were having difficulties in learning to read," Harste, Schullstrom, and Smith write in a draft opposition statement, "and applies it to any and all children learning to read when, in point of fact, a variety of data sources shows that from 70 to 80 percent of all children are having no difficulty learning to read."

I wonder if members of the House Committee will get that these educators are making what they consider to be appropriately veiled criticisms of NICHD's research and Grossen's *30 Years* synthesis paper? In my mind, I can see Harste's exasperation as he struggles to find the wording that will work for a coalition of associations, something that even politically timid professionals would be willing to sign. I imagine the well-chosen expletives peppering the conversation as draft after draft is marked up and written again.

"The bill enables the federal government," the NCTE statement of opposition draft reads, "to determine what is 'reliable, replicable research' and consequently which reading research gets funded, what professional development programs get implemented, as well as what literacy programs get used and supported in our nation's schools."

"[T]hese narrow definitions violate basic principles of local control and democratic decision making," the NCTE group writes in the opening paragraph of the position statement they intend to send with their letter to the House Committee. A draft statement is circulated and reviewed by numerous volunteers, and the educators work to find an effective public voice. In the construction of this document, Goodman has given them a head start. When Carnine and Meeder wrote an article on the hegemonic project, Goodman not only responded directly by writing a letter which *Education Week* published, he also wrote a statement which he circulated that challenges the constitutionality of federal control of how children are taught to read. While Goodman is often criticized by his colleagues, friends and foe alike, for his outspoken political rhetoric, his foresight proves invaluable as the NCTE statement adapts the document that he has written and applies it directly to the Goodling Reading Excellence Act:

ONE: *Neither the Congress nor any federal agency should establish a single definition of reading or research in funding criteria for preservice or inservice teacher education and professional development programs.*

WHY? Research on reading has always progressed through dialogue and debate. Professional forums already promote the exchange of ideas and support ongoing research. Using federal legislation to push any one view to the exclusion of all others is unwarranted, and will do more harm than good in proposing an agenda that may serve some children while excluding or harming others.

TWO: *Neither Congress nor any federal agency should establish a national reading curriculum or a national reading program.*

WHY? The bill includes phrases, such as "research-based programs," which mask favoritism toward particular, commercial reading programs (DISTAR, Open Court). Congress should not pass laws requiring schools or local education agencies to use any specific program or methodology. If all children are to learn to read well, districts, schools, and teachers need to be able to select programs that meet the needs of their students.

THREE: *Neither Congress nor any federal agency should impose a research agenda that restricts investigation to any single definition of reading or any single research model.*

WHY? Scientific research progresses through debate and critique, not through federally mandating one hypothesis over another. Such an imposition would be anti-scientific and limit what could be learned. Assuring that all children learn to read well depends on continued open debate in the professional research on reading.

FOUR: *Neither Congress nor any federal agency should bypass traditional standards and procedures for peer review; nor should they centralize authority for decision making and review by putting these vital functions in the hands of a single individual or extraordinary authorities.*

WHY? In its draft form, the Reading Excellence Act locates decision making in the hands of specially created agencies, panels, and appointed individuals. This select group would control funding without going through established professional peer review.

FIVE: *There should be no blacklisting or stigmatizing of individuals, pedagogies, universities, research agencies, or instructional programs, either directly or by establishing a single set of criteria for eligible programs or grantees.*

WHY? In several states, legislation has been introduced or passed which singles out and even ridicules certain pedagogies, instructional practices, or materials. These include use of predictable texts, invented spelling, determining meaning from context, whole language methods, all of which are implied to be unacceptable. In other cases criteria for acceptable practice are so specific and narrowly drawn that they have the same effect.

SIX: *No federal law or program should be framed in such a way that its effect would be to provide substantial advantage to any commercial reading program. No person should hold an advisory position with any agency or with Congress who could personally profit from any legislation or regulation.*

WHY? Several people who are authors of specific commercial programs are in key advisory roles to the Committee on Education and the Workforce—the committee responsible for drafting and introducing this bill. Some of these advisors are, in fact, on state and federal payrolls, even though they are associated with specific commercial programs.

While NCTE, NCRLL, IRA, and NRC try to negotiate the tedious and time-consuming bureaucratic procedures that make any kind of collaborative decision making a laborious and long-winded process, teachers are more nimble on their feet and they move quickly to respond to H.R. 2614.

If we believe in the democratic process, if we exercise our right to participate, then maybe, just maybe, our voices will be heard

In California, where mathematics instruction is now also under attack,[10] teachers of reading have been forced to respond to their own state legislature's ABC bills, and they are more prepared for the battle that is taking place in Washington, D.C. These brave teachers, who have become role models for many other teachers across the country, use what they have learned about the political process to make their way into the corridors of power which connect with the central chamber.

They telephone and register their disapproval of the bill, and they fax statements and post e-mail messages to members of the House. Rumor has it that some California teachers have actually managed to obtain the home telephone number of Representative Goodling and that they have been calling him at three o'clock in the morning to tell him that there are serious problems with the bill. Needless to say it is also rumored that Goodling is not amused at being woken up in the middle of the night and that he has complained he is being harassed by elementary school teachers. He probably hasn't considered that from their perspective they are being harassed by him.

Some teachers from California go and see Representative Woolsey, who is on the House Committee for Education and the Workforce.

"First off she said that we were her heroes, teachers that is," Kim Suppes writes, describing their meeting with Woolsey.

"We started to tell her our concerns with the Reading Excellence Act," Suppes explains, "mandating one way of reading," before continuing, "and she shook her head not quite agreeing that that would happen. So we started to talk about how it would limit the research available to teachers and how special interests would be served. She wanted to know what special interests, so we explained about Carnine and Meeder." Suppes continues, "We tried to explain the local control issue and how different districts have different needs and she seemed to get that."

"Maybe we need to focus on the special interests aspect with other representatives," Suppes suggests. "It does imply that it might not be best for the kids when people stand to profit financially from this legislation."

In Missouri, teachers contact Representative Clay, who is also a member of the House Committee, and they try to arrange to meet with him. In the meantime they write him a letter which they also send to Representative Talent.

"We are writing to urge you to oppose the Reading Excellence Act," the Missouri teachers write. "The acceptance of this Act would take control of literacy curriculum and instruction, and would take research out of the hands of teachers. It would invest the future of professional development in literacy education in a 'panel of experts.' Douglas Carnine and Hans Meeder argue that reading instruction must be based on 'scientific research.'" Their definition of acceptable research excludes thousands of research studies that provide insight into ways of teaching literacy effectively. They ignore important bodies of research, claiming that any research that is not experimental with control of experimental groups is not 'scientific.'"

I get on with my own letter. "Based on statements by Robert Sweet, a staff member for the Committee," I write, "it is my understanding that the legislation relies heavily on the research of the National Institute of Child Health and Human Development (NICHD) and, in particular, on the reports and presentations of Dr. G. Reid Lyon, the Director of the Institute, and the NICHD research of Dr. Barbara Foorman and her colleagues who have carried out preliminary early reading intervention studies in Houston, Texas."

"I have conducted a critical review and analysis of the research produced by NICHD," I continue, "and I would like to bring to your attention both the serious problems inherent in the research itself, and the serious problems that will occur for the nation's children if NICHD's research is used as the basis for professional development in early reading instruction in schools, or if NICHD research is used as the basis for programs to assist parents with reading activities, or to amend Even Start."

Then I present six areas of major concern, each supported by documentation from this book.

1. The NICHD research of Dr. Foorman and her colleagues is critically flawed. The misrepresentation of data and the treatment of children in their early intervention studies raise serious ethical questions.
2. The contradictory testimony and racist statements made by Dr. Lyon, the Director of NICHD, have serious implications for the scientific veracity of the research generated by NICHD.
3. NICHD research fails to take into consideration the reliable and replicated research on the negative impact of direct instruction in reading on the sociomoral development of young children.
4. NICHD research fails to take into consideration the reliable and replicated research on the relationships between direct instruction in reading and later criminal activity.
5. NICHD research fails to take into consideration the negative effects of direct instruction in reading on young children who are *currently* learning to read.
6. NICHD research fails to take into consideration the reliable and replicated research on the success of reading instruction in many schools across the country which does not involve systematic, explicit phonics or commercial reading programs.

"The preliminary draft of the 'Reading Excellence Act' states that reading research must be both reliable and replicable," I then write. "The NICHD research is neither reliable nor replicable, and this is particularly problematic because both the definition of reading and the approach to reading instruction contained in the 'Reading Excellence Act' are based on NICHD research."

"I sincerely hope that you will give serious consideration to these and other critical issues in the development of the final version of the bill," I state at the end of the letter. "I also hope that there will be opportunities for other voices from the educational community to be heard who can speak to the issues that I have raised about the research of NICHD."

It's Tuesday afternoon, October 7, and it's getting late. I've been told that the House Committee on Education and the Workforce will now discuss the Reading Excellence Act on October 9. David, my husband, and I are collating the attachments and checking the letters to make sure I've signed them. David sticks the labels on as I write them, then he takes the first batch to our local post office, but when he gets there it is already too late. He makes the thirty-minute drive to the central post office. I'm at home addressing labels. We make another run to the central post office before the overnight cut-off at eight, and then stop at El Charro's, the oldest Mexican restaurant in Tucson.

"How did I get into this?" I ask on the way home, feeling that our attempt to influence a committee of the United States House of Representatives is quixotic.

"*Spin Doctors* was supposed to be a twenty-page paper, not a book," David says. "Now it's longer than *Toxic Literacies*. You've got to stop writing."

"Not until we know what's happened to this bill," I answer. I keep thinking that if enough of us are irrationally idealistic, if we believe in the democratic process, if we exercise our right to participate, then maybe, just maybe, our voices will be heard.

Early on October 9, Karen Smith telephones from NCTE. "The bill's been pulled," she says.

"What does that mean?" I ask.

"It's not going to the House," Smith says. "Long telephoned. He said the committee couldn't reach agreement."

Smith says she thinks the documents I sent helped, but I'm not so sure. They might have stirred things up a bit, but nothing more. It would depend on how many other educators sent letters and telephoned. Maybe enough of us have become so politicized that we actually made a difference. I ask her about the statement from NCTE, and she says it didn't go out.

"Did all the organizations sign?" I ask.

"Except for IRA," she says.

"I'm not surprised," I tell her. I think about the McGraw-Hill and

Scholastic exhibits at the annual convention of IRA in Atlanta, and I am back at the beginning of this book. Back before I read the documentation from North Carolina and before I had watched the videos of the May 8 meeting of the California State Assembly. I can see the bright colors and the smiling faces of the sales representatives of the basal publishers, and I think how gullible we can all be and I wonder why we don't object.

"It's not gone," I say to Smith. "The committee will make a few changes and the bill will be back."

The fact that H.R. 2614 has been shelved means we have time to work out how to respond, but we all know it will be an uphill battle. Most of us are in a quandary. We don't have access to the central chambers of the labyrinth; some of us don't even know the labyrinth exists, and many academics still want to be polite to each other. They still want to drift along, fine-tuning grand theories, discussing right-wing alienation, arguing politely, and writing theoretical papers that will take a year to get published in some obscure academic journal. But this isn't an exchange of ideas for the sake of intellectual debate. This is Washington, where deals are cut and trades are made. This is get down-and-dirty, slam-bang, money-grubbing, power-frenzied, horse-trading politics.

The objective is to equate truth with power and to "dominate the public discourse," as Donald Lazere writes, "to repeat the same strident charges over and over again, even after they have been discredited, until they gain credibility through saturation and intimidation."[11]

If battles over control are thrust upon us, we must defend and express our expertise and work to avert attacks on our schools and our children

What chance have academics against this assault? As if in response to my question, I receive a copy of a thoughtful and well-written academic paper that takes me back to North Carolina. It seems such a long time ago that I read about what is happening in that state. But Noel Jones in "Politics and Phonics: 'Sounding Out' the Consequences" brings it all back.[12] Too late, he writes of the "costs and consequences" of legislative proposals and emphasizes that they are "potentially harmful to many children."

"Many children who seem to be successful in the item learning required by these programs (i.e., learning letters and sounds) still cannot read," Jones states. "They find the memorization of associations easy and this becomes their habit of learning. Reading, on the other hand, is complex problem-solving."

"Learning to read is different from learning phonics," Jones continues. "Research seems to converge upon the notion that the complex mental processing and the integration of information from a variety of sources can only be acquired through the process of engaging in reading and writing activity during which the mind is focused on the meaning of the text."

"The proposal to focus beginning reading on intensive, systematic phonics is a proposal to teach to children's weaknesses," Jones cautions. "It assumes that the way to teach is to test, find out what the person does not know, drill on those items, then retest."

Finally, Jones states, "If we truly wish to make our schools productive for all citizens we must continue to engage in discussions that extend knowledge and reexamine unproductive and unwarranted assumptions." Then in the last sentence he urges educators to fight back. "If battles over control are thrust upon us, we must defend and express our expertise and work to avert attacks on our schools and our children."

But many professors of education who made their names encouraging teachers to rethink their pedagogy are still strangely silent, while other researchers, behaviorists, not known for their holistic pedagogical practices, stand up and shout back at their fellow experimentalists.

Show me the RESEARCH!

Back in September, before anyone had heard of the Reading Excellence Act, Dick Allington published a commentary in *Reading Today*, the newspaper published by IRA. On the right side of the page is an Alice in Wonderland caricature of a man with his mouth wide open and above his head he is holding up a banner on which is printed: *Show me the RESEARCH!* Allington was trained as a behaviorist and he has a background in special education, so even though he has shifted over the years and now calls himself a constructivist, I was surprised when I read what he had written.[13] I must admit his commentary made me smile; it sounded much more like me than him. Allington is scholarly in a way that I will never be, and I know that he has not always appreciated my "theoretical graffiti."

"Because of abundant exaggeration and distortion of the research," Allington states at the end of his commentary, "the only strategy I can recommend is that the studies cited be examined carefully for what was really demonstrated."

Now in October, while the *Council Chronicle*, published by NCTE, alerts teachers around the country to difficulties associated with the Reading Excellence Act, *Reading Today* does not even mention H.R. 2614.[14] Instead IRA provides Foorman and her co-researchers Fletcher and Francis with a public forum for their research.[15]

But of course they don't respond to Allington's Lewis Carroll, "Show me the RESEARCH!" Instead, they write of their "large-scale federally funded research" and of "the danger in underselling methods of reading instruction that, when in place, prevent reading failure."

The "results" of Foorman's research have been published in national newspapers, and even *Parents Magazine*.[16] The documentation has been presented to state legislatures, the federal government is about to pass into law a bill that will change the way in which children are taught to read in the United States, but members of the academic community who have spent their lives studying early literacy still are not privy to the data, and they have been consistently denied access to the evidence. It's the ultimate spin. Children have been sentenced to explicit, systematic phonics before the evidence has been reviewed and before the verdict is in.

"No, no!" says NICHD. "Sentence first—verdict afterwards."[17]

"Stuff and nonsense!" Allington says loudly. "The idea of having the sentence first!"

"Hold your tongue!" says NICHD, turning purple.

"I won't!" says Allington.

"Off with his head!" NICHD shouts. Nobody moves.

"Who cares about *you?*" says Allington, who has grown to his full size. "You're just a stack of unverified data!"

I leave a voice message for Allington and eventually he returns my call. We talk about H.R. 2614, what's happening in California and Texas, and about Lyon and NICHD. Allington has been checking references.

Smile. This is a predictable book. I can hear you saying to yourself, "If A cites B."

Allington says Lyon's references are problematic. He talks about specific citations and of a conversation he's had with Lyon about these difficulties. He says he'll send me a paper.

A couple of days later I receive a copy of the piece by Allington and Haley Woodside-Jiron in which they question the adequacy of NICHD research.[18] They discuss how "code-emphasis advocacy efforts" have shifted the curriculum frameworks in California and Texas, and they state that they have "encountered a common advocacy tool" which they identify as the research of NICHD.

"G. Reid Lyon, the Acting Chief and Director of this NICHD program of research, and several NICHD-supported researchers have been active in providing expert testimony to various policy-making bodies in at least two states," Allington and Woodside-Jiron write, naming California and Texas, "and are actively disseminating the results of their research to national audiences."

They focus on Lyon's A-cites-B difficulties, and give as an example a specific reference to the use of an article by Rebecca Felton on the effects of instruction on the decoding skills of children who have phonological processing problems.[19]

"The critical point here," as Allington and Woodside-Jiron point out, "is that much has been said and written about the 'scientific' nature of the NICHD research, often contrasting the experimental rigor of the NICHD studies with the 'anecdotal' evidence found in educational research journals. But the rigor of the research or the quality of the researchers is not the primary question that is being examined and debated."

This is true. But at least by now some of us agree that NICHD's research is being used hegemonically to create a political mythology of how young children learn to read. It is spin doctoring of the very worst kind, filled with factual errors, slipshod documentation, and self-serving circular arguments, but academics have yet to deconstruct the research on which NICHD has built this mythology.

To address this difficulty, Allington and Woodside-Jiron decide to test the rigor of the research, and so they get hold of some of the original studies supported by NICHD.

"Much of this NICHD research has focused on children identified as experiencing reading/learning difficulties," they state, "or identified as at-risk for reading/learning difficulties. Typically, these children have been drawn from the lowest 20–25 percent of the general student population."

"Should findings derived from special population samples be generalized to recommended instructional reforms for the larger general education population?" Allington and Woodside-Jiron ask, as they establish a dialogue with other educators.

"To date, this NICHD research has achieved reliable, replicable effects on developing phonemic awareness and pseudo-word reading performances in children with reading difficulties," Allington and Woodside-Jiron write. But you and I might not want to make even this small concession to NICHD. If this statement is based on the Foorman studies, then Allington and Woodside-Jiron are too generous.

"Are the performance improvements on the targeted populations reported in the NICHD research sufficient to warrant modifying the general education curriculum?" Allington and Woodside-Jiron pose a rhetorical question to members of the academy.

"Most of the NICHD intervention research has employed an add-on instructional design with specially designed instruction delivered by specially trained teachers outside the general education classroom. In many studies this instruction has been tutorial in nature."

"Can findings from such add-on instruction inform us about appropriate general education curriculum reforms?" they ask, as they push academics to question.

Allington and Woodside-Jiron go on to deconstruct the labyrinthian paper on NICHD research written by Grossen, the paper that Silber sent to every superintendent of schools in the state of Massachusetts, that was used in Texas, distributed in California, circulated by right-wing groups on the Web, and according to Sweet, used by the House Committee on Education and the Workforce as the basis of the Reading Excellence Act.

It's another case of A-cites-B. Allington and Woodside-Jiron "compared the recommendations in the document with the findings of the cited research and found little evidence that the research actually offered support for the specific recommendations."

"Rather few papers authored by researchers funded by NICHD were actually cited in the document. Even fewer citations were for the published original research reports," Allington and Woodside-Jiron conclude, "most were reviews or commentaries."

"The general education instructional recommendations offered were overly specific and far more prescriptive than can be derived from the findings reported in the NICHD studies," they state.

"No NICHD research addressed the important variables targeted in four of the recommendations," Allington and Woodside-Jiron go on to state, "and the research is inadequate to support the other three."

The deconstruction of NICHD's research and Grossen's junk science review strikes a blow at the hegemonic mythology of Lyon's "reliable, replicable research." Allington and Woodside-Jiron's research report, which was funded by the Office of Educational Resources and Improvement (OERI), cracks the surface of the official ideology that has come to dictate what counts as scientific evidence, and pushes educators into verbal revolt against the mindless conformism of Lyon's impoverished medical model. Educators who have spent little time on the Internet take lessons from their right-wing counterparts on how to harness the labyrinthian powers of the Web. They establish listservs and connect them up. Post a message on one listserv and it is quickly passed to another. We learn fast, and literally thousands of messages are written, information is shared, views expressed, and strategies are developed by teachers themselves on how to respond to the United States government's establishment of a single definition of "READING," "READING READINESS," and "RELIABLE, REPLICABLE RESEARCH."

"NCTE is gearing up and getting ready to push a button to reach several listservs including CLE," Smith posts on the Web. "This isn't over yet, but I think we've bought some time. We all need to be working on the Senate bill 939 as well. It openly names the NICHD research as the bottom line for all they plan to do," Smith writes, and then adds, "at least it doesn't try to mask things."

"S939 is the Senate bill 'Successful Reading Research and Instruction Act,'" Coles, in New York State, posts, "whose purpose is 'to establish a National Panel on Early Reading and Effective Reading Instruction.'"

"From what I've been able to figure out," Moustafa, in California, posts, noting that S939 appears to be almost identical to H.R. 2614, "while a bill is in committee the critical people to contact are those people on the committee as they are the ones who are voting for or against the bill. The objective is to keep bad bills such as this one from getting out of committee. Hence, the people we need to get our voices to while a bill is in committee are the committee members. If a bill gets out of committee, then we need to be working the people in the districts we live in as well. If this reasoning is correct," Moustafa adds an aside, "and please help me if I'm off target," as if she is working it out as she writes, "we have to be bombarding the committee members whether they are in our districts or not."

In response to Moustafa's posting, Dorothy Watson in Missouri posts the names of the Senators serving on the Committee on Labor and Human Resources so that letters can be sent to the United States Senate as well as the United States House of Representatives.

We are energized. Most of us who are fighting the bill have lost touch with our ordinary lives. Our own research projects have been abandoned. We spend our days trying to get information about what's happening in Washington and around the country. We try to find out who are the generals and what is the role of the subaltern intellectuals. We try to figure out how the conservative think tanks are manipulating what we think and what we believe about how young children learn to read.

"It keeps you awake at night," Harste says.

He's right. No one is getting any sleep. At 2 a.m. I'm up making notes or reading Michael Lind's *Up From Conservativism: Why the Right is Wrong for America*, Sara Diamond's *Facing the Wrath: Confronting the Right in Dangerous Times*, and Cynthia Crossen's *Tainted Truth: The Manipulation of Fact in America*.

Across the United States more and more teachers go home after school and write letters of opposition to H.R. 2614 which they send to members of the House Committee on Education and the Workforce. We are building momentum, participating in the political process, and there are indications that our voices are beginning to be heard. Are we just in time or are we too late?

The generals and their subaltern intellectuals are biting into power and they are determined to get it all. On October 21, for the first time, I realize that they have the ability to control the press and probably the House of Representatives. No, I am not exaggerating, the labyrinth belongs to them.

Propaganda is to democracy what violence is to totalitarianism

"It's bad," Goodman tells me on the telephone when he calls early on the morning of October 21. The article we've all been waiting for by Jim Collins in *Time Magazine* is in the October 27 issue and it is already on newsstands. Goodman reads me sections of the article which has the predictable title of **"How Johnny Should Read."**

As I listen to him, I think about Collins and the day he spent with Ken and Yetta Goodman at the University of Arizona. I was there. I took notes and tape-recorded the interview which lasted the whole day, and in the evening my husband and I took Collins out to dinner as the Goodmans were unable to take him.

In the notes I wrote during the interview I ask, "How will this guy report on what the Goodmans tell him?" Collins makes me nervous. *He's nervous.* I write that he is tall, thin, balding, and wears tortoiseshell glasses. He is a member of the elite. He went to Exeter and wears a blue shirt and cream pants. He sits in the corner in Ken's office looking uncomfortable, sniffing, and frequently blowing his nose. He rarely makes eye contact, and he is evasive when either of the Goodmans asks him a question. As an ethnographer, what fascinates me most is that he does not record the conversation and he makes notes only occasionally on a small yellow lined pad.[20]

Collins asks the Goodmans how they met. He wants to know about their early lives. They answer his questions, honestly. They answer every question and they are not evasive. Listening to them I am struck by the differences between them and Collins. The reporter is so closed and uptight that there are times when he appears to be positively neurotic, and the Goodmans are so open and friendly that they too make me nervous. I am concerned about what Collins will do with the information that the Goodmans share with him. Will he twist what they say?[21]

The Goodmans talk about reading instruction in the United States. They talk about recurring themes going back to the twenties. They focus on civil rights and their work with urban students.

"We didn't start with interventions and then do experiments," Ken Goodman tells Collins. "We did very in-depth kinds of studies of children reading real texts."[22]

"Miscue analysis is always done with complete texts," Yetta Goodman explains, "so we can see what happens across a whole text."

The Goodmans talk about miscue research, which is the most-replicated reading research that has been completed this century. They have all their original data and make it available to researchers who want to do miscue studies.

Yetta Goodman talks of her literacy studies with children as young as two, three, and four. She speaks of Emilia Ferreiro, and the importance of her work, of Don Graves, and of her own writing studies with Native American children.

"If you watch kids in real reading and writing situations, you get a very different picture than if you just test," she tells Collins.

"How would you characterize Adams's position?" Collins asks.

"Scientific word recognition," Ken Goodman says. "The issue is what is the unit of analysis. Is reading words the unit of analysis or whole texts?"

The Goodmans focus on effective reading.

"The reader is as creative in reading a text as the writer is in writing the text," Yetta Goodman explains.

They talk about reader-response theory, Louise Rosenblatt, Umberto Eco, Bakhtin, and then shift back to Lucy Calkins and Don Graves.

Ken Goodman tells Collins that in the miscue taxonomy they identified thirty categories, or data points, for the analysis of each individual miscue. He talks about the importance of the quality of the miscues. He explains that miscue analysis provides teachers with an opportunity to do their own research. Then the conversation moves on to the philosophy of science.

"I can't dismiss Marilyn Adams because I don't like her work," Goodman explains. "I can only look at her work from the perspective of my model."

They focus on the potential for conflict of interest when researchers work for basal publishers and big money is involved.

"I have never had a basal publisher pay for me at a national conference," Ken Goodman says. "Whole language upset traditional patterns of profits for publishers."

"What's happening," Yetta Goodman says, "is that we have kids reading real books."

They talk about teachers and of the attempts by politicians to try to change the way children are taught to read.

"You cannot simply force things on teachers," Ken Goodman explains. "Teachers will resist. California is forcing teachers to change by writing laws. It won't work. Teachers will close their doors, they will fight back, or, most disturbingly, they will leave the profession."

Yetta talks about supporting teachers who are helping kids learn in democratic classrooms. She talks about John Dewey and gives Collins a brief history of progressive education in the United States.

"All kids have language, and all kids should have the opportunity to use their language in the classroom," Ken Goodman tells Collins.

"Shouldn't we respect the knowledge of teachers?" Yetta Goodman asks him.

"Language isn't a bag of words," Ken Goodman says.

They talk of theme cycles, inquiry-based instruction, Jerry Harste, Carolyn Burke. Different views of language learning. Language as a tool and not as an object of study, the functions of language, making learning as authentic as possible, social convention and invention, variant systems and invariant systems, establishing positive views of learning, perception, and cognition—but none of this is reflected in the article that Jim Collins eventually writes.

In the car park on the way to lunch, Collins says that in a good article there have to be sides, and that he is interested in reading because it is a case study in politics and passion. He says a story must touch the emotions but he never talks about fair representation, or accuracy, or truth.

The next day I share my misgivings about Collins with Ken Goodman, and he says the interview depressed him.

"If it's going to be negative," Goodman says, "I'd rather he left me out."

That was six months ago.

"Collins writes that I am 'grandfatherly, with a goatee and longish white hair,'" Goodman says on the telephone, "and I'm 'a charismatic leader' and I'm the author of 'a folksy 100-page paperback' on phonics."

Goodman tells me that he has been communicating with Collins via e-mail, and that just a couple of weeks ago Collins had written that someone from *Time* would be calling him to check quotes.

"No one called," he says.

Goodman ends the conversation by telling me the joke about learning to live under water that will become so important to the struggle in which we are all engaged.[23]

After speaking with Goodman I download **"How Johnny Should Read."** The article is formulaic, hackneyed, and smacks of right-wing reporting hidden beneath the crinoline of a reporter's supposed political neutrality.

Collins writes that Goodman said, "I like people and I'm very happy that my research confirms my prejudices."

Goodman is adamant that he never made this statement; I do not have it in my notes; and I've listened to the five hours of audiotapes of the meeting and I can't find it there either. I go over my notes again and then reread what Collins wrote. Reading him makes it hard for me to write, but I sit at my computer for most of the day even though I don't seem to have a lot to say.

I suppose Collins could equate his conservative perspective with objectivity and truth, but the metal toe caps on his boots are sticking out from beneath his carefully crafted prose. He begins his article with a politically correct horror story, follows it with a crying teacher, and then moves in quickly to demolish Ken Goodman. True to the political rhetoric of our time, Yetta Goodman is conveniently left out.

Let's see if you can predict what Collins has to say.

"The counter-revolution began in 1990 with the publication of another landmark book, *Beginning to Read: Thinking and Learning About Print*, by Marilyn Adams, a cognitive psychologist.

"The concept that Adams brought to the fore was 'phonemic awareness.' Phonemes are the smallest meaningful [sic] sounds in a language. English has 44 phonemes that its speakers combine to make all its words. Cat, for example, has three: 'kuh-aa-tuh.' Adams concluded that in order to read, one must understand that the sounds in a word can be broken up this way."

"As the 1990s progressed, more verification of the importance of phonemic awareness came from studies conducted by the National Institute of Child Health and Human Development at the National Institutes of Health.

"Under the direction of Reid Lyon, researchers have found that problems with phonemic awareness correlate extremely closely with reading failure. Other NICHD studies have reaffirmed the conclusions reached by Chall and Adams—that programs with some systematic phonics instruction lead to better outcomes.

"Finally, brain-imaging studies are beginning to show how poor readers differ neurologically from good readers, and the indication so far is that the former have less activity in the brain's 'phonological processor.'"

"Propaganda is to democracy what violence is to totalitarianism," Noam Chomsky writes in *Manufacturing Consent*. "The techniques have been honed to a high art, far beyond anything that Orwell dreamt of," he states. "[E]liminating rational critical discussion is one of the more subtle means, though more crude techniques are also widely used and are highly effective in protecting us from seeing what we observe, from knowledge and understanding of the world in which we live."

Perhaps some of you are convinced that the delay in the publication in *Time* of the article by Collins so that it arrives on newsstands just as the House Committee on Education and the Workforce is about to reconsider the Reading Excellence Act is nothing more than happenstance.[24] But in my mailbox is the October 27 edition of *Newsweek* and on the front cover is a 1950s little girl and beside her the headline "**KIDS WHO CAN'T LEARN.**"

Inside, "**WHY ANDY COULDN'T READ**" fills half a page, and the article begins with another politically correct horror story which is followed by the types of "learning disabilities" that afflict children: dyslexia, dysgraphia, dyscalculia, dyspraxia, attention deficit disorder, and dysnomia.

"Researchers have identified four distinct steps in learning to read," the authors, Pat Wingert and Barbara Kantrowitz, state. "Breakdowns anywhere in this process can explain severe reading problems. G. Reid Lyon, acting chief of the child-development and behavior branch of the National Institutes of Child Health and Human Development, says that reading for all children begins with phonological awareness. Combinations of just 44 phonemes produce every English word."

"A new study of 285 children in a poor neighborhood in Houston, for example," these authors state, in a totally fabricated interpretation of Foorman's research, "shows those who were taught the forty-four phonemes first to be 10 percentage points ahead of those taught in accordance with whole language theory on a reading comprehension test."

"The whole-language forces have studies of their own," Wingert and Kantrowitz explain, with an aside about Frank Smith stating phonics just doesn't work, "but," they continue, "as Lyon often points out, these studies haven't been successfully replicated."

"Children who will be good readers," Lyon is quoted as saying, "just have a knack for understanding that words are made up of different sounds before they learn anything about the alphabet."

"The next step," Wingert and Kantrowitz explain, "is linking these sounds with specific letters. This can be confusing," they say, "because most letters—in English and many other languages—can have more than one sound. The reading-instruction methods known as linguistics (sound to letters) and phonics (letters to sound) focus on this part of the process by having kids sound out words."

"The third step, Lyon says, is for a child to become a fast reader," these authors continue, "to make the association between symbol and sound virtually automatic so that the child can move on to the final step concentrating on the meaning of words." In brackets they add, "Researchers around the country are testing ways to put these findings into reading programs for all kids, not just learning-disabled children" (p. 60).

"If we do not identify children early, by the end of second grade," Lyon is later quoted as saying, "the majority of them will have difficulty reading for the rest of their lives."[25]

Conrad Bromberg, who was blacklisted during the McCarthy era, says that during that time the press was the "servator of the inquisition." Bromberg says that the "free media" of today is "corrupt, absolutely."[26]

In the October 27, 1997, *US News and World Report*, Lyon is quoted by Thomas Toch, who reviews a book by Diane McGuinness in an article entitled "The Reading Wars Continue." After talking about the forty-three sounds of the English language, Toch predictably quotes Lyon.

"[R]esearch showing the importance of teaching kids the sound structure of language dates to the 1960s and some phonics programs now reflect this, says Reid Lyon of the National Institutes of Health."

I remember that somewhere in one of Ian Fleming's early James Bond novels, Bond says, "The first time it's happenstance, the second time it's coincidence, and the third time it's enemy action."[27]

In the November issue of the *Atlantic Monthly* which is already on the newsstands there is an article by Nicholas Lemann entitled "**THE READING WARS.**" The article focuses on California, and Lemann refers to Honig as a "phonics zealot." Reid Lyon is, of course, referred to in the piece. He is described as "the head of the development and behavior branch of the National Institute of Child Health and Human Development."

"Reid Lyon is a nightmare figure for the whole language movement," Lemann writes, "because he has the means to fund large, scientifically reputable studies of reading instruction methods, the results of which have made him into a wholehearted and very public opponent of dropping phonics."

"Propaganda is to democracy" — there is nothing coincidental about the publication of these articles just as the House Committee on Education and the Workforce is about to consider the Reading Excellence Act. It's a well-organized campaign, mind-numbing, and mind-dumbing.

"For those who stubbornly seek freedom," Chomsky writes, "there can be no more urgent task than to come to understand the mechanisms and practices of indoctrination."

"Brainwashing under freedom," Chomsky calls it, "to which we are subjected and which all too often we serve as willing or unwitting instruments" (p. 29).

"See Dick Flunk," is the heading of Tyce Palmaffy's article in the *Policy Review*, which is published by the ultra-conservative Heritage Foundation. Again the article is formulaic. A political horror story about Alexis, who is inside a National Institutes of Health reading lab. Alexis inserts words, she skips words, she guesses, and she substitutes other words.

"Alexis is one of more than 10,000 participants in an ongoing 30-year, $200-million study of reading disabilities by the National Institute of Child Health and Human Development (NICHD), a division of the NIH," Palmaffy writes, practicing a form of hyperbolic indoctrination. "Acting NICHD Chief Reid Lyon sadly notes that her case is typical of children who have not received proper instruction in how the sounds heard in speech are represented by the letter symbols used in print." Palmaffy explains that means the relationship known as phonics.

"Says Lyon, "There is no way to read if you are not very facile in the use of phonics,'" he writes.

Palmaffy then attacks President Clinton and his America Reads Challenge which, he writes, "declines to incorporate the NICHD findings and recommendations." Predictably he moves to NAEP. Then a swipe at whole language with a quote from Grossen. Then on to Adams, who Palmaffy states is a visiting scholar at the Harvard School of Education. He then notes that North Carolina, Texas, Georgia, Washington, Wisconsin, Oregon, and Ohio have recently passed phonics legislation.

Palmaffy moves on to the national organizations stating that the International Reading Association has reversed policy to "specifically" promote phonics instruction, and that the American Federation of Teachers (AFT) "has come down squarely on the side of skills-based instruction for beginners. A quick mention of the National Education Association and Palmaffy is on to California and a broadside at Goodman. In his primer for the legislature Palmaffy writes of Horace Mann, John Dewey, and the forty-four speech sounds. Then Noah Webster's *Blue-Black Speller*, Rudolf Flesch, and "Why Johnny Can't Read." Another go at Goodman. This time from Lyon.

"'Goodman based his ideas on a poor study whose findings were never replicated,' says Lyon of the NIH. 'It never would have gotten through a National Institutes of Health Review.'"

Palmaffy moves on to Stanovich, and Foorman, before describing the training video that Lyon used in San Francisco. Remember *chu chu chu, cherry pie*, and *jacket*. This is his entree to decodable texts and another quote from Lyon.

"People from literature-based philosophies would freak out if they saw this," he writes that Lyon says. "They don't want to work with kids on these subskills."

"Phonics is non-negotiable," he quotes Lyon as saying.

Once Palmaffy has stacked the deck, he moves in for a frontal assault on the House Committee on Education and the Workforce.

"I've been here all these years and never knew there was an ongoing project on reading at the NIH," he quotes Goodling as saying. Then he adds, referring to the day when Lyon gave testimony, "Neither did his colleagues, and since only 13 members of the 45 member committee even bothered to show up to the hearing, few of them found out about it."

"More disturbing," Palmaffy continues, making sure that Congress gets it, "is the situation on the front lines. The people who should be most familiar with the research—education professors, teachers, and school administrators—have routinely adopted instructional methods and curricula heavily influenced by whole language in spite of the overwhelming body of research evidence supporting phonics.

"Reid Lyon tells of his encounter with a California teacher seeking a doctorate in reading instruction who approached him after a lecture," Palmaffy continues. "Her face wet with tears, she told him that no one had ever exposed her to phonics-based instruction."

"The majority of teachers we've talked to who have been trained over the last 10 years have never even discussed these issues," he quotes Lyon as saying.

Timing is everything

The generals and the subaltern intellectuals are prepared. Through the use of the mass media they have captured the hearts and minds of the American public. A cultural shift has taken place in the way in which the nation believes young children learn to read. Now all that is left is to convert Congress. It's October 22, 1997.

"The House Education and Workforce Committee will be marking up the Reading Excellence Act, H.R. 2614, on Wednesday 10:30 a.m.," Long reports. "This will be an interesting markup because many Republicans on the committee are not in favor of this measure," Long writes, "and the same is true of the committee Democrats." This is encouraging news to the many of us who oppose the bill, and it is particularly gratifying to read what Long writes next. "The administration came out against the bill because of its definitions," which, Long explains, it considered federal intrusion, "and the voucher plan for after-school teachers."[28]

"Most likely the Chairman will put a lot of pressure on enough members to either get their votes or ask them not to show up," Long writes. "In either event I will update you tomorrow."

"Timing is everything," Urquhart says in *To Play the King*, and with the help of the press, Lyon has been used to prepare the House Committee for the bill.

Long misread the situation. Without fanfare, not with a bang, nor with a whimper, and without even a snicker, on October 23, the Reading Excellence Act, H.R. 2614, passes out of committee and is ready for the House of Representatives to consider. There was a voice vote, so no one is on the record.

At the time that the bill passes out of committee, Lyon posts a complaint on CATENet, the listserv of the California Association of Teachers of English.

"I still can not understand how the NICHD research continues to be viewed as supportive of only phonics," Lyon writes in a plaintive reverse spin.[29]

Zinke responds sharply with a quote that could have come from Lyon's testimony at the May 8, 1996, meeting of the California State Assembly.[30]

"'[R]eading scientists, after three decades of well-designed and replicated research, much of it supported by the National Institute of Health,' Zinke quotes, 'have found that reading success depends on specific linguistic proficiencies including awareness of speech sounds, the ability to link speech sounds with written symbols, and the ability to read words fluently and accurately. All this undergirds reading comprehension.'"

"That sounds like a view that takes one cueing system (phonics) much more seriously than the others," Zinke writes. "In my three decades of teaching young children to read, I have noticed much more than phonics undergirding reading comprehension."

"Reid Lyon says different things to different audiences," Goodman posts on CATENet. "To us he professes surprise that anyone thinks that his agency is pushing phonics but he has not publically refuted Bonnie Grossen's summary of 30 years of NICHD research which says it shows that direct instruction systematic phonics instruction is proven to exceed all else."[31]

Keep in mind you're in the hegemonic labyrinth and that many different events are taking place. At the time that H.R. 2614 passes out of committee and the interchange with Lyon takes place on CATENet, Bess Altwerger, who lives and teaches in Maryland, receives an invitation to a luncheon given by the Heritage Foundation.

"Speaking will be Reid Lyon," Altwerger's letter from the Heritage

Foundation states, "chief of child development and behavior at the National Institute of Child Health and Human Development. The NICHD has conducted $200 million of research over 30 years showing that phonics is the most effective way to teach children who do not learn to read at home."

Illiteracy is a health risk, and anything that poses a danger to our children's health should undergo tough scientific scrutiny

At about the same time that Lyon gets ready to speak to the Heritage Foundation, Governor Bush in Texas dedicates a new reading research center (CARS) at the University of Texas Health Science Center.

"By launching this new center, this university is saying we recognize illiteracy is a health risk," Bush declares, according to Melanie Markley of the *Houston Chronicle*, "and anything that poses a danger to our children's health should undergo tough scientific scrutiny."

"Reading researchers Barbara Foorman and associates Jack Fletcher and David Francis will direct the center," Markley writes. "Foorman," she explains, "chaired a task force that recommended a new reading curriculum for the Houston Independent School District." Markley then names the school district, which has tried so hard to remain anonymous, in which Foorman conducted her controversial research, and she writes that Foorman "found that at-risk children learn to read better when they receive a concentrated phonetic foundation."

"Bush said he is taking steps to pressure the teacher colleges to embrace the reading center's research," Markley continues. She then quotes Bush. "For those teacher colleges who are wedded to the past and who refuse to listen to the evidence that comes out of this center," Bush is quoted as saying, "my message is loud and clear: Change."

The news of the new Foorman reading research center is a bitter pill to researchers who are fighting the Reading Excellence Act. They are still denied access to Foorman's NICHD data even though the verdict from the House Committee is in. In the *Houston Chronicle* Markley writes that the center was paid for with public money. Researchers and teachers ask who paid for the center? What public money? NICHD? Is it a hegemonic prize for gross hypocrisy?

The official flyer states, "Supported by over $12 million in grant support over the next five years from the **National Institute of Child Health and Human Development (NICHD)**, the studies of reading instruction in the early grades completed by **CARS** are widely acclaimed in the scientific community for results that help define the components of successful in-school programs." The bold is in the text.

Based on this statement Goodman assumes that Lyon has funded the center, and he shares this information with members of the CATENet listserv.

"He has now also funded a center at the University of Texas Health Center in Houston to do what Gov. Bush called 'field tests' with Foorman and her colleagues in charge," Goodman writes.[32]

"Reid Lyon has not funded our reading center," retorts Jack Fletcher, one of Foorman's co-reseachers, who joins the fray to respond sharply to Goodman's CATENet posting. "The NICHD does fund research centers, but we are not recipients of center support from NICHD."[33]

Goodman persists. "The information about the funding of [the] reading research center in the University of Texas Health Sciences campus came from the program for the celebration of its establishment," he writes on CATENet in response to Fletcher, "at which Governor Bush also referred to its NICHD funding. Please tell us how it is funded if that information is incorrect."[34]

When Fletcher does not respond, Goodman posts another query on CATENet. This time he quotes the sentence on the official CARS flyer which begins "[s]upported by over $12 million in grant support over the next five years from the **National Institute of Child Health and Human Development (NICHD)**. . . ."[35]

"So is the center funded by NICHD?" Goodman asks.

"I was really pleased to see that Dr. Goodman had read the brochure on our reading center," Fletcher responds, politely. "As always, I am glad to respond to questions posed about our research and related activities. He asked 'so is the center funded by NICHD?' the answer, as I previously stated is 'no.' We do not have center support from the NICHD. My grammar is not very good, but the referent to 'supported by over $12 million in grant support' is 'the studies of reading instruction.' Regardless the discussion is silly."

But it's not silly. Foorman's research is the "reliable, replicable research" on which the U.S. government is basing the proposed national definitions of reading, reading readiness, and what counts as research.

"For those teacher colleges who are wedded to the past and who refuse to listen to the evidence that comes out of this center," Bush says, "my message is loud and clear: Change."

"We are very appreciative of Dr. Goodman's close attention to our affairs," Fletcher writes, without disguising his irritation, "and hope that his decoding skills improve since there is too much guessing from expectations."

Again this book is writing me. Analyzing the exchange between Fletcher and Goodman, I decide to interject and post a message to CATENet. "By refusing to give a straightforward answer to a straightforward question," I write at the end of my posting, "Dr. Fletcher leaves at least some of us wondering if there is something about the funding of CARS that he would prefer not to be discussed in public. But, as it appears from statements made by Governor Bush in the *Houston Chronicle* that the center is supported by public funds, then the public has the right to know the source of those funds and how the funds were awarded to Drs. Foorman, Fletcher, and Francis."

"The questions about how CARS is funded are silly," Fletcher responds several weeks later. "To reiterate, we have over $12 M in research funds to Foorman and Fletcher from NICHD for the next 5 years."

Go back and read what Fletcher wrote in response to Goodman's question. "'[S]o is the center funded by NICHD?' the answer, as I previously stated is 'no.' We do not have center support from the NICHD."

It's just one more twist in the hegemonic labyrinth. But there are others. Even though researchers cannot obtain the data from Foorman's Houston studies, both Lyon and Fletcher want to publicly make it seem like they can.

"I do hope though that people in the educational community realize that they can have access to all documents that are in the public domain," Lyon states on CATENet. "They can also call me to discuss the issues or to request available materials."[36]

"People need to know that they can obtain information about NICHD supported studies directly from the research sites," Lyon writes in another CATENet posting.[37]

"There still appears to be confusion about a number of issues involving NICHD research and I would like to try to clarify these issues again," Lyon writes, in yet another posting. "I would also urge that people give me a call and also speak or visit any of the research sites within the research network." Then he adds, "We disseminate information as quickly as we can."[38]

"As always I am glad to respond to questions posed about our research and related activities," Fletcher posts. "Dr. Lyon and I [are] both responsive to inquiries. I can't think of any questions about the Foorman study that one of the authors has not attempted to address."[39]

I am concerned that both Lyon and Fletcher give the impression that they are open and responsive to questions, and that they will readily provide requested information from any NICHD study, and that all that we have to do is ask. Once again the book is writing me. In response to the messages that they posted on CATENet I post a copy of the request for information that I wrote when I was conducting the statistical analysis of Foorman's Houston studies, and I include in the posting the responses I received denying me access to the information which I had requested.[40]

In addition, by now I have a draft of the article by Foorman, Fletcher, and Francis that is to appear in the *Journal of Educational Psychology*, which presents basically the same statistical analysis and findings as Foorman presented at the May 8, 1996, meeting of the Education Committee of the California Assembly. I note that I have a draft of the paper in my CATENet posting.

"[C]ontrary to the e-mail responses from Dr. Fletcher and Dr. Lyon that the paper would answer most of the questions," I write; "it answered only one minor question. In fact, rather than providing answers to the specific questions that we asked, the paper only raises more questions about the scientific veracity of the Houston studies."

"The e-mail responses by Drs. Fletcher and Lyon are disingenuous," I continue. "Both gentlemen must have been aware when they responded to my request that the answers to the questions that we asked could not be obtained from the *Journal of Educational Psychology* paper."

"Dr. Lyon's 'invitation' to replicate the Houston studies also misses the point, and perhaps here we must give Dr. Lyon the benefit of the doubt as he genuinely doesn't seem to get it," I state. "'Replication' does not mean that interested scientists have to redo the entire series of studies. The data has been collected using public money and concerned scientists should be afforded the opportunity to replicate the data analysis."

"In a CATENet posting on Saturday, November 1, 1997," I continue, "Dr. Lyon states in his letter to Michael Pressley which he chooses to make public: 'I have been trained that our job as scientists is to conduct research to falsify hypotheses and not to support them at all costs.'

"Then on CATENet, Friday, November 7, he states, 'Replication is a cornerstone in the development of a scientific data base that can be trusted in the decision-making process. I would ask readers of this post to broadly sample studies within the reading field and ask, 'If I wanted to, does the study contain enough information about the children's cognitive, academic, family education, language, reading, writing, mathematics characteristics, as well as the characteristics of the school and school programs so a similar sample could be selected for replication. Then ask whether the instructional programs and/or methods are described in sufficient detail to ensure that a second study could proceed in the same way. Readers will be surprised at how infrequently this information is provided.'"

"Surprise! Surprise!" I write in my CATENet posting, "The article in the *Journal of Educational Psychology* by Dr. Foorman and her colleagues is sadly lacking in this requisite information. In fact, based on an analysis of 'initial' and 'preliminary' papers and a deconstruction of oral presentations, not only is the necessary information for replication not included in the article, the data that is presented obfuscates critical aspects of the research which are essential for any kind of legitimate and meaningful peer review.

"I would hope that researchers would not be forced to resort to the use of the Freedom of Information Act to obtain the raw data from the Houston studies as both Drs. Lyon and Fletcher suggest in their CATENet postings on October 27. This is an unnecessarily cumbersome, tedious, and drawn-out legal procedure, and is used to obtain documents and information from recalcitrant Federal agencies that are 'reluctant' to provide information in response to simple written requests.

"In their e-mail responses to my written request for information, Drs. Lyon and Fletcher write of 'preliminary analyses' and 'initial phases of the studies,' but as we are all aware, laws have been passed at both the state and national level based in large part upon these studies, and despite their protestations, concerned scientists have yet to be provided with any of the primary data.

"Dr. Fletcher stated in his Monday, 27 October, CATENet posting that the Houston research: 'includes rigorously defined samples that are sufficiently large and representative, relies on measurements that meet established standards of reliability and validity, tests competing theories where multiple theories exist, was subject to peer review before the results were published, and has important implications for effective strategies for improving reading skills.'

"I regard this statement by Dr. Fletcher with considerable scepticism. Based upon the documentation that I have been able to obtain from various sources, including, among other artifacts, early papers distributed at conferences, transcripts of meetings, and videos of presentations, there are very serious inadequacies in the Houston studies," I write. "The research results are neither reliable nor replicable. Although there were large numbers of children participating in the studies, some 'treatment' groups had very few children and the measurements that were used did not meet established standards of reliability or validity.

"In his CATENet posting on 28 October, Dr. Fletcher asked, 'How about a discussion of standards of evidence?' He then expressed the opinion that 'It would be more productive to define research, to talk about standards of evidence, or how research should be used in education. Develop some real differences in opinion or alternative arguments not just distorted reactions to legitimate viewpoints.'

"Excellent. I agree," I write on CATENet. "I would like to invite Dr. Fletcher and Dr. Foorman to present with me at the Spring Conference of NCTE. Let's put the data from the Houston studies on the table, define what is meant by research, talk about standards of evidence, and how research should be used in education. Of course, this would mean sharing the primary data from the studies as Dr. Lyon states is necessary, but I'm sure that if Dr. Fletcher is convinced that the samples were rigorously defined, as well as sufficiently large and representative, and that the measurements meet established standards of reliability and validity, that would not cause any difficulty."

Fletcher responds but ignores my invitation to discuss the Houston studies at the NCTE Spring Conference. He categorically denies that I have a copy of the paper that is to be published and states that many of the questions I ask can be answered by information in the original proposal.

"Many of the other questions are based on preliminary analyses of the data," Fletcher states, and of course he is right, my analysis is based on the preliminary data presented to the California State Legislature and to the Congress of the United States, "and we would be glad to respond to questions about these analyses if there [sic] are still viewed as 'pressing' after the paper is published."[41]

By then it will be too late!

"As far as putting the data on the table," Fletcher continues, "our response is the same as before. Read the paper and ask your question. Denny Taylor should ask herself, however, about the purpose of the questions. We thought she was serious, but she seems to have already reached conclusions about the study. So what purpose would be served by responding? She should get her statistician to help her to summarize their 'concerns' into a paper and submit them to the cold glare of peer review," Fletcher writes, "and see if the concerns pass muster."[42]

Fair enough. Except for the end of the chapter that I am writing, *Spin Doctors* has been sent to five reviewers and five members of the Editorial Board of the National Council of Teachers of English, and while it is clear that I have some editing to do, the manuscript has been unanimously accepted for publication. However, once again I am stuck. The Reading Excellence Act is out of committee and it is essential to deconstruct Foorman's NICHD research before the bill hits the floor of the House of Representatives, but my questions have not been answered and I still don't have access to the raw data from the study.

To hide behind a future journal publication at such a critical moment in time is unethical. I have been told that the copy of the Houston study which has been sent to me is being revised yet again, but in empirical science, the data is the data, surely the numbers won't change? The number of children, the tests used, the procedures, the analysis of the data, surely none of this will change? Moreover, what right or claim does the *Journal of Educational Psychology* have over the data? I've decided to revisit the information on the Houston studies that I have managed to obtain, and on which I built the analysis that I presented at the beginning of *Spin Doctors* and to juxtapose my original analyses with the draft I have obtained of the "final" paper.[43]

Scholars and journalists advance a corporate-friendly agenda

Let me be specific. The analysis that I am going to present to you is based on documentation that has come into the public arena from: (1) the original NICHD proposal for the Houston research; (2) papers which present the preliminary analysis of the data by the principle investigators; (3) the official transcript of Foorman's presentation of the findings of the research to the Business Council of Governor Bush in Texas; (4) the official video of Foorman's presentation of the findings to the Education Committee of the California State Assembly.

The documentation listed above is referred to by both Lyon and the principal investigators as "preliminary analysis" and the "initial phase" of ongoing research, and educational researchers have been told that they should wait before attempting to examine the data and replicate the findings until an article about the research is published at some indeterminate date in the *Journal of Educational Psychology*.

It is important to emphasize that, while members of the research community have been repeatedly denied access to the primary data, and both Lyon and the principle investigators have declined to answer critical questions about the research, state laws have been passed based upon the research, and the United States House of Representatives has used Foorman's research as a basis for H.R. 2614, the Reading Excellence Act, which now awaits a hearing in the Senate. Thus there are serious ethical issues regarding the presentation of this research to policymakers at the state and national level, and these issues should be addressed before any further legislative action is undertaken which relies even in part on the NICHD Houston Reading Studies conducted by Foorman, Fletcher, and Francis, and which have been actively promoted by Lyon. Under these circumstances, my use of the draft of the article that will eventually appear in the *Journal of Educational Psychology* is the only alternative available.

The following critique focuses upon the Title 1 study, in which 375 children, 209 first graders and 166 second graders, received one of three kinds of reading instruction: (1) direct instruction in phonics using the Open Court basal reading program; (2) embedded phonics instruction; and (3) whole language. There was also a fourth much smaller "unseen" control group which received whole language and no curriculum intervention. The study purports to show that direct instruction using Open Court is a superior method of reading instruction, and this "finding" has been presented to state legislatures, to the United States House of Representatives Committee on Education and the Workforce, and has been disseminated nationwide on television and in national and local newspapers and magazines. However, based upon an analysis of the available data, this and other findings presented by Foorman and her colleagues appear to be critically flawed. Let me present the major inadequacies of the research.

The research design and execution are biased in favor of the Open Court/Direct Instruction treatment group.

The Open Court/Direct Instruction curriculum intervention received significant financial and personnel support from SRA/McGraw-Hill, the publisher of the Open Court basal reading program, who clearly stood to benefit commercially from a positive finding in support of Open Court. The subsequent adoption of the Open Court basal reading program in California, Texas, and numerous other states has resulted in significantly increased revenues and profits for SRA/McGraw-Hill.

There is considerable evidence that some of the key results of the study are misrepresented in favor of the Open Court/Direct Instruction treatment group.

For example, the children in the whole language control group who received no extra funds nor extra materials and whose teachers received no extra support actually had higher scores on the Formal Reading Inventory than the children in the Open Court/Direct Instruction treatment group on whom large amounts of money had been spent, whose teachers received extra training, and who had been taught using Open Court. This unadvertised result directly contradicts the widely disseminated "finding" that the Open Court/Direct Instruction program was a superior method of reading instruction.

*The samples are biased in favor of the Open
Court/Direct Instruction treatment group.*

First, the whole language "unseen" control group was only half the size
of the other groups, was drawn from a single school in the poorest neighborhood in the school district, was 70 percent African American, 16 percent Hispanic, 9 percent White, and 5 percent Asian, and 84 percent of
the children were recipients of the Federal Lunch Program. Dr. Foorman
herself has stated that this was "not a good control group." In contrast,
the Open Court/Direct Instruction group was drawn from four different
schools in which there appear to have been very different demographics. For example, the children in one of the schools were 19 percent
African American, 19 percent Hispanic, 33 percent White, and 29 percent Asian, and only 45 percent of the children were recipients of the
Federal Lunch Program. [For the purposes of the study, the researchers
combined Asian children with White children.]

   Second, the children who participated in the study were eligible for
Title 1 and scored in the lowest quartile on the emergent literacy survey
administered by the district. The children with the lowest scores received
tutorials, while children with higher scores were on a waiting list. An
analysis of the available data shows that the samples drawn from the
tutorial and nontutorial groups were biased in favor of the Open Court/
Direct Instruction group. The Open Court/Direct Instruction group was
drawn approximately 45 percent from children in the higher scoring
(nontutorial) group and 55 percent from the children in the lower scoring (tutorial) group. In contrast, the whole language group and the whole
language "unseen" control group were drawn approximately 16 percent
from the children in the higher scoring (nontutorial) group and 84 percent from the children in the lower scoring (tutorial) group.

*Additional, accelerated instruction was provided
only to the Open Court/Direct Instruction group.*

At the suggestion of the Open Court training personnel, approximately
45 percent of the children in the Direct Instruction/Open Court group
received an accelerated treatment program to enhance their ability to
read words and pseudowords. These children received two Open Court
lessons per day instead of one for the first six months of the study. No
other group was given such preferential treatment.

*The numerous defects and the resulting statistical
uncertainties make any conclusions in favor of Open*

*Court/Direct Instruction nothing more than complicated
guesses based upon the biases inherent in the research.*

The statistical modeling of individual growth rates, the statistical methods, the statistical assumptions, and the statistical analyses are unverifiable, false, or inappropriate, as well as simplistic and biased.

In analyzing their data the researchers use a form of analysis known as "parametric statistics," which are based on the assumptions that (1) the samples are randomly drawn and are therefore representative of the population being studied, (2) the sample and population distributions are both normal, and (3) the performance measurements satisfy the requirements of an interval scale. In the Title 1 Houston reading study (1) the samples were clearly not random, (2) the distributions were clearly not normal, and (3) the performance measures were clearly not on an interval scale but are at best nominal or ordinal.

The researchers make the unwarranted and unsupported assumption that each individual child's growth rate on each phonological and word reading performance measure can be represented by a straight line. The researchers make the further unwarranted and unsupported assumption that the relative efficacy of the various instructional practices can be established by collapsing the straight lines from as many as 109 individual children into a single "average" child, so that the individual differences in scores are totally lost. This procedure discards the individual data for each child, and the presentation of the findings provides no information about individual children's progress or scores, and nothing about the range of scores for the children in each treatment group.

In simple terms, this analysis approach implies that the reading abilities of 109 children of different ages, in different grades (first and second grade), from as many as four different schools, from four different ethnic groups, with widely varying social and cultural experiences, and with very different familial experiences and different home languages can be reduced to a single straight line on a chart.[44]

In Sacramento, Open Court is mandated in all elementary schools in the school district, and reading coaches, known to many teachers as "the phonics police," monitor the ways in which they use the basal reading program.

"Teachers work from detailed instructional guides," Deborah Anderluh, writes in the *Sacramento Bee*, "scripted down to the very examples they are to write on the board."

I am back to Chomsky and his manufactured consent. It's in *Time Magazine, Newsweek, US News and World Report,* the *Atlantic Monthly,* and *Policy Review.* We all agree, Lyon says it's so, so it must be. But we *don't* all agree, even though the House Committee on Education and the Workforce now serves willingly or unwittingly as the instrument of the right-wing conservative groups who have promoted Lyon and Foorman's NICHD research. *We don't agree.*

When I was a child my mother used to say "what you don't know can't hurt you," but what we don't know *can* hurt us. The hegemonic project is based on us believing and not knowing, but *we know*.

We know that, as Lazere writes in the October 1997 issue of *College English*, "The conservative foundations function largely as PR agencies for their parent corporations and capitalist ideology in general, expressly recruiting, training, and coordinating scholars and journalists to advance a corporate-friendly agenda."[45]

We know that in the third quarter of 1997 the net income for McGraw-Hill Companies, Inc., grew from 25.3 percent over the comparable 1996 3Q, and that the revenue for the third quarter of 1997 increased 20.5 percent to $1.1 billion. In educational and professional publishing, revenue grew 30.1 percent to $681.2 million, operating profits increased 32.7 percent to $187 million, and operating margins improved to 27.4 percent.[46]

Joseph Dionne, chairman and chief executive of the McGraw-Hill Companies, calls the gains in educational publishing "superb results," and talks of "a record quarter for revenue and profits" on the New York Business Wire.

"**McGraw-Hill's Eduational Publishing Drives Stellar 3Q,**" is the heading of a newsbrief by Jill Goldsmith for the *Dow Jones Newswires*. "A booming market for educational publishers fired up third quarter earnings at McGraw-Hill Cos., (MHP)," Goldsmith writes, "as the company moved to grow and refine its businesses through initiatives at home and abroad."[47]

"In an interview with Dow Jones," Goldsmith adds, "McGraw-Hill President Terry McGraw described a red-hot elementary to high school market that saw his company take a big share in adoption states where a state education board sets the curriculum, and so-called open territories."

"The school division won 60 percent of the $75 million Texas social studies adoption," Goldsmith states. "And new products like Spotlight on Literacy and Collections for Young Scholars garnered the unit 35 percent of the giant $120 million California reading adoption."

"These programs are successful in other markets, too," the press release from McGraw-Hill reports on the New York Business Wire, "illustrating again the benefits of our broad based publishing strategy. For example, the School Division's new reading program took more than half of the adoption in Georgia and is performing well in other adoption states and in open territories. SRA/McGraw-Hill also did well in Georgia, Florida and the open territories."

The Reading Excellence Act will prescribe a "one-size-fits-all" approach to reading instruction and professional development that will seriously damage teachers' ability to help all students learn how to read

We know that the Reading Excellence Act is about great power and huge profits. As I stated at the beginning of this chapter, the war is political and ideological, a product of new capitalism. It is racist and hegemonic.

The more teachers know about H.R. 2614, the more determined they are to fight. I have hundreds of Internet postings regarding the bill. Teachers are now contacting their own members of Congress to register their disapproval of the bill, and NCTE continues to lead the resistance.

"It looks like the Reading Excellence Act may be on the floor of the House as early as Thursday," Long posts, on Tuesday, October 28. "We know that there is a new draft being developed. However we are running out of time to inform you and ask for your help. We need to make one more push on this legislation."

"The agreement that was being worked on between the Republicans and the Democrats looks like it has fallen apart," Long follows up on Wednesday, October 29. "Most of the groups are against the legislation," he states, "different sections are offending different groups. It looks like the Democrats will vote against the legislation and many Republicans don't want the bill either." Long ends by writing, "Over the next day or so we can expect either significant negotiations, or a delay in the vote, or a rejection when it is voted on."

"NCTE, CCCC, NRC, and NCRLL sent a statement of opposition to the House Committee two weeks ago," Karen Smith of NCTE posts the same day. "Tomorrow, we will hand-deliver a letter of opposition to each of the 400 plus Representatives of the House. We are also issuing a press release with an opposition statement. While we are doing what we can at the national level, we urge you to do what you can at the state and local levels by contacting your congressperson with your opinion."

"[T]he legislation will prescribe a 'one-size-fits-all' approach to reading instruction and professional development that will seriously damage teachers' ability to help all students learn how to read," NCTE states in the press release.

"Reading instruction and professional development programs based solely on the kinds of research this legislation favors, studies which are so controlled as to remove any semblance of real-world classrooms, won't help the teachers striving to meet high standards of literacy," Carol Avery, the President of NCTE, is quoted as saying. "Parents and teachers need to be alarmed and to know that effective reading instruction must begin with the learner. Research needs to take individual students into account before it proposes instructional methods for teachers."

There is at least some consensus among teachers who are opposed to the bill that one of the critical issues is loss of local control and the one-size-fits-all approach to reading instruction that is inherent in the Reading Excellence Act. Logically, teachers try to communicate their concern about these issues to members of the House of Representatives. But there is no logic to the House. Like I said before, nothing is what it seems.

The central chamber of the labyrinth is empty and the power lies elsewhere

On October 29, one of the "Special Order Speeches" given by Representative John Shadegg of Phoenix, Arizona, becomes a colloquy with Republican Representative Dave Weldon from Florida, and Republican Representative Peter Hoekstra of Michigan. It is important to note here that Hoekstra is a member of the House Committee on Education and the Workforce which is considering H.R. 2614, the Reading Excellence Act. In close-ups on C-SPAN, but to a totally empty House, they present their ideas on President Clinton's eighth-grade math test. What follows are excerpts from the colloquy. Let's pick up what they have to say as Shadegg pontificates on what is wrong with President Clinton's National Testing Proposal.

"I think this illustrates a larger issue of what is desperately wrong with this National Testing Proposal," Shadegg states, "and that is it puts all the power, and all the focus, and all of the authority in Washington, D.C."

"It comes down to this," Shadegg says later in his speech, "I trust the teachers, the administrators at my daughter's high school," Shadegg names the school. "I trust them. I know them there. If I want my voice to be heard in the curriculum at the school district or the high school, my wife or I can go to their curriculum discussions and have input. We can make our voice heard."

"I don't happen to trust Mr. Reilly and the national experts that will write the federal test and dictate it all across the country," Shadegg is still speaking, "and I think we'd be making a grave mistake if we put all of our eggs in the one basket of a national test."

"The risk of handing over the control of all of our children's education to one single federal test is, I think, an absolute disaster," Shadegg declares a few minutes later.

"What about a single approach to teaching reading?" I ask Shadegg, talking to him as he pontificates on C-SPAN. "What's the difference?" I know the difference, of course: the difference is that the National Test belongs to President Clinton and the Reading Excellence Act is a Republican bill. The arguments that we are making against H.R. 2614 are precisely the same arguments the Republicans are making against the Democratic National Test.

"They're horse-trading children," I say to David, who is watching Shadegg's colloquy with me.

"The question is," Weldon says in a to-and-fro with Shadegg, "is it an appropriate role for the federal government to be instituting a national test? And just to point to Sweden, a country of seven million people or some other foreign little country that has national testing and say they do it, therefore we should do it, is ludicrous in my opinion. This is a country of 260 million people, fifty different states, people of all kind of diverse ethic backgrounds. There's no way that a one-size-fits-all concept could be put on the United States. This is just a different country. But the most important issue that you have brought up today and the biggest reason why I oppose national testing is because I don't have confidence in the federal government to do it correctly."

"But the federal government is going to define reading," I say to the TV. "The government is going to define what counts as research. They'd never do that in Sweden."

"Do you believe that those of us who oppose a one-size-fits-all, national test, that is a federal government mathematics test, written inside the Beltway of Washington, D.C., is a bad idea?" Shadegg's voice rises as he practices his oratory skills by asking a question of the absent opposition. "Do you believe that those of us who believe that it's a bad idea don't care about public education?"

"Delaware started at the grass-roots level," Hoekstra declares. "They got parents involved, they got administrators involved."

I remind David that Hoekstra is a Republican member of the House Committee on Education and the Workforce. I sent him the letter with the attachments which were based on the documentation that I have presented to you in *Spin Doctors*.

"This President in six to eight months," Hoekstra feigns disbelief, "wow, he develops a test. No parental involvement. No local involve-ment. Hasn't gone to the governor of our state!" Later, Hoekstra asks, "What is working in your school district? Or who is making a difference? Why are your schools improving? What is the catalyst? I am still yet to hear someone say, 'It's that new federal program.' The schools that are doing well are typically where a group of parents, administrators, and teachers have taken back their school and said, 'We're going to focus on these kids and we are not going to focus on the bureaucracy or red tape that either comes from Sacramento or Lansing. But we know the kids' names. We know what their needs are. We are going to focus on our kids. We're going to take our schools back.'"

Listening to Hoekstra, for the first time I realize that the central cham-ber of the labyrinth is empty and that the power lies elsewhere. If Hoekstra really believes what he has just said, and if he voted his conscience, there is no way he could vote for the Reading Excellence Act. Again, nothing is what it seems. The real power lies in the small ancillary cham-bers of the labyrinth, where big business and special interest lobbyists lurk, and where there are corridors of power and privilege that lead di-rectly into the central chamber. The bottom line of the bottomed-out mind is that what happens in the central chamber is decided elsewhere.

"I think it will be an absolute disaster if we turn the education of our children in America over to Washington, D.C.," Shadegg argues vehe-mently. "We owe the children of America more than abdicating our responsibility to Washington, D.C., and letting their education be dic-tated millions of miles from their homes and thousands of layers of bu-reaucrats from their own principal and teacher."

"What we have found as we've gone around the country," Hoekstra says, apparently talking about the field visits of the House Committee on Education and the Workforce, "schools that are working and are do-ing a good job of educating our children are those where there is local parental control. Not where Washington is dictating the agenda. This is a battle of where are education decisions for our children going to be made? Is the direction going to be at the local level or is it going to be moved to Washington? All you have to do is go around the country. Take a look at the grass-roots level. You'll be surprised at the wonderful things that are going on in all types of education. Public. Private. Parochial. Religious education efforts. But it's because of grass roots, not because of what we're doing here in Washington."

I press the remote and turn off the TV as the colloquy ends. *If* Hoekstra votes in committee for the Reading Excellence Act, he will vote *for* Washington dictating to local communities how young children are taught to read. I ask myself how can we communicate with members of Congress who can take opposite sides of the same basic issue according to whether it is a Democratic or Republican bill, and then blindly vote their ideology and not their conscience.

There are reports late on Wednesday, November 5, that Goodling met with the president earlier in the day and that a deal has been made. The President will get his national test if Goodling gets his reading bill.[48]

On Thursday I start recording C-SPAN. In the House of Representatives the rules have been suspended and bills are being rushed through an almost empty House before the members go into recess for the holidays. Every two hours I check on the House Web site to see if H.R. 2614 has reached the floor. Then I rewind the tape and start recording again. All day Thursday I write, check the Web, then rewind the tape. Friday it's the same. Record, write, check, rewind, record, write, check. C-SPAN is on the TV in my kitchen and every so often I stop and try to figure out which bill is being discussed.

Late on Friday evening I receive an e-mail from Smith at NCTE relaying a message from Long. "House Bill 2614 will go before the House tomorrow. There will be a 40-minute debate, followed by a voice vote. It may be broadcast on C-SPAN."

There can be no more urgent task than to come to understand the mechanisms and practices of indoctrination

It's Saturday, and the House starts late. A few members take their seats, but most of the seats are empty. There is some discussion about procedures, but there is a videotape in my VCR and I am recording just in case the Reading Excellence Act comes up early. I sit in the kitchen with the last written version of the bill that I have downloaded from the House Web site and go through it while I watch C-SPAN. I focus on the words "reliable, replicable research."

The purpose of the bill is to improve reading skills of children using the findings of "reliable, replicable research."

Eligible professional development providers provide professional development to teachers based on "reliable, replicable research." Eligible research institutions are institutions of higher education in which "reliable, replicable research" is conducted.

"Reliable, replicable research" means "objective, valid, scientific studies" which include (1) "rigorous samples" that are "sufficiently large and representative to support general conclusions drawn"; (2) "rely on measurements that meet established standards of reliability and validity"; (3) "test competing theories"; (4) "are subject to peer review before their results are published"; and (5) "discover effective strategies for improving reading skills."

I pause for a moment and think of Foorman's research. Ironically, the Houston studies do not meet these criteria, and neither do most of the other reading studies supported by NICHD.[49]

The House is bogged down in a discussion of procedures. I continue working my way through the bill. I remember that Farstrup of IRA told me a few days ago that "in theory all money could go into private hands."[50] Farstrup was right to be concerned. There it is in the bill. Private non-profit and for-profit groups are eligible for grants if they provide reading instruction based on "reliable, replicable research." Grant funds can also be used to disseminate "reliable, replicable research."

Subgrantees will use practices based on "reliable, replicable research." Supervised individuals and tutors who have been appropriately trained using "reliable, replicable research" will work with children who are in first, second, and third grade before and after school.

A "panel of experts" will evaluate applications based on "reliable, replicable research." Priority will be given to states that "have modified, are modifying, or providing an assurance that not later than 1 year after receiving a grant the state will modify state teacher certification in the area of reading to reflect reliable, replicable research."

I'm impressed with the thoroughness of the bill. It's a far-right coup d'état, a total mind-meld to ensure a national cultural shift in the way young children are taught to read. Reading is the ability to use phonics skills and knowledge of letters and sounds to decode.

"It's astonishing to me that people define reading as making meaning," Louisa Moats is quoted as saying by Halford in *Infobrief* published by ASCD.[51] "Reading has to do with decoding print."

Meaning is left out. Context no longer exists. The bill makes nonsense of reader-response theory but must make eminent sense to those who believe in censorship. When children are forced to focus on decoding as "reading," the relationships between written language and reality, between language and thought, and between language and the emergence of critical consciousness are distorted and ultimately controlled.

"Language and reality are dynamically intertwined," Freire writes in his essay *The Importance of the Act of Reading*. "The understanding attained by critical reading of a text implies perceiving the relationship between text and context."[52]

"Control language and you control knowledge and the critical understanding of ideas," I say to myself. Go back and read what Chomsky writes about stubbornly seeking freedom. "[T]here can be no more urgent task than to come to understand the mechanisms and practices of indoctrination." It's critical that we understand what is happening because of this bill.

"Reliable, replicable research" is mentioned twenty-seven times in the version of the Reading Excellence Act that I am reading, and NICHD is also mentioned. "The National Institute of Child Health and Human Development and the Secretary of Education will convene the panel to evaluate applications, and representatives from NICHD will be included on the panel."

In the House Committee report that accompanies the bill I pulled off the House Web site "reliable, replicable research" appears over fifty times. There is mention of the series of hearings held by the House Committee on Education and the Workforce which "explored current research on how children learn to read, and the need for strong professional development for teachers of reading on reliable, replicable research on reading."

"Dr. Lyon of NIH testified before the Committee that fewer than 10 percent of our nation's teachers have an adequate understanding of how reading develops or how to provide reading instruction to struggling readers. Less than 2 percent of our teachers have ever seen their professor demonstrate teaching practices with children of diverse skills in a systematic way. About 90 percent of our teachers have never had the theories they have learned—the theoretical information—directly linked to providing instruction to a wide range of children."

Lyon is also quoted as saying that "children who do not learn to read before the end of third grade never actually catch up to their peers." Throughout the report NICHD is mentioned repeatedly.

"[A] member of the NICHD research team made the following observation. . . ."

"Although there has been extensive research in reading instruction conducted over the last thirty years, the most current is that done by NICHD."

"[A]n NICHD researcher noted. . . ."

"Congress mandated that a comprehensive research program be developed in the area of reading and other learning disabilities. NICHD studies have cost the taxpayer more than $200 million and have been conducted at some of the most prestigious universities in America and Canada."

Goodling is finally on C-SPAN.[53] Hoekstra does not appear to be in the House, and he certainly doesn't speak. Clay, whom teachers in Missouri spent so much time trying to educate, also is not visible in the House.

"Mr. Speaker, I rise in support of H.R. 2614, the Reading Excellence Act," Goodling, who is the Republican Representative from Pennsylvania, begins his oratory. "The issue of illiteracy is one of my main interests since I came to work in this body, and over the years I've had the opportunity to work in this bipartisan legislation directed at improving the literacy of our nation's citizens no matter what their age."

"Members will be seated," the Speaker says. "Gentleman will proceed."

"Today we have an opportunity to support a refinement and improvement of all existing literacy programs," Goodling states. "The Reading Excellence Act which will help ensure that individuals of all ages will receive the skills they need to lead productive lives." Goodling explains that the budget agreement said that the President will have a literacy bill. "It is our responsibility as an authorizing committee," he says. "We did not participate in the budget agreement," Goodling emphasizes before continuing, "but it was our responsibility then to make sure that whatever that literacy bill is a well-thought-out bill, and a bill that will work. And so having that in mind, I looked at the President's bill and then I decided on what areas we should really concentrate on if we are going to improve literacy in this country. And the general outline then became: One, make sure that the teachers have the help they need to effectively teach reading based on reliable, replicable research, including phonics."

"Gentleman's time has expired," the Speaker states. "The chair recognizes the gentleman from California, Mr. Martinez."

Martinez, a Democrat, commends the President and his America Reads Legislation. Then he talks about the bill. At the bottom of the TV screen words appear. "Grants could be used for teacher instruction based on 'reliable, replicable research on reading.'"

"The bill provides the much-needed assistance for teachers to receive professional development in teaching children to read more effectively, and it will ensure that professional development is based on reliable, replicable research," Martinez says, as if to reinforce the words on the screen. He then defines what he means. "In other words, proven methods of reading instruction."

Martinez has been sold a bill of goods.

"I strongly believe that the legislation before us today will truly help children to read independently by the end of the third grade and grasp the essential literacy components necessary for employment in our technologically advanced society," Martinez states. "I believe, I also believe that both parties should feel confident that this legislation balances the two very important needs in assuring, in assuring childhood literacy.

Strong professional development for reading teachers and additional tutoring assistance before and after school, on weekends, and during the summer. I urge all members to support this important legislation and reserve the balance of my time."

Goodling yields four minutes to the subcommittee chairman, Congressman Riggs.

"Four minutes," the Speaker says. "Gentleman from California is recognized for four minutes."

Riggs is a Republican from California. He talks about the "proper approach" to spending the money set aside in the budget for a new federal literacy initiative and his opposition to the expansion of the President's America Reads initiative. He says that many teachers have never received "proper instruction" in teaching reading.

No. There is no "reliable, replicable research" to support this proposition.

"If you can imagine," Riggs says. "And I know that speaks volumes about traditional teacher education at colleges and universities, we'd like to address that problem, perhaps we can address it in a bigger way when we get around to the reauthorization of the higher education act."

"But at least here in this bill we've made it a start by providing grants to states and local school districts," he adds. "In those school districts that have the most glaring need is documented by the fact that they have the most Title I students, they have the most so-called school improvement sites, and with those schools and those students that we want to help teachers, classroom teachers, reading specialists obtain the best training based on reliable, replicable research in order to do a better job teaching our young people."

"And lastly," Riggs sums up, "as I said, we also provide money for parents and legal guardians to obtain tutorial assistance for their children. In those instances where a child needs more intensive, one-on-one type of reading instruction from the tutor that they're not able to obtain during the course of the school day, and we say that those grants can be used by parents and guardians to obtain tutoring services from a list of approved and recommended tutors by the local school district. So I think what we've crafted here is a good balanced bill, one that fulfills the obligation that we have on the authorizing committee to come up with the details of authorized legislation to spend the 260 million set aside for the budget agreement."

The Speaker recognizes Roemer, a Democrat from Indiana.

"I rise in strong support of this bill," Roemer states, "both for policy reasons and for some very, very substantive reasons which are included in this bill. First of all on the policy reasons, again we are not recreating the wheel, we are not coming up with a brand new program here, we are trying to find ways to improve the existing program and work with parents and teachers and volunteers and professionals to solve one of the most vexing and heartbreaking problems in America today.

"Illiteracy hurts businesses, costing them billions of dollars when they don't get the right kind of employees coming out of our high schools that can read, it hurts parents who cannot read appropriately to their children, it certainly hurts children's self-esteem when they fall behind."

"This bill comes up with new ideas to fix an existing problem and to improve an existing program. What are these ideas?" Roemer asks. "First of all, we focus on young children in the kindergarten and the first grade, and next year in the Head Start program we hope to move it even further, closer to two and three and four years old and earlier in their education. Secondly, we stress family literacy and encouraging the parent to work as the child's first teacher and encouraging parents to develop literacy skills. Thirdly, we require states to have a professional development program for teachers."

When Roemer's three minutes are up, the Speaker recognizes the gentlewoman from New Jersey for two minutes.

Roukema, a Republican, calls for unanimous consent. "Studies have shown," she says, "I may as well repeat this, it's been stated, that studies have shown that 40 percent of the nation's fourth-grade, graders are below basic reading skills; that's something that has to be improved.

"And I know that there are those here that want to give volunteer help through AmeriCorp," Roukema continues, "that's not the issue here today because there is not a principal or educator in this country who wouldn't say, who wouldn't—would turn away volunteers, but they would also say that the most important essential need is that we train, have *real* reading training for teachers in the classroom, and that's what this bill does, it gives that assistance to the classroom teacher and gives that training."

The Speaker recognizes Miller, a Democrat from California who spends one of his three minutes thanking Goodling and members of the committee.

Miller begins by stating that "we" are "not doing a very good job" of teaching children to read. He then states, "I think that this legislation starts to turn us around in that in terms of the emphasis that it places on the professional development of teachers. It's clear that we have got to have competent, capable teachers in that classroom spending time with those children to help them learn to read, it's clear that we've got to get the parents of these children involved in reading to their children, in encouraging their children, in rewarding their children, for reading competency and it's also very clear that we've got to call upon additional volunteers to come to our schools and to spend time with the children."

Peterson, a Republican from Pennsylvania, is recognized for two minutes, and he talks about tutorial subsistence grants so that "Johnny and Suzy's parents can have the ability to pick from a list" of tutors.

"The gentleman from New York is recognized for four minutes."

"I was shocked to learn that most of the teachers in our schools have never been trained to teach reading," Major Owens, a Democrat, states after his introductory remarks. "There's an article in the *New York Times* editorial page which said the overwhelming majority of the teachers in our schools have never been trained to teach reading and there is a need to have some kind of instruction on how to do that, it will improve the job."

I wonder if the *New York Times* article came out the same week as *Time* and *Newsweek*, and if so, if the article quoted Lyon.

"So the children who will benefit from this, need it now," Owens looks troubled. "We cannot hesitate and wait, we should go on and do all we can, so this is one more small effort to improve education in America, it is just that, a small effort this is like, you know, dipping from the lake of inadequacy with a tea cup, and it is a small program.

"Two hundred million dollars may sound like a lot of money out there, but you know a nuclear submarine costs two billion dollars, more than two billion dollars, if we're really going to deal with the problem of teaching reading we ought to get on to trying to make an impact on the schools of education with some kind of federal program in the future. I don't know if it costs as much as a nuclear submarine or not, probably not, but it would require a bigger effort than this one.

"I hope that these pilot programs, these good common-sense efforts are only a prelude to this Congress going ahead in the future to deal with the overwhelming problem of inadequate and substandard education in America."

Finally, after six months of following the events that are taking place in Texas, California, and Washington, and reading every document I can find, Major Owens is the first public official or researcher to express concern about the infrastructure of schools in the United States and the effect that this problem might have on young children learning to read.

Remember Baldwin? "It's not the lack of quality school facilities," he said. In denial, of course. Right-wing conservatives are not interested in improving the infrastructure of schools. There's nothing in it for them. No power. No privilege. Basal publishers aren't interested either in the adoption states or the "territories." McGraw-Hill's stock won't go up if Congress invests in school buildings so that children have desks and chairs, and politicians won't get elected for making sure that children in inner-city schools don't have to use bathrooms as classrooms when they are learning to read.

"You know the war against substandard education in America cannot be fought by some, with some rifle corps going out, that helps you know, this is a little operation where we're going to send out a few platoons to deal with the problem," Owens continues with his military metaphor, "but you need a real war to deal with substandard education, a real war means that you deal with basic problems like school construction, you know school construction is a basic problem out there, you know a-hundred-twenty-billion dollars to deal with infrastructure of schools all across America."

Go back to the chapter on Louisiana. It may seem out of place in a book about the politics of reading, but it isn't; it's the other side of the argument. The next time you read the politically correct horror story at the beginning of a story about early reading in *Time* or *Newsweek* or the *Atlantic Monthly*, ask yourself why there are no stories about the children in Louisiana. For the tabloid-minded the problem doesn't exist. The children in Red River Parish, Louisiana, the children in East L. A., the children in the Bronx, *they* don't exist. The difficulties they face are reduced by Lyon to a lack of phonemic awareness and systematic, explicit phonics. "They've never even heard these sound systems," Lyon says, absolving politicians of their responsibility to ensure that every child in the United States of America can attend a school where the roof doesn't leak, the boiler works, where there are toilets that flush, where there is a place to eat, and where there are books for children to read. Phonics has become the "anti-poverty pill," but it doesn't work.

"And even if we don't get nearly that much," Owens continues, talking about the 120 billion dollars to fix the infrastructure of U.S. schools, "we ought to do better than we've done so far, you know, to say that we are going to teach reading better and make efforts to make reading or to improve technological instruction or more technology in the schools when the kids are still up against the problem where their boilers are breaking down in the schools and they have to bundle up to go to school in order to stay warm."

"You know that couldn't just happen in Washington, D.C., there's a number of schools all across America that have problems in terms of heat," Owens says, as he slips back into the political rhetoric of an elected official. "So we should see this as a wonderful prelude, as an indication that the Congress cares, for we are just beginning to deal with the bigger problem, we are just beginning to fight the war.

"These are little patrols we are sending out, to reconnoiter, scout out the problems, the problem is much bigger and beyond this program on reading which is about two hundred and ten million dollars, I understand. We need to have a comprehensive approach to education, stimulated and guided by the Congress of the United States despite the fact that the primary responsibility for education is at the local level. We can provide the leadership, we can provide the stimulation, we will never be responsible for education, that's a matter of the states, but we can go beyond the eight, eight percent of education expenditures and move on to a more important role in leading the, this fight to really wage the war against substandard education in America.

"This is the beginning, but let's get ready to fight a bigger war."

"Gentleman's time has expired."

The speaker recognizes Paul, a Republican from Texas, who is the only member of the Congress to speak in opposition to the bill.

"Mr. Speaker, I appreciate the opportunity to express my opposition to the Reading Excellence Act," Paul states. "Which creates yet another unconstitutional, ineffective, 260 million dollar new federal educational program." Paul talks about past federal programs that failed, then ends by stating, "Mr. Speaker, it's ironic that the reason we are considering this bill is because the budget agreement which was supposed to end the era of big government calls for the creation of a federal literacy program. Obviously, the budget does not end big government but preserves and expands unconstitutional interference in areas where the federal government has neither legitimacy nor competence, rather than returning money and authority to the states."

"The gentleman from Delaware is recognized for two minutes."

Castle, a Republican from Delaware, talks about the importance of volunteers and of his own experience in a school near the capitol and talks about teacher training.

"I think teachers' training is imperative," Castle states. "Reading teachers need to learn the best methods for teaching reading based on reliable, replicable research. By giving children the basic building blocks of literacy, learning how to sound out the written word, they will be well on their way to becoming literate adults, and that's exactly what this legislation does, as has been described today. Under this bill, states, through reading and literacy programs, will compete for literacy grants to be used for innovative, inservice reading programs that will be used for classroom teachers and related reading activities based on the best research available.

"And I can't think of anything that is better to do, instilling in our young people the ability to read is absolute. This legislation helps do that and I am again very thankful for all those who put it together. I hope that all can pull together in support. I yield the balance of my time."

"I yield two minutes to the gentlelady from Kentucky," Goodling says, "who worked hard in the state legislature to improve education, Congresswoman Northrup."

"Mr. Speaker, I rise and I am pleased to rise in support of the Reading Excellence Act," Anne Northrup, a Republican from Kentucky. "While we are all concerned about new federal programs, the budget agreement set aside 260 million dollars for a new literacy program. What we could have had is another feel-good, unproven, sounds-good program, the kinds, the kind of program that has failed our children so badly. Forty-four percent of the U.S. students in elementary do not read at a basic level, 32 percent of children of college graduates also have failed to reach this basic level.

"This may be the most important bill that we pass regarding our children and their success in school because what it does, finally and most importantly, is focus on the proven ways of, of reading, teaching children how to read. We know today that the latest scientific research shows that 60–70 percent of all children read any way you teach them but the other children need a very systematic, phonics-based approach to reading if they are ever going to read and be good readers.

"We furthermore know that, science has shown us that, children who do not read by the end of third grade will always have a bigger struggle in reaching that basic level, their opportunity to be good readers is much more difficult if they don't learn to read by the end of third grade, reading opens doors and failure to read slams those doors shut."

No. Science has not shown us this. Lyon has told us. Science and Lyon are not synonymous.

"So what we need to do is to make sure that we use these kinds of scientifically proven methods to teach our children, one that has not been in our schools so often in the past. This phonics-based approach is what teachers will learn as a result of this funding."

Phonics-based instruction has not been scientifically proven. On the contrary, many scientists believe that such approaches are based on overly simplistic interpretations of the reading process which ignore decades of research based on the disciplined systematic documentation of young children as they are learning to read.

"We will also give parents the opportunity to provide tutorial service for their children, their choice based on the most recommended types of tutoring and and reading approach. It also endorses family literacy so we are approaching our, giving our children and also giving the opportunity to schools who teach the right kind of reading and parents who can help those children in the same way. Thank you and I support this bill."

Martinez speaks again briefly and is followed by Goodling again.

"I yield myself the remainder of the time," Goodling says. He sums up and then ends the discussion. "We're not out there to try to create some magnificent program that will end all illiteracy in this country. We are trying to make all of our programs better programs so that every child has the opportunity for quality education. They *must* have it if we are going to succeed in a very competitive twenty-first century. We cannot have 40 percent of our children unable to read properly. Reading readiness, reading skills, at one time you were *literate* if you could read at a sixth-grade level, now you are *functionally illiterate* if you cannot read and comprehend at a twelfth grade level. The only thing that I want from the old schools is discipline. Everything else I want to be *better*, and I yield back the balance of my time."

"Gentleman yields back the balance of his time and his time has expired," the Speaker states, as several members of the House arrive ready to discuss the next bill. "All time has expired." One member of the House continues reading his newspaper. "The question is," the Speaker states, "Will the House suspend the rules and pass the bill, H.R. 2614 as amended?"

"So many as are in favor say aye."

The response is audible even though the House is almost empty.

"Those oppose no."

If there is a response I didn't hear it.

"In the opinion of the Chair two-thirds of those present having voted in the affirmative," the Speaker rattles on, "the rules are suspended, the bill is passed, and without objection the motion to reconsider is laid on the table."

The Speaker recognizes the gentleman from Pennsylvania.

"Mr. Speaker, I ask for unanimous consent that all members may have five legislative days in which to revise and extend their remarks on H.R. 2614."

"Without objection."

Mobilizing a consensus without (extreme) coercion, universalistic literacy allows dominant groups to appropriate popular practices and traditions

"They all sounded so reasonable," I say to David. "It would be so easy to believe them if I hadn't helped a child learn to read."

The bill has been shrouded in crinolines and ruffles. Similar to the California Committee hearing, what the members of the House of Representatives have presented was carefully orchestrated. It was a parody of the democratic process except for Paul, to whom I am grateful, for even though I think there is very little on which he and I would agree, on this day, in the House, his dissenting voice stood for democracy.

In an essay entitled "Hegemonic Practice," James Collins, the social theorist, uses Jenny Cook-Gumperz's concept of "schooled literacy" which Collins says "has slowly become *the* norm for all literacy" (p. 232).[54]

"This universalistic literacy constitutes a strong ideological control or domination," Collins writes, "the sources of which are interesting. Mobilizing a consensus without (extreme) coercion, universalistic literacy allows dominant groups to appropriate popular practices and traditions."

The Reading Excellence Act is hegemonic. Without overt coercion, it transforms our understandings of how young children learn to read while at the same time the act controls how children are taught to read. It's brilliant. Local decision-making is glorified in the political rhetoric while the United States House of Representatives takes control at the national level.

First H.R. 2614 pressures states. To obtain funding through the bill, states will be expected to modify teacher certification to reflect "reliable, replicable research" in reading by the end of the first year.

Second, H.R. 2614 pressures universities. To obtain funding, only research institutions that engage in "reliable, replicable research," in other words, outdated, discredited, reductionist, experimental studies in which children are subjects or a subscript i, need apply.

Third, H.R. 2614 pressures providers of inservice education for teachers. Only providers who use "reliable, replicable research," such as Honig's Consortium on Reading Excellence (CORE), DISTAR, Open Court, or Success for All, will be eligible to receive grants—H.R. 2614 is a cash cow for commercial programs and private companies that sell phonemic awareness activities and phonics skills. Master teachers who have devoted their lives to young children and their early literacy development, such as the teachers I worked with in the Biographic Literacy Profiles Project, will be ineligible for funding.

Fourth, H.R. 2614 pressures providers of before- and after-school tutorial services. Tutors must be trained using reliable, replicable research. H.R. 2614 is a commercial bonanza for companies such as the Sylvan Learning Centers.

Finally, H.R. 2614 pressures family literacy practitioners to base their work with parents and their young children on "reliable, replicable research" which will, no doubt, increase the power base of the self-ascribed

National Center for Family Literacy and will effectively exclude many family literacy practitioners who work with families and their many literacies in liberating ways.[55]

So tell me. How did the right-wing conservatives who sponsored the Reading Excellence Act manage to get the bill through the House when so many of us worked so hard to oppose the bill? Deconstruct the documentation I have presented to you. What are the key elements in getting H.R. 2614 through the House? Make some notes and then check them against this list from Joel Spring, which clearly applies to the right-wing support of systematic, explicit phonics instruction in public schools.

"For the anti-public school movement and other items on the right-wing agenda," Spring writes, with specific reference to school choice, privatization of public schools, and more recently, charter schools, "the following methods are used:

1. Creating foundations and institutes that fund research and policy statements supportive of laws mandating systematic, explicit phonics instruction in public schools.
2. Identifying scholars to do research, write policy statements, and lecture at public forums that support systematic, explicit phonics instruction in public schools.
3. Financing conferences to bring like-minded scholars together for the sharing of ideas and the creating of edited books that support systematic, explicit phonics instruction.
4. Paying scholars to write newspaper opinion pieces that support explicit, systematic phonics instruction that are then distributed to hundreds of newspapers across the country.

"The fourth point is an important element in the trickle-down theory of ideas," Spring states. "It is a big leap from writing a research report to being featured on the Opinion-Editorial (Op-Ed) page of the *New York Times* or other leading newspapers," he explains. "Frankly, it requires connections and a public relations staff to gain quick access to the media. Providing this type of access is one of the important elements in the strategy of spreading the conservative agenda."

Clearly, the passage of the Reading Excellence Act through the House of Representatives is testimony to the effectiveness of the strategies that have been used by the conservative right to mandate explicit, systematic phonics instruction in schools. They were so successful that they were able to use H.R. 2614 to horse-trade with the President.

Several weeks after the bill passed through the House, I received a letter from Mary Jean Le Tendre, the Director of Compensatory Education Programs at the United States Department of Education.

"[T]he 'Reading Excellence Act,'" Le Tendre states, "has some distinct differences from the President's original proposal. Secretary Riley wrote to Chairman Goodling to express his concern about the prescriptiveness of the definitions for "reading" and "reading readiness" . . . This concern for the inclusion of appropriate definitions of reading as well as concerns over other provisions of the bill, including the provision for tutorial assistance subgrants, prevents the Secretary and the Administration from supporting the 'Reading Excellence Act' at this time."

The letter was written on Wednesday, November 5, 1997, the very day that Goodling reportedly went to see the President. You know the rest. One bill was traded for another. The President gets his National Test and Goodling gets his Reading Excellence Act. In the final analysis it's all about biting into power and the getting of it all. It has nothing to do with teaching young children to read, or caring about their well-being, and it has nothing to do with democracy—unless we in the educational community make our voices heard.

We as teachers have got to make our voices heard

Whatever happens with the Reading Excellence Act when it reaches the Senate, for many of us, our lives as teachers have been changed. We do not believe. We have not been co-opted. We have not been brainwashed by all the lies and the spin doctoring.

At the NCTE Annual Convention there is talk of the news blackout that has taken place across the United States. For the first time many of us realize that alternate views on how young children are taught to read are either being distorted or suppressed. The conversation focuses on the misappropriation of research by right-wing groups, and about the bills that are being passed at the state and national level that advantage commercial programs. We discuss how we can make public our opposition to the events that are taking place when we don't have access to the media like right-wing groups. We talk about sound bites.

"Keep politicians out of our classrooms!"

"Use responsible and trustworthy research!"

"Knowledgeable teachers, not a national curriculum!"

"Teachers know a lot about learning and they know a lot about kids!"

Spin Doctors once again becomes a part of what is happening when I share parts of the manuscript with members of the Conference on English Education. Then, in a politically charged presentation, Don Graves and Regie Routman ask "If not us, then who?" as they discuss the

Reading Excellence Act and what we can do.[56]

Graves talks about the "Bolshevik" principle. "[F]irst you must abolish the past in order to have a more glorious future," he says. "Everything in the past has to be condemned. Everything has to be reduced to simplistic terms," Graves tells the audience. Then he explains, "That is, there is a war on. There's the good guys and the bad guys."

"We are looking for enemies," he says. "We've been looking for enemies within ever since, if you will, the East and West controversy withered away, and now we look in our midst for the enemy."

He talks about H.R. 2614. "Continually throughout the document there are these words *reliable, replicable*. If you are to be funded you must have your approach be based on reliable and replicable research. Make no mistake, the panel has been carefully chosen to review all proposals for what is reliable and replicable. Those are two terms that researchers use all the time." His voices rises, "However, when you look at what reliable means in the research community, you should if you have done this research, take the Foorman research, they should then disclose their entire methodologies, the raw data that goes with those methodologies, as well as having to explain their findings in relation to the selection of the population for that study. In short, reliable means that other researchers can take and look at the raw stuff and decide and say "'yes, this is reliable.'"

Again, *Spin Doctors* is writing us as Graves tells the audience that I was denied the information that I requested from Foorman, Fletcher, and Francis about the Houston studies.

"Look at the issues here," Graves says, further on in his presentation. "First, phonics is a shoehorn to get in and control. Make no mistake about it. You can come with all of the answers in the research that you want to," he continues. "And our assumption is that the persons who are promulgating this stuff are thinking logically." Again his voices rises. "They *are* thinking logically, *they are thinking their logical way to control. To control inside the classroom. To control the curriculum.* Phonics is a shoehorn to move in on reading and then move out across the curriculum. We stress meaning because it is essential that a kid be thinking meaning in order to comprehend."

He talks of children who learn to read for meaning coming up with their own ideas. "And that's dangerous," he says. "You would think that in a democracy that it is *not* dangerous, but it is an issue for a certain segment of our population. 'We do not want them to think. We want them to think the way *we* want them to think.' We have to be concerned about that." Graves' voice fills with emotion as he tells the audience that teachers are being denied the freedom to teach in ways which enable them to be responsible for children. Graves is determined. "We must proceed. We must proceed to still be responsive," he says, "to help the kids come through with the meaning."

"And Don, as you and I have talked," Routman says, looking directly at Graves, "and this is something I feel passionately about, the best person to make those decisions is the teacher." She turns and speaks directly to the audience, "And the thing that disturbs me most is that teachers' voices are completely missing. We are not present in the conversation at all, and that's scary."

"I tell you as a teacher," Routman says later in the presentation, "that we as teachers have got to make our voices heard or we are not going to be able to teach the way we know is right and best for children."

"To focus on a methodology is to bypass the teacher, make no mistake," Graves says a few minutes later. " You cannot bypass the professional, you cannot get there from here." There is a sadness in his voice. "And this is why we must begin to fight this as we must."

"Start petitions," Graves and Routman suggest.

"Participate in letter-writing, fax, e-mail, and telephone campaigns.

"Invite a legislator to your school.

"Write letters expressing your opinions to newspapers and other publications.

"Keep informed of important issues being considered by government. Share this information with others.

"Supply your legislators with realistic, truthful information on the conditions of local schools. Let them know how legislative decisions can hurt or help your school programs and your students.

"Encourage others to take an active role in communicating with the government.

"Encourage staff, students of legal age, and community members to vote.

"Educate and utilize the media.

"Create phone trees to share important updates on educational issues.

"Communicate with other teachers through organizations, online bulletin boards, and professional development seminars.

"Donate time and money to organizations you support.

"Attend and speak at public meetings."

Graves and Routman energize. They politicize. They make it clear that teachers have the power. If we organize we can defeat this bill and any bill that is foisted upon us, that we can demonstrate, through research and practical experience, is harmful to the children we teach.

When CORE, the private company owned by Honig and several

others, is one of only two providers approved to receive AB 1986 funds in California, we will speak out. We will make it public that both Adams and Foorman are on the national advisory board of Honig's CORE.[57]

When Adams and Foorman publish a classroom curriculum entitled *Phonemic Awareness in Young Children,* and write "*Phonemic awareness is the buzz word of our times,*" we will remind them that it is their research that made it that way (emphasis in the text). We will continue to question the commercial connections between so-called "reliable, replicable research" and big business, and we will continue to deconstruct the research on phonemic awareness on which fortunes are being made.

In a series of messages posted on several listservs, Steve Krashen deconstructs some of the studies on phonemic awareness on which the national myths are founded.

"Training studies demonstrate that PA can be trained," Krashen writes, "but also show that it develops on its own." Based on his analysis of studies, among others, by Lundberg, Frost, and Peterson; Ball and Blanchman; Cunningham, Bryne, and Fielding-Barnsley; Torgeson; Morgan and Davis; Castle, Riach, and Nicholson; and McGuinness and Donohue, Krashen states, "While experimental groups gain, so do comparison groups, even when the duration of the training is short."[58]

"They show that the effect of phonemic awareness on reading is modest," Krashen writes in his next posting, "[the] studies show that children trained in PA get better in PA." Then to introduce the next section of his analysis, he asks, "But do they get better in reading?"

Krashen states that if the object of phonemic awareness studies is to increase reading comprehension, then the Bradley and Bryant study "wasn't worth it." Of the other studies that he deconstructed, Krashen states, "It is clear that the impact of PA training on tests of phonemic awareness is consistently higher than the impact on PA training on tests of reading comprehension. In fact, there is no overlap at all in the two distributions."[59]

"The modest effect of PA appears to weaken over time," Krashen continues with supporting analysis in another posting, "even when children are tested on reading isolated words."[60]

"The hypothesis that phonemic awareness is the cause of reading ability runs into additional trouble," it's Krashen again, "in the face of studies that show that some children with low PA learn to read quite well."[61]

"There is intriguing evidence that basic aspects of PA are a result of familiarity with the alphabet, which is a result of attempting to read environmental print," Krashen continues in his next posting, with an analysis of a study by Johnson, Anderson, and Hooligan. "In addition, when knowledge of the alphabet is controlled, PA was not a predictor of the ability to read environmental print."[62]

Krashen continues by deconstructing studies of non-alphabetic readers and then in yet another posting he discusses two studies by Scheinder, Kuspert, Roth, and Vise, conducted with German children that he says "replicate the results of the rapidly growing PA literature."

"In both studies," Krashen says, "control groups gain in PA without training, and in both cases the impact of PA training on reading is very modest or completely lacking."[63]

We will speak out. Our voices are loud and we will be heard.

"What is decodable text?" Allington and Woodside-Jiron ask, "and why would educational policymakers recommend its use?"

Allington and Woodside-Jiron attempt to identify and examine the research based on which decodable texts are recommended and even mandated. What they find is that there is no research which offers evidence of what might consitute a decodable text. Indeed, there is no research to support the use of decodable texts.

"We found that many advocacy and policy documents simply asserted 'The research says . . .' but provided no research citations, others provided a general bibliography but no specific references associated with specific assertions.

"We set out to examine all of the research citations offered and found that a few citations were repeatedly referenced."

It's another case of A cites B.

"No NICHD research has manipulated texts on [the] decodability factor," Allington and Woodside-Jiron state, "[there are] no such findings in NICHD research."

"Is that all there is?" they write, paraphrasing Peggy Lee.

"We can find no direct evidence that providing children with decodable text, as defined in the California and Texas educational policy documents, actually enhances reading development or long-term achievement."

"Like many English teachers of my generation, I don't like to talk much about politics," Sheridan Blau tells the audience at the NCTE Convention in his inaugural address, as he explains that he comes from the generation that graduated from college after the intellectual and ethical atrocities of the McCarthy era, but before the Peace Corps and the anti-war marches on Chicago and Washington.[64]

"In statehouses, in local school boards, and in Congress," Blau tells the teachers who are listening to him, "legislators and other policymakers are busy trying to rescue American education by mandating how children should be taught reading, what bodies of research should inform teaching practice in the teaching of reading, and who should be allowed to teach reading teachers and prospective teachers.

"California has adopted legislation [already successfully copied in the House of Representatives] that would fund inservice programs only when the providers of inservice pass tests—not of their academic credentials—but of their subscription to certain acceptable theories of learning, research findings, and instructional practices, forsaking all alternative theories, bodies of research, and unapproved practitioners of research and instruction."

"Such legislation," Blau says, "serves not merely to privilege particular versions of science and scientific truth over others, but to suppress or disenfranchise alternative accounts of what is true and to discount entirely all research or evidence that derives from research methodologies that do not fit a reductivist, positivist, quantifiable, behaviorist version of scientific research."

"In the name of education and science," Blau says, as if he is speaking directly to us, "policymakers and a few of their scientific cronies (most of whom appear to be financially linked to textbooks and publishing companies whose reading programs claim to be based on quantifiable research) are conducting a campaign for intellectual control and the repression of alternative views that not only threatens the principle of academic freedom, but stands opposed to the true aims of science and education themselves."

"Intellectual suppression can produce only false knowledge." Blau explains that false knowledge is "knowledge that prevents further learning." Then he continues, "and a science that substitutes the idolatry of orthodox belief and political expediency for fidelity to the disinterested advancement of learning."

"If political history and the history of ideas in the Western literary and religious traditions teach us anything," Blau says, "it is to distrust those who not only claim to own the exclusive truth, but who insist further on suppressing or punishing all messengers of alternative versions of truth."

"Be vigilant," Victor Navasky, who was blacklisted during the McCarthy Era, tells us. "Be vigilant."[65]

"One of the surest signs of false science has always been its attempt to suppress the arguments and research of those who would challenge its conclusions," Blau states. "Another has been its alignment with sources of political power from which the suppression of alternative ideas always flows.

"Think of the political figures and governments of the past that have embraced one group of scientists to the exclusion of all others, and you will have a catalogue of demagogues and shameful public policies that have used science to justify slavery, racism, genocide, the incarceration of dissidents in mental hospitals, and a host of other injustices."

"But let us not overstate the case," Blau cautions. Then he asks, "Can government agencies and policymakers really be accused of suppressing ethnographic research, case study research and most teacher-research — virtually all qualitative research — merely by deciding that the only fundable inservice programs are those based on quantitative, behaviorist research (which is what the California legislature has done and the House of Representatives has approved in House bill H.R. 2614)?"

"Only if the prejudice of government policymakers translates into diminished opportunities for certain researchers and research-based programs to find support and obtain a hearing within the educational community," Blau answers. "And that, of course, is precisely what is happening, quite aside from the diminished opportunities that are legislatively mandated for politically unacceptable researchers and curriculum specialists."

"The battleground on which we are obliged to make our stand," Blau says, "is the political battleground where we are losing ground to policymakers and legislators who seek to usurp the professional authority that belongs to teachers and professional educators in matters having to do with curriculum, teaching methodology, and materials."

"What business do legislators in California or in Congress have in deciding on an approved curriculum for inservice programs for teachers of reading?" Blau asks. "What moral or ethical or intellectual justification can they offer for arrogating to themselves the authority to declare with respect to a field of specialized learning that one research paradigm and one set of research findings is valid and all others invalid, when the world's most widely respected and most extensively published scholars in the field are engaged in a continuing scholarly debate on those very questions?"

Blau speaks of collegial responsibility. "That legislators have been encouraged by a handful of reading researchers to act with such usurpacious arrogance is much to the discredit of those researchers," he says, "though it may testify more to their naivete than their vulnerability to the attractions of power or the temptations of consulting fees and royalties."

In this period of treachery we cannot be silent, we must speak out.[66]

"Yet surely they must see," Blau says, "or we must ask them to recognize that there is something deeply wrong professionally and ethically when one group of researchers in an academic field supports a congressional bill that declares other respected scholars in the field, including many of the most distinguished and revered figures in literacy studies, unacceptable as sources of knowledge or expertise."

"If as a profession we must lobby our legislatures," Blau then states, "let us lobby for the right of teachers to practice their profession without the interference of non-educators in matters of curriculum, teaching methods, and materials or research methodologies."

"It is a fact," Blau says, "that even a little bit of lobbying can make a difference in shaping policy; and that in many states, if not in the federal government, policy is presently being shaped largely by the efforts of pressure groups who represent a narrow and repressive conception of learning."

Pedagogy should be emancipatory not predatory

The scientific study of reading is founded on observation and documentation, not reductionist experimentation. The reading abilities of young children cannot be reduced to a single line in a single paradigm.

In straight-line research there are no children, only labels, aggregates, and measures. We don't teach "normals," "passive organisms," "subjects," "cohorts." The lives of the children we study and teach cannot be reduced to a subscript "i" in a mathematical formula. We know their names. They are Nicola, Patrick, Erik, Alejandra, and Marisela. They are not anonymous. They are not phenotypes or data points on a scatter plot, "phonologically disabled" or "phonologically deficient," nor "limited English proficient." They are children.

Give copies of Allington and Woodside-Jiron's critical analysis of NICHD's research to members of Congress. Speak out. Take Krashen's deconstruction of the research on phonemic awareness to the legislature. Speak out! Use the strategies provided by Graves and Routman and speak out! Applaud Goodman. When the academic community was silent, he had the courage to speak out. For the children in Texas, speak out! Shout! For the children in California, speak out! Shout! For the children in Louisiana, speak out! Shout![67]

Pedagogy should be emancipatory, not predatory.

When a researcher writes that children are "biologically disadvantaged," speak out! Shout! When children are called "passive organisms," speak out! Shout! Ascription of passivity is a racist activity. Be angry! Speak out! Shout! When the leading researcher on reading in the federal government says the language interactions that inner-city children have had at home are nil, speak out! Shout! Show your passions. Speak out! Shout!

If you teach English as a second language, your struggle is our struggle, and we will speak out! Shout! AB 1086! Speak out! Shout! H.R. 2614! Speak out! Shout! English only! Speak out! Shout! Each time a bill is proposed, Speak Out! Shout!

Don't be silent. Resist the spin. We have the power if we speak out![68]

In which a response is made to the preliminary statistical analyses used to support the nationally publicized findings of the NICHD Houston reading studies

■ ■ ■

In the prologue of *Spin Doctors* I presented a series of findings concerning the NICHD reading studies of Foorman and her colleagues. In this appendix I have provided support for these findings. Of necessity, these preliminary statistical analyses are based on the available summary results of the NICHD reading studies as presented in handouts and overheads and in draft papers. Both NICHD and the principal researchers have declined to produce their underlying data for review and analysis. They have also declined to answer any questions about the statistical analyses that they conducted.

I should emphasize here that, as I stated in Chapter 4, these types of statistical analyses are in fact invalid, because (1) the samples are clearly nonrandom, (2) the distributions are not normal, and (3) the measurement variables do not satisfy the requirements for interval scale measurements.

Nevertheless, putting aside these problems, the findings reported in this Appendix result from an examination of the available results and the application of statistical procedures and tests commonly utilized in this type of reductionist research.

Finding 1: The data for the direct instruction group shows that there is no significant difference between (1) the scores on Foorman's word reading test achieved by the first-grade children after one full year of the Open Court basal reading program, and (2) those children beginning grade 2 who had not had Open Court during their first-grade year and who had only the school district's preexisting reading curriculum.

Support for Finding 1: The means (M) and standard deviations (SD) of the scores on Foorman's word reading test for the children in Foorman's Open Court/Direct Instruction "treatment" group were M=14.19, SD=11.35 for 57 children at the end of first grade in April after one full year of Open Court/Direct Instruction, and M=13.71, SD=11.85 for 48 children beginning second grade in October who had not been exposed to Open Court/Direct Instruction or Foorman's study and had only had the school district's existing reading curriculum. These scores are shown in Figures 1 and 2. Application of the standard statistical "t" test shows that there is no significant difference between these two mean scores, t(103)=0.72, p>0.20.

Finding 2: The data for the Open Court/Direct Instruction group shows that there is no significant difference between (1) the scores on Foorman's phonological processing test achieved by the first-grade children after one full year of the Open Court basal reading program, and (2) those children beginning grade 2 who had not had Open Court during their first-grade year and who had only the school district's preexisting reading curriculum.

Support for Finding 2: The means (M) and standard deviations (SD) of the scores on Foorman's phonological processing test for the children in Foorman's Open Court/Direct Instruction "treatment" group were M=2.25, SD=0.79 for 57 children at the end of first grade after one full year of Open Court/Direct Instruction, and M=1.96, SD=0.71 for 47 children beginning second grade who had not been exposed to Open Court/Direct Instruction or Foorman's study and had only had the school district's existing reading curriculum. Application of the standard statistical "t" test shows that there is no significant difference between these two mean scores, t(102)=1.70, p>0.05.

Finding 3: A third important finding is that in the other three groups, the beginning second graders, who had not received any instruction in Foorman's study, scored significantly better on her word reading test than the first-grade children who had been subjected to a full year of her reading "treatments."

Support for Finding 3: The means (M) and standard deviations (SD) of the scores on Foorman's word reading test for the children in Foorman's Embedded Phonics (EP), Whole Language (WL), and Standard Curriculum (SC) "treatment" groups for (1) children at the end of first grade in April after one full year of Foorman's "treatments," and (2) for children beginning second grade in October who had not been exposed to Foorman's study and had only had the school district's existing reading curriculum were as follows ("N" is the number of children in each group):

Treatment Group	M	SD	N
EP - End First Grade	4.81	7.54	48
EP - Beginning Second Grade	6.83	7.97	42
WL - End First Grade	5.05	7.04	56
WL - Beginning Second Grade	8.46	10.03	39
SC - End First Grade	1.91	2.81	23
SC - Beginning Second Grade	4.53	5.81	32

As is evident from Figures 1 and 2, the mean scores of the beginning second-grade children (no "Foorman study effect") are consistently higher than the mean scores of the ending first-grade children (one full year of the "Foorman study effect"). Application of the standard statistical "t" test shows that the differences between the two mean scores are highly significant for all three treatment groups: For the EP group, $t(88)=3.43$, $p<0.001$; for the WL group, $t(93)=5.51$, $p<0.001$; and for the SC group, $t(53)=4.75$, $p<0.001$.

Finding 4: For the Open Court/ Direct Instruction group approximately half of the children were in the tutorial group and half were in the nontutorial group. For each of the three other treatment groups, more than 80 percent of the children were in the tutorial group and less than 20 percent were in the nontutorial group

Support for Finding 4: The following table provides a breakdown of the numbers (and percentages) of first- and second-grade children who either received or did not receive tutorial instruction for Foorman's Open Court/Direct Instruction (OC/DI), Embedded Phonics (EP), Whole Language (WL), and Standard Curriculum (SC) "treatment" groups:

Group	Tutorial	Non-Tutorial	Total
OC/DI	50 (52%)	47 (48%)	97
EP	62 (81%)	15 (19%)	77
WL	61 (82%)	13 (18%)	74
SC	34 (81%)	8 (19%)	42
Totals	207	83	290
Study Totals	285	90	375
Difference	78	7	85

These numbers are taken from Table 4 of the draft paper by Foorman et al. which presents the results of the May end-of-year achievement tests, including the FRI Text Comprehension. While the FRI test results are not reported for 85 of the children, we know that there were approximately 109 children in each of the OC/DI, EP, and WL groups, and only 48 in the SC group, and so the percentages of children who actually received tutorials in the EP, WL, and SC groups were certainly greater than the percentages given above. The inclusion of the 12 "missing" children for the OC/DI group would change the percentages somewhat, but even if all 12 were in the "tutorial" group (which is unlikely), the percentages would still only be 57%/43% respectively. These data indicate a clear sample bias toward higher achieving (nontutorial) children in the OC/DI "treatment" group.

Finding 5: Both the first- and second-grade children in the Open Court/ Direct Instruction group scored higher on the word reading test than the children in the other three treatment groups at the beginning of the year, and for the second-grade children in particular, the differences in the test scores are highly significant.

Support for Finding 5: The means (M) and standard deviations (SD) of the scores on Foorman's word reading test for the children in Foorman's Open Court/Direct Instruction (OC/DI), Embedded Phonics (EP), Whole Language (WL), and Standard Curriculum (SC) "treatment" groups for the second-grade children at the beginning of the study were as follows ("N" is the number of children in each group):

Group	M	SD	N
OC/DI	13.71	11.85	48
EP	6.83	7.97	42
WL	8.46	10.03	39
SC	4.53	5.81	32

As is evident from Figure 2, the mean score in October of the beginning second-grade children in the OC/DI "treatment" group is consistently higher than the mean score of the corresponding second-grade children in the three other "treatment" groups (see Figure 2). Application of the standard statistical "t" test to these results shows that the differences are highly significant: for the OC/DI/EP groups, t(88)=10.41, p<0.001; for the OC/DI/WL group, t(85)=7.39, p<0.001; and for the OC/DI/SC group, t(78)=14.0, p<0.001.

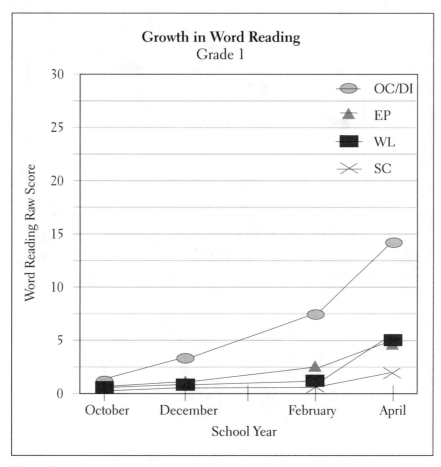

Figure 1

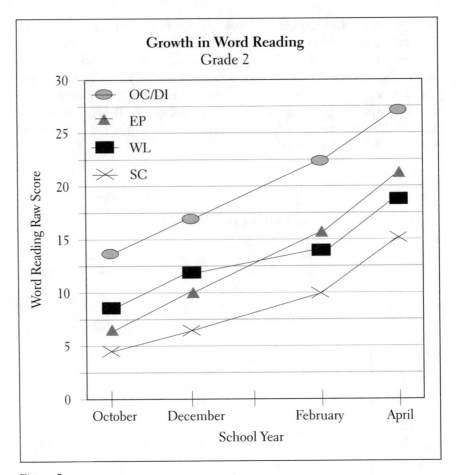

Figure 2

In which late-breaking news about the NICHD Houston reading studies raises further questions about what counts as "reliable, replicable research"

■ ■ ■

Demographics: The 1995–96 Annual Performance Report of the elementary campuses of the school district in which Foorman and her colleagues conducted their reading studies presents (1) detailed data on the percentage of students passing the Texas Assessment of Academic Skills (TAAS) in reading, writing, and mathematics at each grade level; and (2) detailed demographic data on each school, including student enrollment, ethnic distribution, teacher experience, school expenditures, and retention rates.

These data show that the selection of schools for the Open Court/Direct Instruction, Embedded Phonics, Whole Language, and Standard Curriculum treatment groups was biased in favor of the Open Court/Direct Instruction groups:

1. One hundred percent of the Open Court/Direct Instruction treatment group attended schools with passing rates on the TAAS in reading which were above the state average.
2. Fifty-six percent of the Open Court/Direct Instruction treatment group attended two schools with passing rates on the TAAS in reading which were significantly above the state average. None of the children in the Embedded Phonics or Whole Language treatment groups attended these higher-

achieving schools. Moreover, these two schools were added to the study, whereas two schools that were dropped from the study had passing rates on the TAAS which were significantly below the state average.

3. Seventy-eight percent of both the Whole Language and Embedded Phonics treatment groups attended schools with passing rates on the TAAS in reading which were below the state average.

4. Fifty-six percent of both the Whole Language and Embedded Phonics treatment groups attended schools with passing rates on the TAAS which were significantly below the state average. Moreover, one of these schools was added to the study, whereas the school that was dropped from the study had passing rates on the TAAS which were significantly higher than the state average.

5. The Standard Curriculum treatment group attended a school with the lowest passing rate on the TAAS in reading of any school in the district.

The TAAS data for the eleven schools that participated in the NICHD studies of Foorman and her colleagues are presented in Figure 1. It is important to emphasize that there are also differences between the schools in student enrollment, ethnic distribution, teacher experience, school expenditures, and retention rates.

A Comparative Analysis: The findings of the Title 1 study that Foorman presented to the pre-summit meeting of Governor Bush's Business Council in Texas, and to the Education Committee of the California State Assembly, are now published in the *Journal of Educational Psychology*. Thus, comparisons can be made between the information provided to state governments and the information provided to the academy. A comparative analysis raises serious questions about the early claims that were made about the findings of the study, and about the use of these early findings (1) as a basis for laws that have been passed in California and other states, and (2) the textbook adoption of Open Court system wide in many school districts in California and other states.

In Texas at the pre-summit meeting Foorman described Open Court as "very impressive," and in California, at the May 8, 1996, meeting of the California State Education Committee, she spoke of the "impressive gains" of the Open Court treatment group and of the results as "exciting news." However, at the May 8 meeting she also told the Education Committee that the Embedded Phonics and Whole Language

TEXAS ASSESSMENT OF ACADEMIC SKILLS SPRING 1995
3RD GRADE READING SCORES FOR THE SCHOOLS PARTICIPATING
IN THE HOUSTON TITLE 1 READING STUDY

SCHOOL	TAAS 3rd Grade Reading (Spring 1995)			Curriculum Group (Number of Students)	
	% Passing TAAS	Difference from State Average	Grade		
State Average	79.6	0.0			
School 1 (Added)	86.6	+7.0	1	OC/DI (15)	
			2	OC/DI (10)	
School 2 (Added)	84.4	+4.6	1	OC/DI (21)	
			2	OC/DI (15)	
School 3	81.8	+2.2	1	OC/DI (12)	WL (12)
			2	OC/DI (12)	WL (12)
School 4	80.0	+0.4	1	OC/DI (12)	EP (12)
			2	OC/DI (12)	EP (12)
School 5	60.1	-19.7	1	EP (36)	
			2	EP (24)	
School 6 (Added)	78.6	-1.0	1	WL (12)	EP (12)
			2	WL (12)	EP (12)
School 7	73.4	-6.2	1	WL (36)	
			2	WL (24)	
School 8	53.7	-26.1	1	SC (24)	
			2	SC (24)	
School 9 (Dropped)	58.9	-20.9			
School 10 (Dropped)	75.5	-4.3			
School 11 (Dropped)	83.6	+4.0			

TAAS = Texas Assessment of Academic Skills
OC/DI = Open Court/Direct Instruction Curriculum Group
EP = Embedded Phonics
WL = Whole Language Curriculum Group
SC = Standard Curriculum

Figure 1

treatment groups had "the most alarming results of all this." She stated categorically that "the main message of this is that there is very little growth in any of these programs except for the direct instruction group." Foorman contended that, "A child who comes into the direct instruction group has the opportunity to grow," then she insisted, "That's not the case in these other groups to the same extent. That's an alarming picture," she said. "You'd expect to see improvement and when you don't see improvement you've got to ask yourself is this a curriculum disability that we are creating."

But the "impressive gains" and "exciting news" evaporated by the time that Foorman and her colleagues wrote the final version of the paper published in the *Journal of Educational Psychology*. Even the names of the groups were changed. In both Texas and California Foorman referred to the Open Court treatment group as "Open Court" or the "Direct Instruction" group. However, in the final paper this treatment group is referred to as "Direct Code." "Embedded Phonics" has been changed to "Embedded Code" and "Whole Language" to "Implicit Code." The "Unseen Whole Language" group which Foorman included in the analysis which she presented in both Texas and California is excluded from the analysis in the final paper and is referred to as the "Standard Curriculum" group.

More serious disparities exist. Significant changes were made in the data analysis and the presentation of findings between the time in which Foorman made an official presentation of the study to members of the California State Assembly and the publication of the final version of the paper. The numbers of children changed significantly. In California Foorman presented results based on an analysis of data for all of the 109 children originally included in the Open Court/Direct Instruction treatment group. As I discussed in the Prologue and Appendix One, the original Open Court/Direct Instruction group was significantly biased in favor of Open Court. In the final paper, data are presented for only fifty-eight of these children, and the other fifty-one children were excluded from the analysis.

These fifty-one children represent 57 percent of the ninety children who were dropped from the analysis published in the *Journal of Educational Psychology* paper. The researchers themselves state that these ninety children "were better readers" "at baseline" than the children who were included in the analyses. The inclusion of these fifty-one "better reading" children in the results presented to the Education Committee of the California State Assembly clearly biased the findings in favor of Open Court.

The changes in samples had a significant effect on the end-of-year achievement test results. The results presented by Foorman in California, which are based on the highly biased sample of 375 children, showed that the Open Court/Direct Instruction treatment group had significantly higher scores on three of the four achievement test measures than the other three treatment groups. In sharp contrast, if we focus on the Open Court/Direct Instruction and the Whole Language treatment groups, in the final published paper this difference is only statistically significant for one of the four measures. Predictably, that measure is the Woodcock-Johnson Basic Reading Cluster, which is the average of the Letter-Word Identification and Word Attack (pseudoword) subtests. The differences in achievement outcomes are presented in Figure 2.

DIFFERENCES IN END-OF-YEAR ACHIEVEMENT OUTCOMES

	Presented to the Education Committee of the California State Assembly	Presented in the Final Paper Published in the *Journal of Educational Psychology*
Significant difference between OC/DI and WL on WJ-R Decoding Subtest?	YES	YES
Significant difference between OC/DI and WL on the WJ-R Passage Comprehension Subtest?	YES	NO
Significant difference between OC/DI and WL on the KTEA Spelling Test?	YES	NO
Significant difference between OC/DI and WL on the FRI Comprehension Test?	NO	NO

WJ-R = Woodcock-Johnson (Revised)
KTEA = Kaufman Test of Educational Achievement
FRI = Formal Reading Inventory

Figure 2

It should be noted here that the version of the study presented in the *Journal of Educational Psychology* is restricted to those first- and second-grade children who were eligible for and actually received Title 1 services—children who the researchers claim are "at risk for reading failure"—and that no claims are made about the applicability of the study results to the entire first- and second-grade population of 6,413 children in the school district.

In a NRCEMAIL posted on March 27, 1998, Fletcher, Foorman, Francis, and Shatsneider state that "the issue comes down to whether or not the Title 1 children in these schools and this school district are representative of the Title 1 children in the rest of the country." They then make the astonishing admission that they "can only speculate on this representativeness based on the demographic information that we have collected on the children and their families."

Rewriting history, the principal researchers now make no claims as to the applicability of their results to first- and second-grade children outside of their narrow sample of Title 1 eligible children. They further concede that the applicability of the results of their study even to other first- and second-grade Title 1 eligible children in the country is "speculative." This admission is highly problematic given that this study has been represented by the researchers and cited nationwide as "reliable, replicable research" and "scientific evidence" in support of direct instruction in phonemic awareness and the systematic, explicit teaching of phonics for all first- and second-grade children, and has been used as a blatant endorsement for the effectiveness of Open Court.

Prologue

1. Umberto Eco makes this statement in an essay entitled "Between Author and Text" which appeared in *Interpretation and Overinterpretation*, edited by Stefan Collini and published by Cambridge University Press (1992).

2. Later you will find that I have used one of the definitions of a labyrinth discussed by Umberto Eco in the postscript to *The Name of the Rose*. But right now you might just want to think of Adso in the library, or Alice down Lewis Carroll's rabbit hole, or Peter and Judy in Chris Van Allsburg's *Jumanji*, or even Ambrose lost in John Barth's funhouse. The point is that nothing is what it seems and events take place that completely surprise you.

3. As I write, the media is flooded with reports of a highly problematic study conducted by Sally Shaywitz, whose research is funded by the National Institute of Child Health and Human Development (NICHD), which is supposed to have found the neurological basis of dyslexia. The study is reported on March 3, 1998, by the Agence France Presse, U.S. Newswire, PR Newswire, CNN Morning News, AP Online, the *Detroit News*, the *Hartford Courant*, the *Herald Sun*, the *New York Times*, the *Record* (Bergen County, NJ), *St. Louis Post-Dispatch*, *USA Today*, *Ventura County Star* (CA), and the *Washington Post*. Shaywitz was a consultant to the Houston reading studies of Barbara Foorman and, like Foorman, she advocates phonemic awareness training and systematic, explicit phonics. In fact, their arguments are tautological. Foorman references Shaywitz and Shaywitz references Foorman. This is particularly problematic as many researchers consider both studies to be fundamentally flawed. However, the criticisms of their studies are not included in the reports that are published by the media.

4. The Reading Excellence Act (H.R. 2614) has been introduced in the Senate (S 1596) by Senator Coverdell of Georgia. Although the definition of "reading" has been modified, it still privileges phonics and the definition of "reliable,

replicable research" remains the same:

"(6) RELIABLE, REPLICABLE RESEARCH: The term 'reliable, replicable research' means objective, valid, scientific studies that:

(A) include rigorously defined samples of subjects that are sufficiently large and representative to support the general conclusions drawn;

(B) rely on measurements that meet established standards of reliability and validity;

(C) test competing theories, where multiple theories exist;

(D) are subjected to peer review before their results are published; and

(E) discover effective strategies for improving reading skills."

5. The article by Marego Athans, "Schools fail to teach kids how to read," first appeared in the *Baltimore Sun*. It was reprinted in the *Houston Chronicle*, Sunday, January 4, 1998, along with another article from the *Baltimore Sun* by David Folkenflik, "Lack of teacher training behind reading woes."

6. Nicholas Lemann's "The Reading Wars" appeared in the November 1997 issue of the *Atlantic Monthly*.

7. These statements by Lyon are taken from his officially videotape-recorded keynote speech on May 8, 1996, before the Education Committee of the California State Assembly, and are presented in detail in Chapter 14, which describes California's attempts to reinvent how young children learn to read.

8. The refusal of Foorman and her colleagues to make available the data from the Houston reading studies to their colleagues in the field has resulted in a series of responses to requests which are both vitriolic and demeaning. One of the most bizarre interactions occurred at the beginning of March 1998. It began when Ken Goodman raised questions about the Houston reading studies in a critique of a letter from Reid Lyon which was published by *Education Week* on the establishment of a National Reading Panel by NICHD. On March 1, Fletcher made the following statement in a response to Goodman posted on CATENet.

"Dr. Goodman has not asked for the data," Fletcher writes on the public listserv, "but if he makes a request I will personally put the paper and the data in a FedEx envelope and send it to him. No violation of Federal Law; no violation of NIH regulations; no stone-walling."

On March 3, Goodman posts a quick response to Fletcher on CATENet: "I thank him for his offer to provide 'the' paper and the data to me by Federal Express," he states. "I assume until I know differently that by data he means all the data—including the program-specific evaluation data that the Foorman proposal had promised."

On March 9, Fletcher replies on CATENet, "There's no federal law requiring release of unpublished data."

Needless to say, as of March 27, 1998, Goodman has not received either the paper or the data.

9. The October data presented for the second-grade children who received tutorials and who experienced the school district's reading curriculum during their first-grade year is unlikely to have been affected by their participation in Foorman's treatment groups at the beginning of their second-grade year. For the schools involved in the study the start-up dates for the tutorials begin September 26 and end on October 18, 1994.

10. Documentation to support this finding is presented in Appendix One on statistical analyses of the summary of results from the NICHD Houston reading studies—Finding 1.

11. Support for this statement is presented in Appendix One on statistical analyses—Finding 2.

12. Support for this statement is presented in Appendix One on statistical analyses—Finding 3.

13. See Appendix One on the statistical analyses—Finding 4.

14. See Appendix One on the statistics—Finding 5.

15. When I spoke to Ann Lippincott to ask her permission to quote from her listserv message posted February 22, 1998, she added the last sentence: "To assume that Open Court can do all this is very dangerous."

16. The article "Building with Words: City Schools Hope Phonics Boosts Reading" by Deborah Anderluh, was published in the *Sacramento Bee*, Sunday, February 1, 1998. I obtained the article from the newspaper's Web site.

17. I am reminded that in an essay in the book *Interpretation and Overinterpretation*, Umberto Eco writes, "Between the mysterious history of a textual production and the uncontrollable drift of its future readings, the text *qua* text still represents a comfortable presence, the point to which we can stick" (p. 88).

18. In *Releasing the Imagination*, Maxine Greene writes, "My interpretations are provisional," then she adds, "[a]ll we can do, I believe, is cultivate multiple ways of seeing and multiple dialogues in a world where nothing stays the same."

19. Lee Grant spoke with Tony Khan at the seminar Commemorating the Fiftieth Anniversary of the Hollywood Ten.

Chapter 1

1. Barbara Foorman is quoted in the *Los Angeles Times*, Saturday, May 4, 1996, p. A24.

2. Bill Honig is quoted in the *Los Angeles Times*, Saturday, May 4, 1996, p. A24.

3. The Reading Advisory, California State Board of Education, Sacramento. (1994). *Teaching Reading: A Balanced, Comprehensive Approach to Teaching Reading in Pre-K–Grade 3*. Sacramento, California, 1997.

Marilyn Adams, Douglas Carnine, John Shefelbine, and Jerry Treadway are among those who are noted for "their significant contribution" to the program advisory. You will meet Carnine, Shefelbine, and Treadway in *Spin Doctors* when you reach the chapter on California.

4. *Teaching Reading: A Balanced, Comprehensive Approach to Teaching Reading in Pre-K–Grade 3*, p. 4, citing Stanovich, 1986, 1993, and Adams, 1990.

5. Darvin Winick's speech is taken from the court reporter's transcript of the Houston Reading Conference, May 16, 1997, pp. 141–42.

6. Bonnie Grossen is a research associate at the National Center for Improving the Tools of Educators (NCITE), which is located at the University of Oregon and co-directed by Douglas Carnine and Ed Kameenui. There are several versions with minor variations of Grossen's paper that have been widely distributed. In my analysis I have used the version of her paper that Silber sent to school superintendents throughout Massachusetts, and which has been widely distributed to teachers in that state.

7. John Silber to the Superintendents and Charter School Leaders in the State of Massachusetts, April 15, 1997.

8. Documenting the research of Foorman and her colleagues creates an interesting dilemma. In critiquing experimental studies it is standard practice to cite the version of a particular study which has been through a rigorous peer review and is published in a refereed journal. However, Foorman's research has been widely disseminated by the media, presented to state legislatures, and discussed in documents provided to the United States House of Representatives before the academic community has had the opportunity to respond to the studies. Requests for information from Foorman and her colleagues have repeatedly been denied. Given this unusual circumstance, I have used the widely circulated unpublished papers and presentation handouts which have been made available to me as well as transcripts and videotapes that I have been able to obtain. None of the documents that I have used have any restrictions of use printed on them.

Foorman, Barbara, Francis, David J., Fletcher, Jack, M., Schatscheider, Christopher, & Mehta, Paras. (No date). The role of instruction in learning to read: Preventing reading failure in at-risk children. Circulated draft of the paper to appear in the *Journal of Educational Psychology*.

Foorman, Barbara, Francis, David, Fletcher, Jack, Beeler, Terri, Winikates, Debbie, & Hastings, P. (No date). Early interventions for children with reading disabilities and at risk for developing reading disabilities. To appear in Blachman, Benita. (Ed.). *Cognitive & Linguistic Foundations of Reading Disabilities*. Hillsdale, NJ: Erlbaum.

Foorman, Barbara, Francis, David, Beeler, Terri, Winikates, Debbie, & Fletcher, Jack. (No date). Early interventions for children with reading problems: Study designs and preliminary findings. Circulated draft later published in *Learning Disabilities: A Multi-Disciplinary Journal*.

Foorman, Barbara, Francis, David J., Fletcher, Jack, Shaywitz, Bennett, Shaywitz, Sally, & Haskell, Dorothy. NICHD grant application in response to RFA HD-93-09 to examine the effectiveness of early interventions for children with reading difficulties, pp. 45–85.

Foorman, Barbara, Francis, David, Fletcher, Jack. (No date). Growth of phonological processing skill in beginning reading: The lag versus deficit model revisited. This document states that a revised version is to appear in *Scientific Studies of Reading*.

Francis, David. (No date). An introduction to the use of individual growth models in the analysis of change. No further information available.

The official video of the May 8, 1996, Reading Information Hearing of the Education Committee of the California Assembly at which Barbara Foorman presented the findings of the Houston research.

9. For a powerful critique of Stanovich, see Steve Bialostock, (1997), "Offering the Olive Branch: The Rhetoric of Insincerity," *Language Arts* 74(8), 618–29.

10. In *Beginning to Read*, the first sentence Marilyn Jager Adams writes is "Before you pick this book up, you should understand fully that the topic at issue is that of reading words" (p. 3).

11. Hold on to the concept of reading as a labyrinthine process. You will come across other forms of the labyrinth as you read this book.

Chapter 2

1. In this analysis, as I am trying to build an understanding of the research that forms the basis of the political arguments, I will focus on the phonemic awareness studies that have most often been cited in support of a reductionist view of learning to read. In his review of the manuscript for this book, Richard Allington states that it is important to make this clear to readers.

"I think the point to make here," Allington writes, "is that a number of folks have studied PA [phonemic awareness] but only a very few of those folks are cited in the propaganda and mostly they cite a few older studies and selected new ones." Allington continues, "The work of Don Richgels, Lea McGee, Penny Freppon, Margaret Moustafa and hosts of others are never mentioned."

"Phoneme awareness, invented spelling, and word reading," Richgels writes in an article on spelling and word learning, "comprise only a single, albeit a very significant, piece of the larger picture of children's developing literacy knowledge and competence." In the last sentence of his article, Richgels writes that "inventive spellers are especially prepared for the use of phonetic knowledge that beginning reading requires" ("Invented Spelling Ability," p. 108).

McGee, writing with Richgels on learning the alphabet, expresses a concern that "[t]eachers who begin alphabet instruction including phonics instruction without taking into account what children already know about letters and their role may disrupt alphabet letter knowledge that children have already acquired" ("K is Kristen's," p. 224).

Clearly, the point that Allington makes is important, and I urge you to explore these studies in depth and add yet another layer to the argument that I present here.

2. I have included in my analysis articles by the following researchers: Eileen Ball and Benita Blanchman*; Lynette Bradley*† and Peter Bryant*†; Linda Clark*†; Ingvar Lundberg,*† Jørgen Frost,*† and Ole-Peter Peterson*†; Barbara Fox*† and Donald Routh*†; Bonnie Grossen; Morag Maclean, Peter Bryant, and Lynette Bradley; William Nagy,* Patricia Herman,* and Richard Anderson*; Åke Olofsson* and Ingvar Lundberg*; Charles Perfetti,*† Isabel Beck,*† Laura Bell,*† and Carol Hughes*†; Rebecca Treiman*† and Jonathan Baron*†; and Richard Wagner*† and Joseph Torgesen*† (among others). Most of these researchers (noted * above) are relied upon by Marilyn Jager Adams and are referenced many times in her government report. Others (indicated by † above) are also cited by Barbara Foorman and her colleagues.

I want to emphasize that my analysis focuses primarily on Stanovich, Foorman, and Adams, and that while some of the researchers mentioned above might agree with the ways in which their work has been referenced others must be concerned that both the purposes and the findings of their research have been distorted.

3. Note that in the package of materials that have been sent to school districts in California there is a paper in which Adams, writing with Maggie Bruck, uses the Stanovich, Cunningham, and Feeman study to support the contention that "children's knowledge of the correspondences between spelling and sounds is found to predict the speed and accuaracy with which they can read single words, while the speed and accuracy with which they can read single words is found to

predict their ability to comprehend written text" (p. 15). If A cites B. . . .

4. In an essay on studying working intelligence, Scribner states, "Laboratory studies have no intrinsic methodological advantage. The advantage of relevance, however, remains on the side of field-based studies" ("Studying Working Intelligence," p. 37).

5. In an article by John Broder, on "the false God of numbers" in the *New York Times*, Broder quotes Bruce Levin, a statistician at Columbia University's School of Public Health, who criticizes the use of statistics to describe hundred dimensional problems and reduce them to single numbers.

"Professor Levin said," Broder writes, "that politicians labor in vain to apply the discipline of the hard sciences to matters of conjecture and opinion. The physical sciences like chemistry and physics proceed by controlled experimentation, biology and medicine by longitudinal studies and clinical trials."

In such scientific inquiry, Broder reports, according to Levin, "a statistician can locate sources of bias and error and try to correct for them." But how does one measure statistically the success of pre-kindergarten programs?, Levin asks, and we might ask, how does one measure statistically how young children learn to read? It would seem that Levin does not believe these questions can be answered statistically.

6. Ferguson, George. (1971). *Statistical analysis in psychology and education.* New York: McGraw-Hill.

7. Unfortunately, it would seem that even the biblical reference is taken out of context and is misappropriated by Stanovich when he uses "Matthew effects" to describe the "rich-get-richer and poor-get-poorer effects embedded in the educational process."

I learned from my discussions with the Reverend Paul Bretscher, a Doctor of Divinity, that the verse "For unto everyone that hath shall be given, and he shall have abundance; but from him that hath not shall be taken away even that which he hath" (25: 29) from the Gospel according to St. Matthew is the most sacred covenant language.

"We are always first receivers," the Reverend Bretscher says to me. Then he asks, "What is it that we have that is so precious?"

He talks of God's love and of his gifts of hope, honor, and dignity, and he explains that if we are willing to receive these gifts then we will have gifts in abundance, not in the materialistic sense of the rich get richer and the poor get poorer, but in the religious sense of loving and being loved.

8. Oliver Sacks was interviewed by Wim Kayzer in New York City in 1992. The video, *A Glorious Accident: Understanding Our Place in the Cosmic Puzzle*, has been shown several times on PBS and was produced for Films for the Humanities, 1994.

Chapter 3

1. Lave states, "The concept of cultural uniformity reflects functionalist assumptions about society as a consensual order, and cultural transmission as a process of homogeneous cultural reproduction across generations." She goes on to state that "such a strategy legislates away major questions about social diversity, inequality, conflict, complementarity, cooperation, and differences of power and knowledge, and the means by which they are socially produced, reproduced and transformed in laboratory, school and other settings" (*Cognition in Practice*, p. 10).

2. Moll spoke of the cultural mediation of thinking in his keynote address at the 1997 National Reading Conference in Scottsdale, Arizona.

3. See Sylvia Scribner's "Reflections on a Model" in the *Quarterly Newsletter of the Laboratory of Comparative Human Cognition*, 12(3), 90–94.

4. Moll references David Bakhurst's 1995 article "On the Social Constitution of Mind: Bruner, Ilyenkov, and the Defense of Cultural Psychology," in *Mind, Culture, and Activity*, 2(3), 158–71.

5. In my research I focus on the plurality of literacies that are constitutive of the everyday lives of both young children and adults. However, as soon as you shift your view of literacy to include the many complex ways in which a multiplicity of literacies are a part of everyday life, it becomes increasingly difficult to ignore that literacy is embedded in different ideologies, in different political perspectives, and in different political agendas. If we push the envelope a little further it becomes clear that literacy practices—such as teaching young children to read—are specific to the political and ideological contexts in which they occur. Teaching explicit, systematic phonics is grounded in a particular ideological context, and research which ignores culture is itself a political act.

6. Erik, Alejandra, and Marisela are among the children who are learning to read and write that Ferreiro and Teberosky write about in their classic text, *Literacy Before Schooling*.

7. Dyson writes about Jameel, Ayesha, and William in *Social Worlds of Children Learning to Write in an Urban Primary School*.

8. The research of Ferreiro and Teberosky is of critical importance, and so is the research of Dyson. The work of Yetta Goodman, especially her print awareness studies and the many years of research she has conducted on the roots of literacy, are also of particular importance. A description of Goodman's *Longitudinal Study of Children's Oral Reading Behavior* is contained in the 1971 Final Report she wrote for the U.S. Department of Health, Education, and Welfare,

and in the paper that she published entitled *The Development of Initial Literacy*. The research of Marie Clay, available in *Reading: The Patterning of Complex Behavior* and the research of Jerry Harste, Virginia Woodward, and Carolyn Burke, published in *Language Stories and Literacy Lessons*, are also relevant. Add to this list my own research, published in *Family Literacy: Young Children Learning to Read and Write; Learning Denied; From a Child's Point of View;* and, with Catherine Dorsey Gaines, *Growing Up Literate: Learning from Inner City Children.*

9. Critical to the theoretical argument presented in *Spin Doctors* is neo-Vygotskian activity theory. See Vygotsky's *Mind in Society*, which is edited by Michael Cole, Vera John-Steiner, Sylvia Scribner, and Ellen Souberman, and *Voices of the Mind* by James Wertsch.

"When action is given analytic priority," Wertsch writes, "human beings are viewed as coming into contact with, and creating, their surroundings as well as themselves through the actions in which they engage. Thus action provides the entry point into the analysis."

"This contrasts on the one hand with approaches that treat the individual primarily as a passive recipient of information from the environment," Wertsch states, "and on the other with approaches that focus on the individual and treat the environment as secondary, serving merely as a device to trigger certain developmental processes" (p. 8).

Clearly there are important distinctions between "activity" and "task." For Wertsch "activity" is culturally embedded and for Moll culturally mediated. However, in the research of experimentalists such as Stanovich, the concept of "activity" becomes synonymous with the assignment of "task" which is given to the child, who is regarded as the recipient of the information which, of course, is "culture-free."

"It becomes a problem," Moll says in a telephone conversation, "when activity is treated as a normative concept." He talks of his own work and of the importance he attaches to treating *particularly* both "funds of knowledge" and "activity" and not treating them as abstract normative concepts. Another important resource is the paper by Moll which will appear in the fourth edition of the *Handbook of Research on Teaching.*

10. Dyson presents what she calls "the social consequences of written formulas" in *Multiple Worlds of Child Writers: Friends Learning to Write*, p. 221.

11. Louise M. Rosenblatt, *The Reader, the Text, the Poem: The Transactional Theory of the Literary Work*, p. 21.

12. Emilia Ferreiro. (1978.) What is written in a written sentence? A developmental answer. *Journal of Education, 160*(4), 25–39.

13. See L. S. Vygotsky, *Mind in Society*, pp. 45–46.

14. Taylor, Denny. (1993). Early literacy development and the mental health of young children. In *From the Child's Point of View*. Portsmouth, NH: Heinemann Books.

15. I wrote about what happened to Patrick in *Learning Denied*.

16. During my many years of ethnographic research, I have come to understand that there are times when a person's emotional state interferes with this or her ability to read. I have observed this phenomenon both in children in school and in homeless people living on the street. Traumatic events take their toll, but when there is a decrease in stress the ability to read returns.

17. Newman, Denis, Griffin, Peg, and Cole, Michael, (1984). Social constraints in laboratory and classroom. In *Everyday Cognition*, Barbara Rogoff and Jean Lave, (Eds.). Cambridge, MA: Cambridge University Press.

18. These authors support this statement with references to Bartlett, 1958; Cole, Hood, and McDermott, 1978; and Lave, 1980.

19. Rogoff makes this statement in the introduction to the text *Everyday Cognition: Its Development in Social Context*, which she edited with Jean Lave. Rogoff asserts that "Context is an integral aspect of cognitive events, not a nuisance variable" (p. 3).

20. Gough, Phil. (1972). One second of reading. In *Language By Ear and Eye*, J. F. Kavenagh and I. G. Mattingly, (Eds.). Cambridge: MIT Press.

21. Bond, Guy L., and Dykstra, Robert. (1967). The cooperative research program in first-grade reading instruction. *Reading Research Quarterly*, 2(4), 5–126.

22. Samuels, S. Jay. (1971). Letter-name versus letter-sound knowledge in learning to read. *The Reading Teacher*, 24, 604–08.

23. Many years ago, in my first book, *Family Literacy*, I wrote, "The children participating in the present research resisted any such instruction, and yet they all learned the alphabet as they came to use print in the mediation of their experiences of one another" (p. 90).

24. I find myself in a name dilemma. The convention I have established in writing *Spin Doctors* is to use first and last names the first time a name appears and then use last names only thereafter. However, some of the teachers I have quoted appear by their first names in other books and articles that I have written to ensure the anonymity of some of the children that they teach. While I find it unsatisfactory, it is for this reason that I have continued to use the first names of the teachers with whom I have worked.

Chapter 4

1.In his review of a draft of *Spin Doctors*, Richard Allington writes how important it is to state that a report on the NICHD research was released to the media and widely presented there, despite the fact that the research has not been disseminated within the research community.

"The disingenuousness of giving [the] preliminary report to [the] media," Allington says, "but telling [the] research community to wait until the published version appears is [an] incredible indictment of just what sort of spin doctoring is going on."

2. Allington responds in his review of the manuscript to my description of the Foorman experiments by asking whether there is any indication that the experimental PA tasks "were demonstrated to be linked to real world writing and reading." He says he is thinking of Becky Treiman's work on natural spelling and how PA develops.

"If experimental tasks are not related then what is the utility?" he asks, "[and] if they are, why use experimental tasks as opposed to authentic measures?"

"This may be an argument for another book and another author," he continues, "but what does seem ignored in the current politicized debate is the rather deep understanding of how PA is reflected in invented spellings."

3. This description was taken from the abstract of the grant proposal, HD28172.

4. Jean Lave (1988) points out the relationships between the assumption of "cultural uniformity" and "knowledge domains." "'Knowledge' consists of coherent islands whose boundaries and internal structure exist, punitively, independent of individuals," she writes. "So conceived, culture is uniform with respect to individuals, except that they may have more or less of it."

Lave goes on to discuss the "distorted representation of activity" under these conditions and she writes, "[s]uch an approach has nothing to say about the socially situated character of human activity, cognitive or otherwise" (p. 42).

5. Lundberg, Ingvar, Frost, Jørgen, & Peterson, Ole-Peters. (1988). Effects of an extensive program for stimulating phonogical awareness in preschool children. *Reading Research Quarterly*, 23(3), 263–84.

The phonological awareness curriculum was eventually revised and published by Paul Brooks in 1998. The authors are listed as Marilyn Jager Adams, Barbara Foorman, Ingvar Lundberg, and Terri Beeler. The book is called *Phonemic Awareness in Young Children: A Classroom Curriculum*.

6. See Lord MacCaulay's "Minute on Indian Education," reprinted in Ashcroft, B., Griffiths, H., and Tiffin, H. (Eds.). *The post-colonial studies reader*, 428–30. New York: Routledge. (Originally published in *History of the voice: The Devel-*

opment of national language in Anglophone Caribbean poetry, London and Port of Spain: New Beacon.)

7. Hughes, Langston. Dream Boogie. In Giovanni, Nikki (Ed.). (1996). *Shimmy shimmy shimmy like my sister kate: Looking at Harlem through Renaissance poems.* New York: Henry Holt and Company.

8. Giovanni, Nikki. (1996). a poem (for langston hughes). In Giovanni, Nikki, (Ed.). *Shimmy shimmy shimmy like my sister kate: Looking at Harlem through Renaissance poems.* New York: Henry Holt and Company

9. All of these children's rhymes appear in *Jewels,* and were selected by Shelley Harwayne. Published by Mondo.

10. Maclean, Morag, Bryant, Peter, & Bradley, Lynette. (1987). Rhymes, nursery rhymes, and reading in early childhood. *Merrill-Palmer Quarterly, 33*(3), 255–81.

11. Braithwaite, Edward Kamau. (1995). Nation language. In Ashcroft, B., Griffiths, H., and Tiffin, H. (Eds.), *The post-colonial studies reader.* New York: Routledge. (Originally published in *History of the voice: The development of national language in Anglophone Caribbean poetry,* London and Port of Spain: New Beacon.)

12. Riessman, Frank. (1976). *The inner-city child.* New York: Harper and Row.

13. Foorman, Barbara, Francis, David J., Beeler, Terri, Winikates, Debbie, & Fletcher, Jack. (In press). Early interventions for children with reading problems: Study designs and preliminary findings. *Learning Disabilities: A Multi-Disciplinary Journal.*

14. In a discussion of his research on funds of knowledge, Luis Moll refers to this as "the phonics trap." He says, "It goes like this: the teacher holds the theory, as supported by his training and reinforced by the basal reader in use in the school, that beginning English reading, especially for Spanish speakers, must begin with phonemic awareness or phonics. And that until the kids can automatize their phonics skills, with plenty of practice, they really cannot handle more advanced reading or do anything more interesting with text." Moll continues, "Now, the main index of phonics is pronunciation; and since the kids, with an accent similar to mine didn't sound quite right to an English monolingual ear, they were deemed to need more intensive, systematic phonics. The only way to understand (in this context) whether phonics instruction was salient in the teaching of these kids, was to figure out if they understood what they were reading; if they did, then the teacher could move away from teaching intensive, systematic phonics and do more interesting things with text, like help

kids make meaning. But since the logic of phonics instruction rules that out, and since the teacher could not benefit from any counterevidence . . . the teacher kept the focus on phonics, for all the students, all the time." Thus, Moll states, "The students and the teacher were trapped." Moll discussed the phonics trap in his keynote address at the 1997 National Reading Conference in Scottsdale, Arizona.

15. Labov, William. (1972). *Language in the inner city: Studies in the black English vernacular.* Philadelphia: University of Pennsylvania Press.

16. Labov, William. (1984). Field methods of the project on linguistic change and variation. In Baugh and Sherzer (1984).

17. In 1972, Labov wrote what he admitted was a polemic to counter deficit views of nonstandard English. He wrote, "Our work in the speech community makes it painfully obvious that in many ways working-class speakers are more effective narrators, reasoners, and debaters than many middle-class speakers who temporize, qualify and lose their argument in a mass of irrelevant detail" (p. 214). It seems a similar polemic to counter deficit views of reading is also needed.

18. Several years ago I was invited to attend a series of seminars at a well-known university. The seminars focused on research on child abuse, and there were usually between ten and twelve highly respected social scientists who attended the sessions. Most of them were from universities in the United States, but quite often there were also scholars from northern European universities.

Before each seminar, participants were sent copies of the reports of research "in progress" which were to be discussed at the next meeting. Our task was to read and critique them and to come to the seminar ready to respond to the presentation of the social scientist whose paper we had read. Over a period of months I became increasingly concerned about the scientific validity of the reports that I read, and I was uncomfortable with the discussions that took place each time we met. The papers that we were given to critique were typical of the statistical studies in the educational research journals that at one time or another we have all been encouraged to read.

As I critiqued each paper, I shifted paradigms and searched for the underlying philosophical and theoretical assumptions of the researcher. I considered the hypotheses and moved from the introduction to the findings of the research, and I asked myself, what would you have to do to get from the one to the other? Invariably, when I looked at the methodological section and the statistical procedures, I would find that it would take a leap of faith and not a scientific procedure to reach the conclusions put forth by the particular researcher. I'd re-read the conclusions and then turn back to the hypotheses and invariably I'd be left saying "you can't get there from here."

For several months I wrote my critique of the research papers that I was given to read, and I conducted a critical analysis of the statistical procedures.

But at the meetings I rarely spoke. Instead, I listened to the scholars who were gathered there and tried to appreciate the arguments that were presented to make the papers stronger and ready for publication. At no time was there any discussion of the underlying philosophical or theoretical assumptions, or of the statistical procedures that were employed.

Finally, I was sent a paper to critique that focused on the physical abuse of young children. It was an elegant paper filled with the rhetoric of positivist science, and I reviewed it as I had all the other papers. Only this time it was not just the leaps of faith from hypotheses to conclusions that were problematic. The difficulties went much deeper than that. In the study the researcher had used a series of statistical procedures that were highly questionable, but he had also used an interval scale to differentiate between degrees of physical abuse from "slaps" to extreme forms of physical abuse.

"Where are the children in this research?" I asked myself. "Can beatings be represented on an interval scale? How can the lives of children be so reduced?"

Once again I wrote my critique, and I also did a critical analysis of the statistical procedures that the researcher had employed in his sophisticated study. At the seminar I listened as the study was discussed and praised by those seated around the table. There was consensus that it was a landmark study and that the researcher would have no trouble getting it published. As the meeting came to an end I felt compelled to speak.

"Could we perhaps spend a little time discussing the statistical procedures employed in the study?"

The researcher who was in charge of the seminars was stacking the papers he had brought with him and was getting ready to leave. He paused and looked at me as if I had asked a foreign question. Then he smiled. "What would you like to discuss?"

Head down, I stuck to my notes and worked through what I considered to be the flaws in the ways in which the statistical procedures had been used. Each of my criticisms was dismissed, jovially, but with an increasing hint of irritation. Other researchers were getting ready to leave.

"What about the interval scale?" I asked, looking around the room. "Do you think it's been used appropriately?"

The researcher in charge of the seminars was visibly irritated. He spoke sharply, "We've all agreed to use interval scales in the way in which they are used in this research."

"Would a statistician agree?" I asked. At first he didn't answer. "Would a statistician agree?"

He laughed, breaking the tension. "No," he said. "But if we used statistical procedures in the ways that statisticians intended, the social science journals would be empty."

"Then they should be empty," I said, getting up as everybody left.

In retrospect it seems to me that this is the tacit dimension of positivistic science—an understanding passed from one generation of researchers to the next without question, although for some researchers the acceptance of the misuse of statistical procedures must inevitably be a conscious decision. (See Polanyi, Michael. (1983). *The tacit dimension.* Gloucester, MA: Peter Smith.)

19. Foorman is quoted in the Canadian *Globe and Mail,* in an article by Stephen Strauss, entitled "Phonics Reading Method Best, Study Finds Whole-Language Approach Less Effective, Houston Study Shows," February 18, 1997. Strauss becomes part of the spin or else is being spun when he goes on to state that, "The results of the Houston study have resounded almost immediately at the political level in the United States, where the 'back to basics' educational movement has been gathering steam" [n.p., cited from Web version].

"Professor Foorman and her associates," Strauss writes, "have been asked by Texas Governor George W. Bush to speak today to heads of educational facilities and other educators about the results."

"Mr. Bush," Strauss continues, linking phonics instruction with the run for the presidency, "who is often talked about as a potential Republican presidential candidate in 2000, has recently announced a new initiative to raise literacy skills in his state."

20. The letter, which was sent to parents on the University of Houston stationery, is signed by Barbara Foorman and her name is accompanied, without signatures, by the names of David Francis and Jack Fletcher. At the bottom of the last page, beneath Foorman's signature and the names of her colleagues, it states: "THIS PROJECT HAS BEEN REVIEWED BY THE UNIVERSITY OF HOUSTON COMMITTEE FOR THE PROTECTION OF HUMAN SUBJECTS."

21. This statement is made on page 56 of the grant application submitted to NICHD by Foorman and her colleagues in response to RFA HD-93-09 to examine the effectiveness of early interventions for children with reading difficulties.

22. In the NICHD grant proposal, Foorman and her colleagues state, "The Yale Children's Inventory," with reference to Sally Shaywitz and her co-researchers, "is a questionnaire completed by the parent that assesses the presence of ADHD and problems that are behavioral in nature." They give as an example, "oppositional-defiant disorder." Then they continue, "Teachers will complete the Multi-grade Inventory for Teachers, which is a parallel instrument to the YCI." They then state, "It can be used in cases where parental responses cannot be obtained" (p. 57).

23. Although the questionnaire did not include any statements limiting or denying researchers the right to quote, I have only included behavioral descriptors that appear in the article published by Shaywitz, Schnell, Shaywitz, and Towle.

24. The article "The Great Debate Revisited," written by Art Levine, appeared in the *Atlantic Monthly* in December 1994 and is considered by some reading theorists to mark the beginning of the media's war against teachers and teaching practices that are based on a century of empirical evidence on how young children learn to read. Levine writes of "zealots and crazies" who are "hostile to controlled studies." You might want to flip through to the last chapter of *Spin Doctors* and consider Levine's piece within the context of articles that have been subsequently published in *Time, Newsweek, US News and World Report,* the *Atlantic* yet again, and *Policy Review.*

25. Penny Freppon discusses "passivity" in her article entitled, "Low-income Children's Literacy Interpretations in a Skills-Based and a Whole-Language Classroom."

"The outcomes of the current investigation," Freppon states, "suggest that passivity and deferment of personal knowledge is more likely due to skills-based instructional experiences than to the learners themselves" (p. 526).

Freppon writes of children who had been "highly engaged and cognitively active" in a whole language first grade, "shutting down their self-directed and cognitive activities" in response to the "skills-based" instruction they experienced in second grade.

26. For a research perspective which contrasts with the view put forth by Adams, I urge you to read Dyson's *Social Worlds of Children Learning to Write in an Urban Primary School.* Dyson writes of the permeability of the boundaries between home and school literacies.

"When children enter school," Dyson writes on the last page of the book, "they come with complex histories as family and community members. And this history is reflected in the used words, the signs, with which they respond to the interactive spaces we as teachers create."

"As human beings," she writes in the last paragraph, "we seem to be driven to categorizing aspects of the world into neat boxes—the popular, the literary, the folk, the oral, and the literate—developmental lines and sociocultural boxes. But these neat boxes keep all of us, children and adults, trapped."

"Thus," she says, in the final sentence, "in working to create permeable curricula, we further the development of young people with complex visions of themselves, whose varied and varying voices will enrich the cultural conversations of us all."

27. The belief that reading is an "unnatural act" is a recurring theme throughout the documentation that I have deconstructed in *Spin Doctors.* While oral language is considered "natural" from this perspective, reading is regarded as a secondary system. Gee makes this point when he argues that many linguists treat reading as a school subject.

"The point put (too) bluntly is this," Gee writes, "humans have an 'instinct' for language and this aids them in its acquisition (just as certain species of birds have an instinct that helps them build their characteristic nests or sing their distinctive songs)." Gee then states, "We humans have no such instinct for acquiring any school subject like physics or literature, or for learning to read and write" (p. 2). Gee continues by stating that the premise that "literacy is not an instinct . . . is true."

I would argue that in the social sciences, writing of what is "true" or "not true" is highly problematic, and that "scientific" pronouncements must always be viewed with a degree of skepticism to reflect the inherent social bias in all scientific activities. In this case it is the equating of learning to read and write with a particular form of literacy—i.e., school literacy—that causes the difficulty. From both a sociocultural and a sociohistorical perspective such an assumption has to be questioned.

We have only to read *The Psychology of Literacy* by Sylvia Scribner and Michael Cole to appreciate the significance of non-schooled, indigenous literacy practices. In the 1970s, when Scribner and Cole visited West Africa, the indigenous, centuries-old Vai script was taught without formal institutionalization. Scribner and Cole state that the Vai script "ranks among advanced writing systems of the world because of its systematic representation of the sound structure of the language and the originality of its graphic symbols" (p. 263).

Another powerful reminder of the ethnocentricism of positivistic views on reading is provided by Ray McDermott in a paper entitled "Social Relations as Contexts" in which he discusses how the Hanunoo learn to read. The Hanunoo achieve a 60 percent literacy rate in a rare Indic-derived script without formal training in reading and writing. For the Hanunoo, becoming literate is deeply embedded in their social histories and is of significance culturally, but it is not until they reach puberty that the Hanunoo learn to read. The writings of Meyer Fortes are also important here.

There are records of human beings reading and writing some six thousand years ago—long before schools as we know them were invented. Historically, societies developed writing systems when there was a perceived need. By 200 B.C., punctuation had been invented. In 55 B.C., books were invented, marking the beginning of the end for scrolls. Even then reading a book was a political act. In 213 B.C., the Chinese Emperor Shih Huang-ti decreed that history began with his reign and all books published before his ascendency were burned. In Japan at the end of the first millennium reading was restricted to men. In 1933, Joseph Goebbels incited a vast crowd in Berlin to burn the books of "degenerate" writers such as Sigmund Freud, Thomas Mann, Ernest Hemingway, Karl Marx, Emile Zola, H. G. Wells, and Marcel Proust. All of this information comes from Alberto Manguel, who argues in *A History of Reading* that "no society can exist without reading" (p. 7).

"By the time the first scribe scratched and uttered the first letters," Manguel writes, "the human body was already capable of the acts of writing and reading, that lay in the future; that is to say, the body was able to store, recall and decipher all manner of sensations, including the arbitrary signs of written language yet to be invented." Mangual explains, "This notion, that we are capable of reading before we can actually read—in fact before we have even seen a page open in front of us—harks back to Platonic ideas of knowledge existing within us before the thing is perceived. Speech itself apparently evolves along the same pattern." Manguel then refers to *The Interpersonal World of the Infant*, by Daniel Stern, "We 'discover' a word because the object or idea it represents is already in our mind, 'ready to be linked up with the word." It is as if we are offered a gift from the outside world (our elders, by those who first speak to us) but the ability to grasp the gift is our own. In that sense, the words spoken (and, later on, read) belong neither to us nor to our parents, to our authors; they occupy a space of shared meaning, a communal threshold which lies at the beginning of our relationship to the arts of conversation and reading" (p. 35).

Manguel reminds me of Rupert Sheldrake and his radical evolutionary theories of formative causation. The research of Sheldrake, who was interviewed several years ago for the PBS television series *A Glorious Accident*, focuses on form, order, pattern, and structure—the morphic patterns—inherent in both the physical and biological worlds. Sheldrake contends that when you break things down into little bits, you lose the form, the pattern, and the structure intrinsic to the phenomenon that you are studying, thus denying the theoretical possibilities of what he considers the inherent memory of morphic fields.

It is this idea of morphic memory that Manguel hints at in *A History of Reading*. Even though I regard Sheldrake's theories of morphic resonance with some skepticism, I also consider it intellectually indefensible to regard written language as a secondary linguistic system and reading as "an unnatural act." Unfortunately, at the end of the twentieth century many linguists in the United States remain provincial and territorial, and linguists focus on little bits and not on the morphic patterns inherent in how young children learn to read. Perhaps we will not be willing to consider the idea that the ability to read, and to speak, and to do math—as Stanislas Dehaene asserts in an article by Robert Kunzig—is a part of our evolutionary heritage until we are willing to entertain such propositions as Sheldrake's radical evolutionary formative causation theory, or the more easily acceptable scientific arguments presented by Scribner and Cole for the unitary nature of intellectual activity.

A postscript. Just as I was finishing *Spin Doctors*, I received a series of e-mails distributed on a listserv by Steve Krashen in which he deconstructs the research on phonemic awareness. For those of you who want to follow the chronology of *Spin Doctors*, I won't preempt what Krashen has to say. But if you prefer to choose your own adventure, you might want to take a look at the discussion of his argument in Chapter 16.

Chapter 5

1. Manzo, Kathleen Kennedy. (1997). Study stresses role of early phonics instruction. *Education Week, 16*(24), March 12, 1, 24.

2. Manzo, Kathleen Kennedy. (1997). Study stresses role of early phonics instruction. *Education Week, 16*(24), March 12, 1, 24.

3.The letter that Lyon wrote was published in *Education Week* on April 23, 1997. He was responding to a letter criticizing the NICDH Houston studies submitted to *Education Week* by Gerry Coles. Coles posted his letter on several listservs and Lyon posted his response on CATENet. Adams then forwarded his posting to TAWLers.

4. Norman Fairclough makes these statements in *Discourse and Social Change*. He states, "[t]he achievement of hegemony at a societal level requires a degree of integration of local and semi-autonomous institutions and power relations, so that the latter are partially shaped by hegemonic relations, and local struggles can be interpreted as hegemonic struggles" (p. 94).

5. Gramsci defines hegemony in *Selections from the Prison Notebooks*.

6. "That's the power of hegemony," Moll says, in his 1997 NRC keynote address, "it need not be punitive, it is simply sufficient to be sneaky; it's control that is internalized, and just like we internalized semiotic means, we can also come to internalize the ideology of the broader social systems" (p. 14).

7. In a personal communication about *Spin Doctors*, O'Loughlin tells me not to forget Michael Apple.
   "He's a must here," O'Loughlin says. "I think it is a mistake to portray all teachers as helpless pawns," he continues, and I agree with him. "Teachers have shown they can stand up for themselves when they want to," he states, and then adds, "to attempt to defend all teachers leaves you vulnerable to attack by right-wing ideologues who use the Ron Reagan strategy of one awful example to prove their point."
   O'Loughlin gets me to read Apple, whose work I should have read more extensively before. Take a look at *Teachers and Texts*, and *Education and Power*, and also *Schooling and the Rights of Children*, that Vernon Haubrich co-edited with Apple. Add to these texts *Democratic Schools*, which Apple edits with James Beane. All of these texts are important to the arguments that we are discussing here.

Chapter 6

1. The unedited transcript of the pre-summit meeting of Governor Bush's Business Council was distributed at the Governor's first Reading Summit which took place in Austin, Texas, on April 26, 1996.

2. In the transcript Marina Ballyntyne's name also appears as Marina Ballyntine.

3. Once again I urge you to read the original transcript—not the edited version—to read the complete presentations of Osborn, Foorman, and Carnine.

4. In an article entitled "The Creation of Context in Joint Problem-Solving," James Wertsch, Norris Minick, and Flavio Arns discuss the work of Piaget and Vygotsky, and they draw attention to the important distinctions between the social theories of these researchers.

It is important to emphasize here that while the theories of both Vygotsky and Piaget are excluded from theoretical consideration by the advocates of systematic, explicit instruction in phonemic awareness and phonics, their social theories of learning are quite different. Wertsch, Minick, and Arns refer to the research of Piaget as "[t]he most important individualistic theory in modern developmental cognitive psychology," and they note that Piaget, "examined social activity solely from the perspective of how it influences the individual's development" (p. 152). Writing of Vygotsky's social perspective theory, on the other hand, these authors state, "he considered social factors to play a central role in explaining ontogenetic change, and he recognized that the nature and evolution of these factors cannot be explained on the basis of a set of principles relating only to the individual" (p. 153).

As a point of interest, Ferreiro was a student of Piaget, and she continues to work within the Piagetian tradition although her research is distinctively her own.

5. In the report of the study on phoneme-grapheme correspondences directed by Paul Hanna, reference is made to the study of the alphabetic nature of American-English orthography by Ernest Horn. Horn analyzed and noted:

1. More than one-third of the words in a standard reference work on the pronunciation of American English showed more than one accepted pronunciation.

2. Most sounds can be spelled in many ways, one spelling not being sufficient to call it the most 'regular' spelling.

3. Over one-half of the words in a conventional dictionary of American English contain silent letters, and about one-sixth contain double letters when only one letter is actually sounded.

4. Most letters spell many sounds, especially vowels.

5. Unstressed syllables are especially difficult to spell.

6. In the Biographic Literacy Profiles Project, we shared the work of Gunter Grass in *Show Your Tongues*. Writing about it in *Teaching without Testing*, I state, "it is one of the most socially significant examples of symbol weaving that I have so far encountered, just as the illustrated poems of William Blake are artistically/linguistically significant and Benoit Mandelbrot's *The Fractal Nature of Geometry* is scientifically significant." Then, speaking specifically about the project, "Our observations of print in everyday settings support the need we feel to extend the ways in which we think about the symbolic representations

constructed by children. The more we focus our attention upon their productions, the more convinced we have become that our classrooms must be multimedia centers that encourage the exploration of complex symbolic systems" (p. 69).

7. The definition of whole language used by Foorman in the Houston study is not the definition of whole language used by the district, and the project director was not from the district.

8. As of March 1998 the district in which Foorman and her colleagues conducted their research has not adopted Open Court and continues to use a wide variety of approaches and methods to teach reading.

9. Robert Rosenthal's "The Pygmalion Effect Lives" was published in *Psychology Today* in 1973.

10. The project to which Carnine refers was Project Follow Through. His interpretation of the project is challenged in Chapter 14 of *Spin Doctors*, which focuses on the events taking place in California.

11. The 1914 Chambers English Dictionary gives the following descriptions for subaltern: sub´al-tern or su-bal´tern: *adj* a subordinate. - *n*: an officer in the army under the rank of captain.

12. At the beginning of Chapter 14, on California, you will find some alternative perspectives on literacy rates in the United States.

13. In the November 1997 issue of *Worth*, there is an article on Intel. At the end of the article there is a statement which begins in bold caps which states: **"FULL DISCLOSURE**: *A few editorial employees at* Worth *own modest positions in Intel stock, the result of purchases made before this special report was conceived. No purchases were made while this project was in preparation. Under the magazine's conflict-of-interest policy, no employee may acquire shares of a security slated for mention in the magazine. Employees are also required to hold any stock noted in* Worth *at least 30 days past the date that subscribers receive the magazine. None of the senior editors with a hand in this project, including the editor-in-chief, owns shares in Intel"* (p.144).

It's time that academic journals were required to make similar disclosures of their authors' associations with basal publishers.

Chapter 7

1. When I refer to teachers and researchers, I am including teachers in schools and in universities, and researchers in schools and universities.

2. Lyon made this statement in a letter published in *Education Week*, April 23, 1997, p. 50.

3. Grant Wiggins makes this statement in *Assessing Student Performance*, p. 24.

4. Wiggins, *Assessing Student Performance*, p. 26.

Chapter 8

1. North Carolina School Improvement Program in Beginning Reading: Recommendations for Changes to Reflect Research, p. 8. Fall 1996.

2. Lyon sent an e-mail message to Coles which was publicly circulated and distributed throughout the state of California by the Comprehensive Leadership Center at the Sacramento County Office of Education. In the e-mail Lyon expresses his support of the paper written by Grossen about the research of NICHD.

    "Bonnie is basically correct," Lyon writes about NICHD's focus on research which tests competing theories on reading development and reading disorders. Lyon expands upon the point and then writes "Bonnie is correct in writing that sampling issues play a major role in NICHD research." Again, he elaborates before moving to the next point of agreement. "Bonnie is quite correct in reporting that the NICHD data reflect the importance of early intervention." More discussion, then he states, "Bonnie is also correct in reporting that the development of reading skills is not a 'natural act.'" He elaborates, noting that they are in agreement that "skilled readers read words rather than skip them" and that "less skilled readers do rely on context." He notes that "there is a tremendous amount of replicated evidence" to support these statements. He then comments that the information provided by Grossen about the Houston reading studies is "in line with the preliminary findings" and that her review of Stanovich's work "is accurate." Lyon continues with other points that Grossen has made which he regards as "accurate." These include what he describes as the "misguided notion" that children use the context to predict unknown words. Also, that "sound-spelling correspondences should be taught explicitly."

3. Summary of Research Findings for State Bill 1139 as Presented to State Board Reading Committee: Draft, 1-22-96, pp. 1–2.

4. In writing about Maria and Andrew I have paraphrased my account of their work together which appears in the essay "Assessing the Complexity of Students' Learning" which appears in *From the Child's Point of View*.

5. Grossen made this statement on the second page of the version of *30 Years of NICHD Research: What We Now Know About How Children Learn to Read*

that Silber sent to superintendents of schools throughout the state of Massachusetts.

6. This quote is from the e-mail Lyon sent to Coles regarding the Grossen "30 Years" paper on the research of NICHD that was distributed throughout the state of California by the Comprehensive Leadership Center at the Sacramento County Office of Education.

7. See Gee, James. (1992). *The social mind: Language, ideology and social practice*. New York: Bergin & Garvey.

8. Many of these research approaches are referred to by James Gee in "The New Literacy Studies: A Retrospective View" which he presented at the conference on "Situated Literacies" at the University of Lancaster, United Kingdom, July 1997.
     "Obviously these movements, stemming from different disciplines, overlap at many points," Gee states, discussing some but not all of the theories mentioned above. "And they influenced each other in complex ways. While there are genuine disagreements among them, they are . . . beginning to converge in various respects. It is not uncommon, in fact, to see citations to all or most of these movements in current work on sociocultural approaches to literacy and related aspects of education."

9. Gee references *Sociocultural Approaches to Language and Literacy: An Interactionist Perspective*, by Vera John-Steiner, Carolyn Panofsky, and Larry Smith. (1994). Cambridge: Cambridge University Press.

10. This reference is to an article by Carnine, with Linda Carnine and Douglas Gersten (1984), entitled "Analysis of Oral Reading Errors Made by Economically Disadvantaged Students Taught with a Synthetic Phonics Approach" which was published in the *Reading Research Quarterly*, 19(3), pp. 343–56.

11. Pany, Darlene, & McCoy, Kathleen. (1988). Effects of corrective feedback on word accuracy and reading comprehension of readers with learning disabilities. *Journal of Learning Disabilities*, 21(9), 546–50.

12. Joel Brown, along with Ken Goodman and Ann Marek, have produced an annotated bibliography of studies in miscue analysis which is published by the International Reading Association. Miscue analysis has been used to study: adult readers, African American readers, beginning readers, beginning writers, bilingual readers, blind readers, Chinese readers, readers from many different countries. Numerous case studies have been written using miscue analysis. Researchers have used miscue analysis to study chunking, cloze, code-switching, cognitive development, cognitive style, cohesion, college readers, comprehension, computer-assisted learning, concepts of reading, concepts of story, content-area read-

ing, context, dialect, discourse analysis, discourse grammar, English as a second language, error analysis, evaluation/assessment, eye-voice span, graphophonic cues, humor, imagery, immersion, insertions, instruction, intonation, invented spelling, listening, map reading, meaning, morphemes, omissions, orthography, perception, peripheral vision cues, phonemic awareness, phonics, predictability, pronouns, propositional analysis, psycholinguistics, readability, reading development, the reading process, reading proficiency, reading rate, reading recovery, reading strategies, reasoning, regressions, retellings, retrospective miscues, revaluing, reversals, revisions, risk taking, schema theory, self-monitoring, semantic acceptability, semantic cues, sentence combining, silent reading, spelling, style, substitutions, syntactic cues, teacher-student interactions, text analysis, text cohesion, text difficulty, and words. When you look at the miscue studies that have been conducted, the suggestion that there is no research becomes totally absurd. For those of you who are new to miscue research, take a look at the November 1995 issue of *Primary Voices*. The entire volume is devoted to miscue analysis, and it is an invaluable resource.

13. In *Fahrenheit 451* by Ray Bradbury, the sentence actually reads, "The books leapt and danced like roasted birds their wings ablaze with red and yellow feathers" (p. 117).

14. Patrick's teacher used to copy sentences from the decodable texts onto the chalkboard and the children used to sit and copy them on lined paper. Patrick's copying was corrected if his letters were not "sitting" on the line.

15. The article which is supposed to provide supporting evidence is by Keith Stanovich and Paula Stanovich, and is entitled "How Research Might Inform the Debate about Early Reading Acquisition." It was published in the *Journal of Research in Reading*, in 1995. For a powerful critique of this article by Steve Bialostock, see the December 1997 issue of *Language Arts*.

16. All of the text crossed out in this paragraph is crossed out in the documents from North Carolina.

17. As many authors have pointed out," Luis Moll states, "in general, working-class children receive a very different type of schooling than students in wealthier classes. In brief, working-class children receive low-level, rote, drill and practice instruction. As the social class of the community increases there is a shift in instruction towards more process-oriented teaching, from simplicity to complexity, and from low to high expectations for academic success. In other words," Moll says, "there is an unequal distribution of schooling that favors the already privileged: white and affluent students receive more of what is characterized as effective teaching than do other groups; minority and poor students receive an emphasis on low-level basic literacy and computation skills" (p. 10). Moll made

this statement in his keynote address, "Turning to the World: Bilingualism, Literacy, and the Cultural Mediation of Thinking," at the 1997 National Reading Conference in Scottsdale, Arizona.

18. See endnote 27 in Chapter 4 for a discussion on the position of many linguists on learning reading.

19. Gee at Lancaster University, July, 1997.
    "There is a problem," O'Loughlin writes to me in a response to his reading a draft of *Spin Doctors*, "I think it is very important not to dismiss the angst and suspicion of people of color around achievement issues. Poor children of color do very poorly in our schools. They suffer from poor teaching and low expectations. I think it is very important not to appear to slight the argument. Better to acknowledge it and then to point out, even as Delpit does, that back-to-basics reductionism is not the answer. We should all be lined up together on this issue. The Right has a knack for co-opting public anxiety and directing it to its own ends."

20. This statement was made by Delpit in her much-discussed article, "Skills and Other Dilemmas of a Black Educator," which appeared in the *Harvard Educational Review* in 1986.

21. Delpit makes this statement in the second of her *Harvard Educational Review* articles: "The Silenced Dialogue: Power and Pedagogy in Educating Other People's Children."

22. Delpit (1986), *Harvard Educational Review*, p. 384.

Chapter 9

1. See Stephen Rose, in *The Making of Memory*, for a discussion on academic writing.
    I have always found positivist research articles on early reading "acquisition" and the reading process unnecessarily obscure and usually poorly written. For example, historically, articles published in such journals as the *Reading Research Quarterly* are so dense most teachers do not have the time or the inclination to sift through the rhetoric to determine what the researcher is trying so dismally to communicate. Ironically, it is easy to decode studies such as those on phonemic awareness that I've referenced in this book but it is much more difficult to read them for meaning.

2. O'Loughlin, Michael. (1996). Facing myself: The struggle for authentic pedagogy. *Holistic Educational Review*, 9(4), 48–51.

3. The inclusion of oneself in academic writings to shed light on linguistic, pedagogic, or academic issues is sometimes referred to as "narrative criticism." You might want to read Patricia Williams's *Alchemy of Race and Rights: Diary of a Law Professor*, Alice Kaplan's *French Lessons*, Marianne Hirsch's *Family Frames*, or Jane Tompkins's *A Life in School: What the Teacher Learned.*

4. At the International Forum on Family Literacy which was held in Tucson, Arizona, in October 1994, Jennie DeGroat spoke about Navajo family literacy. Jennie said, "It is unfortunate that my life and the stories I have lived are not treated as valid data. I am documentation. This morning I come to you with my experiences. That is all I have" (p. 112).

5. In both the mining villages in which my parents grew up, the four-room row houses in which the miners and their families lived were owned by the collieries. In each village there was one co-operative store which was also owned by the collieries. The miners were totally dependent upon the mines.

6. It is impossible for me to exaggerate the effect that failing the 11+ had on the lives of children in England. It was always with us. We had been put in our place. Our working-class existence assured.

7. I heard about my friend recently. She eventually learned to type and became a secretary. When her children were grown, she went back to school and took the exams she would have taken at sixteen and eighteen if she had stayed in school. She continues to work as a secretary.

8. O'Loughlin (1996), "Facing Myself."

9. The NICHD conclusion that deficits in phonological processing are heritable and highly related to significant differences in neural processing are reported by Reid Lyon and Duane Alexander in "NICHD Research Program in Learning Disabilities," *Their World 1996/1997*, pp. 13–15. This article was attached to the testimony of Reid Lyon before the Committee on Education and the Workforce of the U.S. House of Representatives in Washington, D.C., on Thursday, July 10, 1997.

10. The class system in the British armed forces has recently been criticized by Major Eric Joyce in a paper entitled "Arms and the Man — Renewing the Armed Services," which is published by the Fabian Society. The class divisions in schools reflect the class divisions elaborated upon by Joyce in his critique of the armed services. In an article in the *Times*, Monday, August 4, 1997, page 6, Michael Evans states, "In his article, Major Joyce says the army hierarchy is divided into three classes: the Posh, an exclusively white, male, privately educated elite 'which runs the institution and wholly dominates its culture'; the Professionals, the middle class who provide the technical expertise and middle management; and

the Plebeians, the working classes who account for the great 'use-and-discard' rank and file."

11. The United Kingdom actually has three tiers. The gentry attend private schools which perversely are called "public." Yesterday, in the working class *Express* there was an article on homework in which an old graduate of Eton, where the boys—there are no girls—still wear top hats and tails, talked about getting his report card. The downstairs is still fascinated by the upstairs.

12. O'Flynn, Patrick. (1997, July 7). Labour backs elite pupils. *The Express*, pp. 1, 6, 7.

13. Ward, Lucy. (1997, July 8). Government to have its hand in every school. *The Independent*, pp. 8, 16.

Chapter 10

1. At the end of *Savage Inequalities* Kozol asks a friend in Cincinnati why Hyde Park wasn't going to be included in desegregation, and the friend, a teacher, tells him "that is the question you don't want to ask" (p. 232). He talks about Walnut Hills, a famous high school, and says his friend described it as "a *de facto* private school."

2. "The history of white schooling," O'Loughlin writes in a draft of a book he is writing, "forms the foundation for what we know as public schooling in the United States today. U.S. public education, like its counterpart in England," he continues, "did not emerge from an altruistic desire to bring education to the masses. Public education was born out of the desire of wealthy property owners and business people to protect their interests."

In a telephone conversation, O'Loughlin suggests I read the work of James Anderson on the history of African American experience of learning to read and attending public schools.

"Proposals to educate African American children," Anderson states, "whether in racially integrated or segregated public schools, or even in private schools, invariably aroused bitter opposition in northeastern, midwestern, and western states."

Anderson then gives specific examples and writes of "a white mob" that was "dispersed by a local magistrate" in Canaan, New Hampshire, and of the mayor and alderman of New Haven, Connecticut, denouncing a private academy for "free persons of color" as "destructive to the best interests of the city."

"Ohio's first public school law was passed in 1821, and African Americans were taxed locally to support the public schools, but they were universally excluded from the state's new school system," Anderson writes as he moves across the country describing the exclusionary practices of many states.

"One of the great ironies of this era was that white political leaders," he says, "including those who bitterly opposed educating African American children, contended that widespread illiteracy in the African American population prevented any extension of suffrage or other civil rights" (pp. 26–28).

Add to this picture the response of those with power and privilege to the masses of poor immigrant families who were flooding into the United States. O'Loughlin writes of the "charity schools" which developed that were supposed "to instill moral character and respect for authority in poor children."

"The emphasis in the schools was on rigid discipline and conformity to authority," O'Loughlin writes, "accompanied by a healthy dose of rote learning and recitation."

Keep in mind the parallels between the events taking place at the end of the nineteenth and twentieth centuries regarding the education of children who are poor and children of color. But remember, you will reach Washington, D.C., and the end of *Spin Doctors* before you hear any public official express concern about the inequities in public schooling. Politicians rarely acknowledge that many young children in the United States are learning to read in classrooms that lack even the most basic requirements, such as desks and chairs, or that many children learn without adequate access to books, and without adequate supplies of pencils and paper. Such talk is considered "compassion babble" and is carefully avoided.

3. Ascher, Carol. (1993). Efficiency, equity, and local control—School finance in Texas. ERIC Clearinghouse on Urban Education. ERI/CUE Number 88.

4. Ascher references Jose Cardenas 1992 and William Sparkman and Trudy Campbell 1991 for these figures quoted.

5. Note that Ascher relies on Sparkman and Campbell 1991 and Carenas 1992 for these figures.

6. Ascher references G. Levine's article in the Summer 1991 volume of *Harvard Journal of Legislation.*

7. Delpit writes, in her 1988 *Harvard Educational Review* article, "Let there be no doubt: a skilled minority person who is not also capable of critical analysis becomes the trainable, low-level functionary of dominant society, simply the grease that keeps the institutions which orchestrate his or her oppression running smoothly" (p. 384).

8. Once again Ascher relies on Sparkman and Campbell 1991 for these figures.

9. This statement appears in the paper Gee presented at the 1997 conference on "Situated Literacies" held at the University of Lancaster, United Kingdom.

10. The italics are Gee's.

11. Like the gentry in the United Kingdom, the children of affluence and privilege in the United States attend exclusive private schools.

Chapter 11

1. In presenting the documentation on the Supreme Court case which is currently pending in the state of Louisiana, I have deliberately restrained from interjecting myself into the text. However, I do think it important for you to know that I consider the arguments presented by the ACLU lawyers to be a "window" which allows us to take a look inside one of the closed rooms in the hegemonic labyrinth. In the discussion of how young children should be taught to read there is no conversation which focuses on issues of equity and social justice. But I want to ask you to keep in mind the children of Louisiana as you read what is written and said by researchers, politicians, basal publishers, and the press.

2. Myers, Doug. (1997, March 8). Court rejects lawsuit to force more funding for schools. *Baton Rouge State Times/Morning Advocate*, p. 1A.

3. Supreme Court State of Louisiana: Number (not ascribed). Miriam S. Charlet, et al., Plaintiffs-Applicant, Versus, Legislature of the State of Louisiana et al., Defendants-Respondents, Consolidated with the Minimum Foundation Commission, et al., Versus, the State of Louisiana, et al., Defendants-Respondent. Supervisory Writ Application of Miriam S. Charlet, et al. From the First Circuit Court of Appeal, State of Louisiana, Number: 97-CW-0212. Application for supervisory Writs of Certiorari and Review.

4. The Preamble to Article VIII is quoted in the Writ, in footnote 14 on page 17: "the goal of the public educational system is to provide learning environments and experiences, at all stages of human development, that are humane, just, and designed to promote excellence in order that every individual may be afforded an equal opportunity to develop to his full potential."

5. Once again, I urge you to read the original documents. While I make every effort to stick closely to the documents that I quote, there is always so much more information than can be included.

6. MFP is the Minimum Foundation Program.

7. The MFP—the Minimum Foundation Program—has changed since 1992, and in the 1997 Louisiana Supreme Court writ the lawyers include in an appendix a memorandum from the former State Superintendent of Schools,

Raymond G. Arveson, to the Louisiana Legislative Joint Education Committee. Averson writes, "Although this new formula represents a major first step toward greater equity in per pupil funding from combined state and local resources across the state, the issue of adequacy has not yet been addressed. Louisiana ranks near the bottom in recent statistics measuring per pupil expenditures and average teacher salaries. Given the standards we expect from students, teachers and schools, the provision of adequate resources is imperative to the achievement of those standards."

8. This discussion of teachers' salaries took place in 1992. Since that time salaries have increased but remain low compared with many other states. For the 1996–97 academic year the salaries for teachers in Louisiana ranged from $22,605 for a first-year teacher with a B.A. to $39,955 for a teacher with a Ph.D. and twenty-five years of teaching experience.

9. Myers, Doug. (1995, July 30). Teacher exodus has state officials worried. *Baton Rouge Advocate*, p. 1A.

Chapter 12

1. Kozol, Jonathan. *Amazing Grace*, pp. 243–44.

2. Cecil Picard's comments are repeated in note 18 on page 23 of the Louisiana Supreme Court writ.

3. In Ben's poem he writes of a teacher who leaves unexpectedly and leaves a note for one of her students. "It wasn't about you," the teacher tells the child, "it was all the strings. They tried so desperately to control me in a puppet play, but those strings were tangled up . . ."

4. Stanovich, "Matthew Effects," p. 396.

Chapter 13

1. "The average American child reads quite well compared to children in countries that compose our main trading partners—OECD," Venesky states at the beginning of his presentation. "Among these countries, only Finland has children who read significantly better than American children at ages 9 and 14" (p. 2).
    "In spite of fears raised by NAEP performance levels, which are arbitrary," Venesky continues, "and by other reports of doom and gloom, American 4th and 9th graders are reaching world-class standards" (p. 3).

2. In fact, few, if any, phonemic awareness studies focus specifically on how phonemes are perceived. There are no references to perception in the index of Adams's book *Beginning to Read*, and none of the phonemic awareness studies that I have read address the issue of how words are perceived.

3. Lyon states, "To be sure, there are some children who can read words accurately and quickly yet do have difficulty comprehending, but they constitute a very small portion of those with reading problems" (p. 8).

4. The Foorman NICHD studies are not longitudinal. For the studies to be described as longitudinal, the children would have had to stay in the same "treament" programs for at least five years. An examination of the studies indicates that for many of the children "treatments" were supposed to be changed on a yearly basis. It is important to note that Foorman and her colleagues left the school district in which the highly publicized Title/Chapter One study took place after the first year of the study, and the circumstances of their departure are reported to have been highly problematic.

In his review Allington points out that there are other problems with the reference by Lyon and Chhabra to the NICHD Houston research. "Foorman's study had not even been submitted for publication," Allington points out, "when the Lyon-Chhabra piece was written." Then he asks, "Is it okay for them to cite when the field cannot review until publication in 1998?" It's a good question.

5. All of these terms and statements occur and are used in the article by Lyon and Chhabra.

6. These NICHD research projects were described by Lyon on the CATENet listserv, Wednesday, October 29, 1997, in response to a statement made by Goodman regarding Lyon's reluctance to provide information about NICHD's research programs.

7. These language questions originate in an unpublished paper written by Michael Halliday; they are expanded upon in the author's seminal book *Learning How to Mean: Explorations in the Development of Language*.

Chapter 14

1. Krashen, Stephen. (1997). *The Unz-Tuchman Proposal: A Bad Idea*.

2. Ann McGill-Franzen and Cynthia Lanford have written an important article which describes their research that explores the wide variation in preschools in the opportunities that children have to listen to and engage in conversations about stories. They write specifically of the consequences of the lack of opportunities for a number of the children who participated in their study.

"(W)e believe that limited classroom resources in terms of the number and varieties of books and limited opportunities to participate in literate activities impoverished the story worlds that Daqueesh was able to create," they state, "as well as the expression of Kathy's stories in written text" (p. 273).

3. Krashen, Stephen. (1997/98). Bridging inequity with books. *Educational Leadership*, 55(4), 18–22.

4. Olson, Lyn. (1997, January). Race and demography. (Quality counts: A report card on the condition of public education.) *Education Week* (on the Web).

5. The May 8, 1996, Hearing on Reading of the Education Committee of the California State Assembly is available on five videocassettes from Assembly Rules-Television, State Capitol, Sacramento, CA 95814.

6. Pearson, P. David. (1997, September). The politics of reading research and practice. *The Council Chronicle*, 24, pp. 24, 8.

7. AB 170 directs the California State Board of Education to include in its criteria for adopting elementary instructional materials "fundamental skills," including but not limited to systematic, explicit phonics, spelling, and basic computational skills. AB 170 also states that it is the legislative intent that the State Board of Education ensure that all materials adopted also meet these criteria.

8. AB 1504 specifies that spelling is to be adopted by the State Board of Education in its Language Arts adoption process.

9. In the December 1997 issue of *Language Arts*, Steve Bialostock writes, "By taking advantage of media forums, Honig was able to engender distrust and suspicion toward an issue the public actually knows very little about—reading and reading research." Bialostock continues, "Honig's strongest rhetorical weapon against whole language has been the use of metaphor. Linguist George Lakoff (1992) describes how metaphoric language was used to justify the Persian Gulf War. For example, Secretary of State James Baker referred to Sadam Hussein as 'sitting on our economic lifeline,' while General Schwartzkopf characterized Iran's invasion into Kuwait as a 'rape.' Even though Honig makes numerous references to Keith Stanovich and Marilyn Adams, this powerful metaphoric language carries the effect of his own war—a war on whole language." Bialostock goes on to state, "Just as Lakoff has described the 'fairy tale of the just war,' so Honig has created his own fairy tale, complete with villain, victim, and hero." Later in his paper Bialostock returns to Lakoff, pointing out that the linguist argues that metaphorical thought is "neither good nor bad." "However," Bialostock writes, "Lakoff points out, in the case of war, 'metaphors can kill.' Honig's metaphor has effectively misled and swayed public opinion regarding

whole language, and for all intents and purposes, killed it in California as well as making it a dirty word across the United States" (pp. 624–25).

10. In Yetta Goodman's graduate class on retrospective miscue analysis, Erica is going to read a story. There is a knock at the door, and Erica and her mother are greeted by Yetta and Gopa Goswami, who is Erica's teacher, and a student in class. Erica is ten years old, her long dark hair is pulled back in a pony tail, and even though she is nervous her eyes sparkle when she smiles. Yetta invites Erica to sit at a table at the front of the room so her back is to all the students who are going to listen to her read. Gopa sits with Erica while her mother joins some of the students at the back of the class. It is the first time Yetta has met Erica, and they talk for a few minutes as they get to know each other, and then Yetta invites Erica to read the story *The Man Who Kept House*.

As Erica reads she is unaware that this is a historic moment. Children have been reading *The Man Who Kept House* to Yetta since the 1960s, and every reading is documented and archived for Yetta's research with her husband Ken Goodman on how young children learn to read. Yetta has documented children from many different ethnic communities reading this story, among them children from Maine, Appalachian children, children of Arabic families, Samoan children, urban and rural African American children, Mexican American children, and Native American children. There are approximately six hundred studies on miscue analysis which focus on children and many thousands of citations in the academic literature to this research. But today it is Erica's turn to read, and Yetta and her graduate students are caught up in the moment, and they are not thinking about the historical significance of the enormous contribution that this work on children reading stories has made to the understandings that teachers have of the reading process and how young children learn to read.

Erica is reading, and for a moment the whole class holds their breath as she stumbles over the words of the story. Even Yetta is worried, despite the fact that she has heard so many children read the story before. The story appears to be too difficult for Erica. She reads slowly, word by word, and she frequently encounters words that make her hesitate. She reads "quickly" for "question" then tries again, "ques—," she gives a little shrug and doesn't finish the word. "Bumped" becomes "became," and "knocking" becomes "kitchen." When she reaches "chimney" she starts sounding out with a hard "c," and sometimes she says "pass it" and she skips the word. The students are nervous and so is Yetta. Only Gopa, who has heard Erica read many times in her classroom, seems to be relaxed as she listens to the little girl read.

Erica reads the last line of the story and looks up and smiles at Yetta, and we sit uneasily, knowing that there are many reading researchers who would consider Erica a "lousy reader" who "barks at print." But whatever is written and whatever is said, we have spent our lives observing children and between us have several hundreds years of experience of teaching young children to read, and we wait as Yetta asks Erica to tell us about the story that she has just read.

Erica smiles as she begins her oral retelling, and she gives an account of the story. Gopa smiles as well, because she knew all along that however much Erica stumbled in reading the story she would still be able to tell the tale. Erica recalls all the key elements of the story, and it is clear to us that she understood the plot. She lingers over the little details that seem important to her, she understands the humor and the irony, and she has formed her own opinion of the events that take place in the story.

When a student asks her, "Why do you think that the author wrote this story?" Erica does not hesitate. "Because then a man would know never to complain," she says.

Erica tells Yetta that she can see and even hear what happens in the story and she says, "I could hear the cow falling 'moo, moo' off the roof."

She talks about another story that she has read which is similar to *The Man Who Kept House*. "The donkey gets into the house instead of a pig and he eats the food instead of spilling it," she explains.

Then with some carefully crafted questions from Yetta, Erica talks about the reading strategies she uses when she has difficulty reading a text, and Yetta thanks her for coming to read to us and she tells her that she has helped us as we try to understand how young children learn to read. The students clap as Erica gets up to leave, and Yetta invites her and her mother to come back in two weeks to talk some more about the story she has just read. Erica agrees. When Erica has gone Yetta and her graduate students spend many hours studying the transcript of Erica's reading of *The Man Who Kept House*, and two weeks later when Erica returns she sits and looks at small sections of the transcript with Yetta.

Yetta shows her a sentence from the story that during a first reading she was able to self-correct a particular word. But this time she is unable to read the word. "Why do you think you got it last time?" Yetta asks her. Erica says she "paid more attention." "What were you paying attention to?" Yetta asks. "'Cause I read the whole story," Erica says. "Oh boy," Yetta says, "that's a really terrific thing to say. See, this time you had only one sentence so you weren't sure quite what that was. But before what did you know?"

As Erica tells Yetta about the parts of the story that helped her to read the word the first time and I sit there smiling at this little girl who understands so much about reading, I wonder why so many researchers don't understand that experiments in which children are given only words and pseudowords to read don't tell us much about how young children learn to read. On some intuitive level Erica understands that the meaning of words is embedded in the meaning of the text and that reading words is much easier when they are read in the context of a whole story. I wonder what Honig would have said if he had heard Erica read. Reductionist theories which hypothesize that "good" readers read every word, that automaticity and fluency are important, and that "errors" interfere with comprehension cannot account for the reading I just heard.

11. See the article by Nadeen Ruiz in the November 1995 edition of the *Read-*

ing Teacher in which Ruiz describes the literacy development of her daughter, Elena, who is deaf.

12. The statements made by Sacks remind me of Goodman and his "set for ambiguity."

"Much discussion of phonics is based on the naive assumption that individual letters are recognized and matched with a single sound," Goodman writes in his book *On Reading*, "and the sounds are blended into syllables and words, which are then recognized. And finally, somehow, each string of words is comprehended. That kind of recognition of letters and words implies a brain with templates to recognize and identically match every form."

"What the eye sees and what the ear hears are not precise forms, however," Goodman argues like Sacks, "but a myriad of variable sounds and shapes. The brain does something much more complex and wonderful than recognizing letters and matching them to sounds. It creates perceptions from the ambiguous signals it receives, building order out of ambiguous information."

13. I have written "give to teachers" because, if there is a radical shift to a transmission model—the hand-me-down model—of instruction, it will affect the ways in which teachers are trained to teach reading as well as how children are taught read. It will be (is) no longer acceptable in California to establish critical sites of inquiry with student teachers so that they can learn how to observe and document the qualitative transformations that take place as children learn the alphabetic principle and begin to establish graphophonic relationships.

14. These studies are discussed and referenced in my response to the presentation of Douglas Carnine, who speaks later at the hearing.

15. On October 6, 1997, C-SPAN televised the speech Ezola Foster made to the John Birch Society. Foster preached for the end of public schools, and she encouraged members of the John Birch Society to "pursue strongly and spread the word" that the United States should no longer provide a public education for the nation's children.

16. Eco, Umberto. (1984). *The name of the rose*. New York: Harcourt Brace and Company.

Imagine a labyrinth on many levels, with dark, winding passages, inner rooms, and secret chambers, like Eco's library. Rent the movie *The Name of the Rose* and study the actual physical space that signifies what the library might have looked like in Eco's mind when he wrote the book.

"Why is it so difficult to get our bearings?" Adso asks William in *The Name of the Rose*.

"Because what does not correspond to any mathematical law is the arrangement of the openings. Some rooms allow you to pass into several others, some into only one, and we must ask ourselves whether there are not rooms that do not allow you to go anywhere else. If you consider this aspect, plus the lack of light or of any clue that might be supplied by the position of the sun, (and if you add the visions and the mirrors), you understand how the labyrinth can confuse anyone" (p. 217).

Now use the picture in your mind to imagine an abstract conjectural labyrinth, the "labyrinth of the world" Alinardo calls it in Eco's *Name of the Rose.* In some of the outer rooms in the labyrinth scholars are conducting research. It's their life's work. They want to understand the beginning reading of young children. But in this conjectural labyrinth their movement is restricted to the outer chambers and to the schools in which they do their work. Imagine that it is perfectly possible for them to spend their whole lives in the labyrinth and not know they are inside it. There are others, of course, who occupy this peripheral space. Concerned citizens who have enough time and money to devote their lives to save children from know-nothing teachers who create curricular disabilities when they use holistic practices instead of systematic, explicit phonics to teach young children to read. The inner chambers? They, of course, are closed.

17. The computer research to which Honig refers is highly problematic. Stephen Krashen has examined some of these studies and raises questions about the applicability of the findings to readers reading authentic texts.

"In eye fixation studies," Krashen writes in one long sentence, "readers are asked to read something they did not select, that may be either bland or boring but is surely irrelevant to the reader, are placed in a Clockwork Orange–type contraption while reading, the text is presented on a computer screen, and readers are told they have try to remember what they are reading as they are reading it."

"In addition," he continues, as if taking a breath, "they are sometimes also told that there might be odd spelling errors in the text but they should ignore them." He gives as an example a research study by Zola. "It is hard," he concludes, "to imagine a stranger situation."

Renee Casbergue and Jane Fell Greene add another dimension to the argument when they distinguish between vision and visual perception in a paper which focuses on the industry that has grown up based on the belief that eye training will increase children's ability to read. Quoting Gillet and Temple, these authors argue that there is no scientific evidence to support the underlying assumption that when someone reads the eyes move in some standard, regular way, or that the rate stays the same. They state that "Reading is a vastly complex process which obviously requires visual ability." But they make it clear that perception depends on the reader, what the reader knows, and the reader's purpose in reading.

18. Nicholson, Tom. (1993). The case against context. In G. Brian Thompson, William E. Tunmer, & Tom Nicholson (Eds.), *Reading acquisition processes.* Clevedon: Multilingual Matters Ltd.

19. Ruiz, Nadeen T. (1988). *Language for learning in a bilingual special education classroom*. Unpublished doctoral dissertation, Stanford University.

20. I would like to thank the teachers and children for whom the SPELL-A-THON is an annual event in which the whole community participates for allowing me to quote from the notices and flyers.

21. Degen, Bruce. (1983). *Jamberry*. Story and pictures by Bruce Degen. New York: HarperCollins.

22. Wood, Audrey, & Wood, Don. (1991). *Piggies*. Illus. By Don Wood. New York: Harcourt Brace Jovanovich.

23. Adams's explanation of how young children should be taught to read is fundamentally flawed not only from a sociohistorical and cultural perspective but also from the perspective of connectionism, the theory on which she bases her theoretical interpretation of the reading process.

It's an extreme form of "if-A-cites-B." It goes like this. Adams analyzes the experimental research on beginning reading. She uses connectionist theory to produce her definitive text. It becomes the Bible for researchers studying phonemic awareness, for publishers of basal reading programs, for right-wing phonics-first groups, for conservative anti-public school organizations, and for neoconservative state governments. But no one in any of these groups takes the time to examine the underlying assumptions on which Adams has built her theories. Why would they bother? They have no interest in the flaws in her speculations in how young children learn to read.

Adams has based her theoretical position on what Daniel Dennett ironically calls "ABC" learning. The theories of Dennett, who is known for his machine metaphors, were greatly influenced by the ideas of Alan Turing, who is credited with inventing the digital computer. What Dennett and Adams have in common is that they have both developed mechanistic views of human learning. But, as I am sure you have guessed, Dennett's ABC has nothing to do with the alphabetic principle. He is talking about the cumulative effect of three generations of theorists—Associationists to Behaviorists to Connectionists.

"(W)e are getting quite clear about the strengths and limits of this real but not all-encompassing *variety* of learning," he states, emphasizing *variety*. "Although ABC learning can yield remarkably subtle and powerful discriminatory competences, capable of teasing out patterns lurking in voluminous arrays of data, these competences tend to be anchored in the specific tissues that are modified by training. They are 'embedded' in the sense that they are incapable of being 'transported' readily to other data domains or other individuals" (p. 540).

Dennett explains that the problem with ABC theories is their inability to deal with symbols. The associations or connections are stuck.

"Symbols," he writes, "unlike the nodes woven into connectionist networks, are 'moveable'; they can be 'manipulated'; they can be composed into larger structures where their contribution to the meaning of the whole can be a definite and generatable function of the structure—the syntactic structure—of the parts" (541).

Dennett is ready to augment connectionism with the symbol systems of natural language. He asks, "How could we make a connectionist system *grow* a symbolic system on top of itself?" The point is that there are fundamental scientific flaws in the underlying assumptions that Adams makes in her use of ABC theories to adequately explain how young children learn to read.

So, if you asked me what I think of Honig's "Bible"? Whichever way you look at it, from a sociocultural perspective or from the perspective of connectionism, it doesn't stand a prayer.

24. Lyon received his doctorate from the University of New Mexico in 1978. His doctoral dissertation was entitled "The Neuropsychological Characteristics of Subgroups of Learning Disabled Readers."

I spoke with a neurologist regarding the differences between neurobiology, neurophysiology, and neuropsychology. Based on what he said, it would seem that there is considerable overlap between neurobiology and neurophysiology. The former is concerned with the biology of nervous tissue and the latter with the physiology of nervous tissue, i.e., how cells work at the chemical level. Neuropsychologists are concerned with issues of psychology that have a neurological basis, i.e., they explore such psychological categories as language, memory, and thought. The neurologist told me neuropsychologists know about the neuroanatomy and work in brain disease. He said, "They test a lot."

25. Writing of the mid-nineteenth century, Graff states, "Despite the superficial relationships linking literacy and status and illiteracy and criminality, social inequality represented the primary determinant of criminality" (p. 223). He could have been writing about the end of the twentieth century.

26. See also the articles by Debbie Smith and by Joanna Marasco in *Teaching and Advocacy*.

27. I have found that most people presume that if you work in a literacy center in a poor community you must be teaching people to read. At the center that I established, members of the community came together to find ways to cope with the difficulties that they faced in their everyday lives, and in the process they shared their many literacies.

28. This conversation is painfully vivid in my memory and I have taken the liberty of reconstructing the dialogue. Unless noted, as I have done here, all direct speech comes from transcriptions of actual conversation.

29. Flurkey, Alan. (1997). *Reading as flow: A linguistic alternative to fluency.* Unpublished doctoral dissertation, University of Arizona, Tucson.

30. The reported amount of money allocated to NICHD by the federal government varies. In some accounts the amount is as much as 200 million dollars.

31. A detailed discussion of children's early reading and the documentation of their development of graphophonemic relationships is presented in *From the Child's Point of View.*

32. "One of the aspects of the neuroimaging argument almost no one addresses," Allington states in his review of the manuscript for *Spin Doctors*, "is the potential for certain sorts of instruction/interactions to shape brain responses. Now I don't know if that is true but I cannot help but wonder how being a DISTAR Headstart might 'train' the brain to respond very differently than a High/Scope Head Start. But without any data on either side of the argument it remains an unexplored hypothesis."

33. See Steven Rose (1992), *The Making of Memory.*

34. Lyon is also more cautious in print. In the book entitled *Neuroimaging* which he co-edited with Judith Rumsey, he states in the last article which he also co-authored with Rumsey, "[N]euroimaging remains immature in its applications" (p. 227). Lyon and Rumsey state, "The application of neuroimaging techniques to the study of the developing brain in children poses unique challenges in addition to any technical adjustments that may be required to help the child adapt to the neuroimaging environment (i.e., ensuring a child's comfort, cooperation, and ability to remain motionless for required lengths of time). These challenges include 1) the definition of patient samples, 2) the understanding of normal and abnormal structural brain development, and 3) the ability to achieve a good fit between theoretical constructs and task-related activations in functional studies" (p. 228).

In his review of the manuscript for *Spin Doctors*, Allington also refers to *Neuroimaging* by Lyon and Rumsey. He points out that they state there is no "truly normative database" on the development of brain structure. He backs up this statement with some more revealing quotes from Lyon and Rumsey. On page 230 they state, "Knowledge of normal development will help clarify the need for strict versus relaxed controls for age in studies of developmental disabilities." He points out that on page 233, Lyon and Rumsey write, "Tasks taken from the behavioral literature most typically require modification to fit the constraints of the neuroimaging situation. Complex tasks must frequently be broken down into simpler tasks involving elemental operations." Finally, Allington draws attention to a statement Lyon and Rumsey make on page 234. "Although the tasks that have been used with PET and MRI techniques through 1996 are experimental in nature, it is possible that they eventually will assume a clinically useful role."

The operative word is *eventually*. Maybe. Go back and read what Lyon tells the Education Committee of the California Assembly. Deconstruct the rhetoric. There are serious ethical issues which need to be addressed by the scientific community regarding the use of neuroimaging with young children learning to read.

35. Derrick Bell, in *Faces at the Bottom of the Well*, writes of racism as "an integral, permanent, and indestructible component" of society, against which we continually struggle. Fighting for emancipatory pedagogies and treating universal literacy as a civil rights issue are essential, but illiteracy is not the cause of poverty; we are. What Bell teaches us is that racism and prejudice are integral, permanent, and indestructible components not of society as some abstract idea but of all of us who make up that society.

36. See Kozol (1967), *Death at an Early Age*.

37. Sapphire. (1997). *Push*. New York: Vintage.

38. Lopez-Reyna, Norma. (1996). The importance of meaningful contexts in bilingual special education: Moving to whole language. *Learning Disabilities Research and Practice, 11*(2), 120–31.

39. "Statistics are tools of the scientist," Broder writes in the *New York Times* that Levin, the statistician from Columbia University, said. "But when numbers are crunched in politics, axes are usually grinding too" (p. 4).

40. In the circulated draft of the synthesis paper on the research design and preliminary findings of the Houston reading studies, Foorman and her colleagues state, "In order to control for differences in groups that might have resulted from non-random assignment of children to Chapter1 reading programs, we adjusted for some of the background characteristics of the children in the classroom, viz, verbal IQ and ethnicity" (p. 14). I sent an e-mail to Foorman and her colleagues to request clarification of the meaning of this statement, but, while I did receive a response from Fletcher questioning the purpose of my questions, I did not receive any further information on how the researchers thought they were able to control for differences by making adjustments for verbal IQ and ethnicity.

41. This conversation, which is documented, is quoted with permission, but by request the names have been withheld.

42. I am aware that there are minor disparities between some of the reported numbers, but these disparities are in the original Foorman documents and can

only be reconciled by a review of the original data, which I have been unable to obtain.

43. The fact that the range of scores on Foorman's word reading test was at least 2.5 to 25 for all four treatment groups is immediately evident from the histogram data presented in Figure 3 of the draft of the paper written by Foorman and her colleagues which is to appear in the *Journal of Educational Psychology*. Table 3, in the same draft paper, presents the means and standard deviations of the April Word Reading test scores for each treatment group, and confirms that the range of scores was even greater than I have stated.

44. I telephoned the administrative office for the school district in which Foorman and her colleagues conducted the research, and I asked if the school district would like to respond to the statements that Foorman has made regarding "zero growth" and the questions she raised about the creation of "curriculum disabilities." The person with whom I spoke said that the school district has no comment on the research, and that all enquiries about the research are being referred to Foorman. Then, sadly it seemed to me, the person with whom I spoke said, "We are just carrying on, trying to educate our children."

45. "What can turn bright and eager learners into dull, disenchanted students in a few short years?" Lily Wong Fillmore asks in *California Perspectives*, "Educational programs that treat children as if they were incapable of leaning, programs that begin with the assumption that the children's parents are incapable of preparing them for school, programs that regard Latino children as being in need of remediation before they can be taught the things the school is supposed to teach them, that's what!"

46. This quote is taken from a draft of the paper which will eventually appear in the *Journal of Educational Psychology*. I have been told that substantial changes have been made to the paper, but I presume what was measured will stay the same. [Note: As we go to press, the article has just been published. Ironically, the numbers have been changed.]

47. These histograms appear in the draft of the paper by Foorman and her colleagues slated to appear in the *Journal of Educational Psychology*. The histograms confirm that approximately 15 percent of the results for the Open Court group are missing, and that the histogram bars for the other three groups add up to 100 percent.

48. I have reviewed a videotape of the presentation that Lyon made in San Francisco, and he does indeed state that NICHD does not endorse basal reading programs. However, he also speaks positively about the use of Open Court in Foorman's study and for a considerable period of time he had one of Foorman's misleading straight-line graphs which favor Open Court projected on a screen

behind him as he spoke about reading programs which include exercises in phonemic awareness and systematic, explicit phonics.

49. One of the ironies of the Foorman studies is that she and her colleagues chose to use the Formal Reading Inventory, which is based in part upon the miscue analysis research of Ken and Yetta Goodman. J. Lee Wiederholt is the author of the FRI which is published by PRO-ED, in Austin, Texas. Wiederholt states in the manual, "The FRI can also be used to inventory oral reading miscues. Five types of miscues can be recorded: (a) meaning similarity, (b) function similarity, (c) graphic/phonemic similarity, (d) multiple sources, and (e) self-correction."

50. In the United States "whole language" has become a generic term, a counter concept for the "Phonics Rules!" movement, that includes any and all forms of pedagogy which do not teach graphophonemic relationships as discrete isolated skills. However, while Sharon Murphy estimates that approximately 10 percent of educators are whole language teachers in the United States and Canada, there are many progressive educators whose pedagogies are generally supportive (but not always) of whole language who have different theoretical histories and hold different theoretical positions. For example, my own emancipatory pedagogical stance is informed by more than twenty years of working continuously in ethnographic research which is informed by situated, sociocultural research on practical intelligence and everyday cognition, discourse analysis, critical pedagogy, evolutionary approaches to mind and behavior, and the new literacy studies. What is important to note here is that there are many teachers in our schools, some of whom do define themselves as whole language teachers, and many who do not, who do not support the commercially produced, reductionist approach to beginning reading that Foorman endorses and that is being foisted on teachers across the United States. To suggest, as Foorman does, that holistic practice creates curricular disabilities, when she knows very little about these curricular practices, is highly problematic—especially when these statements are presented to members of the California State Legislature.

51. The pedagogy of the teachers in the school that I have described is holistic, disciplined, and systematic. The teachers have a deep belief in scholarship—their own as well as the scholarship of the children they teach. All labels are avoided. Children are not catagorized as "good readers" and "poor readers." Through systematic observation and careful documentation of children's learning, the teachers build upon the evolutionary processes and transformations that take place as the children they teach are engaged in authentic literacy activities. Ironically, as children read and write, teachers are afforded with an almost infinite number of opportunities to provide explicit instruction in graphophonic relationships, but always within the context of meaningful print. Go back to the third chapter to the descriptions of children's learning provided by Leigh and Martha—who come from different schools—for examples of the

ways in which the teachers in the school described above document children's emerging understandings of "phonics."

52. Halford, Joan Montgomery. (1997). Reading instruction: Focusing the debate on student achievement. *Infobrief, 10.*

53. "California ranks near the bottom in school library holdings," Jeff McQuillan writes in "The California Reading Situation: Rhetoric and Reality." He emphasizes that 25 percent of libraries report cutbacks in children's services. In addition, he adds, "Book budgets in the state had been cut by 25% since 1989, despite increases in California's population" (p. 461).

54. Again I am quoting Toni Morrison in her Nobel acceptance speech.

55. CTC stands for California Teacher Certification.

56. Carnine is correct in his prediction. In a letter sent to members of the Inland Empire Reading Council in California, Barbara Holland, the president of the council, writes that on October 3, 1996, the Curriculum Liaison Commission submitted a memo to the members of the California State Board of Education to remove the Wright Group and Rigby from the materials approved for state adoption, even though they met all the necessary criteria. The Curriculum Liaison Commission also recommended that the State Board *add* to the list SRA/McGraw-Hill and Total Reading even though these publishers did not meet the criteria and were not recommended.

57. This audio-recorded conversation with Brian Husby took place in October 1997. Husby is a professor at Mt. Royal College, Calgary, Canada.

58. Rhine, W. Ray. (1981). Follow Through: Perspectives and possibilities. In W. Ray Rhine (Ed.), *Making schools more effective*. New York: Academic Press.

59. The Bank Street Model is in many ways similar to the British Infants School pedagogical model that is the foundation of my own emancipatory pedagogy.

60. Hodges et al. (1980), *Follow Through: Forces for change in the primary schools*.

61. Weikart, David P., Hohman, Charles, & Rhine, W. Ray. (1981). High/Scope cognitively oriented curriculum model. In W. Ray Rhine (Ed.), *Making schools more effective: New directions from Follow Through*. New York: Academic Press.

62. DeVries, Rheta, Reese-Learned, Halcyon, & Morgan, Pamela. (1991). Sociomoral development in direct-instruction, eclectic, and constructivist kindergartens: A study of children's enacted interpersonal understanding. *Early Childhood Research Quarterly, 6,* 473–517.

63. Burts, Diane C., Hart, Craig H., Charlesworth, Rosalind, & Kirk, Lisa. (1990). A comparison of frequencies of stress behaviors observed in kindergarten children in classrooms with developmentally appropriate versus developmentally inappropriate instructional practices. *Early Childhood Research Quarterly, 5,* 407–23.

64. Verbal permission from Larry Schweinhart, September 26, 1997.

65. Robert Aukerman, in his textbook *Approaches to Beginning Reading* explains that DISTAR is the acronym for "Direct Instruction Systems for Teaching Arithmetic and Reading." He notes that the program was developed by Carl Bereiter, a psychologist, and Siegfried Engelmann, "a former advertising and promotion man." Aukerman states that among the underlying assumptions of DISTAR were as follows:

1. Disadvantaged black children are faced with a serious learning deficit which must be corrected before they enter the competition of the middle-class, white-oriented school system.

2. Culturally-disadvantaged preschool children are generally non-verbal and non-committal when spoken to in a normal classroom manner. The particular cognitive style of their family environment must be overcome so that the children will develop habits of listening and responding. This requires strenuous intervention and direct instruction.

3. The learning process must be teacher-dominated. The responsibility for learning the desired facts, skills and/or behaviors is upon the teacher. The teacher, therefore, must use a clean, structured, step-by-step, fast, specific, absolute, and direct instructional method, together with relevant materials.

4. Direct instruction toward specific learnings will result in specific learnings which can be tested. Thus it can be demonstrated that learning has taken place because it has been taught.

Aukerman includes a quote from James Hymes who states in *Teaching the Child Under Six*, that "the best book to read to appreciate how devastating a program for young children of the poor can be" is *Teaching Disadvantaged Children in Preschool* by Bereiter and Engelmann.

66. I want to thank Joan Zaleski for helping with these references to children's books.

67. I would like to thank Wendy Hood and Bob Hood, who are both kindergarten teachers, for brainstorming the list of books their children like to read.

Chapter 15

1. Janet Hageman Chrispeels has conducted a longitudinal and intertextual analysis of policymaking in California. Chrispeels's article in the *American Edu-*

cational Research Journal is essential reading for anyone who is trying to gather information on what is happening in the state.

2. Paulo Freire, *Education for Critical Consciousness*, p. 152.

3. Pearson, P. David. (1997, September). The politics of reading research and practice. *The Council Chronicle*, pp. 24, 8.

4. Each statement that Baldwin makes is then elaborated upon. It is interesting to note the observations of McQuillan regarding the issue of money.
    "Per capita personal income in California has been dropping steadily since 1989," McQuillan states. He then states that while personal income rose between 1984 and 1988, it returned to 1984 levels by 1993.
    "Interesting," he says, as "this is precisely the pattern we see in third-grade achievement scores through 1987, followed by a decline."

5. Reading the text of Baldwin's speech I am reminded of the book of poems by Denise Duhamel and Maureen Seaton entitled *Exquisite Politics*, and of the last poem in the book, from which the title comes. "Politics is a slug copulating in a Poughkeepsie garden," Duhamel and Seaton write. It's such a repulsive definition, it is indeed exquisite.

6. Weintraub, Daniel M. (1997, April 11). Phonics push may come to shove. *Orange County Register*, pp. 1, 8.

7. Letter sent by Steve Baldwin to Yvonne W. Larsen, President of the California State Board of Education on March 13, 1997. The direct quote is taken from an official document. For copyright reasons the letter is not quoted directly.

8. At a recent meeting a member of a state department of education stated that the question "Do you believe in phonics?" is asked repeatedly at state department meetings and at meetings with members of local communities.

9. At the May 8, 1996, Hearing on Reading, Furry tells the Education Committee, "The key idea here is to get school board members knowledgeable about what is going on, what is the problem in reading instruction, what does the research tell us, and what are our effective reading programs." He explains that the thirty-nine million dollars will be used to educate school board members, administrators, and teacher leaders. He says that the remainder of the money is allocated to schools of education to improve their training on how to teach reading effectively.

10. On January 16, 1998, Allington posts a message on the listserv Nextsteped. The subject heading is "Round Table Discussion: feel free to pass along."

"We have analyzed segments of the Comprehensive Reading Leadership Center in our latest paper: What is decodable text and why are policymakers mandating it?" Allington states, noting that CRLC rarely cites original research reports. It's another case of if A cites B. Instead, Allington writes that CRLC relies on reviews of research or policy documents.

"It seems as if those creating the CRLC documents didn't bother to read the original research cited in the reviews/policy statements they cited," Allington adds, "always a dangerous tactic in policy development."

"If one repeats an unfounded assertion often enough does that make it a research-based citation?" He says he and his colleagues ask at the end of the paper they have written on decodable texts.

It's a good question. Based on the "if A cites B" documents I've reviewed for *Spin Doctors*, I would have to respond "Of course it does."

11. Take a moment and go back to the descriptions written by Leigh and Martha in which they are able to document the complexity of children's emerging understandings of the ways in which oral language can be encoded in print. In Leigh and Martha's classrooms children are actively engaged in the development of graphophonic relationships. In the film used by Lyon, the structure of the lesson made the children the passive recipients of knowledge about digraphs and voiced and unvoiced sounds.

12. Lyon spoke to the administrators for several hours. The quotes presented did not occur consecutively. These statements made by Lyon give you an idea of the tone of his speech and represent some of the ideas he presented.

13. In October, 1997, Nebraska joined the many states which have established new policies for early reading instruction. In the document which was revised on October 10, new policy statements are underlined and deleted statements are struck out:

<u>Establishing a foundation for effective reading is one of the most important functions of schools. Schools will teach systematic phonics in grades K–2 or 1–3. In addition to systematic phonics, students will read and write extensively to apply and develop the reading skills they have learned, including spelling, grammar, and penmanship.</u> ~~Such~~ <u>Local</u> policy should encourage ~~balanced~~ approaches that are based on the needs of the ~~learner~~ <u>student</u> and should include emphasis on appropriate strategies that recognize the developing skills of the <u>learner</u> ~~student.~~

Local policies and procedures should include a process to:
    Identify local needs and assess progress;
    Identify student performance expectations;
    Allow flexibility to design instruction for individual students;

    Support a learner-centered approach to the development and assessment of the program; and

    Provide staff development which supports effective instruction.

~~The Board also supports teacher training that helps teachers acquire and use a variety of skills, techniques, and approaches including systematic phonics for teaching children to read.~~ <u>The Board supports teacher training in systematic phonics and in the use of a variety of skills and techniques for teaching children to read.</u> The Board will promote state level efforts that help schools meet ~~local~~ standards for reading/writing. [Strike-out and underlining of "including systematic phonics" in the text.] State Board of Education: Policy for Reading/Writing Instruction in Nebraska. Adopted December 8, 1995, revised October 10, 1997.

14. In my conversations with researchers in California, they express great concern that there is a concerted effort in the state to dismantle programs in bilingual education. The rewording of this particular statement confirms the serious nature of their concern. *[Note: Since I wrote this comment legislation has been introduced in California to put an end to bilingual education.]*

15. Albright, Madeleine. (1997). Presentation to the Senate Appropriations Committee on NATO Expansion Costs. Tuesday, October 21.

16. While the majority of teachers and college professors remained silent, a considerable number of teachers and a few college professors actively lobbied against 1086. Vaclav Havel once said a soldier's pack is not as heavy as a prisoner's chains. For some teachers who are deeply committed to teaching children to read, it has taken great courage to oppose the California State Legislature. They have both my admiration and deep respect.

17. Teachers in California tell me that if a district decides to have teachers within the district provide 1086 staff development, the teachers do not have to submit materials to the California State Board of Education and they do not have to sign the oath of assurance. But they do have to use what teachers have come to refer to as "the Moats binders," that is the inservice modules developed by Louisa Moats. Apparently teachers are still unsure of how closely they have to adhere to these materials.

18. The oath appears on the last page of the Application for Providers of Professional Development, and is available from the State Department of Education in Sacramento, California.

19. Manzo, Kathleen Kennedy. (1997, November 5). Limitations on approved topics for reading sessions rile teacher trainers. *Education Week* (on the Web).

Chapter 16

1. Conrad, Russell. (1997, March 20). Leave it to the teachers. *London Review of Books*, pp. 16–17.

2. Francis Urquhart is the manipulative British Prime Minister who is a master of greed and corruption in BBC's 1994 production of *To Play the King*, based on the novel of the same name by Michael Dobbs.

3. The articles in Barbara Rogoff and Jean Lave's *Everyday Cognition: Its Development in Social Context*, emphasize that the notion of "reliable, replicable research" is an arcane concept which is difficult to apply in studies of human behavior.

For example, in the study reported by Wertsch, Minick, and Arns, two groups of adult-child dyads were asked to construct a copy of a three-dimensional model. The researchers found that there were notable differences between the dyads in how the tasks were carried out. "Even though they all heard the same instructions, used the same materials, and performed the task in the same physical setting," these researchers state, "the operational aspects of their performance differed radically" (p. 167).

The bottom line is that so-called "reliable, replicable research" produces gobs of superficial data that provide us with very little information about how individual children learn to read and write.

4. Several weeks after I wrote about the possibility that we will one day have an official definition of thinking, I read a posting on CATENet from Sergio Sismondo, who teaches philosophy and sociology at Queen's University in Kingston, Ontario, Canada. Sismondo states, "This past Wednesday, Premier Harris addressed a summit on the future of the universities. On that occasion he said that he sees little value in academic degrees in the humanities, geography, and sociology, in which 'the graduates have very little hope of contributing to society in any meaningful way'" (*Globe and Mail*, November 21, 1997; *Toronto Star*, November 20, 1998).

"I wish I could say that I don't understand what Harris means by 'meaningful,'" Sismondo says, "but unfortunately I suspect I understand all too well. Reflection, education, and research on anything to do with the human world are deemed meaningless unless they immediately make money."

"This is an attack on THINKING," Sismondo writes, coming close to making reality the hypothetical question I ask in *Spin Doctors*. "The Harris government would like to create an Ontario in which 'unproductive' thinking is strongly discouraged. Critical reflection may be good for democracy, for justice, for a virtuous society, for a vibrant culture, but these are not the goals of this government. And Harris is short-sighted enough to believe that he can neglect those goals in favour of business, that business can flourish without any broad education."

5. Each one of the scholars on this list has informed my pedagogy and the instructional practices of the teachers with whom I have worked. They have helped me understand learning from the child's point of view, and they have assisted me as I have worked with children like Nicola whose biographic literacy profile underscores the complexity of children's early literacy development. For this reason I am calling this list of scholars "Nicola's List" and I am inviting other educators to add to the names of those who are already blacklisted in California by the passage of 1086 and will become blacklisted if Washington passes H.R. 2614.

6. I defended my dissertation *Family Literacy: The Social Context of Learning to Read and Write* in November 1980 and deposited it in January 1981.

7. Taylor, Denny (Ed.). (1997). *Many families, many literacies: An international declaration of principles.* Portsmouth, NH: Heinemann.

8. From the preamble to *Many Families, Many Literacies*, p. 4

9. Auerbach, Elsa. (1997). Reading between the lines. In *Many families, many literacies: An international declaration of principles.*

10. "California Goes to War Over Math Instruction" the headlines read on the front page of the *New York Times*, on Thursday, November 27, 1997. The subject is different but the rhetoric is the same. Jacques Steinberg writes about "fuzzy math" and "whole math" and quotes Chester E. Finn, who talks of "Rousseauian romanticism that sees children as wildflowers that bloom naturally when they are ready." Yvonne Larsen, the president of the California State School Board, is also quoted as "lamenting" the lack of grounding in "basic skills" and math that is "fuzzy and watered down" (A1, 34).

11. Lazere, Donald. (1997). Rules for polemicists: The case of Lynne Cheney. *College English, 59*(6), 661–85.

12. Jones, Noel K. (1996). Phonics and politics: "Sounding Out" the consequences. *Literacy, Teaching and Learning: An International Journal of Early Literacy, 2*(2), 3–13.

13. In the commentary, published in the 1997 August/September issue of *Reading Today,* Allington presents five unscientific assertions about reading instruction: (1) no one teaches phonics; (2) there is a phonemic awareness crisis; (3) direct, systematic, and sequential phonics is the only way to go; (4) decodable texts are important; and (5) there is a sucker born every minute.

14. In November 1997, the *Council Chronicle* published by NCTE features a front-page article entitled "Reading Bill Full of Flaws," written by Anna Flanagan,

and the back-page header reads "If You Want To Get Involved . . ." and members of NCTE are urged to "stay abreast" and "get involved." But in *Reading Today* published by IRA, coverage of the Reading Excellence Act continues to be of little interest. Buried in the December/January issue there is a "Washington Update" from Rich Long which has the subheading "Contrasting opinions on education reform." "Even in the highly controversial Reading Excellence Act," Long writes, "with its requirements to use 'reliable, replicable research in reading,' the centerpiece has been to support programs that go beyond a diagnostic, prescriptive model of reading instruction." Long, who obviously doesn't get it, continues, "In the view of Congress, widely used and comprehensive programs such as Reading Recovery and Success for All are seen as more effective interventions than smaller, locally created programs." He then states, "The point of this article is not to judge whether this view is right or wrong, but rather to show that Congress is looking for interventions that are both different and comprehensive. Ideas and programs that are not seen in this light will not be viewed favorably" (p. 26).

15. There are two letters from the Houston research team in the October/November edition of *Reading Today*.

The first is from Foorman and Francis in response. "In our research with first and second graders receiving Title 1 services, we found that the more explicit the instruction in the alphabetic code, the more accelerated the rate of improvement in decoding and overall reading achievement over a two-year period. We gave two tests of reading comprehension," they state. "The groups receiving direct instruction in the alphabetic code had significantly greater reading comprehension than the literature-emphasis groups." Beginning with such basic misinformation as the number of years of the study, one year and not two, this statement is a highly questionable interpretation of their research. In fact, the results of the four achievement tests at the end of the one-year study showed no significant differences between instructional groups for either of the two reading comprehension tests or for the spelling test.

The second letter is from Fletcher and Francis, in which they stick to a medical model of beginning reading. "Only 20 percent of the population develops skin cancer," they state, "but everyone is encouraged to use sunscreen. Vitamin D is added to everyone's milk. Don't the same principles apply to the prevention of reading failure?"

It is also of note that there is a two-page section on family literacy in which the National Center for Family Literacy and Sharon Darling are featured. As the Reading Excellence Act provides significant amounts of money for family literacy programs and actually names NCFL, questions arise about IRA's timing of the article in *Reading Today*. Coincidental? Perhaps. But those with whom I have spoken think that is unlikely.

16. Art Levine quotes Foorman in a special edition of *Parents Magazine* entitled "Parents Report on America's Reading Crisis." Levine writes, "This spring, a

test program in Houston found that Open Court was about twice as effective at improving reading among disadvantaged students as whole-language instruction alone. The Open Court students were brought close to the national average, while the whole-language students languished in the lowest quartile." Levine then writes, "'We were astounded by this kind of growth,' says the University of Houston's Barbara Foorman, who conducted the study that compared the different approaches. 'We learned that direct instruction is very impressive'" (p. 67).

17. I hope Lewis Carroll will forgive me for taking this liberty with *Alice in Wonderland*. When Carroll drops Alice down the rabbit hole, she too enters a labyrinth.

"Alice was not a bit hurt, and she jumped up, but it was all dark over head: before her was another long passage, and the White Rabbit was still in sight hurrying down it" (29). The version I used is *The Annotated Alice* with an introduction and notes by Martin Gardner. (1960). New York: Bramhall.

18. Allington, Richard L., & Woodside-Jiron, Haley. (1997). *Adequacy of a program of research and of a "research synthesis" in shaping educational policy*. National Research Center on English Learning and Achievement. Report Series 1.15.

19. Felton, Rebecca H. (1993). Effects of instruction on the decoding skills of children with phonological processing problems. *Journal of Learning Disabilities*, 26(9), 583–89.

20. As an ethnographer who tries to keep detailed ethnographic notes, I was fascinated by the note-taking style of Collins. My impression at the time was that he was jotting down "memory joggers," words and phrases to remind him of the conversation. But the interview started early in the morning and lasted well into the late afternoon. In my own notes I focused on trying to capture the dialogue. Over the years I have learned the importance of verbatim accounts. The dialogue I report here is taken from my notes. I have five audiotapes of the conversation which I have listened to and which I will eventually transcribe.

21. When the article in *Time Magazine* is published, Marie Ruiz, the Goodmans' administrative assistant, reminds me that after the interview I had shared my concerns with her about Collins and about what he would write. This is before I started writing *Spin Doctors*, but even then I knew that Collins would become a part of the spin.

22. In the Social Science Citation Index (SSCI) there are over 2,600 references in more than 1,500 publications to the miscue research of Ken and Yetta Goodman. Ken Goodman's first and possibly most controversial study, *A Linguistic Study of Cues and Miscues in Reading*, which he conducted when he

finished his doctorate and arrived at Wayne State, is cited over one hundred and thirty times in the SSCI, and an *Analysis of Oral Miscues: Applied Psycholinguistics*, which the Goodmans co-authored, is recognized as a citation classic by the editors of the SSCI.

Miscue studies based upon the Goodmans' research at Wayne State University have been carried out in French, Hebrew, Spanish, Chinese, Thai, Japanese, Yiddish, German, Polish, Persian, Greek, Hindi, and Jamaican Creole. Other studies have been conducted in English with students whose first language is Arabic, Pakistani, Spanish, Italian, Moroccan, Samoan, Navajo, Chinese, and Thai.

All of the Goodmans' original data is archived at the University of Arizona, and they have made their primary data freely available to both doctoral students and established researchers. Between 1965 and 1993 no fewer than 557 studies of reading miscue and related reading issues were conducted (see *Studies in Miscue Analysis: An Annotated Bibliography*, edited by Joel Brown, Ken Goodman, and Anne Marek.) The research studies that the Goodmans have conducted are among the most highly replicated if not the most replicated reading studies of the twentieth century.

23. Goodman posted the story on CATENet on November 8, 1997: The long disused red phone rings in President Clinton's office. It's the Kremlin. "Mr. President, I have terrible news for you," says President Yeltsin. "In the worst days of the cold war the Soviet government developed a doomsday machine. Powerful bombs were planted at the North and South Poles. If they are detonated at exactly the same time, the Atlantic and Pacific oceans will roll over the Western Hemisphere and completely obliterate them. Somehow, wires in the control mechanisms have fallen into disrepair and just now I was notified that in two hours the bombs will explode and there is no way of canceling this catastrophe." Clinton immediately calls all major religious leaders and tells them that they will have to inform the people of their groups and perform whatever last rites are needed. The chief rabbi, hearing the news, says, "If it's all right I'll go last." Spiritual leaders of every religion are carried on all television and radio frequencies preparing their followers for the worst. Finally it is the rabbi's turn. "Fellow Jews," he says. "We survived the exodus, we survived the Pogroms, we survived thousands of years of persecution culminating in the Holocaust. We survived all that. So now we have 20 minutes to learn to live under water." And you don't even have to be Jewish. ******Now we must learn to live under water*******

24. When Collins interviewed Goodman he said that the article would be published before the end of the spring school semester. Then he told Ken Goodman that it would be published at the beginning of the next school year. The article was eventually published six months after Jim Collins came to Tucson and interviewed the Goodmans.

25. In his keynote address at the 1997 National Reading Conference, Moll referred to the *Newsweek* article. He describes Lyon's version of how young children should be taught to read as a "narrower, linear model. Quoting Wingert and Kantrowitz who state that "(r)esearchers around the country are testing ways to put these (NICHD) findings into reading programs for all kids," Moll responds, "now, there is a good example of an ahistorical pronouncement, suggesting that this old, reductionist phonocentric approach is a new insight into reading" (16).

26. Conrad Bromberg made these comments at the seminar Commemorating the Fiftieth Anniversary of the Hollywood Ten, held at the New York School of Visual Arts on October 22, 1997. He spoke in response to a question about the similarities between the McCarthy era and present day right-wing conservative times.

27. In the latest James Bond movie, *Tomorrow Never Dies*, the media mogul Elliott Carver says to 007, "Words are the new weapons."

28. Long sent this e-mail re: H.R. 2614 on October 22, 1997. Smith posted it the same day.

29. Lyon, Reid. (1997). CATENet, 21 October.

30. Zinke, Sharon. (1997). CATENet, 25 October.

31. Goodman, Ken. (1997). CATENet, 25 October.

32. Goodman, Ken. (1997). CATENet, 25 October.

33. Fletcher, Jack. (1997). CATENet, 28 October.

34. Goodman, Ken. (1997). CATENet, 29 October.

35. Goodman, Ken. (1997). CATENet, 1 November.

36. Lyon, Reid. (1997). CATENet, 27 October. I removed the telephone number from the posting.

37. Lyon, Reid. (1997). CATENet, 29 October.

38. Lyon, Reid. (1997). CATENet, 6 November.

39. Fletcher, Jack. (1997). CATENet, 7 November.

40. In conducting a critique of NICHD research I was assisted by a statistician, and based upon the statistical analysis that we conducted, I sent the following e-mail to Drs. Foorman, Fletcher, and Francis:

Dear Drs. Foorman, Fletcher, and Francis:

We have been reviewing those results of your NICHD research projects in the Houston area school district which have either been reported in the national press or on TV, published in preliminary form either by yourselves or by NICHD, or presented at various meetings at both the state and national level. We would like to receive some additional information and clarification concerning the interpretation of some the reported research results from the Chapter 1 Study, which compared Open Court direct instruction (OC or DI), embedded phonics (EP) and whole language (WL or CT) approaches to beginning readers in 1st and 2nd grades. Specifically, we would like to receive your response/input to the following points:

1. An "experimental word list" was used to measure progress where "words were checked for frequency and consistency and for representativeness in the orthographic domain". Was this a word list developed specifically for this project, or was it a word list developed by others that was already in existence? If possible, we would like to obtain a copy of the word list used in the Chapter 1 research, or information about where we can obtain the word list used.

2. In the histograms of "WR Slope" results presented in May 1996 to the California Education Committee, the vertical scales were labeled "density", apparently an output from the SAS program used to process the results. What was the statistical definition of "density" employed by the SAS program? We ask this because the histogram bars do not sum to unity, so apparently "density" was not a normalized density.

3. In the short summary entitled "Preliminary Results from the Chapter1 Study of Foorman et al's NICHD Grant, Early Intervention for Children with Reading Problems (4/17/96)", three histograms are presented, similar to those in (3) above but with the vertical axis labeled "percent of group". The histogram bars for the OC/DI group only sum to about 85%, whereas the other two histograms (CT/EP) both sum to 100%. The 85% total implies that the scores of approximately 16 children from the 108 in the DI population were not included in the histogram presentation, and we would like to know, first why this was done, and second, what were the "Words per School Year" results for these 16 children?

4. In both the histograms in (2) and (3) above, we have assumed that "WR Slope" and "Words per School Year" both refer to the same result, namely the slope of the straight line fitted to the word reading raw score data versus time that you obtained for each individual child. Is this assumption correct, or is there some other derived measure that you used in these histogram presentations?

5. We have also assumed that the histograms in (2) and (3) include the combined data for both the first and second graders and the tutorial/non-tutorial groups included in the study. If they present only the data from one or more subgroups from the study population, which one(s)?

6. *In the various straight line graphs which show for example the "Growth in Predicted Word Reading by Curriculum", we have assumed that the term "Predicted" in the figure titles refers to the fact that the four straight lines (one for each curriculum group) are the means of the growth rate measures derived from the data for each individual child in the group. What is not clear is whether (a) the four "Predicted" lines were obtained by averaging the slopes and intercepts for each child in the group, in which case what do the four data points shown on each line at the October, December, February and April time points mean? or (b) the four "Predicted" lines were generated by fitting straight lines to the means of the individual children's test scores at the 4 time points when these were measured, in which case it seems unlikely that the four data points would lie exactly on the fitted lines for all four curriculum groups. We would like you to confirm whether one of these two approaches or some other method was used to generate the "Predicted" lines for each curriculum group. If approach (a) was used, we would like to obtain a tabulation of the means and standard deviations of the slopes and intercepts for each curriculum group; if approach (b) was used, we would like to obtain a tabulation of the numbers of children, means and standard deviations for each of the 16 data points presented in these graphs; and if some other approach was used, we would like to obtain the equivalent data. We presume these summary data (or the actual raw data obtained for each child in each curriculum group) are either readily available, or if published somewhere, perhaps you could supply a reference.*

7. *Same information as (6) for the phonological and orthographic processing scores obtained at the four time points.*

8. *We would also like to obtain a tabulation of the numbers of children and the means and standard deviations for each achievement measure reported from this Chapter 1 study, i.e. the WJ-R Basic, WJ-R Broad, KTEA and FRI (tutorial and non-tutorial group) test scores, or a reference to a publication that presents these more detailed data. How were these achievement outcomes "controlled for verbal IQ and ethnicity"?*

9. *We would like to be able to access the raw data collected during this study (or the series of five studies) for further analysis. Who do we contact to obtain access to the data—yourselves the researchers, NICHD, or the school district?*

10. *Three schools were apparently dropped from the original proposal list and three different schools were substituted. Could you provide the same characteristic data for these three schools as were tabulated for the original eight schools, i.e. enrollment, %FL, %AA, %Hisp, %A, %WA and %ESL?*

11. *What was the rationale for using the lowest SES school, as the "district control WL" school, and why was the control population from this one school less than half the size of the DI, EP and WL (project directed) multi-school populations?*

12. *In the NICHD proposal for the five studies, you indicated that a "Behavioral and Environmental Information battery will be collected yearly at the beginning of school." Children were to be given the Children's Title Recognition Test and the Harter Perceived Competence Scale; parents were to complete the*

Henderson Environmental Learning Process Scale, the Family Resource Scale, the Yale Children's Inventory and the Hollingshead Questionnaire; and teachers were to complete the Multi-Grade Inventory for Teachers and the Teacher Report Form of the Child Behavior Checklist. We have assumed that each of the instruments in this battery was actually employed, and we are particularly interested to know what use was made of the data collected by means of the "Behavioral and Environmental Information battery" in analyzing either the growth rate data for individual children or the end of year achievement test results in the Chapter 1 study, and also what use was made of this data in the Reading Disabilities study?

Thank you in advance for helping with these questions.
Denny Taylor

Dr. Fletcher sent the following response on behalf of himself and Drs. Foorman and Francis:

Thank you for your inquiry concerning our research. We appreciate your interest. Most of your questions are addressed in the paper reporting the Title 1 study, which will be published in the *Journal of Educational Psychology*. We suggest that you review this paper when it is published. The material you describe represents preliminary analyses, so the final report should be consulted. At that point, we would be happy to entertain additional inquiries concerning the study.

Sincerely,
Barbara Foorman
Jack Fletcher
David Francis

Dr. Lyon also received the e-mail, even though I did not send it to him, and he also responded:

Thank you very much for forwarding your letter to Drs. Foorman, Fletcher, and Francis to me. The questions you have asked are very productive. The full report of the first series of studies undertaken in Houston is in press in the "Journal of Educational Psychology". This expanded version of the study should provide the majority of the details you are seeking.

Your questions are also critical to our current studies and replication efforts. As we conduct ongoing intervention studies in Albany, Syracuse, Boston, Atlanta, Houston, Tallahassee, Gainsville, Seattle, Washington, D.C., and Toronto we are able to supplement existing protocols so that reliable intermediate results inform possible changes in direction or that questions that arise from the initial phases of the studies can be addressed and answered in the context of the ongoing study. In essence, the intervention studies are framed according to our NIH clinical trials format and provide the flexibility necessary to address questions that emerge from the data.

We are very interested in stimulating replication studies and the methodological details that will be provided in the forthcoming JEP article should allow scientists to independently and fully replicate the Houston studies. Indeed, it would be of tremendous benefit to the field if several labs or research programs could conduct their own prospective, longitudinal studies that both replicate and expand the existing NICHD intervention efforts. I would be very open to discussing these ideas for new studies with you. At the present time, the NICHD is supporting a new five-year replication of the Houston effort in Washington, D.C. and these data should provide additional information to help us answer the question:

For Which Children are Different Instructional Components Most Beneficial at Which Stage of Reading Development and For Which Reading Behaviors?

Thanks again for forwarding your letter to me. Please give me a call if you would like to discuss how the NICHD could help support your conducting a replication trial or a new study that addresses reading development and reading instruction.
G. Reid Lyon, Ph.D.
Chief
Child Development and Behavior Branch
National Institute of Child Health and Human Development
National Institutes of Health

41. Fletcher, Jack. (1997). CATENet, 24 November.

42. Fletcher suggests that the response be sent to the journal in which the article will eventually appear and this I will do.

43. Once again there are "if-A-cites-B" problems with the references.

44. Most importantly, even if the inadequacies outlined above were rectified, the researchers make the scientifically indefensible assumption that training children to read words and pseudowords will enable them to read cohesive texts. The results of their own study demonstrate clearly that this is not the case.

45. It's difficult to think positively when we know that the forces we are fighting are also organizing within the academy. Especially when we read in Sara Diamond's *Facing the Wrath* about the National Association of Scholars (NAS), which she describes as "the Right's first sustained organization of university faculty nationwide." In 1996, at the time that Diamond is writing, she states that NAS has "a network of 3,000 faculty members, organized into 29 state affiliates" (p. 126).

Gerald Graff, in *Beyond the Culture Wars*, adds to this discussion when he asks, "When is something political?" He talks about "an impressive interlocking network of right-wing foundations such as the Olin Foundation, the American Enterprise Institute, and the Hudson Institute spending millions of dollars to establish conservative centers and institutes in major universities in the fields of law, economics, government and political science."

"Organizations like Olin," Graff writes, "make no secret of their goal of reversing the gains of multiculturalism and affirmative action and returning education to 'traditional values,' yet this agenda," Graff adds paradoxically, "and its formidable financial backing have at this writing still escaped the general label of 'politicization' that the press attaches to its targets of criticism" (166–67).

46. The McGraw-Hill Companies Reports 25% Increase in Third Quarter. (1997, October 16). *The New York Business Wire.*

47. Goldsmith, Jill. (1997, October 16). McGraw-Hill's Educational Publishing Drives Stellar 3Q. *Dow Jones Newswires.*

48. Long, Rich. Forwarded e-mail message. Wednesday, November 5, 1997.

49. I am not aware of any NICHD reading study which fulfills the criteria for reliable, replicable research as defined in the Reading Excellence Act.

50. Alan Farstrup made this comment to me during a telephone conversation on Monday, October 27. When I asked him why IRA had not joined the other organizations when they developed a joint statement, he said, "We're trying to support money for staff development. We didn't want to give a blanket rejection."

51. Louisa Moats is a visiting scholar at Sacramento State University. She was hired by the state to work with teachers to ensure that they follow the ABC laws. Moats has developed a series of modules which are used for teacher inservice education.

52. Freire, Paulo. (1991). The importance of the act of reading. In Candace Mitchell & Kathleen Weiler (Eds.), *Rewriting literacy: Culture and the discourse of the other.* New York: Bergin & Garvey.

53. I have used excerpts from a full transcript of the presentation of H.R. 2614 in the House of Representatives.

54. Collins, James. (1989). Hegemonic practice: Literacy and standard language in public education. In Candace Mitchell & Kathleen Weiler (Eds.), *Rewriting literacy: Culture and the discourse of the other.* New York: Bergin & Garvey.

55. To explore the many ways in which family literacy practitioners work as activists addressing ethical issues, communicating human rights concerns, and

fostering social justice, read some of the essays in *Many Families, Many Literacies: An International Declaration of Principles*.

56. Routman has addressed many of the issues that teachers face today in her book *Literacy at the Crossroads* (1996).

57. On November 14, 1997, the California State Board of Education approved two applicants to provide professional development in reading in accordance with the provisions of AB 1086. The first is the Consortium on Reading Excellence, Inc. (CORE). When I telephoned CORE to inquire about AB1086, I was told that the person who usually answered questions was at a school doing a training session. "Bill Honig has all the information about 1086," I was told by the person who answered the telephone, "You can call him direct. He owns the company."

According to CORE's "service options" that were sent to one school district, there are at least four training models provided by Honig and his company. To give you one example, it states in the document that for Option 1 "(t)raining can accommodate up to 65 participants for 2 CORE instructors at a cost of $18,000 for the 6 Day Primary Series." For smaller groups the cost drops. "For groups of up to 45 participants, the cost for 1 CORE instructor is $9,000." In addition "Coaching Days at school sites are charged at $1,500 per CORE instructor day." Added to that "(t)ravel expenses are also charged." Then there are the CORE notebooks. They cost $55, plus tax and shipping, of course. However, school districts can buy an annual licence for "unlimited reproduction" of the primary notebooks for $3,000.

"Do the math!" a California teacher tells me, as she counts up schools and districts.

I tell her I already did. When I worked on the Biographic Literacy Profiles Project I was paid $200 a day, at a total cost not to exceed $2,000 for the year for each of the six schools. There were no extra charges for travel or charges for materials. I include this information, even though I may sound self-righteous, because there is an important point to be made. It has to do with how we position ourselves within the work that we do. The teachers and I worked together as advocates for the children in their classrooms who were learning to read. It wasn't a commercial enterprise.

Teaching is a profession, not a business. Indeed, many of the university researchers and college educators that I know who work in schools with teachers don't charge a fee for the work that they do. Others write grants so that scarce financial resources aren't siphoned out of children's classrooms. However, instead of receiving applause, these educators who are committed to public education, to teachers, and to young children, are vilified by policymakers and their more commercially minded colleagues for their holistic or progressive philosophies. Packaging "reading" instruction and selling it to districts might make you rich, writing about reading—as I do—might make you well-known, but teaching children to read and write is what it is all about.

The second provider is the Institute for Continuing Education in Metairie, Louisiana, which is owned by Jane Fell Green. Calls to her office provided no further information about the AB 1086 funding her company has received.

58. Steve Krashen originally posted this documentation on the listserv of the California Literacy Educators on November 14, 1997.

59. Original posting on the CLE listserv, November 14, 1997.

60. Posting on the CLE listserv, November 16, 1997.

61. Posting on the CLE listserv, November 18, 1997.

62. Posting on the CLE listserv, November 18, 1997.

63. Posting on the CLE listserv, November 23, 1997.

64. Sheridan Blau's commentary on his antipathy for political discourse is critical to understanding the reluctance of the reading field to enter the political arena. Blau's inaugural address "Toward the Separation of School and State" is a landmark speech. Blau made it socially acceptable for academics to respond to the rhetoric of right-wing extremists who are dictating how children are taught to read. As one eminent researcher said to me at the 1997 NCTE Annual Convention, "It's become acceptable to say the p-word." My first thought was phonics or phonemic awareness as politics has always had a prominent place in my lexicon. "The p-word?" I queried. "Politics," came the reply, "It's okay to be political."

65. Victor Navasky made these comments at a seminar at the New York School of the Visual Arts on October 22, 1997, Commemorating the Fiftieth Anniversary of the Hollywood Ten. Navasky, who is now the editor of the *Nation*, was responding to a question about the similarities between the McCarthy era and events taking place in the present time of right-wing conservatism.

66. In response to a question from the audience at the seminar Commemorating the Fiftieth Anniversary of the Hollywood Ten, Navasky spoke of the silencing and of those who were silenced. He said that keeping silent didn't work, and he talked of the importance of accounts of individual acts of bravery.

67. In the December 1997/January 1998 edition of *Reading Today*, there is a letter in support of Allington from Sharee Cantrell of Texas. Cantrell writes, "Actually, most reading teachers are becoming disgusted with school boards and legislatures that have been brainwashed by publishers trying to make a buck with their 'new and improved' ways to teach. No curriculum will fix what is wrong with reading instruction. Better preparing teachers to make decisions

about instruction in their classrooms is the only effective way to increase learning." Cantrell continues, "You can purchase millions of dollars worth of phonics materials, put them in the hands of a poorly trained teacher, and they are worthless. Along the same lines, you can take a teacher able to make strong instructional decisions with limited resources, and kids learn to read. Imagine what would happen if we provided teachers with the materials they are asking for, rather than what noneducators are smothering them with constantly. I am appalled at the waste of my tax dollars and the children who suffer as a result." (p.18).

68. As I reach the end of *Spin Doctors* other educators are finishing books which focus on the politics of early reading instruction. Among them is Coles's new book *Reading Lessons: The Debate Over Literacy*; then there is *In Defense of Good Teaching: What Teachers Need to Know About the "Reading Wars"* which is edited by Ken Goodman and includes articles by Goodman, Carole Edelsky, Ellen Brinkley, David and Yvonne Freeman, Linda Ellis, Frances Patterson, Constance Weaver, Richard Allington and Haley Woodside-Jiron, Sharon Murphy, and Bess Altwerger; Jeff McQuillan has written *The Literacy Crisis: False Claims, Real Solutions*; and Constance Weaver has edited a volume entitled *Reconsidering a Balanced Approach to Reading*. Write back! Speak out!

REFERENCES

Adams, Marilyn Jager. (1990). *Beginning to read: Thinking and learning about print.* Cambridge, MA: The MIT Press.

Adams, Marilyn Jager, & Bruck, Maggie. (1995). Resolving the "great debate." *American Educator, 19*(2), 7–20.

Adams, Marilyn Jager, Foorman, Barbara R., Lundberg, Ingvar, & Beeler, Terri. (1998). *Phonemic awareness in young children: A classroom curriculum.* Baltimore: Paul H. Brooks.

Albright, Madeleine. (1997). Presentation to the Senate Appropriations Committee on NATO Expansion Costs. Tuesday, October 21.

Allington, Richard L., (1997, August/September). Overselling phonics. *Reading Today, 15*(1): 15–16.

Allington, Richard L., & Woodside-Jiron, Haley. (1997). Adequacy of a program of research and of a "Research Synthesis" in shaping educational policy. (Report Series 1.15). Albany, NY: National Research Center on English Learning & Achievement.

Anderluh, Deborah. (1998, February 1). Building with words: City schools hope phonics boosts reading. *Sacramento Bee.* Posted on CATENet (catenet@listserver.cybercon.com).

Anderson, James D. (1995). Literacy and education in the African-American experience. In Vivian Gadsden & Daniel Wagner (Eds.), *Literacy among African-American youth: Issues in learning, teaching, and schooling,* (pp. 19–37). Cresskill, NJ: Hampton Press.

Aronowitz, Stanley. (1992). *The politics of identity: Class, culture, social movements.* New York: Routledge.

Ascher, Carol. (1993). Efficiency, equity, and local control—School finance in Texas. ERIC Clearinghouse on Urban Education. New York: ERIC/CUE no. 88.

Athans, Marego. (1998, January 4). Schools fail to teach kids how to read. *Houston Chronicle*, pp. 8A–9A.

Aukerman, Robert C. (1971). *Approaches to beginning reading.* New York: Wiley.

Averson, Raymond, G. (1997). Louisiana State Superintendent of Schools memorandum to the Louisiana Legislative Joint Education Committee.

Baker, Scott B., Simmons, Deborah C., & Kameenui, Edward J. Vocabulary Acquisition: Synthesis of the Research. Document prepared by the National Center to Improve the Tools of Educators, funded by the U.S. Office of Special Education Programs. (darkwing.uoregon.edu/~ncite/).

Bakhurst, David. (1995). On the social constitution of mind: Bruner, Ilyenkov, and the defense of cultural psychology. *Mind, Culture, and Activity*, 2(3), 158–71.

Baldwin, Steve. (1997, May 27). *Teacher training for phonics.* Memo to the Board Members of the San Diego Unified School District.

Ball, Eileen W., & Blanchman, Benita A. (1991). Does phoneme awareness training in kindergarten make a difference in early word recognition and developmental spelling? *Reading Research Quarterly*, 26(1), 49–66.

Barth, John. (1968). *Lost in the funhouse.* New York: Doubleday.

Bartlett, Frederic Charles. (1958). *Thinking: An experimental and social study.* New York: Basic Books.

Becker, Wesley C., Engelmann, Siegfried, Carnine, Douglas W., & Rhine, W. Ray. (1981). Direct instruction model. In W. Ray Rhine (Ed.), *Making schools more effective: New directions from Follow Through* (pp. 95–154). New York: Academic Press.

Bell, Derrick. (1992). *Faces at the bottom of the well: The permanence of racism.* New York: Basic Books.

Bialostock, Steve. (1997). Offering the olive branch: The rhetoric of insincerity. *Language Arts*, 74(8), 618–29.

Blake, William. (1826/1984). London. *Songs of experience.* New York: Dover.

Blau, Sheridan. (1997). *Towards the separation of school and state.* Inaugural Address. NCTE Annual Convention, Detroit, November.

Bond, Guy L., & Dykstra, Robert. (1967). The cooperative research program in first-grade reading instruction. *Reading Research Quarterly 2*(4), 5–126.

Bradbury, Ray. (1953/1996). *Fahrenheit 451.* New York: Del Ray/Ballantine.

Bradley, Lynette, & Bryant, Peter. (1983). Categorizing sounds and learning to read—A causal connection. *Nature, 301,* 419–21.

Brathwaite, Edward Kamau. (1995). Nation language. In Ashcroft, Bill, Griffiths, Gareth, & Tiffin, Helen (Eds.). *The post-colonial studies reader* (pp. 309–13). New York: Routledge. (First published in *History of the voice: The development of nation language in Anglophone Caribbean poetry.* (1984). London and Port of Spain: New Beacon.)

Broder, John. (1997, August 24). Big social changes revive the false god of number. *The New York Times,* pp. 14–15.

Brown, Joel, Goodman, Kenneth S., & Marek, Ann M. (Eds.). (1996). *Studies in miscue analysis: An annotated bibliography.* Newark, DE: International Reading Association.

Brummett, Bill, & Maras, Lisa Burley. (1995). Liberated by miscues: Students and teachers discovering the reading process. *Primary Voices K–6, 3*(4), 23–31.

Burts, Diane C., Hart, Craig H., Charlesworth, Rosalind, & Kirk, Lisa. (1990). A comparison of frequencies of stress behaviors observed in kindergarten children in classrooms with developmentally appropriate versus developmentally inappropriate instructional practices. *Early Childhood Research Quarterly, 5,* 407–23.

Burts, Diane C., Hart, Craig H., Charlesworth, Rosalind, Fleege, Pamela O., Mosley, Jean, & Thomasson, Renée. (1992). Observed activities and stress behaviors of children in developmentally appropriate and inappropriate kindergarten classrooms. *Early Childhood Research Quarterly, 7,* 297–318.

Cardenas, Jose A. (1992). *Myths and issues in school finance.* Paper presented at the Summer Conference of the Institute for Urban and Minority Education, Teachers College, Columbia University, New York, NY, July.

Carnine, Douglas, & Meeder, Hans. (1997, September 3). Reading research into practice. *Education Week on the Web* (www.teachermagazine.org).

Carnine, Linda, Carnine, Douglas, & Gersten, Russell. (1984). Analysis of oral reading errors made by economically disadvantaged students taught with a synthetic phonics approach. *Reading Research Quarterly, 19*(3), 343–56.

Casbergue, Renee M., & Greene, Jane Fell. (1988). Persistent misconceptions about sensory perception and reading disability. *Journal of Reading, 32*(3), 196–203.

Charlet v. Louisiana. No. 97-CW-0212 (Louisiana 1st Cir. Ct. App.)

Chomsky, Noam. (1986). *The manufacture of consent.* Minneapolis, MN: Silha Center for the Study of Media Ethics and Law.

Chrispeels, Janet Hageman. (1997). Educational policy implementation in a shifting political climate: The California experience. *American Educational Research Journal, 34*(3), 453–81.

Clarke, Linda K. (1988). Invented versus traditional spelling in first graders' writings: Effects on learning to spell and read. *Research in the Teaching of English, 22*(3), 281–309.

Clay, Marie. (1979). *Reading: The patterning of complex behavior.* Portsmouth, NH: Heinemann.

Cole, Michael, Hood, Lois, & McDermott, Raymond P. (1978). *Ecological niche picking: Ecological invalidity as an axiom of experimental cognitive psychology.* New York: Laboratory of Comparative Human Cognition and Institute for Comparative Human Development, Rockefeller University.

Coles, Gerald. (1988). *The learning mystique: A critical look at "learning disabilities."* New York: Pantheon Books.

Collins, James. (1991). Hegemonic practice: Literacy and standard language in public education. In Candace Mitchell & Kathleen Weiler (Eds.), *Rewriting literacy: Culture and the discourse of the other* (pp. 229–54). New York: Bergin & Garvey.

Collins, James. (1997, October 27). How Johnny should read. *Time Magazine Online, 150* (17), (www.pathfinder.com/time/).

Cronbach, Lee J. (1984, 1990). *Essentials of Psychological Testing.* (4th ed., 5th ed.) New York: Harper and Row.

Crowell, Caryl G. (1995). Documenting the strengths of bilingual readers. *Primary Voices K–6, 3*(4), 32–38.

Dahl, Karin L., & Freppon, Penny A. (1995). A comparison of innercity children's interpretations of reading and writing instruction in the early grades in skills-based and whole language classrooms. *Reading Research Quarterly, 30*(1), 50–74.

DeGroat, Jennie. (1997). Navajo family literacy. In Denny Taylor (Ed.), *Many families, many literacies: An international declaration of principles.* Portsmouth, NH: Heinemann.

Delpit, Lisa D. (1986). Skills and other dilemmas of a progressive Black educator. *Harvard Educational Review, 56*(4), 379–85.

Delpit, Lisa D. (1988). The silenced dialogue: Power and pedagogy in educating other people's children. *Harvard Educational Review, 58*(3), 280–298.

Dennett, Daniel C. (1993). Learning and labeling. *Mind and Language, 8*(4), 540–47.

DeVries, Rheta, Reese-Learned, Halcyon, & Morgan, Pamela. (1991). Sociomoral development in direct instruction, eclectic, and constructivist kindergartens: A study of children's enacted interpersonal understanding. *Early Childhood Research Quarterly, 6*(4), 473–517.

Donaldson, Margaret C. (1979). *Children's minds.* New York: Norton.

Duhamel, Denise, & Seaton, Maureen. (1997). Exquisite politics. In Denise Duhamel & Maureen Seaton, *Exquisite politics* (p. 70). Chicago: Tia Chucha Press.

Dyson, Anne Haas. (1989). *Multiple worlds of child writers: Friends learning to write.* New York: Teachers College Press.

Dyson, Anne Haas. (1993). *Social worlds of children learning to write in an urban primary school.* New York: Teachers College Press.

Eco, Umberto. (1990). *The limits of interpretation.* Bloomington, Indiana: Indiana University Press.

Eco, Umberto. (1992). Between author and text. In Stefan Collini (Ed.), *Interpretation and overinterpretation* (pp. 67–88). New York: Cambridge University Press.

Eco, Umberto. (1994). *The name of the rose: A novel*. New York: Harcourt Brace & Company.

Erikson, F. (1987). Transformation and school success: The politics and culture of educational achievement. *Anthropology and Education Quarterly, 18*(4), 335–56.

Evans, George Ewart. (1976). *From mouths of men*. London: Faber & Faber.

Evans, Michael. (1997, August 4). Officer calls for end to class system dividing the forces. *The Times*, p. 6.

Fairclough, Norman. (1989). *Language and power*. New York: Longman.

Fairclough, Norman. (1992). *Discourse and social change*. Cambridge, MA: Polity Press.

Felton, Rebecca. (1993). Effects of instruction on the decoding skills of children with phonological processing problems. *Journal of Learning Disabilities, 26*(9) 583–89.

Ferguson, George A. (1971). *Statistical analysis in psychology and education* (3rd ed.). New York: McGraw-Hill.

Ferreiro, Emilia. (1978). What is written in a written sentence? A developmental answer. *Journal of Education, 160*(4), 25–39.

Ferreiro, Emilia, & Teberosky, Ana. (1982). *Literacy before schooling*. (Karen Goodman Castro, Trans.). Portsmouth, NH: Heinemann. (Original work published 1979).

Figueroa, Esther. (1994). *Sociolinguistic metatheory*. New York: Pergamon.

Fillmore, Lily Wong. (1991). Language and cultural issues in the early education of language minority children. In Sharon L. Kagan, (Ed.), *The care and education of America's young children: Obstacles and opportunities*. The 90th Yearbook of the National Society for the Study of Education (pp. 30–49). Chicago: National Society for the Study of Education.

Fine, Michelle. (1991). *Framing dropouts: Notes on the politics of an urban public high school*. Albany, NY: State University of New York Press.

Fletcher, Jack M., Foorman, Barbara, Francis, David J., & Schatschneider, Christopher. (1997, October/November). Only 15–20 percent... *Reading Today, 15*(2), 18.

Flurkey, Alan D. (1995). Taking another look at (listen to) Shari. *Primary Voices K–6*, 3(4), 10–15.

Flurkey, Alan D. (1997). Reading as flow: A linguistic alternative to fluency (Vol. I). Unpublished doctoral dissertation, University of Arizona, Tucson.

Foorman, Barbara. (1997). Quoted in Strauss, Stephen (1997).

Foorman, Barbara, Francis, David, Fletcher, Jack, Beeler, Terri, Winikates, Debbie, & Hastings, P. Early interventions for children with reading disabilities and at risk for developing reading disabilities. To appear in Blachman, Benita. (Ed.), *Cognitive & Linguistic Foundations of Reading Disabilities*. Hillsdale, NJ: Erlbaum.

Foorman, Barbara, Francis, David, Beeler, Terri, Winikates, Debbie, & Fletcher, Jack. (In press). Early interventions for children with reading problems: Study designs and preliminary findings. To appear in *Learning Disabilities: A Multi-Disciplinary Journal*.

Foorman, Barbara, Francis, David J., Fletcher, Jack, Shaywitz, Bennett, Shaywitz, Sally, & Haskell, Dorothy. (1996, April 17). Grant application: Preliminary results from the Chapter 1 study of Foorman et al.'s NICHD grant: Early interventions for children with reading problems.

Foorman, Barbara R., Francis, David J., Fletcher, Jack M., and Schatschneider, Christopher. (1998). The role of instruction in learning to read: Preventing reading failure in at-risk children. *Journal of Educational Psychology*, 90(1), 37–55.

Foorman, Barbara, Francis, David, & Fletcher, Jack. (In press). Growth of phonological processing skill in beginning reading: The lag versus deficit model revisited. Revised version to appear in *Scientific Studies of Reading*.

Fortes, Meyer. (1938). Education in Taleland. *Africa*, 11(Supplement)4.

Foster, Ezola. (1997, October 6). C-SPAN televised speech to the John Birch Society.

Fox, Barbara, & Routh, Donald. (1975). Analyzing spoken language into words, syllables, and phonemes: A developmental study. *Journal of Psycholinguistic Research*, 4(4), 331–42.

Freire, Paulo. (1985). *The politics of education: Culture, power, and liberation.* Hadley, MA: Bergin & Garvey.

Freire, Paulo. (1989). *Education for critical consciousness*. New York: Continuum.

Freppon, Penny A. (1991). Children's concepts of the nature and purpose of reading in different instructional settings. *Journal of Reading Behavior, 23*(2), 139–63.

Freppon, Penny A. (1995). Low-income children's literacy interpretations in a skills-based and a whole-language classroom. *Journal of Reading Behavior, 27*(4), 505–33.

Gee, James Paul. (1992). *The social mind: Language, ideology, and social practice*. New York: Bergin & Garvey.

Gee, James Paul. (1996). *Three critiques of progressivism: Linguistics, politics, and the mind*. NCTE Workshop, Chicago, November 25.

Gee, James Paul. (1996, November 25). Three critiques of progressivism: Linguistics, politics, and the mind. NCTE Workshop "English Studies and English Education: Language, Literacy, and Public Policy." Chicago.

Gee, James Paul. (1997). *The new literacy studies: A retrospective view*. Paper presented at the conference on "Situated Literacies" held at the University of Lancaster, United Kingdom.

Gilkeson, Elizabeth C., Smithberg, Lorraine M., Bowman, Garda W., & Rhine, W. Ray. (1981). Bank Street Model: A developmental-interaction approach. In W. Ray Rhine (Ed.), *Making schools more effective: New directions from Follow Through* (pp. 249–88). New York: Academic Press.

Gillet, Jean Wallace, & Temple, Charles. (1986). *Understanding reading problems: Assessment and instruction*. Boston: Little Brown.

Giovanni, Nikki. (1996). *Shimmy shimmy shimmy like my sister Kate: Looking at the Harlem Renaissance through poems*. New York: Henry Holt.

Giroux, Henry A. (1988). *Schooling and the struggle for public life: Critical pedagogy in the modern age*. Minneapolis: University of Minnesota Press.

Giroux, Henry A. (1988). *Teachers as intellectuals: Toward a critical pedagogy of learning*. Granby, MA: Bergin & Garvey.

Goodman, Kenneth. (1974). Urban dialects and reading instruction. In Joseph P. Kender (Ed.), *Teaching reading: Not by decoding alone* (pp. 61–75). Danville, IL: Interstate Printers and Publishing.

Goodman, Kenneth S. (1996). *Ken Goodman on reading: A common-sense look at the nature of language and the science of reading.* Portsmouth, NH: Heinemann.

Goodman, Kenneth S. (1997, September 24). Capturing "America Reads" for a larger agenda? (Response to Reading Research into Practice by Douglas Carnine & Hans Meeder, September 3, 1997). Letter to the Editor, *Education Week on the Web.* (www.teachermagazine.org).

Goodman, Kenneth S., Smith, E. Brooks, Meredith, Robert, & Goodman, Yetta M. (1986). *Language and thinking in school: A whole-language curriculum.* New York: Richard C. Owen Publishers, Inc.

Goodman, Yetta. (1971). *Longitudinal study of children's oral reading behavior.* Final Report: U.S. Department of Health, Education and Welfare. Project No. 9-E-062.

Goodman, Yetta. (1984). The development of initial literacy. In Hillel Goelman, Antoinette Oberg, & Frank Smith (Eds.), *Awakening to literacy: The University of Victoria Symposium on Children's Response to a Literate Environment: Literacy before Schooling* (pp. 102–09). Portsmouth, NH: Heinemann.

Goodman, Yetta M. (1995). Miscue analysis for classroom teachers: Some history and some procedures. *Primary Voices K–6, 3*(4), 2–9.

Gough, Phil. (1972). One second of reading. In James F. Kavenagh & I. G. Mattingly (Eds.), *Language by ear and eye.* Cambridge, MA: MIT Press.

Graff, Gerald. (1992). *Beyond the culture wars: How teaching the conflicts can revitalize American education.* New York: Norton.

Graff, Harvey J. (1995). *The labyrinths of literacy: Reflections on literacy past and present.* (Revised and Expanded Edition). Pittsburgh: University of Pittsburgh Press.

Gramsci, Antonio. (1971). *Selections from the prison notebooks of Antonio Gramsci* (Quintin Hoare & Geoffrey Nowell-Smith, Trans.). New York: International Publishers.

Grass, Gunter. (1989). *Show your tongue* (John E. Woods, Trans.). San Diego: Harcourt Brace Jovanovich.

Graves, Donald, & Routman, Regie. (1997). If not us then who? Responding to issues presented by the media. NCTE Annual Convention, November 20–25.

Greene, Maxine. (1995). *Releasing the imagination: Essays on education, the arts, and social change.* San Francisco: Jossey-Bass.

Greene, Maxine. (1997). The heart of the matter: Reflections. *Liberal Education* (Spring), 26–35.

Grossen, Bonnie. (No date cited.) *30 years of NICHD research: What we now know about how children learn to read, technical report.* Santa Cruz, CA: Future of Teaching and Learning as the Publisher.

Grossen, Bonnie. (No date cited in paper.) What does it mean to be a research-based profession? National Center to Improve the Tools of Educators Online. (darkwing.uoregon.educ/~bgrossen/resprf.htm).

Gunn, Barbara K., Simmons, Deborah C., & Kameenui, Edward J. (No date cited in paper.) Emergent literacy: Synthesis of the research. Document prepared by the National Center to Improve the Tools of Educators, funded by the U.S. Office of Special Education Programs. NCITE Online. (darkwing.uoregon.edu/~ncite/).

Haberman, M. (1991). The pedagogy of poverty versus good teaching. *Phi Delta Kappan,* 73, 290–94.

Halford, Jean M. (1997). Focusing the debate on student achievement. *Infobrief: An Information Brief of the Association for Supervision and Curriculum Development,* 10, 1–7.

Halliday, Michael A. K. (1975). *Learning how to mean: Explorations in the development of language.* London: Edward Arnold.

Hamilton, Mary, Barton, David, & Ivanic, Roz. (1994). *Worlds of literacy.* Philadelphia, PA: Multilingual Matters, Ltd.

Hanna, Paul R., Hanna, Jean S., Hodges, Richard E., & Rudorf, Jr., Edwin H. (1996). *Phoneme-grapheme correspondences as cues to spelling improvement.* Washington: U.S. Government Printing Office.

Harste, Jerome, Woodward, Virginia A., & Burke, Carolyn L. (1988). *Language stories and literacy lessons.* Portsmouth, NH: Heinemann.

Hartocollis, Anemona. (1997, August 28). In schools, more new space than additional students. *The New York Times,* p. 83.

Hearing on Reading of the Education Committee of the California State Assembly, May 8, 1996, official videocassettes, Assembly Rules.

Hirsch, E. D., Jr. (1997, April 10). Mathematically correct (Address to the California State Board of Education). (ourworld.compuserve.com/homepages/mathman/edh2cal.htm).

Hirsch, Marianne. (1997). *Family frames: Photography, narrative, and postmemory.* Cambridge, MA: Harvard University Press.

Hodges, Walter, Branden, Ann, Feldman, Richard, Follins, Johnnie, Love, John, Sheehan, Rob, Lumbley, Jack, Osborn, Jean, Rentfrow, Robert K., Houston, John, & Lee, Carson. (1980). *Follow through: Forces for change in the primary schools.* Ypsilanti, Michigan: The High/Scope Press.

Holland, Barbara S. Personal communication from the president of the Inland Empire Reading Council entitled "No more Wright Group or Rigby??" Riverside, CA.

Honig, Bill. (September 1997). Reading the right way. *The School Administrator,* 6–15.

Hood, Wendy, J. (1995). I do teach and the kids do learn. *Primary Voices K–6,* 3(4), 16–22.

Horn, Ernest. (1926). *A basic writing vocabulary: 10,000 words most commonly used in writing.* Iowa City, Iowa: College of Education, University of Iowa.

Horn, Ernest. (1960). Spelling. In Chester Harris (Ed.), *Encyclopedia of educational research* (pp. 1337–54). New York: Macmillan.

Hughes, Langston. (1994). *The dream keeper and other poems.* New York: Knopf.

Husby, Brian. (1997, October). Audio-recorded conversation. Husby is a professor at Mt. Royal College, Calgary, Alberta, Canada.

Jencks, Christopher. (1972). *Inequality: A reassessment of the effect of family and schooling in America.* New York: Basic Books.

Jensen, Julie M. (Ed.). (1984). *Composing & comprehending.* Urbana, Illinois, National Conference on Research in English: ERIC Clearinghouse on Reading & Communication Skills.

John-Steiner, Vera, Panofsky, Carolyn P., & Smith, Larry. (1994). *Sociocultural approaches to language and literacy: An interactionist perspective.* Cambridge: Cambridge University Press.

Jones, Noel K. (1996). Phonics and politics: "Sounding out" the consequences. *Literacy, Teaching, and Learning, 2*(2), 4–13.

Joyce, Eric. (1997). *Arms and the man—Renewing the armed services.* London: Fabian Society.

Kaplan, Alice. (1993). *French lessons: A memoir.* Chicago: University of Chicago Press.

Kozol, Jonathan. (1967). *Death at an early age: The destruction of the hearts and minds of Negro children in the Boston Public Schools.* Boston: Houghton Mifflin.

Kozol, Jonathan. (1991). *Savage inequalities: Children in America's schools.* New York: Crown.

Kozol, Jonathan. (1995). *Amazing grace: The lives of children and the conscience of a nation.* New York: Crown.

Krashen, Stephen. (1997). Comments on "Bilingual Education for Children in Public Schools" by Unz and Tuchman. *CABE Newsletter, 21*(3), 14–17.

Krashen, Stephen. (1997/98). Bridging inequity with books. *Educational Leadership, 55*(4), 18–22.

Krashen, Stephen. (In press). Eye fixation studies do not disprove the Goodman-Smith hypothesis. In Dreyer, Philip (Ed.) Claremont Reading Conference Handbook.

Kunzig, Robert. (1997, July). A head for numbers (the research of Stanislas Dehaene). *Discover,* 108–15.

Labov, William. (1972). *Language in the inner city: Studies in the Black English vernacular.* Philadelphia: University of Pennsylvania Press.

Labov, William. (1984). Field methods of the project on linguistic change and variation. In John Baugh & Joel Sherzer (Eds.), *Language in use: Readings in sociolinguistics* (pp. 28–53). Englewood Cliffs, NJ: Prentice-Hall.

Lakoff, George. (1992). Metaphors and war: The metaphor system used to justify war in the Gulf. In Martin Pütz (Ed.), *Thirty years of linguistic evolution: Studies in honour of René Dirven on the occasion of his sixtieth birthday* (463–81). Philadelphia/Amsterdam: John Benjamin Publishing Company.

Language as moral action. (1997, September). *The Council Chronicle*, 7(1), 11.

Lave, Jean. (1980). What's special about experiments as contexts for thinking. *The Quarterly Newsletter of the Laboratory of Comparative Human Cognition*, 2(4), 86–91.

Lave, Jean. (1988). *Cognition in practice: Mind, mathematics and culture in everyday life*. Cambridge: Cambridge University Press.

Lazere, Donald. (1997). Ground rules for polemicists: The case of Lynne Cheney's truths. *College English*, 59(6), 661–85.

Learning to Read/Reading to Learn Campaign. (1996). Helping children with learning disabilities to succeed. National Center to Improve the Tools of Educators online. (darkwing.uoregon.edu/~ncite/).

Lemann, Nicholas. (1997, November). The reading wars. *The Atlantic Monthly*, 128–34.

Lerner, Richard, & Busch-Rossnagel, Nancy (Eds.). (1981). *Individuals as producers of their development: A life-span perspective*. New York: Academic Press.

Levin, Diane. (October 1996). Critique of "The new reading program advisory: Teaching reading." *California Curriculum News Report*, 22, (I), 6–7.

Levine, Art. (1994, December). The Great debate revisited. *The Atlantic Monthly*, 38, 40–44.

Levine, Art. (1996). Parents report on America's reading crisis: Why the whole-language approach to teaching has failed millions of children. *Parents Magazine* (October), 63–68.

Levine, G. (1991). Meeting the third wave legislative approaches to recent judicial school finance rulings. *Harvard Journal of Legislation*, 28(2), 507–42.

Lopez-Reyna, Norma. (1996). The importance of meaningful contexts in bilingual special education: Moving to whole language. *Learning Disabilities Research and Practice*, 11(2), 120–31.

Lundberg, Ingvar, Frost, Jørgen, & Peterson, Ole-Peters. (1988). Effects of an extensive program for stimulating phonological awareness in preschool children. *Reading Research Quarterly*, 23(3), 263–84.

Lyon, George Reid. (1978). *The neuropsychological characteristics of subgroups of learning disabled readers.* Unpublished doctoral dissertation, University of New Mexico, Albuquerque.

Lyon, G. Reid, & Rumsey, Judith M. (1996). Neuroimaging and developing disorders: Comments and future directions. In G. Reid Lyon & Judith M. Rumsey (Eds.) *Neuroimaging: A window to the neurological foundations of learning and behavior in children.* Baltimore, MD: Paul H. Brooks Publishing Company.

Macaulay, Thomas. (1995). Minute on Indian education. Reprinted in Bill Ashcroft, Gareth Griffiths,& Helen Tiffin (Eds.), *The post-colonial studies reader* (pp. 428–30). New York: Routledge. (First published in *History of the voice: The development of nation language in Anglophone Caribbean poetry.* London and Port of Spain: New Beacon, 1984).

Maclean, Morag, Bryant, Peter, & Bradley, Lynette. (1987). Rhymes, nursery rhymes, and reading in early childhood. *Merrill-Palmer Quarterly,* 33(3), 255–81.

Mandelbrot, Benoit B. (1983). *The fractal geometry of nature.* New York: W. H. Freeman and Company.

Manguel, Alberto. (1996). *A history of reading.* New York: Penguin.

Manzo, Kathleen Kennedy. (1997). Study stresses role of early phonics instruction. *Education Week,* 16(24), 1, 24.

Marasco, Joanna. (1997). Who'll take care of my baby? Advocating for Serena. In Denny Taylor, Debbie Coughlin, & Joanna Marasco (Eds.), *Teaching and advocacy.* York, ME: Stenhouse.

Markley, Melanie. (1998). Battling illiteracy. *Houston Chronicle.* Sunday, March 1. 21A

Martens, Prisca. (1995). Empowering teachers and empowering students. *Primary Voices K–6,* 3(4): 39–44.

McBride, James. (1996). *The color of water: A black man's tribute to his white mother.* New York: Riverhead Books.

McDermott, Ray P. (1982). Social relations as contexts for learning in school. In Eric Bredo & Walter Feinberg (Eds.), *Knowledge and values in social and educational research* (pp. 252–270). Philadelphia, PA: Temple University Press.

McDermott, Ray P. (1987). The explanation of minority school failure, again. *Anthropology & Education Quarterly*, 18(4), 361–64.

McGee, Lea M., & Richgels, Donald J. (1985). Teaching expository text structure to elementary students. *The Reading Teacher*, 38(8), 739–48.

McGee, Lea M., & Richgels, Donald J. (1989). "K is Kristen's": Learning the alphabet from a child's perspective. *The Reading Teacher*, 43(3), 216–25.

McGill-Franzen, Anne, & Lanford, Cynthia. (1994). Exposing the edge of the preschool curriculum: Teachers' talk about text and children's literary understandings. *Language Arts*, 71, 264–73.

McGill-Franzen, Anne, Lanford, Cynthia, & Adams, Ellen. (1997). *Learning to be literate: A comparison on five urban early childhood programs.* (Report series 2.28.) Albany, NY: National Research Center on English Learning and Achievement. (ERIC Document Reproduction Service No. ED 403 584).

McQuillan, Jeff. (1998). The California reading situation: Rhetoric and reality. In Constance Weaver (Ed.), *Reconsidering a balanced approach to reading.* Urbana, IL: NCTE.

Merton, Robert K. (1968, January 5). The Matthew effect in science. *Science*, 159, 56–63.

Moll, Luis. (1997). Turning to the world: Bilingualism, literacy, and the cultural mediation of thinking. Keynote address, National Reading Conference, Scottsdale, Arizona, 5 December.

Moll, Luis C. (in press). Through the mediation of others: Vygotskian research on teaching. In V. Richardson, (Ed.), *Handbook of research on teaching* (4th ed.). Washington, DC: American Educational Research Association.

Morrison, Toni. (1994). *The Nobel lecture in literature: 1993.* New York: Knopf.

Myers, Doug. (1997, March 8). Court rejects lawsuit to force more funding for schools. *Baton Rouge State Times/Morning Advocate*, pp. 1A, 6A.

Nagy, William E., Herman, Patricia A., & Anderson, Richard C. (1985). Learning words for context. *Reading Research Quarterly*, 20(2), pp. 233–53.

National Center to Improve the Tools of Educators. (1997). NCITE Homepage (darkwing.uoregon.edu/~ncite/).

Newman, Denis, Griffin, Peg, & Cole, Michael. (1984). Social constraints in laboratory and classroom. In Barbara Rogoff & Jean Lave (Eds.), *Everyday cognition: Its development in social context* (pp. 172–93). Cambridge, MA: Harvard University Press.

Nicholson, Tom. (1993). The case against context. In G. Brian Thompson, William E. Tunmer, & Tom Nicholson (Eds.), *The reading acquisition processes* (pp. 91–104). Clevedon: Multilingual Matters Ltd.

O'Flynn, Patrick. (1997, July 7). Labour backs elite pupils. *The Express,* pp. 1, 6, 7.

Olofsson, Åke, & Lundberg, Ingvar. (1985). Evaluation of long term effects of phonemic awareness training in kindergarten: Illustrations of some methodological problems in evaluation research. *Scandinavian Journal of Psychology, 26,* 21–34.

O'Loughlin, Michael. (1992). Engaging teachers in emancipatory knowledge construction. *Journal of Teacher Education, 43,* 336–46.

O'Loughlin, Michael. (1992). Rethinking science education: Beyond Piagetian constructivism toward a sociocultural model of teaching and learning. *Journal of Research in Science Teaching, 29,* 791–820.

O'Loughlin, Michael. (1996). Facing myself: The struggle for authentic pedagogy. *Holistic Educational Review, 9*(4), 48–51.

O'Loughlin, Michael. (In press). *Being a teacher.* New York: Houghton Mifflin.

Palmaffy, Tyce. (1997, November/December). See Dick flunk. *Policy Review: The Journal of American Citizenship* (www.policyreview.com/heritage/p_review/nov97/flunk.html).

Pany, Darlene, & Coy, Kathleen M. (1988). Effects of corrective feedback on word accuracy and reading comprehension of readers with learning disabilities. *Journal of Learning Disabilities, 21*(9), 546–50.

Pearson, P. David. (1997, September). The politics of reading research. *The Council Chronicle 7*(1), 24, 8.

Pearson, P. David, & Stephens, Diane. (1994). Learning about literacy: A 30-year journey. In Ruddell, Robert B., & Singer, Harry. (Eds.). *Theoretical Models and Processes of Reading,* 4th ed. Newark, NJ: International Reading Association.

Perfetti, Charles. (1984). Reading acquisition and beyond: Decoding includes cognition. *American Journal of Education*, 92, 40–60.

Perfetti, Charles A., Beck, Isabel, Bell, Laura C., & Hughes, Carol. (1987). Phonemic knowledge and learning to read are reciprocal: A longitudinal study of first grade children. *Merrill-Palmer Quarterly*, 33(3), 283–319.

Plomin, R., DeFries, J., & Loehlin, J. (1977). Genotype environment interaction and correlation in the analysis of human behavior. *Psychological Bulletin*, 84, 309–22.

Polanyi, Michael. (1983). *The tacit dimension*. Gloucester, MA: Peter Smith.

Posnick-Goodwin, Sherry. (1996, November). A balanced approach to reading, long advocated by teachers, gains acceptance. *California Educator*, 7–9.

Rhine, W. Ray. (1981). Follow Through: Perspectives and possibilities. In W. Ray Rhine (Ed.), *Making schools more effective: New directions from Follow Through*. New York: Academic Press.

Rhine, W. Ray, Elardo, Richard, Spencer, Leilani M. (1981). Improving educational environments: The Follow Through approach. In W. Ray Rhine (Ed.), *Making schools more effective: New directions from Follow Through* (pp. 25–46). New York: Academic Press.

Richgels, Donald J. (1987). Experimental reading with invented spelling (ERIS): A preschool and kindergarten method. *The Reading Teacher*, 40(6), 522–29.

Richgels, Donald J. (1995). Invented spelling ability and printed word learning in kindergarten. *Reading Research Quarterly*, 30(1), 96–109.

Richgels, Donald J., Poremba, Karla J., McGee, Lea M. (1996). Kindergartners talk about print: Phonemic awareness in meaningful contexts. *The Reading Teacher*, 49(8), 632–42.

Riessman, Frank. (1976). *The inner-city child*. New York: Harper and Row.

Rogoff, Barbara. (1984). Introduction: Thinking and learning in social context. In Barbara Rogoff & Jean Lave (Eds.), *Everyday cognition: Its development in social context* (pp. 1–8). Cambridge, MA: Harvard University Press.

Rogoff, Barbara. (1990). *Apprenticeship in thinking: Cognitive development in social context*. New York: Oxford University Press.

Rogoff, Barbara, & Lave, Jean (Eds.). (1984). *Everyday cognition: Its development in social context.* Cambridge, MA: Harvard University Press.

Rose, Steven. (1992). *The making of memory: From molecules to mind.* New York: Doubleday.

Rosenblatt, Louise M. (1978). *The reader, the text, the poem: The transactional theory of the literary work.* Carbondale, IL: Southern Illinois University Press.

Rosenthal, Robert. (1973, September). The Pygmalion effect lives. *Psychology Today,* 56–63.

Routman, Regie. (1996). *Literacy at the crossroads: Crucial talk about reading, writing, and other teaching dilemmas.* Portsmouth, NH: Heinemann.

Ruiz, Nadeen T. (1988). *Language for learning in a bilingual special education classroom.* Unpublished doctoral dissertation, Stanford University.

Ruiz, Nadeen T. (1995). A young deaf child learns to write: Implications for literacy development. *Reading Teacher, 49*(3), 206–17.

Russell, Conrad. (1997, March 20). Leave it to teachers. *London Review of Books,* 16.

Rutter, Michael, & Madge, Nicola. (1976). *Cycles of disadvantage: A review of research.* London: Heinemann.

Sacks, Oliver. (1970/1990). The president's speech. *The man who mistook his wife for a hat and other clinical tales.* New York: HarperPerennial.

Sacks, Oliver. (1990). *Awakenings.* New York: HarperPerennial.

Sacks, Oliver. (1994). Featured in *A glorious accident: Understanding our place in the cosmic puzzle.* [Film]. Films for the Humanities.

Samuels, S. Jay. (1971). Letter-name versus letter-sound knowledge in learning to read. *The Reading Teacher, 24,* 604–8.

Sapphire. (1997). *Push: A novel.* New York: Vintage.

Scarr, S., & McCartney, K. (1983). How people make their own environments. *Child Development, 54,* 424–35.

Schweinhart, Lawrence J., & Weikart, David P. (1997). *Lasting differences: The High/Scope preschool curriculum comparison study through age 23.* Monographs of the High/Scope Educational Research Foundation. Ypsilanti, MI: High/Scope.

Scribner, Sylvia. (1984). Studying working intelligence. In Barbara Rogoff & Jean Lave (Eds.), *Everyday cognition: Its development in social context* (pp. 9–40). Cambridge, MA: Harvard University Press.

Scribner, Sylvia. (1990). Reflections on a model. *The Quarterly Newsletter of the Laboratory of Comparative Human Cognition, 12*(3), 90–94.

Scribner, Sylvia, & Cole, Michael. (1981). *The psychology of literacy.* Cambridge, MA: Harvard University Press.

Sebald, Winfried George. (1996). *The emigrants* (Michael Hulse, Trans.). London: The Harvill Press.

Share, David L., Jorm, Anthony F., Maclean, Rod, & Matthews, Russell. (1984). Sources of individual differences in reading acquisition. *Journal of Education Psychology, 76*(6), 1309–24.

Shaywitz, Sally. (1998). Dyslexia. *The New England School of Medicine, 338*(5), 307–09.

Shaywitz, Sally E., Schnell, Carla, Shaywitz, Bennett A., & Towle, Virginia R. (1986). Yale Children's Inventory (YCI): An Instrument to Assess Children with Attentional Deficits and Learning Disabilties I. Scale Development and Psychometric Properties. *Journal of Abnormal Child Psychology, 14*(3), 347–64.

Sheldrake, Rupert. (1994). Featured in *A glorious accident: Understanding our place in the cosmic puzzle.* [Film]. Films for the Humanities.

Shockley, Betty, Michalove, Barbara, & Allen, JoBeth. (1995). *Engaging families: Connecting home and school literacy communities.* Portsmouth, NH: Heinemann.

Siegel, Sidney. (1956). *Nonparametric statistics for the behavioral sciences.* New York: McGraw-Hill.

Smith, Courtney, Constantino, Rebecca, & Krashen, Stephen. (1997). Differences in print environment for children in Beverly Hills, Compton and Watts. *Emergency Librarian, 24*(4), 8–9.

Smith, Debbie. (1996, Spring). (Re)defining and responding in an alternative high school. *Arizona English Bulletin,* 19–25.

Smith, Debbie. (1997). Tagging: A way to make meaning. In Denny Taylor, Debbie Coughlin, & Joanna Marasco (Eds.), *Teaching and advocacy* (pp. 125–37). York, ME: Stenhouse.

Smith, Sylvia Barrus, Simmons, Deborah C., & Kameenui, Edward J. (no date cited). Synthesis of research on phonological awareness: principles and implications for reading acquisition. Document prepared by the National Center to Improve the Tools of Educators, funded by the U.S. Office of Special Education Programs (darkwing.voregon. edu/~ncite/).

Sparkman, William E., & Campbell, Trudy A. (1992). Cultural diversity and political turmoil: The case of school finance in Texas. In James G. Ward & Patricia Anthony (Eds.), *Who pays for student diversity? Population changes and educational policy* (pp. 141–59). Newbury Park, CA: Corwin Press.

SRA/McGraw-Hill. (1997). Reading/language arts and mathematics 1997 catalogue.

Stanovich, Keith E. (1986). Matthew effects in reading: Some consequences of individual differences in the acquisition of literacy. *Reading Research Quarterly, 21*(4), 360–406.

Stanovich, Keith E. (1991). Discrepancy definitions of reading disability: Has intelligence led us astray? *Reading Research Quarterly, 26*(1), 8–29.

Stanovich, Keith E., Cunningham, Anne E., & Cramer, Barbara. (1984). Assessing phonological awareness in kindergarten children: Issues of task comparability. *Journal of Experimental Child Psychology, 38*(2), 175–90.

Stanovich, Keith E., Cunningham, Anne E., & Feeman, D. J. (1984). Intelligence, cognitive skills, and early reading progress. *Reading Research Quarterly, 19*(3), 278–303.

Stanovich, Keith E. & Stanovich, Paula J. (1995). How research might inform the debate about early reading acquisition. *Journal of Research in Reading, 18*(2), 87–105.

Stern, Daniel, N. (1985). *The interpersonal world of the infant: A view from psychoanalysis and developmental psychology.* New York: Basic Books.

Sternberg, Robert. (1985). *Beyond IQ: A triarchic theory of human intelligence.* New York: Cambridge University Press.

Strauss, Stephen. (1997, February 18). Phonics reading method best, study finds. *The Globe and Mail,* (www.theglobeandmail.com/).

Summary of Research Findings for State Bill 1139 as Presented to State Board Reading Committee: Draft 11-22-96, pp. 1–2.

Systemic Reform at the Top—Setting Standards for Educational Leaders (1996, May). National Center to Improve the Tools for Educators online (darkwing.uoregon.edu/~ncite/).

Taylor, Benjamin J. (1997). The traveler, the trucker, the schoolboy and the mechanic. Unpublished poem.

Taylor, Denny. (1983). *Family literacy: Young children learning to read and write.* Portsmouth, NH: Heinemann.

Taylor, Denny. (1990). Teaching without Testing: Assessing the Complexity of Children's Literacy Learning. *English Education, 22*(1), 4–74. Reprinted in 1993, in *From the child's point of view.* Portsmouth. NH: Heinemann.

Taylor, Denny. (1991). *Learning denied.* Portsmouth, NH: Heinemann.

Taylor, Denny. (1993). *From the child's point of view.* Portsmouth, NH: Heinemann.

Taylor, Denny. (1996). *Toxic literacies: Exposing the injustice of bureaucratic texts.* Portsmouth, NH: Heinemann.

Taylor, Denny. (Ed.). (1997). *Many families, many literacies: An international declaration of principles.* Portsmouth, NH: Heinemann Trade.

Taylor, Denny, Coughlin, Debbie, & Marasco, Joanna (Eds.), (1997). *Teaching and advocacy.* York, ME: Stenhouse Publishers.

Taylor, Denny, & Strickland, Dorothy S. (1986). *Family storybook reading.* Portsmouth, NH: Heinemann.

Teaching reading: A balanced comprehensive approach to teaching reading in preK–grade 3. (1997). Reading Program Advisory, California State Board of Education: Sacramento, CA.

Toch, Thomas. (1997, October 27). The reading wars continue. US News Online (www4.usnews.com/usnews/issue/971027/27read.htm).

Tompkins, Jane P. (1996). *A life in school: What the teacher learned.* Reading, MA: Addison-Wesley.

Torneus, M. (1984). Phonological awareness and reading: A children and egg problem? *Journal of Educational Psychology*, 70, 1346–58.

Treiman, Rebecca, & Baron, Jonathan. (1983). Phonemic-analysis training helps children benefit from spelling-sound rules. *Memory and Cognition*. 11(4), 382–89.

Tunmer, William E., & Nesdale, Andrew R. (1985). Phonemic segmentation skill and beginning reading. *Journal of Educational Psychology*, 77, 417–27.

Van Allsburg, Chris. (1981). *Jumanji*. Boston, MA: Houghton Mifflin.

Vanity Fair (1997, November). A portrait of world power, (pp. 216–76).

Veltema, Jean. (1997, March). Reading between the lines. *California Educator*, 17–18.

Vygotsky, Lev S. (1962). *Thought and language*. Cambridge, MA: MIT Press.

Vygotsky, Lev S. (1978). *Mind in society: The development of higher psychological processes*. Cole, Michael, John-Steiner, Vera, Scribner, Sylvia, & Souberman, Ellen. (Eds.). Cambridge, MA: Harvard University Press.

Wachs, T., & Mariotto, M. (1978). Criteria for the assessment of organism-environment correlation in human developmental studies. *Human Development, 21*, 268–88.

Wagner, Richard, & Torgesen, Joseph. (1987). The nature of phonological processing and its causal role in the acquisition of reading skills. *Psychology Bulletin, 101*(2), 192–212.

Walberg, Herbert J., & Tsai, Shiow-Ling. (1983). Matthew effects in education. *American Educational Research Journal, 20*, 359–73.

Ward, Lucy. (1997, July 8). Government to have its hand in every school. *The Independent*, p. 8, 16.

Weikart, David P., Hohmann, Charles, & Rhine, W. Ray. (1981). High/Scope cognitively oriented curriculum model. In W. Ray Rhine (Ed.), *Making schools more effective: New directions from Follow Through* (pp. 401–47). New York: Academic Press.

Weintraub, Daniel M. (1997, April 11). Phonics push may come to shove. *Orange County Register*, pp. 1, 8.

Wertsch, James V. (1991). *Voices of the mind: A sociocultural approach to mediated action.* Cambridge, MA: Harvard University Press.

Wertsch, James V., Minick, Norris, & Arns, Flavio J. (1984). The creation of context in joint problem-solving. In Barbara Rogoff & Jean Lave (Eds.), *Everyday cognition: Its development in social contexts.* Cambridge, MA: Harvard University Press.

Wiggins, Grant P. (1993). *Assessing student performance: Exploring the purpose and limits of testing.* San Francisco: Jossey-Bass.

Williams, Patricia J. (1991). *The alchemy of race and rights.* Cambridge, MA: Harvard University Press.

Williams, Patricia J. (1995). *The rooster's egg: On the persistence of prejudice.* Cambridge, MA: Harvard University Press.

Wingert, Pat, & Kantrowitz, Barbara. (1997, October 27). Why Andy couldn't read. *Newsweek*, 56–64.

Zola, David. (1984). Redundancy and word perception during reading. *Perception and Psychophysics, 36,* 277–84.

CHILDREN'S LITERATURE CITED

Ahlberg, Allan, & Ahlberg, Janet. (1980). *Funnybones*. New York: Greenwillow Books.

Asbjornsen, Peter Christian. (1973). *The three billy goats gruff*. Illustrated by Paul Galdone. New York: Seabury Press.

Asch, Frank. (1983). *Mooncake*. Englewood Cliffs, NJ : Prentice-Hall.

Asch, Frank. (1981). *Just like daddy*. Englewood Cliffs, NJ: Prentice-Hall.

Barton, Byron. (1982). *Airport*. New York: T. Y. Crowell.

Barton, Byron. (1986). *Airplanes*. New York: T. Y. Crowell.

Barton, Byron. (1986). *Trains*. New York: T. Y. Crowell.

Barton, Byron. (1993). *The little red hen*. New York: HarperCollins.

Barton, Byron. (1995). *The wee little woman*. New York : HarperCollins.

Bennett, Jill. (1985). *Teeny tiny*. Story retold by Jill Bennett, illustrated by Tomie De Paola. New York: G.P. Putnam's Sons.

Brown, Margaret Wise. (1942). *The runaway bunny*. New York: Harper.

Brown, Margaret Wise. (1975). *Goodnight moon*. New York: Harper & Row.

Burgess, Thornton W. (1960). *Old mother west wind*. Boston: Little Brown.

Carle, Eric. (1976). *The very hungry caterpillar*. Cleveland: Collins & World.

Carle, Eric. (1984). *The mixed up chameleon*. New York: T. Y. Crowell.

Clifton, Lucille. (1983). *Everett Anderson's goodbye*. New York: Holt, Rinehart & Winston.

Cohen, Lillian. (1995). *First grade takes a test*. New York: Bantam Doubleday Dell Books for Young Readers.

Cook, Bernadine. (1956). *The little fish that got away*. Illus. by Crockett Johnson. New York: W. R. Scott.

Cowley, Joy. (1983). *Greedy cat*. Wellington, New Zealand: School Publications.

Cowley, Joy. (1984). *I'm the king of the mountain*. Wellington, New Zealand: School Publications.

Crews, Donald. (1978). *Freight train*. New York: Scholastic.

Degen, Bruce. (1983). *Jamberry*. Story and pictures by Bruce Degen. New York: HarperCollins.

DePaola, Tomie. (1978). *Pancakes for breakfast*. New York: Harcourt Brace Jovanovich.

DePaola, Tomie. (1984). *Mary had a little lamb*. New York: Holiday House.

Flack, Marjorie. (1933). *The Story about Ping*. New York: Viking Press.

Flack, Marjorie. (1965). *Ask Mr. Bear*. New York: Macmillian.

Fox, Mem. (1988). *Guess What?* Illustrated by Vivienne Goodman. San Diego: Harcourt Brace Jovanovich.

Fox, Mem. (1994). *Tough Boris*. Illustrated by Kathryn Brown. San Diego : Harcourt Brace Jovanovich.

Galdone, Paul. (1975). *Gingerbread boy*. New York: Seabury Press.

Galdone, Paul. (1987). *Enormous turnip*. Troy, Michigan: International Book Center

Gibbons, Gail. (1981). *Trucks*. New York: Crowell.

Gibbons, Gail. (1982). *Tool book*. New York; Holiday House.

Gibbons, Gail. (1983). *Boat book*. New York: Holiday House.

Gibbons, Gail. (1987). *Dinosaurs*. New York: Holiday House.

Gibbons, Gail. (1987). *Trains*. New York: Holiday House.

Gibbons, Gail. (1988). *Farming*. New York: Holiday House.

Gibbons, Gail. (1992). *Sharks*. New York: Holiday House.

Gibbons, Gail. (1993) *Spiders*. New York: Holiday House.

Hill, Eric. (1980). *Where's Spot?* New York : Putnam.

Hoban, Tana. (1994). *Little elephant*. New York: Greenwillow.

Hoff, Sid. (1958). *Danny and the dinosaur*. New York: Harper.

Hoff, Sid. (1959). *Julius*. New York: Harper.

Hoff, Sid. (1960). *Who will be my friends?* New York: Harper.

Hoff, Sid. (1961). *Little chief*. New York: Harper.

Hurd, Thacher. (1984). *Mama don't allow: Starring Miles and the Swamp Band*. New York: Harper & Row.

Hurd, Thacher. (1986). *The pea patch jig*. New York: Crown.

Johnson, Crockett. (1955). *Harold and the purple crayon*. New York: Harper & Row.

Keats, Ezra Jack. (1962). *The snowy day*. New York: Viking.

Kellogg, Steven. (1991). *Chicken Little*. Old Greenwich, CT: Listening Library.

Kraus, Robert. (1972). *Milton the early riser*. New York: Windmill Books.

Krauss, Ruth. (1945). *The carrot seed*. New York: Harper & Row.

Krauss, Ruth. (1955). *Is this you?* New York: W. R. Scott.

Lionni, Leo. (1959). *Little Blue and Little Yellow*. New York: I. Obolensky.

Lionni, Leo. (1963). *Swimmy*. New York: Pantheon.

Lobel, Arnold. (1970). *Frog and toad are friends*. New York: Harper & Row.

Lobel, Arnold. (1972). *Frog and toad together.* New York: Harper & Row.

Lobel, Arnold. (1977). *Mouse soup.* New York: Harper & Row.

Lobel, Arnold. (1982). *Ming Lo moves the mountain.* New York : Greenwillow Books.

Martin, Jr., Bill. (1970). *Brown bear, brown bear, what do you see?* New York: Holt, Rinehart, & Winston.

Martin, Bill, Jr., & Archambault, John. (1989). *Chicka chicka boom boom.* New York: Simon & Schuster Books for Young Readers.

McDermott, Gerald. (1993). *Raven, a trickster tale from the Pacific Northwest.* San Diego: Harcourt Brace.

McDermott, Gerald. (1994). *Coyote, a trickster tale from the American Southwest.* San Diego: Harcourt Brace.

Minarik, Else Holmelund. (1957). *Little bear.* New York: Harper.

Munsch, Robert. (1982). *Mud puddle.* Illustrations by Sami Suomalainen. Toronto : Annick Press.

Munsch, Robert. (1985). *Mortimer.* Art by Michael Martchenko. Toronto: Annick Press; Scarborough, Ont.: Distributed by Firefly Books.

Munsch, Robert. (1986). *Love you forever.* Illustrated by Sheila McGraw. Scarborough, Ont. : Firefly Books.

Munsch, Robert. (1988). *Angela's airplane.* Art by Michael Martchenko. Toronto: Annick Press.

Prelutsky, Jack. (1986). *Ride a purple pelican.* Pictures by Garth Williams. New York: Greenwillow Books.

Rosen, Michael. (1989). *Going on a bear hunt.* Illustrated by Helen Oxenbury. New York: Margaret K. McElderry Books

Sendak, Maurice. (1963). *Where the wild things are.* New York: Harper & Row.

Stolz, Mary. (1959). *Emmit's pig.* New York: Harper.

Thayer, Mike. (1989). *Teacher from the black lagoon.* New York: Scholastic.

Viorst, Judith. (1972). *Alexander and the terrible, horrible, no good, very bad day.* New York: Atheneum.

Wood, Audrey, and Wood, Don. (1991). *Piggies.* Illus. By Don Wood. New York: Harcourt Brace Jovanovich.

Yolen, Jane. (1985). *Commander Toad & the dis-asteriod.* New York: Coward-McCann.

Yolen, Jane. (1987). *Owl moon.* New York: Philomel Books.

Yolen, Jane. (1990). *Dinosaur dances.* Illus. by Bruce Degen. New York: Putnam.

Zemach, Margot. (1983). *The little red hen.* New York: Farrar, Straus & Giroux.

INDEX

speech at Governor Bush's Business Council, 72–80

testimony to California Education Committee, 199–213

tests used by, 49–51

Forces for Change in the Primary Schools, 230

Formal Reading Inventory, 40–41, 209–10

Fossey, Richard, 140

Foster, Ezola, 373 n 15

Foster, Murphy J. (Mike), 133–34, 141

Fortes, Meyer, 355 n 28

Framing Dropouts, 184

Francis, David, 33–35, 277, 293–94, 388 n 15

Freire, Paulo, 32, 306

Freppon, Penny, 354 n 26

FRI. *See* Formal Reading Inventory

From the Child's Point of View, 69, 377 n 31

Frost, Jørgen, 36

Frye, Michael, 94

Furry, Alice, 191, 250

Furry, Bill, 219, 383 n 9

Gadsden, Vivian, 158

Gee, Jim, 100, 115, 131–32, 361 n 8

Geertz, Clifford, 70

Geeting, Greg, 255

Genetically advantaged children, 55

Genetic etiology, 47, 114, 159

Georgia State University, 163

Gilkeson, Elizabeth, 229

Giroux, Henry, 62, 84, 93,
on right-wing groups, 60

Goldsmith, Jill, 300

Goodling, William, 262–63, 266, 305, 307–8, 314, 315

Goodman, Ken, 37, 57, 69, 90, 179, 193, 245, 249, 259–60, 270, 281–85, 291, 340 n 8, 361 n 12, 373 n 12, 389 n 22
on dialect, 74–75

Goodman, Yetta, 57, 69, 108–10, 281, 370 n 10, 389 n 22

Gough, Phil, 25

Gould, Stephen J., 163

Governor Bush's Business Council 1996, 62, 334

Graff, Gerald, 395 n 45

Gramsci, Antonio: on hegemony, 59–60, 83, 93

Grant, Lee, 341 n 19

Graphophonemic cueing system, 57

Graphophonic cueing system, 106–8, 111

Graves, Don, 282, 318–20

Greene, Jane Fell, 374 n 17

Greene, Maxine, 70, 341 n 18

Grey Oral Reading Test III, 49

Griffin, Peg, 24

Grossen, Bonnie, 4–5, 33, 46, 96, 101, 113, 250, 268
on neuroimaging technology, 191
on phonemic awareness in African American children, 47
on research findings, 100
on school funding, 178

Growing Up Literate, 22, 32, 47, 57, 69, 71, 97, 185

"Guide to the California Reading Initiative", 95

Halford, Joan Montgomery, 218, 380 n 52

Halliday, Michael, 69, 369 n 7

Hancock, Herbie, 194

Handbook of Research on Teaching, 347 n 9

Haney, John, 231

Hanna, Paul, 26, 69, 358 n 5

Haring, Keith, xxiv

Harste, Jerome, 268–69, 283

Hart, Craig, 232

Harter Perceived Competence Scales, 51

Harvard Educational Review, 366 n 7

Head Start, 260

Kunzig, Robert, 356 n 28

Lakoff, George, 370 n 9
La Montagne, Margaret, 64, 71
Language: English as a second, 38
  process of understanding, 22
*Language for Learning in a Bilin-
  gual Special Education Class-
  room*, 374 n 19
Langworthy, David, 63
Larsen, Yvonne, 248, 383 n 7, 387 n
  10
"Last Empire, The", 256
Lasting Differences, 233
Lave, Jean, 24, 39, 69, 90, 254, 349
  n 4
  on cultural uniformity, 19
Lazere, Donald, 275, 300
Leadership Conference of the
  California Reading and Litera-
  ture Project, 249
Learning Denied, 106, 213
Learning First Alliance, xx
Learning How to Mean, 369 n 7
"Legislative Alert", 261
Lemann, Nicholas, xvi, 286
Le Tendre, Mary Jean, 317–18
Levin, Bruce, 345 n 5
Levin, Harry, 69
Levine, Art, 388 n 16
Libraries: condition of in Louisiana,
  145–48
Lind, Michael, 280
Linguistic-cognitive deficits, 91
Linguistic deficits, 54
Linguistic subsystems, 38
Lippincott, Ann: on Open Court, xxi
Literacy, 66, 267
Literacy development, 100–01
Local Cultures, 70
Loggins, Van, 234
Long, Rich, 158, 258, 260–61, 288,
  387 n 14
Lopez-Reyna, Norma, 198, 378 n 38
Louisiana Board of Elementary and

Secondary Education, 133–34
*Louisiana Handbook for School
  Administrators*, 136, 142, 145
Lundberg, Ingvar, 11–12, 36, 90–92,
  265
  on statistics, 16
Lyon, Reid, xvi, xx, 34, 95, 158, 161–
  63, 183–84, 187–89, 191–99,
  208, 260, 268, 277–78, 286–88,
  289, 292–93, 340 n 8, 376 n 24,
  377 n 34
  credentials of, 183–84
  on education professors, 89
  e-mail to Taylor, 394 n 40
  on Foorman study, 58
  on measurements, 100
  on neuroimaging, 191–92
  on teacher-preparation practices,
    77
  speech at Hearing on Literacy
    (1997), 159–60
  speech to San Francisco adminis-
    trators, 198–99, 253–54
  testimony to California Education
    Committee, 184–92, 196–98
  testimony to House Committee, 307

Maclean, Morag, 36
Making of Memory, The, 190, 363 n 1
Making Schools More Effective, 229,
  381 n 58
Manguel, Alberto, 9, 355 n 28
Manufacturing Consent, 284
Many Families, Many Literacies,
  266–67
Manzo, Kathleen Kennedy, 256
Marasco, Joanna, 376 n 26
Marek, Ann, 361 n 12
Markley, Melanie, xvii
Martinez, Matthew, 308–9
Mashishi, Letta, 86
Mastery Learning, 102
Matthew Effects, 55
  term explained, 8, 345 n 7
"Matthew Effects in Reading", 3, 7–

Phonics trap, 350 n 14
Phonological awareness, 63, 349 n 5
Phonological differences, 75
Piaget, Jean, 69, 90, 358 n 4
Picard, Cecil, 133, on Louisiana
    school system, 154–55
"Politics and Phonics", 275
Portfolio assessment, 77
Practical intelligence, 19
Prediction, 107
Principal: case study of, 214
"Principles of Reading Instruction",
    242
Project Follow Through, 228–29,
    233, 246
Psychological experiments, treat-
    ment of children in, 52–54
Psychology of Literacy, The, 355 n 28
Public and Its Problems, The, 70
Publishers: affiliations with research-
    ers, 85–86, 218
Pygmalion effects, 76–78

Qualitative research, 97–99
"Quality Counts", 168
Quantitative research, 97
Quasi-experimental designs, 97

Race, 91
Racism, 128
Rapid Automatized Naming, 50
Ravani, Gary, 167–68
Reading, 275–76, 306
    labyrinthine process of, 9, 343 n
        11
    social activity for children, 90
Reading as Flow, 376 n 29
Reading deficits, 91
Reading development: factors that
    hinder, 160
Reading disabilities, 40, 72–73, 78,
    161–62
    genetic etiology of, 47, 114
    heritability of, 47, 114

Reading Disabilities Early Interven-
    tion Study, 49
Reading Excellence Act, xvii, xxiii,
    262, 265, 268, 270, 272, 273–
    74, 288–89, 301–2, 303, 305,
    307, 308, 316, 317, 339 n 4
    opposition to, 313
Reading Mastery, 71, 79, 85, 97, 102
Reading methods, 67
Reading problems: Grossen's
    solutions to, 5
Reading readiness: government
    definition of, 263–64
Reading Recovery, 225
Reading Task Force, 170, 221
Reading Teacher, 372 n 11
"Reading the Right Way", 172
Reading Today, 172, 175, 276, 388 n
    15
Reading wars, 259
"Reading Wars, The", xvi, 286
"Reading Wars Continue, The", 286
Recipe for Reading, 42, 45
Reciprocal causality, 91
"Recommendations for Changes to
    Reflect Research", 113
Red River Parish, Louisiana, 86
Reed, Lenox, 64
Reese-Learned, Halcyon, 231
"Report Card on California, The",
    169
Research: basis of phonemic
    awareness, 7, 91
    bias of Houston, 333–38
    characteristics of, 97–99
    criticisms of phonemic awareness,
        89–90
    government definition of, 264,
        305–6
    problematic nature of phonemic
        awareness, 15–18, 89, 207–8,
        270–71, 273–74, 278, 297–99
    Project Follow Through, 228
    reliable defined, 340 n 4
Researchers: affiliations with

AUTHOR

Photo: Benjamin J. Taylor

Denny Taylor receives international recognition for her research and writing. Her awards include the Mina P. Shaughnessy Prize from the Modern Language Association of America, the Elva Knight Award from the International Reading Association, and the Richard C. Meade Award from the National Council of Teachers of English. For the last twenty years she has been continuously engaged in literacy research in families, communities, and schools, in urban, suburban, and rural settings. Her ethnographic research is the basis of all her books, including *Growing Up Literate* and *Learning Denied*. One of her most recent books, *Toxic Literacies*, has been attributed with introducing a new genre of academic writing to those who study language and literacy.

BEGINNING TO READ AND THE SPIN DOCTORS OF SCIENCE

Composed by Electronic Imaging in Adobe's Electra
with display lines in Interstate, designed by Tobias Frere-Jones.
Printed by Braun-Brumfield on
50-lb. Acid Free Offset.